(continued from front flap)

commanding, Daniel Guggenheim and William Cooper Procter on the advantages of a democratic workplace, Katherine Graham on the importance of credibility, Jack Welch and Ross Perot on leading in adversity, Ray Kroc on self-appraisal, and Ben Cohen and Jerry Greenfield on value-based leadership, to name just a few.

For easy reference, the 52 essays contained in *The Book of Leadership Wisdom* are organized into eight categories covering leadership qualities, dealing with adversity, visions of progress, labor relations, company culture, habits and idiosyncrasies, motivating employees, and leading change. Each essay is preceded by a brief introduction that places it in historical perspective and offers interesting and insightful information about its author's life and career. And throughout each essay, passages have been highlighted that call attention to each contributor's most pithy, profound, or quirky ideas.

Offering timeless wisdom from the most successful business leaders ever, *The Book of Leadership Wisdom* is must reading for managers at every level, from the junior executive cubicle to the presidential suite.

The BOOK OF LEADERSHIP WISDOM

The BOOK OF LEADERSHIP WISDOM

Classic Writings by Legendary Business Leaders

Edited by Peter Krass

John Wiley & Sons, Inc.

New York • Chichester • Weinheim • Brisbane • Singapore • Toronto

This book is printed on acid-free paper.♾

Published by John Wiley & Sons, Inc.

Published simultaneously in Canada.

ISBN 0-471-29455-1

Printed in the United States of America.

10 9 8 7 6 5 4 3 2 1

Contents

Introduction

What makes a leader? What special character traits do they need or already possess to meet the challenge of business leadership? In times of world crises, superhuman statesmen such as Franklin Delano Roosevelt and Winston Churchill inspire nations to unite. In battle, demigod generals such as Robert E. Lee and George S. Patton inspire their troops to face certain death. Their astounding capacity to lead, however, is the result of unique circumstances. Now consider the businessperson who is in the trenches of corporate life, day in and day out. Certainly, T. Coleman du Pont, Katherine Graham, Andrew Grove, and Jack Welch are *not* ordinary people, but they also are not faced with unique crises that require superhuman efforts and mystical powers of persuasion. So, in the daily grind of business, what makes them rise to the top to become leaders?

Such a mythology has developed around yesterday's and today's corporate leaders that we have begun to believe they were born with something special, something innate as opposed to learned. Part of this mythology is driven by the money these people are awarded in both salary and stock, which puts them on a level with Hollywood superstars and franchise athletes. Part of it is sheer power. Not only do businesspeople such as Bill Gates rival President Clinton when it comes to global influence, but the public accepts that what is good for their companies is also good for the United States. In other words, in a post–cold war world, our national strength relies on the health of our corporations, not on the size of our army. So now the chief executive officer is placed on the pedestal once occupied by Dwight D. Eisenhower. The advice of CEOs is sought on issues beyond the scope of how to make widgets. Today's business leaders are pop icons and household names. But it wasn't always so.

The evolution of the business leader reflects the evolution of business management and even that of American industry, all beginning with unrefined resources and crude methods. In the 1700s America was mostly an agricultural country, with small pockets of industry driven by such men as Samuel Colt, Ben Franklin, and Eli Whitney, who were more inventors than big businessmen. Alexander Hamilton's influential 1799 *Report on Manufacturers* called attention to the country's need to develop a manufacturing base and become less dependent on farming. According to Hamilton, women and children, who were less capable of arduous field work, should be employed in the factory, and immigration should be encouraged as another source for cheap labor. Hamilton and others regarded people simply as a basic resource critical to the survival of a young nation—and so it would be for another century.

The second half of the 1800s brought robber barons, including John D. Rockefeller and Cornelius Vanderbilt, whose ideas on business leadership were based on the darwinian theory of survival of the fittest. By transferring Darwin's ideas on biology to business, the tycoons were convinced that if they survived, then they were inherently good. Business was about brute power and the rules of the jungle, not about cultivating loyalty and empowering employees. As working conditions declined, an organized labor movement took hold with the formation of the Knights of Labor in 1869 and the National Labor Union and Samuel Gomper's American Federation of Labor (AFL), both in 1886. That same year of 1886 witnessed the bloody Haymarket Massacre in Chicago, in which scores of policemen and labor protesters were hurt and killed. It and other labor disputes, such as the 1892 Homestead Steel Strike, which ended in a bloodbath and ten dead, brought attention to the unbalanced relationship between capital and labor. All of this labor upheaval forced the captains of industry to realize that they must take a more enlightened approach to leadership.

Among the first companies to acknowledge the need for change and to do something about it was Procter & Gamble, which introduced profit-sharing in 1886. Even hard-nosed Andrew Carnegie softened his views on labor and understood the importance of making his top managers limited partners. A concrete idea of what it meant to be a business leader, however, was still a few decades away. First, the actual methods for managing a large business concern had to become more of a science than a gut feeling; managing had to shift from merely mining raw material with brute power to more sophisticated methods.

One of the pioneers of scientific management, Frederick Winslow Taylor, contributed to this evolution. Through time and motion studies, he melded man and machine to make work less arduous. Such thinking resulted in Henry Ford's revolutionary assembly line, which was implemented in 1913. Alfred Sloan, who took the helm of General Motors in 1920, is credited with being the first modern CEO who essentially took the time and motion studies and applied them to an organizational chart. While Sloan did move the business executive toward recognizing how best to organize a company's operations, ultimately he himself remained a great manager, not a great leader. But what is the difference? As a manager it is assumed you have people reporting to you, so in a sense you must be a leader also, right? Is it just a matter of semantics?

Students of business, such as Warren Bennis, have made it clear that the difference is definitely more than just semantics; a manager and a leader have very different roles. In his book, *An Invented Life,* Bennis lists differences between the manager and the leader. He includes: "The manager administers; the leader innovates. The manager is a copy; the leader is an original. The manager maintains; the leader develops. The manager focuses on systems and structure; the leader focuses on people." The difference between the two is clear, and the first steps taken to define these two roles better began in earnest in the 1930s.

This next step in the evolution of business leadership involved a character by the name of Chester Barnard, whose essay "The Active Qualities of Leaders" is included in this collection. Barnard became chief of Bell Telephone in 1927 and is considered the first captain of industry truly to study the role of executive leadership within a company. His seminal 1938 book, *The Functions of the Executive,* outlines his thoughts on the subject. Barnard pinpoints some specific traits, from the creative to the ethical, that the business leader must bring to the table to succeed. He focuses on how the executive can inspire unity and cooperation, and warns his readers that an authoritarian form of leadership cannot force cooperation. A leader, according to Barnard, is someone who naturally commands respect and is able to communicate purpose.

While over the years business executives became more conscious of their role as leaders, they remained largely managers and bureaucrats right through the 1970s, because, by and large, American industry could do no wrong. Reengineering, breaking down barriers, innovation, change—none of this was necessary. However, the high inflation and economic slump in the late 1970s and early 1980s, combined with the rapid rise in foreign competition, provided the wakeup call. In fact, more than half of the essays included in *The Book of Leadership Wisdom* were written in the 1980s and 1990s. The volume is not purposefully weighted this way; rather, much more material is available in the last two decades, a fact that reflects the attention leadership now receives in a leaner, meaner business world.

The idea of leading has been around since the first caveman whittled himself a spear and gathered together a group of

Cro-Magnons to kill a mastodon. The actual verb "to lead" has been in our vocabulary since at least the twelfth century and finds it roots in the Old English word *laeden,* which comes to us from the Old High German word *leiten.* While many authors in this collection put their own spin on the definition of being a leader, the crux of what it is can be found in *Webster's Ninth New Collegiate Dictionary,* which defines to lead as "to guide on a way especially by going in advance." Being able to guide means having a good sense of direction or a vision; it means going first into uncharted territory where others fear to tread; it means encouraging your troops to follow even though hazards block the way. The core idea of leadership has not changed much since Cro-Magnons hunted in groups 40,000 years ago, since the wise King Solomon began his rule in 972 B.C., and since Abraham Lincoln presided over the tragic Civil War. And every essay in this collection embodies the same timelessness; they are all both universal and poignant.

Of course, what is different are the circumstances under which each author was writing and the very different skill sets that they needed for those different situations; so as with the first book in this series, *The Book of Business Wisdom,* this collection is organized into eight thematic parts specifically to address those different skill sets. *The Book of Business Wisdom* covered a variety of general topics pertinent to businesspeople, from how to get ahead, to investing, to leadership. Leadership continues to be so critical to the success of both individuals and companies that we decided to pull it out from the first collection and focus on it alone. Each section of *The Book of Leadership Wisdom* is introduced with a few lines to summarize its purpose and to define the dominant theme. From the basic qualities needed for leadership, to dealing with adversity, to understanding the historical relationship between management and labor, to leading revolution, it's here and alive in the words of America's legendary business leaders.

Another difference is the leaders themselves, their character traits, and their philosophies of how to go about leading.

Each essay is preceded by an introduction that provides some insight into the authors and their philosophies. Their very different ideas (as well as their similarities) really emerge in the pieces. For example, Louis F. Swift, who headed one of the world's largest meatpacking and packaged foods companies, talks about the bully tactics used by his father. He wrote, "Sarcasm was his tool for keeping his subordinates alert and free from mistakes which should not be repeated." In contrast, Electronic Data Systems (EDS) founder and two-time presidential candidate H. Ross Perot talks about encouraging openness, candor, healthy skepticism, and creativity. "The total emphasis in our company is on results, not procedures," he said. "EDSers just hate procedures."

A unique view is offered by catalog pioneer and retailing genius A. Montgomery Ward, who believed a leader must be physically strong: "A man physically weak is at a disadvantage always when he comes in contact with robust personalities." Andrew Grove, chairman of Intel, takes a humbler perspective, writing, "Leaders, we are told, embrace change. They transform their organizations with bold actions based on their abiding vision of the shape of how things need to be." But then he goes on to say that you don't need a grand vision to be a leader, you don't need to be superhuman, but what you do need is the ability to communicate effectively—and that's something everyone can learn to do.

Among these various characters, in fact, the general consensus is that leaders are made, not born. The mythology of some mystical ability that surrounds these leaders is just that—myth. As to the question: What makes a leader? The answer is here in *The Book of Leadership Wisdom.* The key is to connect with what works best for you as you read each selection; to take bits and pieces from here and there and put them together; to absorb these leaders' ideas, expand on them, and tweak them to best fit your own needs.

The
BOOK OF
LEADERSHIP WISDOM

PART I

The Necessary Qualities

My job is to unlock the inhibitions and fears of my people, declares the late chairman of IT&T Harold Geneen in the opening essay of this section. The ability to build a creative and challenging environment is one quality that defines the business leader. So do physical strength, decisiveness, credibility, and the clear articulation of goals, among others. But what does Andrew Grove mean by "Taking the Hype Out of Leadership"? Grove makes the point that leadership is not just for an elite group, delves into how any employee can develop skills to improve on-the-job performance dramatically, and reveals the secret to success. Roberto C. Goizueta, the legendary chairman of Coca-Cola who died in 1997, prefers to boil down his mission to *creating shareholder wealth*. But under this condensed statement are a number of supporting and dynamic ideas that made him the best at it. The essays in Part I provide a broad foundation that serves as a starting point for this collection.

Harold S. Geneen
1910 – 1997

Under Harold S. Geneen's command, ITT helped develop control systems for the U.S. government's all-important Strategic Air Command (SAC) and maintained the president's hot line to Moscow at the height of the cold war. These examples typify the glamour Geneen brought to a once-stodgy and drifting international telecommunications company. He also brought discipline. After taking over the helm in 1958, Geneen initiated a merciless reorganization and, through acquisitions, managed to pump up annual sales from $690 million to $2 billion over the next eight years. When he retired in 1979, sales had rocketed to $22 billion. Eventually ITT was transformed into what was then considered a new breed—the conglomerate. Geneen preferred to call ITT "a unified-management, multiproduct company."

And if that's not a mouthful, to achieve his earnings goals Geneen expected his managers to follow "a philosophy of aggressive anticipation of goals and problems and of effective advanced counteractions to insure our attainment of final objectives." (Perhaps the generals at SAC had some influence on his rhetoric.) Ultimately, Geneen understood that for a multinational conglomerate to operate efficiently, control was everything. To maintain his own handle on operations, he kept a dozen-odd attaché cases packed with memos and balance sheets, and he always carried two or three with him wherever he went.

Geneen's managers took the brunt of his unrelenting scrutiny within a system of checks and balances. In staff meetings he questioned his people aggressively because he felt charged exchanges would lead more quickly to solutions. Geneen was characterized as a strong but harsh leader by a company historian. And according to Rand V. Araskog, who succeeded Geneen as ITT's chairman in 1980, "Geneen did not encourage an entrepreneurial bent among his top executives. He inspired it in the field, but it was his own province at headquarters." Geneen admitted that every leader must have an ego, but it has its proper place and purpose. In *Leadership* he describes the fine qualities that separate a leader from a commander and a leader from a manager.

Leadership

Harold S. Geneen

Leadership is the very heart and soul of business management. No one really manages a business by shuffling the numbers or rearranging organizational charts or applying the latest business school formulas. What you manage in business is people.

Management and leadership are of course inextricably intertwined, but for the sake of clearer understanding, I think of business management as something objective: You want to accomplish an objective, to get from here to there, and your performance can be measured. You can be taught the tools of your trade in a school of business administration. In fact, if you pass all your examinations, you are rewarded with the title "Master of Business Administration." But the legion of young men and women who come out of the business schools each year, armed with calculators and computer science, are at best enlightened business administrators, not leaders. Leadership is something else again. It is purely subjective, difficult to define, virtually impossible to measure objectively, and cannot be taught in school, any more than a baseball player can learn to throw a curve ball by reading a manual. And yet it is always palpably there in every enterprise, setting the personality of each individual company, a reflection of the character and personality of the chief exec-

...ive and his top management team of players. To my mind, the quality of leadership is the single most important ingredient in the recipe for business success.

Leadership, of course, is the ability to inspire other people to work together as a team, following your lead, in order to attain a common objective, whether in business, in politics, in war, or on the football field. No one can do it all alone. Others must want to follow the leader. I don't particularly subscribe to the theory that there are natural, born leaders. Leadership is learned, although I cannot explain entirely how it is learned. The ability to lead and inspire others is far more instinctual than premeditated and it is acquired somehow through the experiences of one's everyday life, and the ultimate nature and quality of that leadership comes out of the innate character and personality of the leader himself.

The legion of young men and women who come out of the business schools each year, armed with calculators and computer science, are at best enlightened business administrators, not leaders.

My own style of leadership at ITT was not deliberately calculated to accomplish set goals. In fact, it was not calculated at all. It was much more instinctual. I established high, challenging goals for the company because that was the kind of man I was when I came to ITT. I did not even think of it in those terms at the time. But now, upon reflection, I can see that it probably goes back to my days as a student at Suffield Academy. I worked conscientiously because I liked to get good marks and it bothered me if I got a poor one. I was delighted when a teacher wrote "well done" or "interesting" on one of my papers. I learned at Suffield that I had to earn whatever I got, but I also discovered that good marks made me feel good, even proud. They stimulated me to do more. When I worked all kinds of hours to sell classified ads for the old *World-Telegram,* I did it because I was scared. I was afraid not to work hard. I did not want to fail. Out in the business world, I wanted to do as well as or better than the next fellow and I was willing to work hard for that distinction. I came to realize that the challenge the business world offered was exciting and I was positively delighted with the feeling of accomplishment when I exceeded even my own expectations in getting a particularly difficult job done.

So, at ITT I instinctively sought to instill something of the same kind of spirit into the management of the company. I had always enjoyed going to work. In fact, I never thought of it as work. It was a part of my life, a part of the environment in which I lived and breathed. I often told colleagues that business was as much fun as golf, tennis, sailing, dancing, or almost anything else you might want to name. The pleasures were different from those of eating an ice-cream sundae. Business provided intellectual challenges that stimulated and fed one's mind. They were every bit as good in their own way as the momentary pleasures of gobbling down one's dessert, and they were more durable. The sweetness lasted longer. Business could be a great adventure, a lot of fun, something to look forward to every day, and the rewards went much further than one's annual salary and bonuses.

When I worked all kinds of hours to sell classified ads for the old World-Telegram, *I did it because I was scared. I was afraid not to work hard. I did not want to fail.*

I wanted to create that kind of an invigorating, challenging, creative atmosphere at ITT. I wanted to get the people there to reach for goals that they might think were beyond them. I wanted them to accomplish more than they thought was possible. And I wanted them to do it not only for the company and their careers but also for the fun of it. I wanted them to enjoy the process of tackling a difficult piece of business, solving it, and going on to bigger, better, and tougher challenges. I wanted them to do this, not for self-aggrandizement, but as part of a greater team effort, in which each player realized his own contribution to the team, knew that he was needed and appreciated, and took pride and self-satisfaction from playing a winning game. My job as chief executive, as I saw it, was to unlock whatever inhibitions or fears bound these people in chains of insecurity. The way to do that was to create at ITT a climate of growth and opportunity, a climate in which each fellow would want to carry his own share, and would be driven to excel not only because I pushed him but because of peer pressure and pride.

Consider two men of generally equal intelligence and ability: One works eight hours a day for ten years; the other works twelve hours a day for ten years. . . . Which one would you hire?

The best hope of achieving that, given my own sense of leadership, was to jump in the boat, grab an oar, and start pulling along with the other men. I suppose you might call it participatory leadership. I didn't want to be the captain sitting in the back of the boat, exhorting his men to do all the work while he sat there doing nothing. Nor did I want to be like the master of a galley, frightening his slaves half to death with the giant whip in his hands. I worked as long and as hard as any man at ITT and they knew it. I worked those twelve- and sixteen-hour days, traveled back and forth to Europe, carried briefcases of work home with me every weekend—not because I wanted to set an example. I did it because I had to do it in order to get my own work done competently. But I did set an example, an honest example, which traveled down the ranks of management and, to an extent, established a standard of performance for the whole company. After all, if I could do it, so could the next man—if he had any measure of pride in his own ability.

My job as chief executive, as I saw it, was to unlock whatever inhibitions or fears bound these people in chains of insecurity.

The rationale for the value of working extra hours is clear-cut in my mind. Consider two men of generally equal intelligence and ability: One works eight hours a day for ten years; the other works twelve hours a day for ten years. At the end of ten years, one man has ten years' experience; the other will have fifteen years' experience. Which one would you hire? Consider two rival business managers or two chief executives in a competitive situation, one working an eight-hour day, the other a ten- or twelve-hour day. Which one is more likely to become the better businessman?

On the practical side, the first obligation of any chief executive is to set the goals for his company. It is his responsibility to point his people in the direction of the goalposts, and tell them how to get there. He is the only man who can do it. That, too, will come out of his personality and character as a leader. If he is satisfied with mediocre results, that's what he will get. In a railroad company, the primary goal might be to ensure that the trains will run on time; in a utility, that the electric, gas, or telephone service will not be interrupted. At ITT, I set a much more competitive and challenging goal: a steady, stable growth of 10 to 15 percent increase in earnings per share for each and every year. Together, we set out to double our earnings in five years.

I never let up. I talked about growth, how we were going to achieve it, and I talked about more growth. In the beginning at ITT, I spent night after night talking with our management teams about what we were going to do with the company, discussing how we intended to do it. As the years went on, every time we acquired a new company we would give a welcoming dinner for the new company's management and we would talk about our goal of at least 10 percent annual growth. It did not make any difference if times were good or bad. When they were good, we should be able to make our goal easily; when they were bad, we had to work harder. But we had to make our goal each and every year. That was the message. And the new company managements believed us, because they knew that we meant what we were saying.

We set out to hire the very best people in the industry that we could find. I did not want glamorous, glib-talking men who got by on their coiffured good looks or family connections.

Now, it must be understood that we were not *ordering* these men to increase their earnings by 10 to 15 percent each year. We were telling them that we were all going to do it together, that the headquarters management team, including the chief executive, was there to help them achieve these goals. In short, we were all in the same boat, sink or survive, and we all would be rowing very hard, but in the end it would all prove to be worthwhile for all of us.

In every well-organized company there must be a sense of balance that is understood by every man and woman who works there. If you are seeking the best people available, and if you expect them to stretch beyond the ordinary, even beyond what they think are their capabilities, you have to reward them commensurately. One of the first things we did at ITT when I got there was to move onto the fast track. We set out to hire the very best people in the industry that we could find. I did not want glamorous, glib-talking men who got by on their coiffured good looks or family connections. Nor did I want geniuses who were so smart that they could not get along with the rest of us mere mortals. No, what we sought were capable, experienced men who were motivated, who wanted to achieve and to make something of their lives, and who were not afraid to work hard for what they wanted. Of course, we wanted people who were intelligent, knowledgeable, and experienced, but in choosing among candidates who had those attributes, I wanted men around me who shared my enthusiasm for work.

The "firing line" is perhaps the most acute test of a company's leadership. Who gets fired and why and when and even how goes to the very heart of the character of a company, its management, and its leadership. Obviously, it is the responsibility of the leader, whether he be the manager of a plant, a group vice president, or the chief executive, to weed out of the system those people who are not contributing or who are impeding the general efforts of all the others. Unfortunately, there always are some people in every company who simply do not want to work. They may be lazy or disturbed or resentful or otherwise preoccupied, but, for whatever reason, they don't do their share, nor do they want to. Then there are those people with personality traits which make it difficult for them to work with their peers or their subordinates. It is easy enough to recognize such people on the assembly line in the factory. In the ranks of management, it is considerably more difficult. Nevertheless, everyone around such a person recognizes that he or she is a faker, a phony, or whatever word you might want to use. Nor will others ordinarily tell the "boss" what is going on. But they will be watching and judging. And it is the duty of the leader to recognize that kind of person and to get rid of him. It may take a bit of time before the laggard's excuses, glib talk, or downright lies catch up with him. But the alert leader will recognize the clues and will move forcefully as soon as he learns the facts. And when he does, he will earn the respect of all the others who are hardworking, imaginative, and productive and who have long resented the freeloaders in their ranks. In that sense, firing people can be a constructive role of a company's management. It clears the air and improves the climate.

Firing people is always difficult. It's the moment of truth for a business leader. You never face the problem of firing somebody without truthfully, honestly examining the question of how much you yourself have contributed to the situation. Are you firing him because the company is under pressure to cut costs, because of general economic conditions, or because you are losing business and market share? If so, then it isn't his fault, it's yours. You were supposed to run the company so that it would be strong enough to weather bad economic conditions without laying off people and smart enough not to be caught in the crunch of new products or marketing trends.

Who gets fired and why and when and even how goes to the very heart of the character of a company, its management, and its leadership.

You may be firing him because he has done a poor job. Even he knows it. But you have to ask yourself: Did he do a bad job because he was not helped? He was entitled to help. If he couldn't do the job alone, you were supposed to be smart enough to be able to help him. Maybe it's not all his fault. Maybe you failed again. Perhaps a man is failing because he inherited a tough problem that no one else can solve; or he is caught in a situation completely beyond his control.

The most difficult task of all is firing a man who *is* working hard, doing the best he can, but whose confidence in himself far outstrips his abilities. He's over his head. His judgment or lack of judgment might even be a serious danger to the whole operation. It breaks your heart to have to tell such a man that he is incompetent. After all, you probably gave him raises and promotions for ten years. It was you who put him in deep water over his head.

Or consider the man who has faithfully served the company well for twenty or thirty years, and now is in failing health and ability. He is only two or three years away from retirement. What would you do with him?

There is no simple formula for firing people. There will always be, and should be, exceptions to every rule you devise. How you handle each of the above cases, however, will determine what kind of leader you are, how much respect you command and deserve from your colleagues, and ultimately the personality and character of the company you lead. You have to take action. You have to clear the decks for all the other people who are performing up to your standards and perhaps are carrying the extra burden of those who are not. They expect it of you.

In physics it is well known that for every action there is a reaction. Every time a chief executive takes an action for or against someone in the company, either firing or promoting a man, there is a reaction throughout the company. The reaction is not simply between the boss and the man he is dealing with. The way he handles the situation involves not only the action and reaction between them. It reverberates to all the others down the line and they pass judgment upon what the boss did and the way he did it, and they react accordingly.

So you have to let all those people go—except for that last fellow so close to retirement. He has earned his right to stay on in his job, even at the expense of efficiency. Perhaps you can move him laterally somewhere, so that someone else can take over his former position. He knows the score. So do all the others around him. If you fired him, the message would be clear: It's the company policy to pay you as long as you are useful and then throw you on the junk heap when you're old and gray. Who would give loyalty to a company like that? As for the others, it is your duty to let them go, however unpleasant it may be. But you can do it as decently and as painlessly as possible. The willing but over-his-head manager can be helped to find another job for which he is better suited without destroying his self-confidence. Demoting him would do him (and the company) more harm than good.

Ultimately, a good leader should do the decent thing. He should know what the decent thing is; everyone else does. No one wants his or her leader to be tolerant of incompetence through ignorance, indecisiveness, or weakness. No one wants to follow a weak leader. He is the worst kind. You cannot rely upon his judgment because you don't know what he will do in a difficult situation. Much more respect and loyalty is given to the tough leader, the one who is not afraid to make difficult and even unpopular decisions, just as long as he is perceived to be decent and fair and reliable in his dealings with his subordinates.

One final word on firing the man who is not pulling his oar, as such episodes apply to the crucial role of the leader. Others in the organization will not come and tell you about him. But in time, almost instinctively, a good executive will recognize the faults as well as the attributes of the men working for him. Almost always his reactions to the man will be the same as those of others who deal with him, whether he is unreliable, vacillating, or insufferably arrogant, or whatever. And when you, as the leader, give the man his walking papers, only then will the others come forward and comment. They had all been wondering how long it would take you to wake up to the reality of the situation.

By the same token, when a good person is in trouble (and it happens to the best) it is incumbent upon a leader to support and help that person as far as possible. You owe that person your loyalty because loyalty is always a two-way street. Once again, your actions will reverberate through the whole company.

No one wants his or her leader to be tolerant of incompetence through ignorance, indecisiveness, or weakness. No one wants to follow a weak leader.

As president and then chairman of ITT, I was perceived from the outside as a tough man to work for. I was often portrayed that way in the press. The stereotype of the difficult, ruthless s.o.b. driving his subordinates to early graves in his quest for quarterly profits makes good copy and sells magazines. Actually, the management team that stayed with ITT through the years, and took over when I retired, thrived on the fast pace and on the action and growth that we engendered. In recent years, since my retirement, I have received many letters from men who said that those early, growing years with ITT had been the most thrilling time of their lives.

As a matter of policy, which was stamped upon the management of all 250 profit centers of ITT, we treated every company manager as an individual entrepreneur. We were demanding but decent. I often made the point that the facts of any given situation were making the demands upon the man, not me. I might criticize what he had done or failed to do, but my attacks were never personal. At meetings large and small, I never demeaned a man's ability or threatened him. Sarcasm or personal attacks were not countenanced at any level. I've seen more good, imaginative ideas nipped in the bud by a clever, sarcastic remark than by logical, informative criticism. Open communication meant that every man was entitled to speak his piece. I wanted my people to be as imaginative and creative as they could possibly be. When I thought a man deserved a dressing down for something he had done or failed to do, I did it privately. I wanted *him* to know how I felt, not others.

Good ideas are hard to come by and I always felt that as chief executive it was incumbent upon me to welcome and foster imaginative thinking. The chief executive is the man in the best position to take the risk of allocating money for a seemingly wild idea. At least he should be. Those under him are too often in fear of making a mistake which might jeopardize their careers. Big companies, like ITT, with all their financial resources, can afford to take such risks. Many of our new ventures added spice and excitement to our working environment. Some succeeded beyond even our own expectations and that, in and of itself, helped build confidence in our ability to reach even further out into the unknown. Imagination and creativity are the two elements most lacking in most large American corporations.

Everyone says he believes in team play, reciprocal loyalty, corporate decency, the dignity of labor, and fair remuneration, but when the crunch comes, how many chief executives abide by those "beliefs"?

In accord with the principle of treating each of our managers with the dignity and respect due an entrepreneur, I made it a policy never to *order* a division or company manager to do something with which he disagreed. No chief executive should. You can order a man *not* to do something: Don't burn the building down. Don't build another $500 million plant this year. But if you want him to do something with which he disagrees, you have to persuade him. If you order him to do it, you have taken over the responsibility for that decision. Then he has the right to come back to you later and say, "I did what you ordered and the whole thing fell apart, and it's not my fault." In fact, subconsciously, he was almost committed to proving that your idea would not work, and that he was right and you were wrong.

What do you do when you fail to persuade him? It happens not infrequently. Chief executives of subsidiary companies can have as much ego and self-confidence as chief executives of parent companies. You try to persuade him to take course A; he insists upon course B. He's the operating man and it is his responsibility. You tell him, "Okay, John, we [at headquarters] think you're wrong," and you tell him your reasons. "But if you still think we are wrong and you're right, then go ahead and try it."

If he turns out to have been wrong, then you hope he has learned something. The second time it happens, if he is still stubborn, you say, "Look, you're in charge, so go ahead. But we [at headquarters] are going to be kept well informed on everything you do and we are going to follow this closely, and we're going to advise you of what we think all along the way. Now, you're an intelligent guy and we expect you to sort out what we tell you, what's right and what's wrong. If you have doubts, raise them with us. If the thing is a fifty-fifty toss-up, and neither of us really knows, then you call the shot. You're the operating man. You know more about this than we do. We're not going to order you to do anything and we're not going to go behind your back. But if you go ahead, you better do your homework and know what you are doing. Don't act out of some kind of blind nonsense. If we discover that you've turned out to be wrong because you did not go far enough into the facts of the situation, then you're in trouble. With that understanding, go ahead." That's treating a man with respect. Even though you believe he is wrong, you hope he is right. The important thing is not who is right, but what is right.

Leadership is practiced not so much in words as in attitude and in actions. Everyone says he believes in team play, reciprocal loyalty, corporate decency, the dignity of labor, and fair remuneration, but when the crunch comes, how many chief executives abide by those "beliefs"? How many risk their own careers to stand up for their management team and their labor force? Or how many really are looking out for Mr. Number One? Up and down the management ladder, an executive need only double-cross a subordinate once—saying one thing and in a crunch doing something else—and he will lose that man's respect and loyalty for evermore. And the word will travel far and wide. Everyone who hears that story will think and rightly so: "If he did it once, he might do it again. He might even do it to me. He can't be trusted. I have to watch out for myself, guard my flanks, maybe think of finding another job, because this one has suddenly become insecure."

I don't think anyone can fake it. In all the companies in which I worked I invariably found that right down to the elevator boy, the maintenance man, or the floor sweeper, the people in the company carried with them a firm opinion about the character of the chief executive, the vice presidents, and their own immediate bosses. In one company I went around inquiring about our two top executives.

"What do you think of so-and-so?" I asked.

"Oh, he's a great guy."

"What do you think of so-and-so?"

"Oh, he's a real [expletive]!"

"Have you ever met either of them?"

"No, but I know . . ."

He did know. Those were his opinions based upon what he had learned and they were seldom wrong. Those men closer to the executive in question had more facts to support their opinions, but the opinions usually were the same up and down the line. And it was an accumulation of those opinions which set the tone, atmosphere, and spirit of the company. It shows up, too, in performance. Everyone knows it is a pleasure to work for someone you respect and admire, and it is hell to work grudgingly for a blankety-blank expletive.

So, as far as I can see, the best way to inspire people to superior performance is to convince them by everything you do and by your everyday attitude that you are wholeheartedly supporting them. You have got to mean it and demonstrate it. Deep down, they have to feel that support. That's the part of grabbing an oar when they are in trouble. In the beginning at ITT, the complex monitoring system that I instituted—with all the detailed reports and the meetings and the rigorous staff checks and rechecks—was resented by most if not all of our subsidiary company managers. No one likes to have someone looking over his shoulder and checking up on him. Their first reaction was fear. It took some time before they recognized and accepted the fact that our monitoring system was there so that we at headquarters could help them succeed in their line operations; and that when they succeeded, with or without our help, they would receive full credit for their achievement. They had to check me out, test my intelligence, my ability, my honesty, my character, my dependability, just as I had to check them out. But as time went on, trust and respect and a certain sense of camaraderie and loyalty set in, as well as a measure of pride in what we were accomplishing together.

Everyone knows it is a pleasure to work for someone you respect and admire, and it is hell to work grudgingly for a blankety-blank expletive.

The dedicated, unfailing support of a chief executive is like a lifeline or a safety net to his management team and, in fact, to the whole company. They have got to rely upon him to feel safe in their jobs so that their families and college-bound children will not suffer by a sudden notice of dismissal. Only then will they feel free to unleash their imaginations and creative energies. They have to feel free to admit to an honest mistake without fear of unfair reprisal. I've had men come into my office and admit they goofed, that the mistake cost the company several millions of dollars, but then they presented a plan by which they would rectify the situation. As long as they came in with a plan to remedy the disaster, they had my support.

As I've said, a true leader has to have a genuine open-door policy so that his people are not afraid to approach him for any reason. A man should feel free to tell his chief executive to his face, "I think you're dead wrong about such and such, and here are my reasons." A chief executive who has conquered his own ego problems listens to such criticism, for even if it is wrong, he will probably learn something. He can then set the man straight with the facts. If the man is right, the chief executive has cause to thank him profusely and then set about correcting the situation. That action will sweep down the corridors of the company and inspire others to speak their minds freely. No one, after all, has a monopoly on brains in any company.

One of the essential attributes of a good leader is enough self-confidence to be able to admit his own mistakes and know that they won't ruin him. The true test is to be able to recognize what is wrong as early as possible and then to set about rectifying the situation. I made my share of mistakes at ITT and they did not ruin me. I admitted them at General Managers Meetings, often with the expression "I guess I pushed the wrong button," and then I outlined my plan to save as much as could be saved from the situation. Usually such *mea culpas* were well received. Anyone who has goofed gets a little enjoyment out of seeing the man up there admit to a mistake. There's nothing lost and much to be gained by admitting that you're human.

The authority vested in the chief executive of a large company is so great, so complete, and the demands made upon his time are so consuming, that most chief executives slip into authoritarian roles without realizing that the process is going on. In the vast majority of large American companies, the chief executive lives in a world of his own. He is sequestered in his luxury executive suite high up in the headquarters building. His word is law. Everyone kowtows to him. They adjust to his moods and to his idiosyncrasies. He runs the company from his inner sanctum. The people "out there" seldom catch a glimpse of him. Reports reach him through layers of management after being processed by committee after committee. He writes "yes" or "no" and initials them. He may subscribe to everything I have said about business leadership, but he cannot find the time to pay attention to those intangibles which do not show up on the profit-and-loss sheet. Subtly, he changes. It is easier and less time-consuming to be authoritarian. He has changed from a leader into a commander.

A man should feel free to tell his chief executive to his face, "I think you're dead wrong about such and such, and here are my reasons."

A leader leads his people; a commander commands them. There are, of course, gradations between the two, but essentially, by his attitude and by his actions, the commander is telling his people, "I want this done and by this date, and if it is not done, then heads will roll!" And he follows through. He who fails is fired; he who succeeds gets a pat, a promotion, or a bonus. His subordinates toe the line. He rules by fear. One chief executive, an old associate of mine, confided in me that as a matter of policy he visits each of his company's division managers every three months and "scares the hell" out of them. And it works. His P&L looks just fine.

To the degree that business commanders strike fear in the hearts of their management team, they have turned the American business world into a jungle in which scared people compete *within* a company for their own personal survival. In the long run, I am certain that it is counterproductive. First of all, frightened people play office politics; they won't come forward and admit their problems early enough for them to be solved. The most capable, independent people leave, not willing to work under those conditions. Good people won't want to come into such a company. Imperceptibly at first and then more and more, all these negative conditions and attitudes will feed upon one another until, in the end, the company will slide into a decline that the commanding chief executive and his board of directors will find difficult to fathom.

The person who heads a company should realize that his people are really not working for him; they are working *with him* for themselves. They have their own dreams, their own need for self-fulfillment. He has to help fill their needs as much as they do his. He has to prove to them that he is working as hard as they are, that he is competent in his own role as chief executive, that he will not lead them over the cliff and jeopardize their livelihoods, that he can be relied upon to reward them properly and fairly, that he is willing to share the risks as well as the rewards of their enterprise.

The person who heads a company should realize that his people . . . have their own dreams, their own need for self-fulfillment. He has to help fill their needs as much as they do his.

No chief executive can prove to his board of directors or shareholders how much, if anything, this leadership contributes to the bottom line in the profit-and-loss statement of the company. It is all intangible. He may have difficulties with his board in demanding seemingly high rewards and a firm support system for the men on his management team. But I am convinced that leadership is the single most important ingredient in business management, and that those attitudes of the chief executive which inspire his people to stretch and to excel contribute as much as 80 or 90 percent of a company's success.

Finally, as I said in the beginning, no one can teach you leadership. Everyone reads the same books and yet one manager will get a 40 percent effort out of his management team and the other will get 80 percent, and it will depend upon the manager himself and the hundreds of little things done every day that reveal character. There is a delicate balance that exists in the hierarchy of every company and the balance swings upon all those little things that the chief executive does instinctively, intuitively, spontaneously, or out of experiences, good and bad. Leadership, like life, can only be learned as you go along.

ANDREW S. GROVE
1936 –

Born Andras Grof in Budapest, this refugee hunted first by the Nazis and then by the Soviets, fled to the United States in 1956 during the failed Hungarian revolution. The journey began in cowering fear and ended in joy. Once in the United States, Grove studied a subject that left little to emotion: science. Eventually he was awarded a Ph.D. in chemical engineering from the University of California, Berkeley. Grove took a job with Fairchild Semiconductor, doing research under Gordon Moore and Robert Noyce. They were among the first to discover how to use silicon effectively in chip making. In 1968 Moore and Noyce left to start their own company, Intel. Grove followed and, with Moore as his mentor, became president of Intel in 1979 and then CEO in 1987.

During his tenure, Grove has built Intel into a microchip Goliath; their chips are in almost 90 percent of the world's personal computers. His mission is his product, and he is terse when he hears accusations that the computer hasn't made the world more efficient. For Grove, computers have speeded up the tempo of work; he is able to gather information faster and then make decisions faster. He once wrote, "Like a natural force, technology is impossible to hold back. It finds its way no matter what obstacles people put in its face."

Grove is tough on critics, and he was also once tough on employees. *Fortune* magazine named him one of America's toughest bosses back in 1984 but he's mellowed with time. At the office, Grove sits in a cubicle like everyone else to encourage an open environment and to collect internal company information that can't be had on the Web. He said, "The type of information most useful to me, and I suspect most useful to all managers, comes from quick, often casual conversational exchanges." For Grove, the gathering of information is the crux of his managerial work. When it comes to seeking truth, friends characterize him as being ruthlessly honest. Grove prefers to call it fear, a paranoia bred in his youth that demands facing the truth to survive and to become a leader. In *Taking the Hype Out of Leadership,* Grove presents a lesson on why he told a middle manager the facts of life.

Taking the Hype Out of Leadership

Andrew S. Grove

One of our divisional marketing managers recently asked for a meeting with me. A man in his mid-30s, he reports to a division general manager, who reports to the group general manager, who in turn reports to me. I know that this fellow works hard at his job, and also that he pays attention to his progress up the ladder. As he said quite openly when asking for the meeting, the purpose of the session was to have a "career checkup": He wanted to know if he was doing all the right things for the company to continue his rise through the ranks.

Our discussion went smoothly at first. He told me of some things he had done in the past year that he was particularly proud of and a bit about what he planned to do. Then he asked what I thought he should be working on. I countered with another question: What were his strengths? He quickly replied that he prided himself on his organizational skills, his understanding of his product area and the market, and his rapport with the corporate sales force—the people who, while not under his authority, use his marketing strategies to sell the division's products. Next I asked where he thought he was lacking. After considerable hesitation, he gave an answer that didn't mean a whole lot to me: "I am afraid I don't provide enough leadership."

He isn't the only one thinking about leadership these days. Whether the question is our national competitiveness, the decay of ethics in government, or just about any other problem facing our society, sooner or later someone will identify the root cause as a lack of leadership. Leaders, we are told, embrace change. They transform their organizations with bold actions based on their abiding vision of the shape of how things need to be. In the avalanche of books and articles on the subject that have come down around our heads recently, most of the commentary centers on the President or on the chief executives of major corporations.

So how does all this relate to my divisional marketing manager?

He is one of perhaps five million American middle managers. For the most part, these people don't possess grand visions for their companies but instead worry about procedures for approving loans, methods of reducing the setup time for some newfangled and terribly expensive piece of machinery, approaches for introducing new products, and the like. Can such managers be leaders? Do they need to be?

Whether the question is our national competitiveness, the decay of ethics in government, or just about any other problem facing our society, sooner or later someone will identify the root cause as a lack of leadership.

A few weeks after my meeting with the man, I happened to see him in action. He was giving a presentation—an important one—to a group of corporate sales managers, explaining his division's marketing plans for the next six months: what to sell, to whom, how, and for how much. His aim was to ensure that his products would receive a healthy "share of mind" among the sales managers, who sell products from all of Intel's divisions.

This was no piece of cake. As I listened from the back row, one sales manager after another raised objections to the plans being presented. "How can we sell against the competition if we don't have the such-and-such feature?" one demanded. "Unless we have a complete family to offer, we are wasting our time," another said. And so it went, each comment just stimulating another even more critical one.

Leaders, I thought to myself, are individuals who make ordinary people do extraordinary things in the face of adversity.

The young marketing manager acted as if he basically agreed with the comments, even when they were obviously exaggerated. It seemed to me that the sales managers were mainly trying to make their own lives easier. The perfect product is easy to sell; no salesman enjoys having to make up for a product's imperfections by dint of extra work. But the marketing exec was so bent on appeasing this group that he just went with the flow, agreeing with whatever they said. When his time was up, he left behind a very disgruntled group of sales managers.

As I watched this scene, a picture of what had gone wrong formed in my mind. It struck me that most famous examples of military leadership arise in situations where the Great Leader spurs his underarmed and bedraggled followers, on their last legs and with no ammunition left, to great feats of valor. Winston Churchill's greatest moment came when London was being bombed and an invasion of England seemed imminent. Leaders, I thought to myself, are individuals who make ordinary people do extraordinary things in the face of adversity.

What the marketing manager needed to do was to make this ordinary group of salesmen commit themselves to do their extraordinary best in selling his imperfect and incomplete product line. The more his products were underdogs to the competition, the more he needed to elicit such a commitment. But he didn't rise to the occasion. His earlier comment about his lack of leadership skills was, unfortunately, quite correct, perhaps even more true than he realized.

Nonetheless, I hope the man will not try to go about improving himself by reading too much of the current literature on leadership. Being told that leaders and managers are inherently different people would be less than helpful; indeed, the message might discourage him from trying to develop his skills. Nor would the suffocating preoccupation with larger-than-life business figures like Lee Iacocca and Jack Welch do him much good: His role in the business world is so far removed from theirs that he might as well read about the exploits of Alexander the Great.

The lesson my young marketing executive must learn is that an effective manager needs to blend altogether different skills but does not need to be superhuman. On the one hand, he needs administrative skills, skills based on logic and used according to predictable rules. On the other hand, he also needs an ability to convey his strong feelings about a subject when that's appropriate, as it would have been with the sales managers. What he should have said, and with obvious conviction, is something like this: "Here's our product line. We know it's not perfect and we will work to improve it continually. But, for now, this is, what we—and you—have to work with, and what you must sell. I *know* it can be sold because I have sold it myself. You can call me anytime, day or night—here is my home phone number—if you need help to work out an approach that's right for your customer. Give me 24 hours and I will be there to go with your salespeople to call on any account that needs it."

My would-be leader also needs to learn to gauge the right moment to inject his emotion into a business situation. Leaders get the timing right. Had he burst into his speech too early, he would have come across to the sales managers as insincere. As it happened, he missed the right time altogether and came across as a weak, wishy-washy, uncommitted manager. The perfect moment probably would have been after he replied strongly to the first couple of objections.

. . . an effective manager needs to blend altogether different skills but does not need to be superhuman.

How will my subordinate learn such things? Not by reading about great leaders whose experience is so foreign as to make it impossible for him to identify with them. Nor, in my view, by going to wilderness retreats and climbing poles and rafting down white-water rivers. He will learn the same way each of us has learned the important, unteachable roles in our lives, be they that of husband or wife, father or mother: by studying the behavior of people who have made a success of it and modeling ourselves after them.

I went back to the divisional marketing manager after the sales presentation and told him that he was right, he did indeed lack in leadership skills. I described how I saw him come across at the meeting, and the opportunity he had missed. He wasn't at all happy to have his suspicions confirmed, but, knowing him, the next time he makes a presentation to the sales managers, I'm expecting a major display of leadership.

Katherine Graham
1917 –

For several decades Katherine Graham was one of the most influential people in the United States as chair of the Washington Post Company; and for a long time, the only woman to run a Fortune 500 company. She was born to a New York multimillionaire banker, who bought the *Washington Post* newspaper in 1933 when it was financially ailing. Before joining her father's company, Graham attended Vassar College, left the stodgy school for the University of Chicago, then took a job as a reporter for the *San Francisco News* in 1938. A year later her father reeled her in. She began work in the circulation and editorial departments of the *Post*'s Sunday edition. In 1948 her father sold the newspaper to her and her husband, and they proceeded to turn it into a media conglomerate, adding *Newsweek* and other periodicals as well as radio and television stations.

When Graham's husband committed suicide in 1963, she became president, actively running the company until 1991. In stating her mission, she quoted one of her father's axioms: "In the pursuit of truth, the newspaper shall be prepared to make sacrifice of its material fortunes." Later, when the company went public, she had to assure Wall Street that she wasn't just a madwoman concerned with editorial issues. She operated under the assumption that journalistic excellence and profitability go hand in hand. "I thought if you did one thing well—focused on a quality product—the results would follow." That excellence included Carl Bernstein and Bob Woodward's Watergate reporting. As Watergate unfolded, Graham was attacked by Nixon's allies for harboring ulterior motives and being unpatriotic. John Mitchell, Nixon's advisor and ex-attorney general, went so far as to threaten Graham if a breaking story was published.

While Graham often was embroiled in complicated issues, she always supported her people and never dictated editorial policy. She once told an interviewer, "You want intelligent, large-scale thinkers and writers, and nobody for whom you have any respect would take an edict from on high." A leader's ability to inspire confidence was of the utmost importance to her, which she tackles in the aptly named *If "Business Credibility" Means Anything.*

If "Business Credibility" Means Anything

Katherine Graham

It's become stylish to bemoan the loss of public confidence and trust in institutions, and everybody seems to have a poll that documents his own profession's low estate.

Indeed, the loss of credibility seems to have become a national malaise, as widespread and persistent as the common cold. But like the cold, the notion of "credibility" has become a barrier to clear thinking. For one may be sure that any word that's used so often, in so many kinds of situations, is being misused at least part of the time.

One source of difficulty is that often when people plead for more credibility, they are really asking for more acceptance, and uncritical acceptance at that. That is a very human desire, but it ought to be couched in much more modest terms. Surely mature people, especially those who have or seek any power or influence, do not expect to be universally loved and supported. It was never thus, not in a free, competitive society—and particularly not in a time of social and economic stress.

Thus it is wishful thinking for many executives to expect public affection. Even so, they may at least desire to be believed—to have some credence given to their motives and their views. Yet this kind of "credibility," too, should be stated in modest and qualified terms.

In most situations some people won't or can't give credence to the other side. Consumer advocates cannot afford to give businesses much credit for compassion or concern—not without undermining their own arguments and losing their hold on their constituencies. In the same manner, many corporate lobbyists pay their rent by playing up the threats from what they paint as irresponsible citizens' groups and power-hungry bureaucrats.

Even if overstatements can be minimized, the fact remains that often nobody expects to be literally believed. That is the case with advertising, which is perhaps the greatest native American art. Even under today's restrictive codes, the advertising game allows a large range for exaggeration, selectivity and dreams. The same is true in politics.

Believability depends on an intricate calculus involving words, performance, and the standards that are being applied. And this, I think, gets us closer to the real source of difficulty today—for in many areas of our national affairs something has gotten out of line. The gaps between words and actions and standards seem to be unreasonably large.

People are asking more of leaders and institutions, and tolerating much less. I think this has a great deal to do with the so-called credibility problems that now exist, because the evolution of values, like everything else, has the defects of its merits.

Believability depends on an intricate calculus involving words, performance, and the standards that are being applied.

It's certainly not wrong to impose higher standards of morality and ethics in public affairs and in the marketplace. In fact, I think this change is overdue. But difficulties do follow, inevitably, when the new standards are not yet too clear—and when they are applied ex post facto in judging practices that evolved in a more lenient yesterday. The "everybody did it" defense does not excuse political corruption or accounting frauds.

On another front, it's certainly good to seek more safety for workers and consumers, and more protection for the environment. Yet these healthy campaigns have created many problems, not only because the changes involved may be costly but because they often test the frontiers of technology and the ingenuity of managers.

Finally, it is certainly healthy to ask for more accountability and openness in public affairs, and to afford more groups more access to decision-making and more ways to seek redress of grievances. But all these trends compound the time, paperwork and cost required to get anything done. Even worse, they abet the natural tendency of Americans to be litigious and to take every issue to Congress, a regulatory body, or the courts.

The challenge, I think, is to find ways to reduce the difficulties without abandoning the gains. The passage of time will help; environmental laws are already becoming more familiar. But since endurance is no substitute for effort, we should ask what we can do to minimize hostilities and promote a climate in which communications will be easier and real conflicts can be worked out.

But if we ask what business can do honestly and specifically, I think the answer is that "business," as such, can do very little—any more than "Congress" or "the public" can. Even to think of "business" as a distinct coherent group is to engage in the kind of generalities and platitudes that need to be rooted out. Thus I would focus on what individuals and companies can do—and several routes seem worth exploring.

Wanted: More Candor

The first step is to define one's operating standards and develop better ways of policing oneself. Lawyers, accountants, and broadcasters, to name a few, are wrestling with these problems.

The second is to inject more candor into all communications, and to be more willing to explain policies and acknowledge mistakes. It seems almost too obvious to mention, but companies can avoid many problems by being more forthcoming with reporters, consumers and investors, and by volunteering information about products and practices. This applies especially to annual reports, which are most firms' major summary of their own view of themselves.

A real erosion of public confidence occurs, I think, when a major breakdown takes place, catching the public by surprise, and it later turns out that warning signals were suppressed from public notice and remedy by good manners, personal friendships, habits of discretion, and very understandable human optimism. Such optimism is of course important. It can be the foundation of confidence in institutions whose stability and well-being in turn affect the well-being of millions of people. But it ought to be based on facts.

Given the high public stakes in all this, it can be argued, and frequently is, that the press has an obligation to contribute to the maintenance of such confidence and the optimism on which it rests. But I would argue that while we must be responsible, our responsibility does not include a kind of blind Pollyanna reporting of business affairs and business conditions. On the contrary, our responsibility may point in a different direction on occasion. And that is because the other side of this optimistic bent of mind can be profoundly destructive of the very business soundness and general welfare it is intended to promote.

Too often corporate executives who are extremely up-to-date in other ways describe the free enterprise system, at least publicly, in terms that could have been plagiarized from the robber barons of the 19th century. The language about freedom from government control may never have been wholly true. It is certainly inaccurate now, when government is involved in most aspects of corporate operations—and when industries have encouraged regulation of everything from entry into the airlines business to official definitions of peanut butter and potato chips.

Too often corporate executives who are extremely up-to-date in other ways describe the free enterprise system, at least publicly, in terms that could have been plagiarized from the robber barons of the 19th century.

It would be a remarkable advance if we could describe our economic system in terms that better reflect the real complexity of these relationships. It would also help to discuss deregulation the way we tend to lobby for it—selectively.

The third step is to show more hospitality to critics—to grant them, in short, the same legitimacy we ask for ourselves.

And the fourth is to seek substitutes for litigation as a way to work out conflicts. Though conciliation is not a panacea, it is certainly better than going to court. There are many possibilities—but they all depend on a real commitment by top managers to listen to criticism and respond.

I have carefully avoided bringing up the role of the news media in this. I don't want to encourage in any way the argument that the credibility problems of businesses or any other group would be reduced if the media would only do more to foster public confidence. That line of thinking involves major misconceptions of the nature of news and the role of the media.

First, it assumes that there is a great mass of something called "good news" that the media aren't covering. The system doesn't work that way. By definition, news is the dramatic, the disastrous and the unusual. When millions of workers go home at night without being poisoned on the job, or when new cars do not break down, that is important—but it's seldom news.

My counsel on the subject of credibility therefore adds up to this: Don't think about it. *Focus instead on honesty, perspective, and performance.*

Second, it isn't the role of the media to promote, to ration bad news or to feature an editor's idea of what is good or cheering for society. It's even less our job to try to compensate for someone else's mistakes. When the wheels fall off police cars, there's not much the media can do to help the company involved.

That's not to say there's nothing that news companies can improve. The public can certainly ask—indeed, demand—coverage that is accurate, fair, and grounded in real understanding of events. It can ask for much better economic coverage, an area in which much of the press has been quite superficial until recently. And it can ask news companies, even more than others, to explain their standards and policies, to acknowledge weaknesses and correct mistakes. Our performance, like that of other companies, will improve only if individuals apply higher standards and take specific steps.

My counsel on the subject of credibility therefore adds up to this: *Don't think about it.* Focus instead on honesty, perspective, and performance. The gains that result may be modest—but they are likely to be real.

But although I would banish the word, I think the quality of credibility is essential. For "credibility" is simply shorthand for the basic level of trust and mutual regard on which our whole economy and democracy depend—that foundation which enables competition to thrive, arguments to rage, and accommodations to evolve, however inefficiently. This is essential to preserve.

The system is not as free or successful as its apologists may claim; but it is surely not as exploitive, repressive or rickety as its critics allege. It does face serious challenges. But it has provided, over two centuries, a greater measure of freedom, opportunity and prosperity for more citizens than any other social arrangements yet devised.

Chester I. Barnard

Chester I. Barnard, who served as president of New Jersey Bell from 1927 to 1948, is considered the first executive to truly address the issue of what it means to be a business leader. He wrote prolifically on the subject, including his renowned book, *The Functions of the Executive* (1938). After attending Harvard University for three years, Barnard joined AT&T in 1909 as a clerk in the statistical department. Not long afterward he was sent to Europe to study telephone organizations in detail. By 1915 Barnard was considered a foremost expert in telephone practices and given the task of overhauling Bell's system to create greater efficiency. His study of the business and ability to improve on existing operations eventually led to his being named president.

Barnard's breadth of experience also encompassed a variety of interests outside of Bell. He became president of the venerable Rockefeller Foundation and chairman of the National Science Foundation. Also, he was elected president of the United Service Organization (USO) in 1942, a group dedicated to building clubhouses for and entertaining America's armed forces. When he took over the operation, it had 700 units; within three years it had 3,000 plus. Another of his major accomplishments with the USO was spearheading the provision of services to African American soldiers. Of this achievement, he said, "In the long run this accomplishment may be more important than anything we have done, for unity amid diversity is a fundamental problem of world peace."

In Barnard's study of business leadership, he focused a great deal on how the executive can inspire unity and cooperation, writing "The work of cooperation is not a work of leadership, but of organization as a whole. . . . But leadership is the indispensable fulminator of its forces." To Barnard, a leader is someone who naturally commands respect and is able to communicate purpose. While one of the first to dissect the executive, he admitted, "The elements and processes of leadership are observed and abstracted with great difficulty." Regardless, in *The Active Qualities of Leaders* he does a good job of pinpointing five necessary traits.

The Active Qualities of Leaders

Chester I. Barnard

Leaders, I think, are made quite as much by conditions and by organizations and followers as by any qualities and propensities which they themselves have. Indeed, in this connection, I should put much more emphasis upon the character of organizations than upon individuals. But this is not the common opinion; and I certainly should not fail to discuss that quite variable component, the individual.

I shall list and discuss briefly five fundamental qualities or characteristics of those who are leaders, in their order of importance as regarded for very *general* purposes. Probably I shall not include qualities that some think essential. I would not quarrel about what may be only a difference in names or emphasis. Perhaps, also, there will be disagreement about the order I have chosen. This I shall mildly defend, my chief purpose being to correct for a current exaggerated and false emphasis. The list follows: (I) Vitality and Endurance; (II) Decisiveness; (III) Persuasiveness; (IV) Responsibility; and (V) Intellectual Capacity.

I. Vitality and Endurance

We should not confuse these qualities with good health. There are many people of good health who have little or moderate vitality—energy, alertness, spring, vigilance, dynamic qualities—or endurance. Conversely, there are some who have poor health and even suffer much who at least have great endurance. Generally, it seems to me vitality and endurance are fundamental qualities of leadership, though they may wane before leadership capacity does.

Notwithstanding the exceptions, these qualities are important for several reasons. The first is that they both promote and permit the unremitting acquirement of exceptional experience and knowledge which in general underlies extraordinary personal capacity for leadership.

The second is that vitality is usually an element in personal attractiveness or force which is a great aid to persuasiveness. It is sometimes even a compelling characteristic. Thus few can be unaffected by the violent energy with which Mussolini throws his arm in the Fascist salute, or by the vehemence of Hitler's speech, or by the strenuous life of Theodore Roosevelt. Similarly, we are impressed by the endurance of Franklin D. Roosevelt in campaign.

. . . vitality and endurance are fundamental qualities of leadership, though they may wane before leadership capacity does.

The third reason for the importance of vitality and endurance is that leadership often involves prolonged periods of work and extreme tension without relief, when failure to endure may mean permanent inability to lead. To maintain confidence depends partly on uninterrupted leadership.

II. Decisiveness

I shall be unable to discuss here precisely what decision is or involves as a process, but I regard it as the element of critical importance in all leadership, and I believe that all formal organization depends upon it. Ability to make decisions is the characteristic of leaders I think most to be noted. It depends upon a propensity or willingness to decide and a capacity to do so. I neglect almost entirely the appearance or mannerism of being decisive, which seems often to be a harmful characteristic, at least frequently misleading, usually implying an improper understanding and use of authority, and undermining confidence. Leadership requires making actual appropriate decisions and only such as are warranted.

Capricious and irresponsible leadership is rarely successful.

For present purposes decisiveness needs to be considered in both its positive and negative aspects. Positively, decision is necessary to get the right things done at the right time and to prevent erroneous action. Negatively, failure to decide undoubtedly creates an exceedingly destructive condition in organized effort. For delay either to direct or to approve or disapprove, that is, mere suspense, checks the decisiveness of others, introduces indecisiveness or lethargy throughout the whole process of cooperation, and thus restricts experience, experiment, and adaptation to changing conditions.

III. Persuasiveness

The fundamental importance of persuasiveness I have already mentioned. Here I refer to the ability in the individual to persuade, and the propensity to do so. Just what these qualities are defies description; but without them all other qualities may become ineffective. These other qualities seem to be involved, yet not to be equivalent. In addition, persuasiveness appears often to involve or utilize talents, such as that of effective public speaking or of exposition or special physical skills or even extraordinary physique, and many others. The relation of specific talents to leadership we cannot usefully consider further here. But at least we may say that persuasiveness involves a *sense* or understanding of the point of view, the interests, and the conditions of those to be persuaded.

IV. Responsibility

I shall define responsibility as an emotional condition that gives an individual a sense of acute dissatisfaction because of failure to do what he feels he is morally bound to do or because of doing what he thinks he is morally bound not to do, in particular concrete situations. Such dissatisfaction he will avoid; and therefore his behavior, if he is "responsible" and if his beliefs or sense of what is right are known, can be approximately relied upon. That this stability of behavior is important to leadership from several points of view will be recognized without difficulty; but it is especially so from that of those who follow. Capricious and irresponsible leadership is rarely successful.

V. Intellectual Capacity

I have intentionally relegated "brains" to the fifth place. I thereby still make it important, but nevertheless subsidiary to physical capacity, decisiveness, persuasiveness, and responsibility. Many find this hard to believe, for leaders especially seem to me frequently to be inordinately proud of their intellectual abilities, whatever they may be, rather than of their more important or effective qualities.

A. Montgomery Ward
1844 – 1913

A. Montgomery Ward began his illustrious business career as a humble apprentice to a cobbler, before working in a barrel factory for 25 cents a day. But as he once recalled, he was not "mentally or physically equipped" for such work. Since hard labor was ruled out, it made sense that Ward would enter and one day rule over the catalog business. Ward was inspired to enter the business while working as a traveling salesman for a dry-goods wholesaler based in St. Louis. He visited many rural towns where the local general store charged far more for the same products sold in the city. The farmers suffered, so Ward put together a plan to buy large orders of goods direct from the manufacturers and sell them for cash to the farmer.

In 1871 Ward had saved enough money to start his catalog business, only to lose his entire inventory in the Great Chicago Fire. Finally, in 1872 he mailed out a one-page catalog of 150 items. Five years later the catalog was 150 pages, and the now-threatened rural storekeepers were burning them in protest. Ward wrote his own copy in a folksy style, focused on the quality of goods and delivery time, offered a money-back guarantee, and sold to everyone regardless of race or color. But the key to Ward's early success was that he aligned himself with the National Grange, a popular farmers' association.

Ward spoke at hundreds of Grange meetings to overcome his customers well deserved suspicions of mail order. He took a paternalistic view concerning his farmers, lecturing to them on how to judge quality, how to buy, and how to save. He even tried to protect farmers against various price-gouging trusts that sprang up by waging public relations battles against them. And, of course, he urged his customers to bring in other customers because it was their Christian duty to help their neighbor. Ward worked hard at perfecting his catalog: "We study methods of improving our business as we would a science. We imitate no one." His own personality, of course, was also a force in his success. In *The Elements of Personal Power,* Ward delves into what it takes to have power and how a leader's personality can make or break a business.

The Elements of Personal Power

A. Montgomery Ward

Just as a firm's reputation is summed up in its personal name, so is the personal power of all its employees summed up in the personal power of the firm itself.

That personal power determines sooner or later the firm's success or failure.

It may begin with one man, but it never ends there. It is true that one man's name frequently stands for all the rest. A. T. Stewart's name stood for a great commercial institution employing an army of buyers and sellers, and for a great commercial success.* It was the personal guarantee to thousands of people of Stewart treatment, Stewart honor, Stewart merchandizing, but it was Stewart personality expressed in his employees that made Stewart a great man. He had principles. He had ideas. He had personal magnetism.

He impressed his principles, his ideas, his magnetism upon his associates, and they impressed them upon the vast concourse of people who bought of A. T. Stewart because he was A. T. Stewart.

Stewart personality was duplicated, radiated, ramified through the people employed. Through them it reached out

*A. T. Stewart (1803–1876) is considered America's first great retailer.

to influence an enormous purchasing constituency. Each customer who came to the store felt it was Stewart personality that was expressed in the policy that governed the selling, and each one who wrote in to order goods felt Stewart personality in the reply that came in the shape of the letter of acknowledgment and the goods.

This is the primary personality of business—the firm founder or head whose name stands for its policy. And around the personality is built up the organization which expresses that personal power in all the firm's transactions.

Thus we find Carnegie founding the steel trust. He throws Carnegie personality into the organization. Carnegie power goes in also. Carnegie guarantee likewise—and we find the steel trust's girders and beams labeled not "United States Steel Corporation," but "Carnegie."

Now, that personality of his influences every employee, stimulates every manager, creates duplication of each good idea upon the broadest plane until each part of the great combination is enjoying the best that each other part has, and finally finds imperishable expression in that lettering on the steel framework of the enormous buildings and bridges and elevated structures which are a greater monument to Carnegie than his libraries.

What is it that constitutes Carnegie personality?

Much of it is common to all great men—for instance, optimism. Carnegie is a man of great hope and courage. He sees great things to do. He believes they can be done. He goes ahead and does them. He inspires others with great hope, great courage and great achievement. Probably not a healthy and intelligent citizen of this country who can read and write, but who feels he can do greater things because of what Carnegie has done and enabled others to do.

These qualities of hope, optimism, courage, are common to Stewart, Hill, Lincoln, Washington, Gladstone—any great man you can mention; and they are common to millions of men you cannot mention because they are unknown, but yet are doing great things.

They are common to thousands of employees in great commercial establishments—to buyers, to salesmen, to managers, to stenographers, to shippers, to wagon drivers, to cashiers, to office boys. This is the great blessing of our age and day. The attributes of men like Carnegie, Stewart, Lincoln, are made known to the masses and are duplicated today in every walk of life.

We all know that each establishment depends on the personal power of every man employed by it.

Enormous organizations, instead of crushing the personal, have made it stronger, recognized it, stimulated it, advertised it, banked on it, rewarded it.

Carnegie has made millionaires of a whole battalion of his young lieutenants. He has made managers of thousands of men who worked in the ranks. He has offered books, education, emancipation from manual labor to millions more. He has said to his employees: "Give the world the best in you. The world will reward you. If we are your world we will reward you. If not, you will find equal reward no matter what line you go into."

I use Carnegie's name not to specialize him, but because he represents the fact that we all recognize—namely, that we want more of the personal power in business.

We all know that each establishment depends on the personal power of every man employed by it. It cannot make an exception of a single man or boy, woman or girl. Each has personal power to do the firm harm or to help it.

Take the chain of facts that are associated with merchandizing. There is first the buying. That is in the hands of buyers who must depend on their own personal judgment. They must have tremendous personal power. That power must be of various kinds. It must be mental to enable them to study up styles, sizes, colors, demand special lines. It must be moral, to enable them to resist temptation. Every buyer has all manner of temptation thrown in his path. He is invited to dine, to the theater, to smoke, drink, drive, at the expense of those who wish to sell him goods. He is given the chance to make a few dollars on the side. He is always in line to receive presents sent out to his house or his hotel. He is the subject of keenest study by those who sell. They size him up, A to Z. If he has a weak spot, they will find it. And if he has powerful personality, his weak spot will show in his selections. He will fail to buy what will sell best, miss it on quality or price or style, or something that he would not have missed it on if his personality had been strong enough to keep the seller at a distance and pass upon his purchases solely by his own judgment.

He must also be physically strong. A man physically weak is at a disadvantage always when he comes in contact with robust personalities. We all know these things to be true. We see it every day.

The buyer's personality must also be secretive. He must keep his ideas to himself. He must not throw open his mind to those he is dealing with. He must resist every effort to penetrate his inner man. He must be cautious, suspicious, self-confident.

He is buying not to please those he deals with, but the millions of people all over the country and in foreign countries who will eventually judge us by the personality of the buyer worked out into goods for the home, the person, the dairy, the farm. He does not come in direct contact with these customers of ours—but we wish he could.

We like him to feel they are his customers and that he is personally responsible to them. That helps him and helps them. That is why we have some of our buyers write their own advertising, setting forth the reasons why they have bought certain goods and signing the advertisements with their own names. That not only gives the buyer the direct personal interest we want him to have in his work, but it gives the purchaser the feeling that he or she is not buying from a big impersonal mail order establishment, but that we are still a personality or a group of them, no matter how many millions the business may totalize.

The goods bought and the process of selling them begun, the power of personality enters into the correspondence and the advertising. You will find a page or so of personal talk from myself to the people who buy of us, many of whom I feel are my personal friends, many of whom I have met personally or written to personally and millions of whom have personally visited us here in Chicago. It is their confidence that has built the business. I impress upon everyone who writes a letter or meets a customer the fact that we are doing business with people personally and not impersonally.

We want every letter that goes out to be personally written. We want it to have the personality of the firm in it and the personality of the writer. We would like to have the stenographers and typewriters take a personal interest in these letters. Perhaps, if they did, they would not so frequently make us feel that they regard themselves as machines instead of personalities.

It now takes about fifteen letter inspectors to read the letters that go out of here daily and detect mistakes that would never occur if each stenographer would look upon her work as something personal, striving to understand as well as transcribe what is said. As it is, lack of personal interest is responsible for over a hundred and fifty letters daily being rejected by the inspectors and rewritten by the typists.

A man physically weak is at a disadvantage always when he comes in contact with robust personalities.

Promotion is not very rapid for those who make these mistakes, and yet promotion is what we seek more strenuously than even our employees do! In a business growing as fast as this is there is plenty of promotion for all who will show personal interest and personally qualify themselves for higher places.

In cheerful contrast to the lack of personal interest of the few is the enthusiasm and eagerness shown by the many. I am thinking particularly of young men who have banked strongly on the personal and won out. They are found all through the place, but several heads of departments stand out conspicuously as demonstrating the value of those qualities which we find in Carnegie and Lincoln—optimism and self-confidence.

"I am going to make it a half-million this year," said the head of our furniture department one day.

He had not touched the quarter-million mark then. I liked his talk.

There is nothing secret about our bookkeeping. The whole place is wide open. Everything is simple and plain.

I have watched the effect of such talk. It sounds large. It is frequently condemned. Our furniture man got the half-million all right, but before he got it he was talking a million, and before he got that he was talking a million and a half, and thence onward so fast that he never had time to remember his previous goals before he had gone entirely past them.

You see, men who talk that way have to make good or be humiliated. Their boastful words would be hard to swallow in case of failure. So they lie awake nights thinking how to win, get down early and hustle. The whole place gets full of the infection. The other departments wake up and enter the race. And the result is a heavy gain all along the line and a fine esprit de corps that keeps things on the go.

See the people entering our place any day. They may be from Arizona or Mexico or Australia. They may never have been in town before, may have been buying of us for years and always wanted to come up and see what we look like. The minute they come in the door there is a personal welcome for them. A man is on duty with a pleasant personal greeting, a friendly way of telling them where to find what they want and the art of making them feel that the personality the customer has been banking on all these years is right here and all over the place, expressed in every employee and just as real as the goods we sell.

There is a young man making out refund vouchers. He wants the customer to sit right down alongside his desk and get acquainted. There is a row of chairs by the desk. He is glad to have the customer see the whole process. There is nothing secret about our bookkeeping. The whole place is wide open. Everything is simple and plain. There are no mysteries or ceremonies. The firm is out in the open. We don't believe in getting behind the wall. Now this is not policy merely. It is the real footing we have. Our customers are our friends, and we want them to feel we are glad to see them.

There are desks out in the office with names of employees on them. Why not? We want them to feel they do not sink their personalities when they come with us. They find that we are looking for personality, even in the packing departments. Go in there and you will find our packers taking almost as much personal interest in each box or bundle they make up as those who will receive it.

You will find that spirit all through the place, for personal enthusiasm has its reward. It takes the form of tangible appreciation.

That means more money and better positions. We do not know of any substitute for that. Employees cannot be convinced that personal attention to business, learning personally how to promote the interests of the firm, exhibiting personal power applied to our success, is worthwhile unless we show personal interest in them. Turkeys and baskets at Christmas, payment for overtime, advancement as fast as justified, convince employees they are part of our success, and thus make them feel like proving we are right in our policy.

They get to think pretty much alike along the lines of optimism, hope, courage and get a good deal of happiness out of their work. They see that it is a personal proposition all through, from the general policy of treating each customer the best we know how, money back if wanted, goods lost in shipment replaced and all that, down to the specific policy of personal success for each person who works for us.

They get their ideas of personal force in business by an unconscious process of absorption. They start in feeling possibly that we are a big concern that has not time or inclination to bother about the personal side of things at all. The average city employee comes in usually with a deep sense of personal injury and regards work as something to be endured, but never to be enjoyed.

That is because the city is so vast and so impersonal that it crushes out personality in its young people. The average country employee comes with the feeling that there is no success possible without personally deserving it and working for it, and that, if it is paid for in loyalty, fidelity and hard work, it will be delivered.

No matter how large the business grows, it is always an expression of personal force, just as the personal force of a nation is the sum total of the personal force of its people.

But even the country employee does not believe he or she will count much personally. After a while it dawns on them that the personal side does count, that we do take notice and work for those who work for us.

They see we do not watch to detect weak spots but that we do find out the strong spots while the undeserving fall by the wayside of their own weight. Thus each employee discovers his or her personality in making a success or failure for that employee and also for us. It does not take long to drive truth into intelligent minds.

They see that those who deplete their energies with late hours and dissipation come down late and indifferent to their work: They are sour, snappy, self-condemnatory.

They see those who lead reasonable lives store up energy, develop geniality, make friends, do things and get ahead. They see that it is all personal from habits, clothing, language, to morals and brains.

They see the high-salaried ones are those of the best personality. They see that selling goods, managing people, writing advertisements—all depend on personal force and thus personal force becomes inculcated, along with the feeling that right personality expressed in a system reaches out for vast results and is endorsed by the dollars and confidence of the millions.

So no matter how large the business grows, it is always an expression of personal force, just as the personal force of a nation is the sum total of the personal force of its people.

We believe that our customers and employees feel that our business is as much a matter of personality today as it was in the beginning. Behind each transaction is personal guarantee, and we trust that behind each customer is personal interest in the growth and the perfecting of a system that seeks to interpret the personal desires of each man, woman and child who deals with it.

Thus its policy is a composite of the ideas of all its customers, expressing their will in all its undertakings, while its increase and success are, we believe, as much matters of personal pride and gratification to our patrons as they are to ourselves and our employees.

Roberto C. Goizueta
1931 – 1997

Roberto C. Goizueta, who has been recognized as the greatest builder of shareholder wealth in the 1990s, served as Coca-Cola's chairman from 1981 until his death. Goizueta began his career with the company in 1954 as a chemical engineer in the Havana, Cuba, plant. Life in Cuba had always been good for his family; as a young man he attended a prep school in Connecticut to improve his English, which paved his way to Yale University. In 1959, however, Fidel Castro seized power and confiscated many businesses, including Coca-Cola's facility. So in 1960 Goizueta and his wife fled to Miami with $200 and 100 shares of Coca-Cola stock. Of the experience, he said, "It was a shocker. . . . It brings a sense of humility. It builds a feeling of not much regard for material things." Goizueta carried these endearing traits with him through his career.

Fortunately, Coca-Cola kept him on after the revolution, and by 1966 he was vice-president in charge of technical research and development. But he didn't have specific career aspirations: "I never set a goal to be this or that. I always believed that if you could do the best job you can, somebody will notice you sooner or later." Goizueta's experiences as a chemist proved incredibly beneficial when, as chairman, he championed the development of the ever-popular Diet Coke and caffeine-free versions in the early 1980s. Of course, the notorious introduction of the new Coke formula in 1985 and accompanying public protest was considered either a blunder or a marketing coup, depending on your view. The return to the classic formula ninety days later strengthened the beverage's market position.

Goizueta brought to Coca-Cola the willingness to shake up an entrenched and tentative culture by taking risks. He never abandoned the core traditions surrounding the world's "most valuable product." However, he said, "It is extremely important that you show some insensitivity to your past in order to show the proper respect for the future." In the middle drawer of his desk, he always kept the company's mission statement: to create value over time for the owners of our business. In the following selection Goizueta explains why he never felt the need to make shareholders comfortable, only richer.

The Real Essence of Business

Roberto C. Goizueta

At The Coca-Cola Company, our publicly stated mission is to create value over time for the owners of our business. In fact, I would submit to you that in our political and economic system, the mission of any business is to create value for its owners.

Usually, wherever I go, people are full of questions for me. Today, I am here to ask you one simple question: Why should company managements focus so strongly on creating economic value?

Why shouldn't the mission of business be to produce something? Or why shouldn't it be to serve our customers? Or why not philanthropy? Why is it not to make products of the highest quality? Or why not to create jobs?

So . . . why share-owner value?

This question has a three-part answer. First, increasing share-owner value over time is the job our economic system demands of management. Second, by increasing share-owner value, we are able to contribute to society in meaningful ways. And, third, it keeps management from acting shortsighted.

Let's look at these answers one by one. First, creating value is a core principle on which our economic system is based; it is the job we owe to those who have entrusted us with their assets.

We live in a democratic capitalist society. Here, people create specific institutions to help meet specific needs. Governments are created to help meet civic needs. Philanthropies are created to help meet social needs. Churches are created to help meet spiritual needs.

And companies, such as the ones that you and I work for . . . are created to meet economic needs. One role of government, in turn, is to provide the necessary climate for business to carry out its function.

My job is to make The Coca-Cola Company grow profitably, which inherently stokes the economy . . . here and everywhere else in the world we do business.

While performing its role, business distributes the lifeblood that flows through our economic system, not only in the form of goods and services, but also in the form of taxes . . . salaries . . . philanthropy.

Society benefits from commerce, in fact, it thrives on it. And make no mistake, our companies, in turn, benefit from a healthy society. We benefit from educated employees, from a high quality of life in our cities, from roads and waterways . . . from all the services for which the government is the preferred provider. Still, business is the main driver of economic growth.

Thus, we cannot hold any administration in our nation's capital solely responsible for the performance of the economy. That would be like holding me responsible for the performance of the United States Marines.

It is not my job.

My job is to make The Coca-Cola Company grow profitably, which inherently stokes the economy . . . here and everywhere else in the world we do business.

But we can and should hold government responsible for keeping the aisles clean for business, so that business can carry out its economic role while assuring that business acts without impairing the civic needs of the rest of society.

But unfortunately today, these roles of business and government have become blurred in the minds of many people, and the result is most discomforting. It is discomforting because when institutions try to broaden their scopes beyond their natural realms, they eventually run into trouble.

On the one hand, through increasing regulations, government impinges negatively on the ability of companies to effectively and efficiently meet economic needs to play the role for which companies were created.

And on the other hand, the demands, economic and otherwise, on those same companies are growing every day. Customers and consumers, employees and communities: We are asked to serve many masters, and in many different ways.

So, in the face of all these distracting and shifting currents and countercurrents, we must return to one simple but lasting truth: We work for our share owners. That is literally what they have put us in business to do.

That may sound simplistic. But I believe that just as oftentimes the government tries to expand its role beyond the purpose for which it was created, we see companies that have forgotten the reason they exist to reward their owners with an appropriate return on their investment.

They forget because they may become complacent with success paying no mind to the fact that respect for the future is best displayed through a healthy insensitivity to the past.

Or they may wrap themselves in the company flag. They may, in the name of loyalty, prevent change from taking place, or they may assume their business must be all things to all stakeholders.

In the process, these companies totally miss their primary calling, which is to stick to the business of creating value.

I believe it would be wrong, even bordering on arrogant, for business to think it can be all things to all people.

But it also would be wrong for the government to think the same way.

I have to tell you, I find it ironic that as democracy and capitalism are spreading around the world, as one country after another has rejected the failed ideologies by which government promises all things to all people, here, in history's most successful democratic capitalist society, some groups of our fellow citizens have a difficult time grasping the fact that government's job is not to solve all of society's ills.

But neither is it the job of business. Nevertheless, we must always be mindful of one hard fact: While a healthy company can have a positive and seemingly infinite impact on others, a sick company is a drag on the social order of things. It cannot serve customers. It cannot give to charity. And it cannot contribute anything to society.

So, again, why share-owner value? The second answer is that, if we do our jobs, we are allowed to contribute to society in very meaningful ways.

I believe it would be wrong, even bordering on arrogant, for business to think it can be all things to all people.

It puzzles me that many Americans want our government to "fix" our economy or even protect our jobs when much of the rest of the world is thrilled to have government finally playing its appropriate role. Just ask the people of the former socialist world how much they enjoyed having governments "fix" their economies and "guarantee" their jobs. I have asked some of them, and I can tell you their answers were very direct and blunt.

Our Company has invested millions of dollars in Eastern Europe since the fall of the Berlin Wall, and the people of Eastern Europe understand the effects of our investments.

They will not soon forget that we came early to meet their desires and needs for jobs and management skills.

And in the process, they are becoming loyal consumers of our products, while we are building value for our Company's share owners, which was our job all along.

I know firsthand what happens when a system in which people provide for themselves and their families is replaced by a system that promises to provide for everyone. It's the reason I came to this country from Cuba.

That is why I feel so strongly about this subject. It is no sin for us to deliver for the people who have hired us. It is no sin for us to work for the people who have entrusted their retirement savings to us or bought stock in our companies to send their children to college.

In fact, it's our job.

Certainly, we, as a Company, take it upon ourselves to do good deeds that directly raise the quality of life in the communities in which we do business.

But the real and lasting benefits that we create don't come because we do good deeds, but because we do good work . . . work that is focused on our mission to create value. We must not fail to fulfill this mission. There are far too many people depending on us.

Seventy-six million shares of The Coca-Cola Company are owned or held right here in Illinois.* Today, those shares are worth some four billion dollars.

Seven public pension plans in this state, including the Illinois State Teachers Retirement System, hold stock in The Coca-Cola Company that is worth 231 million dollars. Chicago-based charitable foundations and nonprofit organizations hold in their endowments stock in The Coca-Cola Company that is worth approximately 50 million dollars.

Tens of thousands of Illinois people whose financial futures depend on the continued growth of their investment in our Company are depending on us to fulfill our mission.

*Goizueta delivered this speech before the Executive Club of Chicago.

In the United States, more than 8 percent of our total outstanding shares are owned by foundations and other nonprofit institutions. That's 211 million Coca-Cola shares valued at more than 11 billion dollars.

In 1996, we will distribute more than 105 million dollars in dividends to these charities, endowments and foundations. Or, another way to look at it is that, through the appreciation in our stock price this year alone, The Coca-Cola Company has created nearly 3 billion dollars in additional wealth for nonprofit organizations across this country.

The gravity of this responsibility reminds us that we must remain focused on the core duty asked of us: creating value, over time, for the many people and institutions which own the business in which we work.

Please note that I said creating value "over time," not overnight. Those two words are the core of the third answer to my question, "Why share-owner value?" Because focusing on creating value over the long term keeps us from acting shortsighted.

The long-term nature of our commitment keeps us disciplined to creating value for all our stakeholders on an enduring basis.

In 1996, The Coca-Cola Company has created nearly 3 billion dollars in additional wealth for nonprofit organizations across this country.

I believe our share owners want to put their money in companies they can count on, day in and day out.

If our mission were merely to create value we could suddenly make hundreds of decisions that would deliver a staggering short-term windfall. We could gouge our customers and suppliers. We could cut salaries and benefits. We could stop behaving like good corporate citizens. We could even put our business up for sale to the highest bidder.

But that type of behavior has nothing to do with sustaining value creation over time. To be of unique value to your owners over the long haul, you must also be of unique value to your consumers, your customers, your partners and your fellow employees over the long haul.

That is why I am against a scorched earth adherence to profit at all costs.

I am against slashing today to boost the numbers tomorrow, with no regard to what happens the following day.

Certainly, harsh competitive situations can sometimes call for harsh medicine. But in the main, our share owners look to us to deliver sustained, long-term value. We do that by building our businesses and growing them profitably.

At The Coca-Cola Company, we have built and grown for more than 110 years remaining disciplined to our mission which has brought us to remarkable places.

. . . I am against a scorched earth adherence to profit at all costs.

I am against slashing today to boost the numbers tomorrow, with no regard to what happens the following day.

Not long ago, we did some research and came up with an interesting set of facts.

A billion hours ago, human life appeared on Earth.

A billion minutes ago, Christianity emerged.

A billion seconds ago, the Beatles performed on *The Ed Sullivan Show.*

A billion Coca-Colas ago was yesterday morning.

And the question we are asking ourselves now is: What must we do to make a billion Coca-Colas ago be *this* morning?

By asking ourselves that question, we discipline ourselves to that long-term view.

In his newest book entitled *Business As A Calling* the widely known lay theologian Michael Novak cites a thought from David Packard, of Hewlett-Packard. That thought goes as follows:

"When a group of people gets together and exists as an institution that we call a company . . . they are able to accomplish something collectively they could not accomplish separately. Together they make a contribution to society, a phrase which sounds trite but is fundamental."

We, in business, do have a calling. We have a calling to reward the confidence of those who have hired us and to build something lasting and good in the process.

Sir John Templeton has said: "If the service is beneficial, then every useful work is a calling and a blessing for all people."

We have a calling to reward the confidence of those who have hired us and to build something lasting and good in the process.

We should not be shy in proclaiming our calling. Nor should we ever need to apologize for having found our calling in business.

As a current country song proclaims, "You've got to stand for something, or you'll fall for anything."

PART II

Dealing with Adversity

Adversity offers the greatest challenges and the greatest opportunities for leaders to prove themselves. Feisty H. Ross Perot provides insight on how to motivate people under bleak circumstances. Lean-and-mean Jack Welch likens a spring day to economic recovery and hammers home the need to be more competitive to withstand future recessions as well as international competition. And using military metaphors, J. Paul Getty explains how to turn adversity into advantage. Those dire situations can include dealing with economic crises that effect business, countering aggressive competitors, responding to unforeseen emergencies, and handling personal attacks at the hands of the media or the stockholders. All the authors in Part II tackle tough problems and their solutions.

H. Ross Perot
1930 –

H. Ross Perot, a folk hero of business, is descended from French traders who settled in Texas prior to the Civil War. As a kid Perot held a variety of jobs, from breaking horses to roofing barns. He never imagined great glory for himself; any indoor job would have been all right. But then he won an appointment to the U.S. Naval Academy by writing letter after letter to his congressman. Perot has always been known for his persistence. After a stint with the navy, he became a top salesman for IBM but detested the company's bureaucracy. In 1962 he founded Electronic Data Systems (EDS), took it public in 1968, and eventually sold EDS to General Motors for $2.5 billion in 1984.

At EDS Perot was concise in his instructions to subordinates: "Do what makes sense" and "Spend the [company's] money like it was your own." Compensation in the form of stock made such simple walking orders possible. His primary commandment to his management team was even simpler: "All people who manage in an authoritarian way will be fired." The feisty Texan wanted results-oriented leaders who encouraged fresh ideas; he feared that his company would become another stodgy IBM. As a leader, Perot is characterized as a righteous warrior who never compromises, and his constancy is a prime example of what makes him a leader; he can be depended upon. For example, in 1978, two EDS executives were taken prisoner in Iran under questionable circumstances. The next year Perot orchestrated a successful rescue mission that was led by a former army Ranger.

In more recent years, the wily Texan is best known for his runs at the White House as a third-party candidate. While he came up short in 1992 and 1996, his desire for a better America defies cynicism and typifies his maverick brand of leadership; namely, bucking the system to make it better. In a speech he once admitted, "As a young man I wanted to be a pearl. Unfortunately my lot in life is to be the grain of sand that irritates the oyster." In the following selection he provides insight into how he took care of his pearl, EDS, as well as how to stir up the troops when threatened with both complacency and foreign competition.

Business Leaders: It's Up to Us to Recover the Industrial Leadership

H. Ross Perot

It's up to us, the business leaders, to recover the industrial leadership which we've given up in this country. It is our responsibility to keep our people at work.

Recently I had someone ask me, "Ross, why do you care so much about this?" It's very simple. I grew up in the Depression. I saw good people looking for work and there were no jobs. I don't ever want to see that again because if you have seen it, you know exactly what I'm trying to say.

There's another thing. The working American is an economic miracle. Make no mistake about where the tax base is in this country. I love the politicians who say, "Let's tax the rich, let's tax the big corporations." I've gone on record publicly for years saying, "Take it all. Then let the American working people see that that won't run the country for very many days." On the strong broad shoulders of the American working men and women rests the tax base and if they're not working our two trillion dollar deficit goes into a tailspin in a hurry.

We must remain the world's largest customer and we can't be that if our people aren't working.

And now we've got this funny phenomenon going that says "Well, gee, why don't we get rid of all our basic industries and go to a service economy?" Now the thing that just breaks my heart is the best and brightest out of Asia are learning skills that will create jobs. Our best and brightest all want to be Wall Street bankers, consultants and other things that contribute little to the real worth of this country, and contribute very little to creating jobs. Their priorities are certainly much better than ours. We cannot give up our basic industries. This is a joke. Who are all these consultants going to sell their services to? They don't sell to one another.

Now, let's get more fundamental than that. Whether we like it or not, the odds are there will be wars in the future. Just try to imagine our country fighting a war without being able to have its own steelmaking capacity, its own electronic capacity. Is there any question in your minds whether or not we could have won World War II without converting these car plants? Absolutely not. So, no problem, we'll get all that stuff from Japan. How would you like to be the captain of a ship carrying steel across the Pacific with satellites watching you every minute of the way? It's just a question of where they want to sink you.

This is the goofiest idea in the world. For our country to be anything like the country our parents gave us, we absolutely must keep our basic industries and we can. So, the service economy concept is a mirage.

Well, how did we get in this mess? At the end of World War II, we were the supplier to the world. Today many of our business leaders grew up in an era where there was little competition. The world has changed dramatically in the last few years. Many of us that grew up in this era complain that the playing field is not level. The playing field is never level. Too many of us grew up in a world where we owned the bat, the ball, the stadium, both teams and the lights. Now, let's be honest. It was so bad we had to create intramural sports within our companies, right? All the competition was within the companies, the big U.S. companies. Not among the companies—within the companies.

OK, it's changed. It's NFL time now. We've got some first-class teams on the field and they're tearing our heads off. So, what are we going to do about it? We've got a weird phenomenon in our nation. Everybody understands sports and nobody understands business.

Let's think about it. One of the things that most impresses me and I've had two or three situations where I was negotiating with Communist officials in my life, and the one thing that really impressed me is, they may have just parroted it, like a child parrots Bible verses, but they knew their dogma. We don't understand our system. The average student gets a college degree and has no understanding of business or the free enterprise system, but they all understand sports.

The playing field is never level. Too many of us grew up in a world where we owned the bat, the ball, the stadium, both teams and the lights.

OK, we've got a losing team. Let's say the great teams here in Detroit have lost all season. You're the owners, what are we going to do? You're going to replace the quarterback, you're going to replace the coaches. In business, we criticize the players and the lower level managers. And the average American sits there and says, "Well, yeah, that's all right."

We've got to change that. In other words, we are the leaders and we must provide the leadership.

At a time when many American industries are turning out second and third-rate goods, I've had the great good fortune to be associated with a little company that doesn't play second fiddle to anybody—not the Japanese, not the Germans, not anybody. This little company is generally considered to be the best in the world at what it does. After studying EDS carefully, the Japanese declared it the only Japanese-style company they had found in America.

They went on to declare us fanatics. I reacted to that, and then they went on to explain what they meant. They meant it as a compliment. They said, "Your entire organization is driven to win; you're driven to be the best. You work together as a tightly-knit unified team. You waste no energy on non-essentials. You spend all of your energy on the product and on the service."

IBM made EDS more successful than I because we knew if we ever blinked, they'd kill us.

And then people say, "But you can't do that in the United States, we're such individualists." You couldn't find a bigger collection of characters anywhere around than at EDS. If you met the people, they're really an interesting collection of characters, best summarized when Prince Charles came out to visit us one time, he walked in the room and all the key guys were there and he said, "What do you normally do in this room if I'm not here?" And one of the guys said, "This is where we come to fight with one another."

So, there is plenty of room for individualism in our company. I'll go back to sports. Did you ever find a better collection of characters than the Chicago Bears? But when they go out on the field they play as a team, right? And that's what we have to do in this country.

Let me make it very clear, I'm not the reason for EDS's success. Let me tell you a little bit about this company and why it has been successful because I think it contains some of the clues as to what we have to do. Twenty-four years ago it was a one-man operation, had $1,000, had no customers, no market for our services, and IBM totally dominated the computer field. Using the playing field analogy, when we started, our playing field was a cliff and we were at the bottom. IBM, one of the greatest companies in the world, was at the top.

You'll never hear me say anything bad about IBM, but if I took my shirt off, you'd find their scars on every part of my body where they've beaten it up in competition. IBM made EDS more successful than I because we knew if we ever blinked, they'd kill us. I used to get up every morning and pray it would be the Japanese instead of IBM—nearly anybody except IBM. We were at the bottom of the cliff, they were at the top. We had no money, they had everything. We couldn't even rent a computer, we were so poor.

Day after day and month after month a handful of little dedicated EDSers—and I wish I had time to tell you who they were and what their backgrounds were—scaled the cliff. Armed only with their brains, wits, their creative ability, they just proceeded to clobber the living hell out of IBM. Nobody has beaten IBM as often as ratty little EDS. Any time we go to war with IBM, it's a holy war.

Now, what's my message? Brains, wits, the creative abilities of the American people are an incredible substitute for capital. And so we certainly don't have to lose, even if that's all we have.

Many of our great ideas came from people too young, too inexperienced to have an idea of that quality. But they had it. So you've got to listen to all of them.

The whole success of the company centers around people, not finances. It had to because we didn't have any money. The whole story of my financial success hinges on the fact that nobody would buy any of the stock. I was stuck with it all.

That's the truth.

I shared the ownership of the company with the people who built the company and, believe me, that focused their heads on what was important. This little company has made more people wealthy than any other company I know of in the last 25 years.

So the story of EDS is a story of people. It's a story of average Americans who are capable of extraordinary achievement. Everything you see at EDS today was at one time some person's idea. Since we had no money, we had to listen to the people who did the work. We had to tap their creativity.

So, my first message is, listen, listen, listen to the people who do the work. If you can have two-way communication, that's wonderful. But my experience over the years has been, as long as I hear from the folks that are doing the work, we're going and making money. If they don't hear from me, everything works out pretty well. If I start sending orders down to them and I don't hear from them, I get in trouble in a hurry.

There are guys all over American industry that spent 30 years eating dirt. They finally got in a position of responsibility and they see their role in life is to make everybody eat dirt that works for them.

Many of our great ideas came from people too young, too inexperienced to have an idea of that quality. But they had it. So you've got to listen to all of them.

At EDS there's only one class of person, a full partner. At EDS we encourage people not to look up to one another because it stifles communication. If I find anybody looking down on anybody else, we fire them because that really hurts the team effort in a company. You never hear the words "management" and "labor" used in EDS. Those things separate people. There are no job descriptions in EDS. There are no work rules.

I had a guy come in not too long ago and say, "Ross, I've just got to have a work rule."

I said, "OK, use your initiative. Use your initiative. Do whatever it takes to win, as long as it's honest and ethical."

We tolerate no politics in the company. We want people who want to move ahead based on what they contribute and not at the expense of others. We have a philosophy in EDS that you can manage inventory, you can manage things, but you must lead people if you want to tap their full potential.

Let me give you some examples. If I worked for you, are you wiser to have me enjoy my work or hate my work? There are guys all over American industry that spent 30 years eating dirt. They finally got in a position of responsibility and they see their role in life is to make everybody eat dirt that works for them. Are we going to be able to win and have the best products in the world in that environment? Absolutely not.

Are you wiser to have me work for you or with you? The answer is obvious. Are you going to get the best out of me unless you have my trust and respect? The answer is obvious. How do you get it? You earn it every day. You can have earned it for 20 years and you can lose it in a moment.

We believe in strong, simply stated philosophies that can be communicated and understood by thousands. What is EDS? Every EDSer can answer this. EDS is the finest computer services company in the world. Nobody beats EDS on the quality of its services or the competitiveness of its price.

What is an EDSer? An EDSer is a person that goes anywhere, anytime, 24 hours a day, 7 days a week, to make sure that EDS is the finest computer service company in the world and that nobody beats us in competition.

We tell young people that in their first interview and a lot say, "Gee, if I had wanted to do that, I would have been a doctor."

I say, "No, doctors get Wednesday off."

I think it's very important to tell these young people before they get in the door that, by golly, this is not just a way to make a living, this is a crusade where we are going to always be the best in the world.

What type of person do we look for? Well, that's the fun part. I wish I had more time on this because I'd give you some examples. We look for people who are smart, tough, self-reliant; people who have a history of success since childhood; people who are used to being the best at what they do and people who love to win.

And from time to time, the recruiters have come to me and said, "Gee, Ross, what if we run out of people who want to win?"

I said, "Go look for people who can't stand to lose."

Bring in a person like that, you can give them bad leadership, bad training, bad everything, and they'll make your company a success. Give them good leadership, good training, you've optimized your chances.

The definition of an EDS leader is, he won't ask anyone to ever do anything that he or she hasn't done before and wouldn't do again in a minute. And we would never, ever ask anyone to do anything that was improper or unethical.

In our company there's no penalty for honest mistakes. They're like skinned knees on children. They're painful, they're superficial, but they heal quickly. We encourage the creativity of our people. We encourage openness and candor. I could tell you stories by the hour on that one. We encourage a healthy skepticism about everything that's going on. The total emphasis in our company is on results, not on procedures. EDSers just hate procedures.

They just say, "Tell me what you want me to do, but don't tell me how to do it."

There are over 7,000 people here today. Did any of you ever successfully complete anything the way you thought you would when you started? No. You need to give the people the freedom to use their brains, their wits, their creativity, as they proceed towards the objective.

Our people thrive on huge challenges, the bigger the better; the longer the odds, the more excited they get. You can ask them to do the impossible, they'll do it. We can ask them to do something that's easy and stupid and we'll have a revolt on our hands.

Our business is dynamic and changing. We have avoided having thick books of HOW-TOs. There are only three things in EDS that we won't change. The quality of our service, the competitiveness of our price to our customers is Number One. How we treat one another is Number Two. And Number Three, we will never compromise on our ethical standards.

In our company there's no penalty for honest mistakes. They're like skinned knees on children. They're painful, they're superficial, but they heal quickly.

We look on competitions as wars. I'll tell you a few quick stories that will tell you the flavor of EDS. I have a thousand here I can't tell you because of the time.

We were invited to participate in the largest competition in the history of the computer industry a few years ago. It was so big and so complicated, only EDS and IBM showed up. Two teams on the field, the New York Yankees and the Bad News Bears.

You know, one guy had his older brother's glove; some guys were wearing two left shoes; so on and so forth. We pulled together a team of our brightest people. They were working on it. About 30 days later, our President, Mort Meyerson, walked into a room and his team was saying, "Well, gee, we can't win but it will be a great experience."

Mort went to the front of the room and proceeded to write on the blackboard the seven criteria by which we would be judged. He said, "Look, fellows, we're better than IBM at this. You know it and I know it and the fact that the world doesn't know it is a secondary issue. But we know we're better and we are. Now the issue is not whether we will win or lose. There's only one issue. We're going to beat IBM 7–0." Now that's leadership.

Two years later I had the good luck to be with the team the night they won. At EDS we believe in paying for excellence right on the spot, so we rewarded them with the bonuses, the cash, the stock and so on and so forth while they're still sweating. That took place that afternoon. I was with them that night when we were celebrating. They were dead tired. That's a constant after one of these two-year competitions. I've always told our people, "You're going to be so sick and tired of it when it's over, you might as well win." Feel good about something, right? To be that tired and lose is really bad. So they felt great that they had won. They felt great that they had gotten the stock. They felt great that they had created thousands of new jobs and so on and so forth. But do you know what they felt better about than anything else? Do you know what they'll talk about when they're old men and women sitting in rocking chairs? They'll talk about the time they went up against the best in the world and beat them 7–0. Nobody was going to have it be a 6–1 or a 5–2. Hell, a 4–3 would have won, right? We went for 7–0 and got it.

My second story—we went into an even bigger competition a couple of years later and it was so miserable everybody started dropping out. IBM was working for us as a subcontractor on this one, so we were working together. Everybody else had dropped out except one company. The company walked in and said, "We're throwing in the towel because EDS will win." And the customer said, "Wait a minute. Are you saying we're showing favoritism?"

"Absolutely not."

"Then why are you quitting?"

He said, "Look, this thing is so miserable, we're not sure anybody can run these big benchmarks. You have to lash together five acres of the biggest computers in the world, which nobody's ever done, and do all these things, but we don't think anybody can do it. But those miserable people,"—and they didn't use the word "people"—"from EDS won't eat, won't sleep, if necessary will walk barefooted through the snow and march straight through the gates of hell, and when it's finished they will make it run, and they will win. So, rather than go through all of that, we're quitting now."

They didn't intend that as a compliment but I contend that that's the nicest compliment ever paid to EDS. That kind of spirit, that kind of drive has made EDS a $4 billion company, employing over 45,000 people around the world today. It's a story of ordinary Americans working together to achieve extraordinary results. It's a story of a great team. I think this little company shows, we don't have to be losers in competition, even when you don't have the tools to win. They've proved that average Americans can still be the best.

I hope it's apparent to all of you that the people in EDS occupy a very special place in my life. Next to my family, they are the very best part of my life. I don't just like the people in EDS, I love the people at EDS, and I suggest that wouldn't be a bad attitude for everybody that runs a company in this great country.

Because, by golly, the people who do the work in this country are easy to love. To all EDSers here today, I urge you to always be the best. Never compromise your standards. Carefully guard the three things we've said we'd never change but would always improve. EDS has a cutting edge like a scalpel today. Don't ever lose it because that's the difference between winning and losing.

Keep the great spirit that causes every EDSer to rally around to help another EDSer or his family when a problem arises.

To all the business leaders today, I suggest that only we can create the jobs. Millions of fine, decent Americans are more than willing to work, but they cannot create their jobs. All they can do is work if we create the jobs. Their ability to have a job rests squarely on our leadership and our policies. I urge you to redouble your efforts to make the finest products in the world and sell them at a competitive price.

Once again during our careers let's make "Made in the USA" the world standard for excellence. Keep the people at work. Don't just hold the line. Create thousands of new jobs. It won't be easy, but that's our job. This is the job of the business leader. We have to do it.

To all the business leaders today, I suggest that only we can create the jobs. Millions of fine, decent Americans are more than willing to work, but they cannot create their jobs.

Our business is tough. We teach our people that from the time they join us. Every EDSer likes to get in a fight. And then, young people come and say, "He hit me." Well, that's what a fight is, right? You're not going to get to throw all the punches. A fight's a two-way street. You've got to expect to get hit hard, you've got to endure the pain. And as I've talked to people in EDS for years and I suggest to all the business leaders here, in a boxing match you can lose the first 14 rounds. All you go to do is get that sucker before the last 10 seconds of the 15th round and you're the heavyweight champion, right?

At EDS, we've got another philosophy. If we don't do that, we declare the old rules in effect—just keep the fight going until he's too tired to come out. That's the kind of spirit we have in sports and that's the kind of spirit we need in our companies in order to keep our country what it has always been.

With that spirit, our best days are in the future, not in the past. I am certain that with that spirit we too will leave a better world for our children and our grandchildren.

Finally, in closing, I urge every EDSer and every business leader here, and every American working person who's here or hears this speech, to never forget the rallying cry that we at EDS have used many times over the years. When we were tiny and small and didn't have the tools, when we were outgunned, when we were outnumbered and the odds of victory seemed hopeless, our rallying cry when we felt that we simply were too tired and beaten to answer the bell for the next round, the rallying cry that gave us renewed determination to get back in the ring and win was Winston Churchill's shortest speech.

Here it is in its entirety: "Never give in, never give in, never, never, never."

John F. Welch, Jr.

1935 –

John (Jack) F. Welch grew up in the gritty town of Salem, Massachusetts, where there was little to look forward to except sports. He became captain of the hockey and golf teams, and when he went to the University of Massachusetts, he joined a jock fraternity. "We drank more beer and had more fights than anybody there," he recalled, but quickly added, "And I had great grades." The same macho attitude has defined his tenure at General Electric. As one colleague said, you've got to prepare for meetings like you would a football game. And not long after Welch took over as CEO of General Electric in 1981, he was dubbed "Neutron Jack" by *Newsweek* magazine as he eliminated or divested one-third of the company's workforce (170,000 jobs) over the next five years.

The reorganization was based on Welch's simple and direct strategy: Every GE business unit had to be one or two in its respective industry, or it was gone. In other words, you either adapted to what he correctly anticipated as "a rapidly changing high-tech global market," or you were vaporized. Some attacked this philosophy as too arbitrary, too unconcerned with the nuances of particular industries. Welch admitted, "I don't know what color the refrigerator is or how it all works, but generally speaking, we know what the higher issues are. . . . It's sort of a smell, a scent, a trust in the people."

Welch focuses on creating a boundaryless organization that listens to every rank-and-file employee, to every customer, to every supplier, all in the name of winning greater efficiency. As he once said, leadership "isn't someone on a horse commanding the troops. It's the ability to succeed through other people's successes." To create a fluid organization that puts a premium on spirited teamwork, Welch and company built their own management school. It was so successful that *Fortune* magazine labeled it "the Harvard of Corporate America," and other companies literally stole its textbooks. In the following speech, delivered on the heels of the economic recession of the early 1990s, Welch elaborates on being boundaryless and the changes that are necessary to win in a leaner, meaner world.

Global Competitiveness: America in the Eye of the Hurricane

John F. Welch, Jr.

There is something about a spring day that improves one's view of life and the world. And there is something about economic recovery—improved orders, growing exports and robust profits—that does the same. This afternoon I would like to step back from the excitement of this domestic-driven economic recovery and give you one view of America's competitive position in the global economy. I share many of the same experiences with you as a participant in the same global trade wars; and since my Company is fortunate to be a significant supplier of goods and services to the auto industry, I am someone with an enormous interest in your success.

And your recent success—and the success of the American manufacturing sector in general—has been impressive. America's competitiveness in the global arena *has* improved; and this recovery is all the more impressive when you lay its vital statistics next to its more-or-less typical predecessor, which took place between 1982 and 1985.

In that recovery, we saw volume pick up at an annual rate of 4.5 percent, we got almost a point and a half of price, and we saw manufacturing profits climb 7 percent.

That recovery, while strong, was a lot different from this one. In this one, we've only seen *half* the volume increase—

and almost nothing in the way of price—and yet profits are 40 percent higher than in the last recovery.

How do you get this profit improvement out of relatively little volume and no price? The answer to that is one word: productivity. In the '82–'85 recovery, we generated a routine 2 percent productivity increase and let the volume and price lift us. In this recovery, manufacturers more than *doubled* that productivity, and we helped to lift ourselves.

America became more productive. It got more out for less in. Those gains in appliances or light bulbs or vehicles per employee, the kinds of numbers with which all of us are familiar, are impressive. Quality improvements, which are linked to productivity growth, were impressive, as well. I know you take great pride in your progress in quality, and that pride is justified. And almost every American industry, by almost every measure, has seen improvement in its productivity and its relative competitive position.

And, if I can give you just one more number, this improvement in competitiveness is reflected in another statistic: exports as a percentage of GDP—a key measure of competitiveness—are up more than 50 percent from a decade ago.

We certainly can't complain that we're not getting credit for all this. The business press, which wrote articles about us just a few years ago that could have been confused with obituaries, is now ebullient about our comeback and lavishing its sympathy on our troubled competitors in Europe and Japan. I remember a prominent article in the business section of *The Sunday New York Times* just a couple of months ago that I can only describe as euphoric . . . even giddy. According to it, "American industry is back with a vengeance." Our managers are tougher and more farsighted. Our European and Japanese competitors are now envious of, and I quote again, "our country's cleverness in churning out everything from jobs to jeeps." In fact, we are "the envy of the industrialized world."

Lest any doubt remain, there is this conclusive centerpiece of data, and again I quote: "Rush Limbaugh, who likes to brag about America's prowess, is one of the most popular radio talk show hosts. By contrast, Bruce Springsteen, the balladeer of dying American factory towns, hasn't had a hit in a couple of years."

Yes, the numbers are pretty good, and there's nothing wrong with a puffy valentine from the press every now and then.

Now, I'm an optimist—someone who is often accused of seeing the glass as always half full. And I'm probably guilty as charged. But today, I'd like to step out of character for a few minutes and make a case for at least a second look at this newly acclaimed supremacy of American manufacturing.

I'd like to think of what we have come through over the past decade as the leading edge of a hurricane . . . buffeting and turbulent. We got through this front edge with some of the things we read in our press clippings: innovation, higher productivity, pain and sacrifice. Now we find ourselves in what I believe to be not the clear air of fair weather but rather the deceptively tranquil center of the storm—the eye of the hurricane.

Those of you who have ever weathered a hurricane will probably never forget the experience—howling wind, darkness, damage, and then, when the eye passes overhead, there is a sudden period of calm, sunshine, the birds start up again; but that calm is temporary, and everyone knows that what is to come will be at least as severe as what has come before.

That eye of the hurricane is, in my view, where we stand today in much of manufacturing in America.

Exhibit "A" in the case for that view is the currency situation.

In 1985, the yen was 270 to the dollar. Today, it's roughly 150 percent stronger, at 105. In 1985, the D mark was 3.30. It's now about 50 percent stronger at 1.65. That's a lot of productivity for us to find. How much would we be selling, how bold and innovative would we American managers be, how envious would the world be of our manufacturing prowess if that yen and that D mark were at the same strength they were not ten years ago—at 270 yen to the dollar—but only three—about 140 to the dollar?

Currency is a critical element in a country's competitiveness, and it is increasingly volatile and explosive in its effect on competitiveness. When Italy and Great Britain left the ERM in the summer of '92 and devalued their currencies against the franc and the mark, Italy's export growth went from 4.6 percent annually to over *18 percent.* Great Britain shot from a 3.5 percent growth in exports to *14 percent—in a year.*

The biggest danger lies in believing our press clips—toasting the end of a storm that has not ended . . .

The euphoria is enhanced in this pleasant interlude by the way the U.S. situation contrasts with the difficult times competitors are having with their national economies. The well-deserved affluence and success of the Japanese dulled their competitive edge a bit, and the deflating of their bubble economy—caused by forays into overpriced real estate from Tokyo to Rockefeller Center to Pebble Beach—has taken its toll. In Western Europe, the bloated bureaucracies of their companies and the social policies of their governments finally caught up with them and severely reduced the competitiveness of their industry. And the West German acquisition of East Germany, while strategically sound, created a heavy goodwill amortization burden on their short-term performance.

And finally, while some in this country often complain about share owner activism, impatience and demands for performance, I believe that the indulgence and the patience of the European and Japanese share owners has had the effect of lessening the bite, the urgency and the overall competitive edge of their companies.

So, yes, we have plenty of reason to enjoy the relative improvement we see in our manufacturing industries, but only if we understand the role currency shifts, the weakening economies of our traditional competitors and the indulgence of their share owners played in this relative improvement in our performance. The biggest danger lies in believing our press clips—toasting the end of a storm that has not ended—and hosting a party for all our constituencies to share in the fruits of this apparent success.

That way lies danger. Because while we pat ourselves on the back, global competitors are working with feverish intensity to overcome the disadvantages of their economies and their currencies. The annual report of Toyota, one of the world's greatest manufacturing companies, lays out very clearly solution number one to the problem of the yen, and I quote, "*We will cut costs like we have never cut costs before.*"

Over the past few months, I've met with several Japanese CEOs of customer companies and GE venture partners, and their grim determination is to do exactly that: cut costs, and then cut them again, not in nibbles but with what one of our Japanese associates calls "bullet-train thinking"—not incremental performance improvement but order-of-magnitude improvement. The CEO of one of our partners plans a *30–50 percent* cost takeout in 18–24 months, and they are well on the way toward these goals. Others say they put no stock in predictions of a weaker yen and are preparing themselves to compete at 90 yen to the dollar.

Think about it. An enormously resourceful Japan, handicapped by a strong yen, *still* exports a record $350 billion of merchandise in 1993, grows to what some consider the world's largest manufacturing economy, and is talking about cost takeouts of 30–50 percent. Company after company is increasing the percentage of goods and components now produced outside high-cost Japan as they confront the currency problem head-on.

I could make the case that the powerful yen is the *best* thing that ever happened to Japanese competitiveness.

And look at Europe. There's a new, aggressive, smart breed of CEOs, privatization is spreading across the continent, companies are increasing their sourcing from low-cost areas within Europe and Eastern Europe, and share owners are increasingly becoming interested in performance and profits. Companies are delayering, restructuring, attacking bureaucracy, getting faster. And when they rein in their social bureaucracies, cut their costs, and feel the heat of the share owners, they will become more competitive than we have ever imagined they could be.

America's global competitors are taking actions right now that will push it from the deceptive tranquility of the eye back into the turbulence of the hurricane, a hurricane that this time will come with a ferocity that could be intensified should the currency go the wrong way.

Currency is a wild card in global trade. Exchange rates are growing in their volatility because of enormous and sudden international capital movements that are independent of the traditional tinkering of central banks. For us to bet on the permanence of a rising yen or D mark makes as much sense as assuming the permanence of a rising tide.

The consuming passion of each of our companies must be to become so fast and so lean and so close to that customer that the value nub is always in our sights.

What are we going to do when a restructured and hungry Europe and a lean, low-cost Japan, with improved local economies, come roaring back? Show them our press clippings? And what happens if the yen swings back to over 130, as it was just two years ago, and/or the D mark moves toward 2?

What, then, do we do?

First, we've got to stop believing the press and the politicians. They were wrong when many of them wrote us off as dinosaurs. And now those that have taken the opposite view are equally wrong. This "happy days are here again" talk is just talk. You know it. I know it. Our competitors know it. Now we need to make sure each of our constituencies knows it as well, and we need to buttress the urgency of our situation with actions today that prepare us for tomorrow: relentless cost-cutting, rational labor-management conversations, resisting the expansionist schemes of a tax-hungry government, and waging an unending war on bureaucracy and bureaucrats. If the Japanese are preparing to compete at 90 yen, we must be ready to compete at *130,* and until we are, we delude ourselves if we think we are in control of our own fate.

Second, we must focus enormous energy on growth. We must concede no markets—and no customers—because our competitors do not. You know with car models, and I know with turbines and jet engines and CT medical scanners, that there is a value nub, an intersection, where low cost and just-the-right features intersect. That value nub, when hit, causes products to fly off the shelves and out of the showrooms. The consuming passion of each of our companies must be to become so fast and so lean and so close to that customer that the value nub is always in our sights.

We must forfeit no geographic markets, particularly those of high growth. Asia is the greatest growth market we will see in our careers. It is our future. All of us who consider ourselves global companies have to be active players there. We use a little aphorism around our Company that goes, "If you're not in Germany, you're not in Europe. And if you're not in Asia, you're nowhere."

We must have growth. Growth is the *only* hope for the future of those good-paying jobs our companies provide. Growth in successful companies is a mindset. In the future, it must become the *obsession* of all of us.

Growth can be everywhere, from emerging countries to the so-called "maturest" of markets.

To give you a small, but to me fascinating, example of the growth mindset in action, every year we have a management meeting at a hotel in Florida, and every year it seems the hotel touts its "new," "improved," "redesigned" golf course. The "redesign" consists of amputating parts of the holes and building million-dollar homes and condos on them. The "improvements" mean you now have 18 better—but shorter—fairways and 18 better—but smaller—greens. But it also means that 400-yard par fours are now just over 300 yards, and there seem to be more par threes every year. And then they have the imagination to advertise the homes anywhere near the little pond on what's left of the short par four as having, and I quote, "water views."

This may be a little extreme, but you have to admire the mentality that takes a seemingly finite asset—in this case acreage—and finds growth. "Mature" isn't just an adjective anymore, it's an excuse for not finding growth. There's no such thing as a mature business or a mature market.

We now know where productivity—real and limitless productivity—comes from . . . It comes from engaging every single mind in the organization.

What business could be mature when you have economies with more than two billion people in India, China and Southeast Asia?

What market could be mature when subjected to the creativity we know resides in all of us?

Third, and finally, we must—just *must*—get more productive. Productivity growth is the ultimate measure of competitiveness and the source of every nation's standard of living. None of us should rest easy at night if any competitor can produce appliances or turbines or jet engines or cars with higher real productivity than we can.

The country or the company with the highest absolute productivity may be buffeted by the winds of competition or the fluctuations of currency, but in the long run it controls its own fate.

Growing productivity must be the foundation of everything we do. We've been chasing it at GE for years. We once thought we could manage it into business operations, with controls and hierarchies and vinyl books with charts. All we did was stifle people, sit on them, slow them up and bore them to death. In the early eighties, we fell in love with robots and automation and filled some of our factories with them as our employees looked on sullenly and fearfully. It didn't work.

We now know where productivity—real and limitless productivity—comes from. It comes from challenged, empowered, excited, rewarded teams of people. It comes from engaging every single mind in the organization.

To get this productivity, we use a big, clumsy word we call "boundaryless" to define behavior. This behavior works in any culture anywhere in the world to harness every volt of productive energy—and every good idea—from every source.

Boundaryless behavior evaluates ideas based on their merit, not on the rank of the person who came up with them. It assumes that there isn't a customer in the world who doesn't have something valuable to share with you, so why not hand them a coffee mug and bring them into the room when you sit down to design a new product?

Boundaryless behavior recognizes that the supplier knows more about the component he makes than our engineers do, so why not let the supplier do more of the design?

Boundaryless behavior laughs at the concept of little kingdoms called finance, engineering, manufacturing and marketing sending each other specs and memos, and instead gets them all together in a room to wrestle with issues as a team.

Boundaryless behavior in our Company leads a medical business based in Milwaukee . . . to empower a Swedish manager in Asia . . . to use a Japanese associate . . . to make diagnostic equipment with components sourced from India and China . . . for sale in Europe.

Boundaryless . . . behavior works in any culture anywhere in the world to harness every volt of productive energy—and every good idea—from every source.

Boundaryless is the language, the behavior definer, the culture, the soul of a true global enterprise. It ignores geography, borders, accents, currencies, and unites people of all cultures.

Once you begin to attack these boundaries, anywhere in the world, many of which are rooted in tradition and the essentially military structure of the post–World War II U.S. corporations, they begin to fall like dominoes.

Boundaryless behavior is tough to embed in a culture like GE's that is steeped in over a century of tight management, but we're getting there; and even our early progress has grown our productivity from the poky national pace of 2 percent in the early eighties to nearly *triple* that today. But I'm not boasting about that, because I know it's simply not good enough to face what's ahead. But at least, and at last, we know the source of what we need.

Our only chance to succeed in these fiercely competitive years ahead lies in engaging every mind, making everyone part of the action, and allowing everyone to have a voice—a role—in the success of the enterprise. The paradox is that these brutally competitive times will be the most exciting, rewarding and fulfilling of all for those fortunate enough to be part of boundaryless companies.

I'm in my 14th year of running a global company, and I've been wrong about a lot of things in those 14 years; but one prediction I've made at least 14 times that has always come true is that things are going to get tougher, the shake-outs more brutal and the pace of change more rapid. When we, someday in the future, look back on this sunny time in 1994, I hope it will be with the satisfaction of knowing we understood it for what it was—and used it to get ready for what was to come.

Rene C. McPherson
1924 –

The maverick Rene C. McPherson became famous for his progressive management style. When he took the helm of Dana Corporation, a sprawling international auto parts manufacturer, his first task was to eliminate the tangled bureaucracy. First, he cut 350 people from a corporate staff of 500. Second, he replaced the seventeen-inch-thick operating manuals with a concise policy statement. Third, he put an end to the numerous management reports that generated over 400 pages every month and replaced them with a closed-circuit TV for information sharing. Fourth, managers were barred from sending memos to communicate with their subordinates; they had to meet face to face. And fifth, he had all time clocks removed from their facilities.

Despite these somewhat liberal and radical actions, the Harvard MBA was still concerned with the bottom line. McPherson said, "We know that profit is like our heartbeat—no heartbeat, no life; no profit, no company . . ." To get the performance he desired, he decentralized the organization, forcing managers to become decision makers, and he set goals that were understandable and quantifiable. McPherson despised ambiguity: "How many people in this world really know what's expected of them in a positive, factual way?"

McPherson founded Dana University for in-house training, and employees were recruited to study manufacturing processes abroad and to share what they learned. He enjoyed saying that the company was made up of only 10 percent money and 90 percent people, so he knew where to make the best investment. And he asked the employees to invest in the company by offering a stock-purchasing program through payroll deduction. The purpose of the program was to make employees feel that they were working with management instead of for it. *The People Principle,* written in 1980 when inflation was in double digits, exemplifies McPherson's belief that people are always the solution to problems. Instead of calling for government help, he expects business leaders to show the way to economic recovery.

The People Principle

Rene C. McPherson

We need new leaders, better plans, improved morale, fewer rules and regulations, and modern equipment. But, most important, we need our people—the millions who have suffered economically in the front lines, making and adding value to our products and services—to successfully carry the war against inflation to its conclusion.

THE PRINCIPAL ANTIDOTE

The principal antidote to inflation is productivity. I am opposed to the idea that less government, fewer regulations, capital-formation incentives and renewed research and development activity are what we need most to improve productivity. My suggestion: Let our people "get the job done." Expand rather than reduce the input side of productivity measurements. Look for something more than a unit of labor, or hard work from people. Listen to them. Learn from experts.

Smart money managers who are charged with maximizing returns look first at their largest concentration of assets.

While people cannot be carried on the books of account as assets, many companies spend more money by far for them than for any other category. Yet human input ranks distressingly low—from my experience with industry attempts to improve productivity—as a feasible solution to the problem.

No Doubt About It

People are the keys to the continued prosperity of any organization. While we all think our products and services are superior, we cannot depend solely on their relative quality for our success. Our ability to sell and market more aggressively, manage our money more creatively, utilize our assets more effectively, plan our future more comprehensively and meet change more vigorously provides the vital margin for success. The people we employ thus make the difference.

> *People were reduced to the status of schoolchildren as soon as they stepped into the plant, their time ruled by an elaborate system of time clocks, bells and buzzers . . . in today's setting that is a sure formula for disaster.*

We had better start admitting that the most important people in an organization are those who actually provide a service or make and add value to products, *not* those who administrate the activity. Likewise, the most important managers are the line supervisors. Until we believe that the expert in any particular job is most often the person performing it, we shall forever limit the potential of that person, in terms of both his contribution to the organization and his own personal development. Consider a manufacturing setting: Within their 25-square-foot area, nobody knows more about how to operate a machine, maximize its output, improve its quality, optimize the material flow and keep it operating efficiently than do the machine operators, material handlers, and maintenance people responsible for it. Nobody.

TIME CLOCKS, BELLS AND BUZZERS

For years much of industry did not recognize, or refused to accept, that principle. People were reduced to the status of schoolchildren as soon as they stepped into the plant, their time ruled by an elaborate system of time clocks, bells and buzzers, their work dictated by an enormous volume of procedures and production standards. Improving production efficiency was thought to be the sole province of management, and the people actually making the product were seldom asked for suggestions. Nor did they feel inclined to offer any. The big game was to beat the system, not change it.

In today's setting that is a sure formula for disaster. People today work very hard, and we should not approach productivity only from the standpoint of working harder. There is another, more rewarding and exciting solution. The experience, perspective and basic operating intelligence possessed by our people represent a large asset that is still vastly underutilized. Our primary objective, therefore, must be to draw from our people the ideas, suggestions, solutions and commitment to purpose necessary for the continued success of our organizations and our economic system. This process starts first with recognizing people as an invaluable, knowledgeable resource, seeking and responding to their ideas, and treating them with the respect productive people deserve. Our managers should manage people; let people manage their assignments.

The Force of Authority

Whatever risk we may find inherent in that idea is due primarily to the insecurity of management and not to a lack of confidence in the potential of people. Frankly, it is much easier for managers to rule with the force of total authority than to share with their people the challenge of accomplishing a task.

This working atmosphere of placing people at the forefront of all objectives can be achieved in many ways. There is no single style of management or method of involving people within an organization. Such a climate is much more difficult to develop, however, where authority is centralized. Having worked in both types of organization, I much prefer that which is highly decentralized, placing the operating and decision-making authority where it best belongs—as far away as possible from headquarters.

Five Ways to Do It

There are a few contributions toward a productive climate that are basic enough to fit any organizational application:

- *Nothing more effectively involves people, sustains credibility or generates enthusiasm than face-to-face communication.* As a total group, both within departments and on an individual basis, our people must meet regularly to discuss goals, objectives, financial performance, the status of suggestions, the future or whatever else is on their minds. I do not believe in corporate procedures; they are counterproductive and restrict the flexibility of people to respond to the unpredictable. They also retard the inventiveness, professional development and accountability of managers. Among the few corporate policies that must survive, however, is the one requiring managers and leaders to meet with *all* of their people regularly—to talk, to explain and to *listen.*

I do not believe in corporate procedures; they are counterproductive and restrict the flexibility of people to respond to the unpredictable.

- *It is critical to provide and discuss all organizational performance figures with all of our people.* Bad news is as important as good news, and candor is essential. If we are managing well, our people have tough goals to meet, and they must know how they are doing as judged against performance yardsticks. Regular meetings help ensure that our goals are understood, and offer the opportunity to share the recognition for having met the challenges.
- *We have an obligation to provide training and the opportunity for development to our productive people who want to improve their skills, expand their career opportunities or simply further their general education.* Tailor the programs to their specific requirements and listen to their evaluations of those programs. Forget about trying to cost-justify education; rely instead on instinct. Everyone responds positively to needs that are, or can be, satisfied. Smart companies during the last recession used the period as an opportunity.
- *This is the most difficult: It is essential to provide job security for our people.* Concentrate on eliminating cyclitility and business fluctuation as well as on establishing an environment where layoffs and work shortages are not considered to be as inevitable as they once were. Most of our people are well insulated from the shock of a layoff to their earnings through a series of income-protection plans. But no matter how sheltered our peo-

ple are by supplemental unemployment benefits, layoffs are bad. They create an attitude of uncertainty, disrupt productive programs, undermine our credibility and erode the spirit of optimism and aggressiveness so important in our work areas. They have the effect of saying to our people, "As hard as you work, and as valuable as your ideas are, we don't need you right now." We do need them, and we need to correct situations that cause employment interruptions. It takes excellent leaders and exceptional long-term planning to accomplish this.

- *Create incentive programs that rely on ideas and suggestions, as well as on hard work, to establish a reward pool.* Then distribute this pool as a percent of income to *everyone* in the particular operation, without respect to rank. Group cohesion is vital.

I learned years ago that most organizations are too large to be run from one office or through the sheer dynamism of a few individuals. I also learned that if we do not listen to our people, encourage them to participate and recognize the immense talent they have, we shall fall short of our growth expectations and our obligation to provide our constituencies the performance they expect.

WHAT DO *YOU* THINK?

The return from investing money in new equipment is fairly predictable: We know the equipment's potential. The return from an investment of time in people—simply by asking, "What do you think?"—is incalculable: That return is productivity.

The productivity we need to beat inflation during this decade will not come from boardrooms, executives or administrators. Dramatic productivity gains cannot be manipulated. However, developing a productive atmosphere in which our people are motivated is the responsibility of leaders. Once that atmosphere is created, it is self-perpetuating. People, our most valuable asset, will respond as enthusiastically as they always have to the challenge facing us. But they will only perform as superbly as their leaders allow.

MAX DEPREE

Under Max DePree's leadership, Herman Miller, Inc., a furniture manufacturer, was ranked regularly by *Fortune* magazine as one of the top-ten most admired companies. His father founded the company in 1923, naming it after his father-in-law, who was well respected in the community (and a major investor in the new enterprise). For DePree and his father, furniture design involved more than being chic; it was also a moral issue that included simplicity, utility, and high quality. In recent years DePree extended the ethical concern to include what type of woods are used in manufacturing; for example, the firm no longer uses the endangered rosewood.

DePree brought the same humanist qualities to leadership, defining it as "liberating people to do what is required of them in the most effective and humane way." When DePree took the helm from his brother in the 1970s, one of his first initiatives was a plan that allowed employees to become shareholders in the company. Employees also must be treated as important contributors, DePree said, believing "everyone has a right and duty to influence decision making and to understand the results." Diversity was another button DePree pushed: "Understanding and accepting diversity enables us to see that each of us is needed. It also enables us to begin to think about . . . admitting that we can't know or do everything." His humaneness paid off as company sales skyrocketed from $49 million in 1975 to $492 million in 1985.

DePree learned a critical lesson concerning leadership, he said, when a granddaughter was born extremely premature and the baby's father skipped out. DePree was appointed surrogate father and charged with caressing and talking to the baby every day. The key, a nurse instructed, was for the baby to connect the voice with the touch. The same goes for a business leader; his message must be consistent with his actions. The unexpected challenge DePree met as a grandfather is an example of what he calls "roving leadership." In the following selection DePree explains what roving leadership is and why it's a key element to a company's success when it is faced with unforeseen adversity.

Roving Leadership

Max DePree

It was Easter Sunday morning and the large church was filled. The processional was ready to begin. The three pastors, the senior choir, two children's choirs poised at the back of the church—weeks of planning and preparation about to be fulfilled.

As the organist struck the first chord, a middle-aged man in the center of the church began to sweat profusely, turned an ashen gray, rose partially out of his seat, stopped breathing, and toppled over onto his daughter sitting next to him.

And what did these pastors, organists, and choirs do? They did nothing.

But in less than three seconds, a young man with experience as a paramedic was at the stricken man's side. Quickly and expertly he opened the airway and restored breathing. After several minutes, making sure the sick man's condition was stabilized and on a signal from the paramedic, six men lifted him carefully and carried him quickly to the back of the church where he was laid on the floor to await the arrival of the ambulance, which, having been called for immediately by some unknown person, was already on its way.

When the man was laid on the floor near the waiting children's choir, two youngsters fainted. Two doctors from the congregation were immediately on the scene. One stepped in to help the young man care for the patient; the other immediately looked after the two children.

At this point a man thrust his head into the group gathered around the patient and said, "Are you going to want oxygen?" And when the doctor said, "Yes," he immediately handed it to him having anticipated the need and gone to find the oxygen bottle.

It is difficult for a hierarchy to allow "subordinates" to break custom and be leaders. The people who did *respond swiftly and effectively are roving leaders. . . . those indispensable people in our lives who are there when we need them.*

While all these things were going on, the man's wife (who was in the senior choir and did not know what was happening—only that the service was being momentarily delayed) was sensitively informed and brought to her husband's side. Others quieted the children's choirs, reassured them that the man was going to be okay and that they should begin to compose themselves for the service. The paramedics arrived, put the man in the ambulance, and took him to the hospital.

Roving leaders are those indispensable people in our lives who are there when we need them.

As you can imagine, a tender and poignant service now began. At the end of the service, the pastor was able to announce that the man had suffered a severe allergic reaction; his condition was stable; the outlook was positive.

The point in telling you this story is to show that while this church has a hierarchy of more than thirty appointed and elected professionals, committee members, board members, and others, the hierarchy did not respond swiftly or decisively. It is difficult for a hierarchy to allow "subordinates" to break custom and be leaders. The people who *did* respond swiftly and effectively are roving leaders. Roving leaders are those indispensable people in our lives who are there when we need them. Roving leaders take charge, in varying degrees, in a lot of companies every day.

In special situations, the hierarchical leader is obliged to identify the roving leader, then to support and follow him or her, and also to exhibit the grace that enables the roving leader to lead.

More than simple initiative, roving leadership is a key element in the day to day expression of a participative process. Participation is the opportunity and responsibility to have a say in your job and to influence the management of organizational resources based on your own competence and your willingness to accept problem ownership. No one person is the "expert" at everything.

Roving leadership demands a great deal of trust and it demands a clear sense of our interdependence. Leadership is never handled carelessly—we share it, but we don't give it away.

In many organizations there are two kinds of leaders—both hierarchical leaders and roving leaders. In special situations, the hierarchical leader is obliged to identify the roving leader, then to support and follow him or her, and also to exhibit the grace that enables the roving leader to lead.

It's not easy to let someone else take the lead. To do this demands a special openness and the ability to recognize what is best for the organization and how best to respond to a given issue. Roving leadership is an issue-oriented idea. Roving leadership is the expression of the ability of hierarchical leaders to permit others to share ownership of problems—in effect, to take possession of a situation.

When roving leadership is practiced, it makes demands on each of us—whether we're a hierarchical leader, a roving leader, or a good follower. It's a demanding process. It demands that we be enablers of each other.

Roving leadership also demands discipline. . . . Discipline is what it takes to do the job.

Roving leadership demands a great deal of trust and it demands a clear sense of our interdependence. Leadership is never handled carelessly—we share it, but we don't give it away. We need to be able to count on the other person's special competence. When we think about the people with whom we work, people on whom we depend, we can see that without each of us, we are not going to go very far as a group. By ourselves we suffer serious limitations. Together we can be something wonderful.

Roving leadership also demands discipline. Interestingly, though in organizations like ours we need a lot of freedom, there's no room for license. Discipline is what it takes to do the job.

It is not a matter primarily of whether or not we reach our particular goals. Life is more than just reaching our goals. As individuals and as a group we need to reach our potential. Nothing else is good enough. We must reach toward our potential.

The condition of our hearts, the openness of our attitudes, the quality of our competence, the fidelity of our experience—these give vitality to the work experience and give meaning to life. These are what it takes to make roving leadership possible. And roving leadership, freely and openly practiced together, is the vehicle we can use to reach our potential.

Olive Ann Beech
1903 – 1993

Olive Ann Beech, the "First Lady of Aviation," cofounded the Beech Aircraft Corporation with her husband in 1932, in spite of the Great Depression. Walter Beech, a World War I Army Air Corps veteran, already had been involved in several other airplane ventures, including a partnership with Clyde Cessna—Travel Air Manufacturing Company. But he wanted to pursue his own vision and design for an aircraft. While Walter Beech focused on design, Olive ran the day-to-day operations. A financial wiz, she met her husband when she was hired by Travel Air to manage the office, becoming one of twelve employees—the other eleven were pilots.

Beech's early experiences were interesting, to say the least. "When I first started working at Travel Air," she said, "I didn't know the empennage of an airplane from the wing. After a great deal of teasing from the staff when my letters were confused, I had our own chief engineer give me a complete breakdown drawing of an airplane. . . ." When the company entered a 1936 transcontinental air race, Beech insisted they hire two female pilots to fly for them. She reasoned a woman pilot offered "convincing proof that unlike some airplanes of that day, brute strength was not required to operate a Beechcraft." They won both the race and great publicity. During World War II the company really took off, winning a number of military contracts. In 1943 Beech was named one of America's twelve most distinguished women by the *New York Times.*

When her husband died in 1950, Beech took over and continued his spirit of innovation, building, for example, the world's smallest jet to train fighter pilots. Beech retired as president in 1968 but remained on the board of directors. The company merged with Raytheon in 1980, and a few years later Beech retired from the board, ending more than fifty years in the business. She knew she had the capabilities to lead a company, as did many other women in her time. Her only handicap was the constant distractions she faced answering questions related to women in the workplace, especially at the hands of journalists, which she discusses wryly in *The Woman Executive.*

The Woman Executive

Olive Ann Beech

Women in business have long been important in many sectors of our American economy, but their general role may have escaped proper evaluation because of their universal tendency to avoid ungracious and undue publicity and their inborn conviction that, subject to physical limitations, there isn't anything a man in business does that a woman with training and diligence cannot do also.

And yet it seems that throughout business and industry, women executives patiently expect to be called upon from time to time to discuss their ideas "about misapprehensions which are widely prevalent with regard to woman executives' duties and performance." I believe many, many women in management throughout the nation must share with me certain quite human reactions to the many inquiries which, with some humor and no malice, one might separate into a few convenient categories.

Reporter and Researcher

First, there is the occasional cub-reporter somewhat overawed during an initial visit to a large business or industrial scene of multiphased activity. In this newest age of aerospace conquests, it's relatively easy to point out how many women there are at work today "breaking the sound barriers" in their particular fields, just as in aviation there are not only women who serve as professional pilots and test pilots but many others whose special talents contribute greatly through a wide range of business, technical, financial, and managerial assignments.

. . . it's relatively easy to point out how many women there are at work today "breaking the sound barriers" in their particular fields . . .

Second, there is the quiet researcher who seems bent on seeking out "unknown missing facts" in that era between today and that time two decades ago when the Sunday supplements glamorized "Rosie, the Riveter." To such an inquirer, who usually has overindulged in the history of yesteryear, it's simply a patient chore to point out what great strides American ingenuity has taken on behalf of American business. Women production workers today profit through the use of advanced equipment equivalent to the progress made in converting the old-time celluloid-collared bookkeeper to a modern miss who can make the most complicated computer almost think.

Interviewer and Reviewer

Third, there is the special interviewer who, by experience, is a master of repartee with men in management across the land but who oftentimes quite uneasily seems to hesitate in "getting down to facts" with the woman executive. On such occasions I find that my sense of humor serves to break the ice and clear the atmosphere. Certainly if a woman might be permitted a good strong "D- - -" upon being caught with too many points in her hand during a friendly gin rummy game, then women executives should be appraised as being equally adept at expressing their convictions when chairing a board of directors meeting. And we are, and we do!

Fourth, there is the individual who asks for a "special opportunity to review in depth" the whole field of "facts and fancies about the role of women executives." It is at times like this that we women executives need to proceed forthrightly to a discussion of the hard facts of business life—to point out that talent is where you find it, that it is no respecter of men or women, young or old. And therein lies the secret. As long as there exists a shortage of thinkers, as long as there remains a demand for doers, women executives will be at work helping build a better nation in a better world.

Challenges as Opportunities

Today these hard facts of life confront business and industry with a whole host of *challenges* that may be accepted realistically as *opportunities—if* executives have and practice daily the right kind of human business philosophy!

Women executives in their important role of management today are no different than men executives.

In an age when there exists great concern about past tendencies to over-emphasize *security,* I wonder how many of us have neglected some of our basic management responsibilities. How much are we doing to develop and encourage sound profit-and-loss business conceptions among all levels of management, supervision, and labor? How hard do we endeavor to instill the Right Mental attitude? How often do we invest in the future by taking time now to teach and train and develop younger men and women in the true fundamentals which, in a perhaps oversimplified summary, means just one thing: "Everyone is like a tack and can only go as far as the head permits."

Tasks and Qualities

Women executives in their important role of management today are no different than men executives. Their primary tasks are to define the long-range objectives and direct the execution of such programs. For the accomplishment of their plans they need qualified people. People with ingenuity, talent, dedication, faith, loyalty.

Though the decor of our individual offices may vary, the daily problems on our desks are no different. The kind of a woman who can function in an executive job is one who can handle that job, and it's just about that simple.

Certainly it is essential today that our successors have the highest possible professional competence and the energy and leadership qualities to carry on. Their courage, insight, and dynamic action on all fronts will be needed then as they are now.

Though the decor of our individual offices may vary, the daily problems on our desks are no different. The kind of a woman who can function in an executive job is one who can handle that job, and it's just about that simple.

"What kind of a woman?" we're asked. The correct answer from any board of directors of any business or industry would be, I believe: "The foremost in the field; the best available."

J. Paul Getty
1892 – 1976

J. Paul Getty, oil tycoon and once the world's richest man, made no apologies for his wealth: "I have worked hard for my money, producing things people need. I believe that the able industrial leader who creates wealth and employment is more worthy of historical notice than politicians or soldiers." He was a good practical geologist and a "working boss" who could perform any task at a drill site. That's because he had learned the business from the ground up as a young boy. His father, originally a lawyer from Minneapolis, was one of the first wildcatters of Oklahoma. Young Getty followed his father through the oil fields, fascinated by the machinery and the roughnecks.

When Getty graduated college he was thinking of becoming a diplomat, but his father urged him to join in the hunt for oil. He agreed; however, it was almost a year before he made his first strike. From then on good fortune was on his side. Getty made his first million in 1916 at the age of twenty-four. During the Great Depression he bought oil stock when everyone was selling, adding greatly to his burgeoning empire. In 1949 he realized one of his greatest coups when he was awarded rights to drill in the Middle East. Part of his success in negotiating with foreign dignitaries resulted from the once-aspiring diplomat learning the ways of other cultures. In addition, Getty was fluent in five languages and had meticulous manners.

As an underdog challenging giants like Exxon and Mobil, Getty needed to work every angle to win business. Fortunately, as an independent he didn't answer to committees or boards; he was free to make on-the-spot decisions and beat others to the punch. If Getty needed a temporary railroad or pipeline to access a site, he built it. To give himself greater mobility, he built the biggest supertankers which also made his competitors' fleets obsolete. Getty, who revered Napoleon, once wrote, "I think business has to be guided by military history. You've got to plan campaigns and strategies. . . . You've got to plan for all the things that can go wrong." Getty advises on how to deal with those setbacks in *The Businessman at Bay.*

The Businessman at Bay

J. Paul Getty

Crises, setbacks, obstacles—these will certainly be met by any executive in the course of his career. The measure of a man in such circumstances is not only how he copes with adversity, but also how he turns it to his advantage. Business is always a battle—for sales, improvements, efficiency—and an executive must lead very much as a general would: to win.

I remember learning as a youth an invaluable lesson from a man who even then had extensive business holdings and who later became one of America's wealthiest industrialists. Although I knew him fairly well, I hadn't seen him for several months before bumping into him one day in the lobby of a Chicago hotel.

"How are things going?" I asked him after we'd exchanged the customary greetings.

"Not good—terrible, in fact," he replied with a placid smile. "One of my companies has been shoved into a tight corner by the competition. Another is operating in the red—and a third hasn't the cash to meet its short-term debts that fall due this month."

"You certainly don't act as though any of it worries you very much," I remarked in surprise. I found it hard to believe that any businessman who was in so much apparent trouble could be so casual about his problems.

"Hell, Paul, I'm not in the least bit worried," he answered. "To tell you the truth, I needed something like this to get me up on my toes; everything had been going entirely too smoothly for far too long. An occasional crisis is good for a businessman. There's no better exercise for him than to have a few messes to clean up every now and then."

Business is always a battle—for sales, improvements, efficiency—and an executive must lead very much as a general would: to win.

Later, I learned that it had taken my friend less than six months to clean up all his "messes." Despite the fact that he owned or controlled many other business enterprises, he plunged enthusiastically into the task of personally reorganizing and revitalizing the three faltering companies.

He quickly pulled the first one out of the corner into which it had been driven by its competitors. He began improving old products, developing new ones and launching an imaginative, aggressive sales campaign that turned the tables on competing firms. He then put the second firm back on its feet by initiating new policies and programs, reducing production costs and increasing output. As for the third company, he arranged refinancing of its obligations, made needed changes in management personnel and soon had the firm on a sound financial footing and operating at a comfortable profit.

"I had quite a workout getting things in order," he told me sometime later. "But I sure enjoyed it—it's always more fun to win a hard fight than an easy one."

"Adversity is the first path to truth," Lord Byron said more than a hundred years ago.

"Calamity is man's true touchstone," Francis Beaumont and John Fletcher wrote in the early 17th century.

Now, Byron and Beaumont and Fletcher were not businessmen and they did not concern themselves with business in their writings. Yet the basic truths implicit in their lines are applicable to every present-day businessman and to anyone who hopes to make a success of a business career.

A machine that is functioning perfectly needs only nominal care. By the same token, a highly prosperous business that operates year after year without problems requires little more than caretaker management. No exceptional ability is needed to run such an enterprise. Unfortunately, the "perfect business" does not exist. Snags, difficulties and crises crop up in every business. For the businessman—as for any individual—the true test of his mettle comes at the time when he is faced with adversity.

How do executives or businessmen act and react when they are at bay?

First, there are those who sit by helplessly, allowing whatever adversity they face to overwhelm them completely. They are like rabbits which, transfixed by the headlights of an automobile rushing toward them on a highway, make no move to save themselves and are consequently crushed under the vehicle's wheels. Such men take no action to change the course of events and prevent disaster because they are incapable of comprehending what could or might be done. When they have been finally overwhelmed, they are stunned, totally unable to understand what went wrong and why.

For the businessman—as for any individual—the true test of his mettle comes at the time when he is faced with adversity.

Then, there are those who surrender meekly or flee in fear as soon as things start to go wrong. Such men have little or no sense of proportion; they are likely to panic and view even minor slumps and setbacks as unavoidable major catastrophes. While individuals in the first category fail to fight back because they do not know how to fight, businessmen who can be classed in this second group fail to fight back because they are afraid to do so.

Next come those men who react to adversity in an unreasonable, almost hysterical fashion. Terror-stricken, they snarl and snap, striking back blindly and ineffectually, squandering their energies in the wrong directions. These men invariably rail and curse against the "impossible odds" and "rotten breaks" they claim defeated them. Just as invariably, they seek to lay the blame for the predicaments in which they find themselves on shoulders other than their own.

The truly great general views reverses calmly and coolly; he is fully aware that they are bound to occur occasionally and refuses to be unnerved by them.

In another category are those businessmen who fight good, tenacious—and, very frequently, entirely successful—defensive actions whenever things start to go wrong. They are courageous, reliable individuals who unflinchingly meet threats and solve problems as they arise, acting to the best of their not-inconsiderable abilities. But there they stop. Their minds are geared to thinking solely in terms of plugging the holes in the dike as, if and when they appear. The men in this group do not have the imagination and initiative—or lack the experience—to think and plan in terms of building entirely new and much stronger dikes in which holes will be far less likely to develop.

Finally, there are those businessmen who are the real leaders. These are the imaginative, aggressive individuals who base their business philosophy on the ancient military axiom that attack—or, at the very least, energetic counterattack—is invariably the best defense. Obviously, they can't—and don't—always win, but then no general in the world's history has ever won *every* battle he fought.

On the other hand—to carry the analogy between business affairs and military campaigns a bit further—the generals who win the wars and have the highest percentage of victories to their credit are those who can mastermind defensive strategy as well as an offense.

The truly great general views reverses calmly and coolly; he is fully aware that they are bound to occur occasionally and refuses to be unnerved by them. When driven back, he prevents retreat from turning into rout and then adroitly transforms the retreat into an orderly retrograde movement.

By so doing, he disengages his forces from those of the enemy with a minimum of additional loss, saving the bulk of his manpower and material resources so that they can be regrouped and made ready for a counterattack. Naturally, he leaves behind rear guards to protect the withdrawal. He accepts the losses these covering forces must inevitably suffer with philosophical stoicism, realizing that it is sometimes necessary to sacrifice a part in order to save the whole.

When his troops have been rested and reinforced and his supplies replenished, the successful general launches his carefully planned counterattack. Having studied the situation with great care and having learned much about the enemy's capabilities and habits from an analysis of what has gone before, he employs a combination of every resource at his command. He makes feinting and diversionary assaults, aims his major blows at the weakest points in the enemy line and holds back his reserves until he can commit them at the right—at the decisive—times and places.

Like the successful military leader, the successful, veteran businessman understands that he cannot master every business situation, that he cannot emerge victorious from every business "battle." He knows that, sooner or later, he will encounter problems which cannot be solved quickly or easily, that he will find his progress blocked by obstacles which will require much time and effort to overcome or which will even force him to retrace his steps and take a new route. He knows that reverses and losses are sometimes inevitable.

The seasoned business campaigner is well aware that the line charting the course of any company's history or any businessman's career on a graph would be a jagged one. The graph would reflect a series of alternating peaks and lows. But such ups and downs do not bother the seasoned businessman unduly. He recognizes that the significant and telling proof lies in whether the line at the right edge of the chart terminates at a point that is higher or lower than the point at which it begins on the left.

True business leaders—the real *leaders*—often give their most impressive demonstrations of leadership and brilliance at the very times when they are temporarily forced to go over to the defensive, at the times when they are at bay. And this is precisely what sets them apart and raises them above the level of other, less successful businessmen.

Take, for example, the case of my friend who found himself in three serious business predicaments simultaneously. There were several courses of action this businessman might have followed. He could have done nothing, allowing matters to take their own course. He could have closed or sold one or more of the companies, utilizing whatever money he realized from any sale or sales to shore up whatever remained. He might have been content merely to plug the holes.

But he neither surrendered nor panicked. Nor was he satisfied with doing a hasty job. A good general, he surveyed the situation thoroughly, reorganized his forces, brought up replacements and reinforcements and made his plans. Then, marshaling all his resources, he launched successful counterattacks on all three fronts.

The history of American business and industry is replete with examples of how the great business leaders of the nation handily turned serious reverses into major triumphs . . .

I've encountered my share of adversity and reverses. I've spent fortunes drilling many thousands of feet into the ground at one time or another—to strike nothing but sand. I've had other wells that cost other fortunes run dry or blow up and burn. I soon learned to accept such misfortunes philosophically and to take them in my stride, for I realized that I would not be able to stay in business very long if I permitted them to discourage me. In fact, each setback seemed to serve as a special incentive and stimulus to try again—but even harder the next time.

The seasoned business campaigner is well aware that the line charting the course of any company's history or any businessman's career on a graph would be a jagged one.

There were many other, more complex trials and blows, too. I recall, for example, the sharp break in crude-oil prices that occurred in 1921, when oil, which had been selling at $3.50 per barrel, dropped to $1.75 per barrel in less than 10 days—and the price continued to spiral down in the days that followed. At least one of the companies in which I held a substantial interest became hard-pressed for cash as a result of the price crisis.

When I met with other directors of the company, there were those among them who verged on panic. Fortunately, the majority remained calm and objective. Any suggestions that the company close its doors were immediately voted down. Instead, it was agreed to retrench and the directors agreed to obtain the money needed to keep the company going. They also agreed to slash their compensation to the bone and reduce management salaries until the crisis was past. In time, the petroleum market became stabilized once more—and as soon as conditions returned to normal, the directors and management implemented an ambitious program which greatly increased the company's sales and profits within a very short period.

I also have vivid recollections of a memorable campaign my associates and I conducted to obtain control of a large company. The incumbent—and well-entrenched—directors of the company fought us fiercely at every step. However, although the financial resources at our disposal were far less than those of the opposition, we managed to do a bit more than merely hold our own and the battle seesawed for a considerable time.

Then, at one point, the opposition sensed that I had almost exhausted my financial resources by buying the company's stock—and that for a time I would be unable to purchase any more. As I was still far short of having a controlling interest in the company, the incumbent directors believed that they now had the upper hand. Swiftly changing their tactics, they decided to allow the issue to be decided by all the stockholders.

This, of course, meant a proxy contest. In a burst of chivalrous magnanimity, the opposition entered into a sort of "gentleman's agreement" with our side. To prevent the proxy contest from degenerating into a rough-and-tumble fight that could injure the company's reputation, solicitation of proxies would be limited to one reasonably worded letter from each side. The two letters—one urging the stockholders to give their proxies to the incumbent board—would be mailed in the same envelope to each stockholder. Thus, the individual stockholder would have both sides of the story before him—and he could make his own decision as to which of the two groups best deserved to control the company.

My associates and I unhesitatingly accepted what we considered to be a gentlemanly agreement. Our letter was duly composed, reproduced and sent off together with the one prepared by the opposition. When that had been done, I assumed that the die was cast and that nothing further would be—or could be—done to influence the outcome.

Then, only a few days before the scheduled stockholders' meeting, one of my aides burst into my office. His face was livid with anger and he clutched a piece of paper in his hand.

"Read this!" he exclaimed, thrusting the paper at me. I took it and found that it was a letter—a *second* letter—which the opposition had sent out to the stockholders only a day or two earlier. And what a letter it was!

The gist of the no-holds-barred missive was a virulent personal attack on me and a highly objectionable—and entirely baseless—implication that my motives for seeking control of the company were, at best, dubious. I called my associates and held a hasty council of war. What could be done at that late stage of the game? Not much, some of my associates declared dispiritedly. There wasn't enough time.

"I'm afraid this licks us, Paul," one man said, shaking his head in resignation. "Nothing in this letter is true—but it's going to have a tremendous impact on the stockholders. Not having any way of checking up on the charges that have been made, they'll play it safe and give their proxies to the other side."

"You really think we're licked?" I asked, glancing around at the men in the room with me. Some heads nodded assent. The faces of some other men showed that they weren't entirely convinced that all was lost. A few of my associates indicated that they refused to accept defeat that easily.

"Nuts!" one of them snorted. "We still have a chance!"

"I think so, too," I said. "Now, let's get to work."

Working feverishly against a deadline that was far too close for comfort, we composed our own second letter. Instead of calumny, we stated facts and figures that demolished every argument and charge advanced by the opposition.

Then, working straight through the day and night and the day that followed, we—secretaries, clerks, typists, executives, my associates and I—reproduced the letters, addressed envelopes to thousands of stockholders, folded and inserted the letters and sealed and stamped the envelopes. At last, we finished the staggering job—and exhausted men and women carried bundles of the letters to the nearest post office for mailing.

Would the letters reach the stockholders in time? We could only hope, and wait to see what happened at the stockholders' meeting a few days later. But we didn't have to wait that long. The response to our second letter was astounding. Replies began to pour in from stockholders two days before the meeting.

"We might make it yet," one of my aides remarked. And we did make it. Cold facts, stated clearly and plainly, proved to be more convincing to the stockholders than were the heated, personal attacks and irresponsible charges that had been made by the opposition. To the shocked amazement of the incumbent directors—and the delight of my associates and myself—the voting at the stockholders' meeting resulted in a clear-cut victory for our side!

Just a few years ago, it appeared that I was facing another serious—and potentially catastrophic—impasse. Exploration and drilling operations conducted by a company in which I held a very large interest indicated that the Middle Eastern areas in which it held drilling concessions would soon be producing crude oil in fantastic quantities. Unfortunately, various factors and restrictions would prevent importing more than a fraction of the production into the United States.

On the face of things, the outlook was anything but bright. Before long, immense quantities of crude oil would be pouring up out of the ground—but, unless something was done, and quickly, most of it would be virtually worthless. Crude oil is, after all, only a raw material. It must be refined into other products which must then be distributed and marketed.

As time went on and more and more wells came in, there were those who openly predicted that I would soon find myself in a position from which I could not extricate myself.

After spending staggering sums on obtaining the concession and on exploration and drilling, the company would be left with oceans of crude oil which it could not market. There were even those who gleefully rumored that it wouldn't be long before Paul Getty would be in serious financial trouble.

I'll admit the corner was getting a bit uncomfortable—but it was far from being so tight that there was no way out of it. To the chagrin of those who were predicting that the Getty interests would soon drown in their oceans of excess crude oil, we found—in fact, we virtually created—new outlets for our production. If we couldn't ship all our crude to the United States for refining and sale, we would ship it elsewhere, even if we had to buy or build our own refineries in other countries. And that is precisely what we did, buying one almost brand-new refinery in Italy, building another one in Denmark and finding other refinery capacity elsewhere. Now, of course, the Getty interests are avidly searching for *more* crude oil in the Middle East and elsewhere in the world.

Experiences such as these—and there have been many of them—have taught me that the time for the businessman to think and fight hardest is when the tide seems to be running against him and his prospects appear bleak. He can frequently turn even the worst of bad business situations to the advantage of his company, his stockholders and himself.

The successful businessman—the true business leader—is the individual who develops the ability to retain his composure in times of stress and in the face of setbacks. The young businessman should strive to acquire and develop this and the related traits I have previously mentioned—and he should try very early in his career, for it will not be long before he encounters his first reverses and adversities. The manner in which he meets the first few tight situations in which he finds himself will often set the pattern for the rest of his career.

Plainly, it is not possible for anyone to give a businessman specific, step-by-step advice on what he should—or should not—do when he suffers business reverses. There are far too many variables; each situation differs greatly from the next. On the other hand, there are certain fundamental principles which will greatly aid any businessman in meeting adverse situations and transforming setbacks into successes:

1. No matter what happens, do not panic. The panic-stricken individual cannot think or act effectively. A certain amount of trouble is inevitable in any business career—when it comes, it should be met with calm determination.
2. When things go wrong, it is always a wise idea to pull back temporarily—to withdraw just long enough and far enough to view and evaluate the situation objectively.
3. In the opening stages of any developing adverse situation, it may be necessary and advisable to give some ground, to sacrifice those things which are least important and most expendable. But it should be a fighting withdrawal, a retrograde action that goes back only so far and no further. It must never be a disorderly retreat.
4. Next, all factors in the situation must be examined with meticulous care. Every possible course of action must be weighed. All available resources—cerebral as well as financial, creative as well as practical—must be marshaled.

In the opening stages of any developing adverse situation, it may be necessary and advisable to give some ground, to sacrifice those things which are least important and most expendable.

---

5. Countermoves must be planned with the greatest care and in the greatest of detail—yet with allowances for alternative courses in the event unforeseen obstacles

are encountered. Counteraction must be planned on a scale consistent with the resources available—and the goals set must be conceivably attainable. It is well to bear in mind, however, that the impetus of a properly executed counterattack very often carries the counterattacking force far beyond the point from which it was driven in the first place.

6. Once everything is ready, action should be taken confidently, purposefully, aggressively—and above all, enthusiastically. There can be no hesitation—and it is here that the determination, personality and energy of the leader count the most.

The businessman—young or old—who guides himself according to these principles when he has suffered reverses will not remain at bay very long.

PART III

Visions of Progress

Throwing away old methods, retrying things that didn't work before, carving away the complex to arrive at the simple are some of the maxims of the visionaries in Part III. This section is organized chronologically to provide an opportunity to compare and contrast the authors' visions of how people, machines, and technology work together to contribute to progress. Vision is one of the most intangible qualities of leadership, but it is certainly not the stuff of science fiction. Some of the greatest of visions often start with simple goals. Thomas Edison, for example, wanted simply to emancipate man from arduous tasks by introducing more machines into the workplace, and he methodically charted a course to achieve his goals. Whether it is Edison discussing machines in 1926 or Charles B. Wang, founder of Computer Associates, discussing information technology in 1994, all of the authors recognize the moral issues involved in advancing civilization and discuss the implications in graphic terms.

Thomas A. Edison
1847 – 1931

The man who became a cultural icon for inventing the phonograph was mostly deaf from the time he was a boy. Thomas A. Edison, who grew up relatively poor in Michigan, never considered the ailment a disadvantage. To the contrary, he said, "In my isolation (insulation would be a better term) I had time to think things out." His formal education was minimal, but even in his youth he was hungry for information, so he frequented the Detroit Public Library. "I didn't read a few books," he said. "I read the library." Edison's first jobs included that of a newsboy and later a telegraph operator. Telegraphy really sparked his interest in electricity, and Edison began his experiments in earnest.

One of Edison's few friends was Henry Ford, who once worked for one of the inventor's companies. Ford said that when it came to inventing, Edison was not a mystical visionary as many thought. Rather, Edison's vision was a methodical thinking through of things, of understanding how pieces to the puzzle fit together. Ford also said that it took Edison only five minutes to sketch his first model of the phonograph. Yet early success eluded Edison. His first invention was an electric vote counter, which he tried to sell to the U.S. Congress; it was turned down. (It would have made them too honest.)

While Edison was the guiding force of his organization, he surrounded himself with intelligent people. "Competent men in our jobs mean success for us; incompetent men in them would mean failure," he said. As scientific and industrial progress accelerated at the turn of the century, Edison recognized that the average person was not mentally equipped to grasp or to utilize many of the new products. He explained, "If modern industry and invention expected to have a market for its products it had to turn school-master on an elaborate scale." One of his often-repeated messages was that man needed to incorporate more machines into daily life to emancipate himself from the drudgery of physical tasks, which is clearly stated in *Machine and Progress.* Once emancipated, man would have more time for thinking and civilization would truly advance.

Machine and Progress

Thomas A. Edison

It has been charged abroad and occasionally at home that we of the United States have become a machine-ridden people, that we are developing upon lines too completely mechanical. The very reverse is the truth. We are not mechanical enough. The machine has been the human being's most effective means of escape from bondage. Too many people, even now, remain bond-slaves to laborious hand processes. Not through fewer, but through more machines, not through simpler, but through more complex machines, will men find avenues that lead into lives of greater opportunity and happiness.

We must substitute motors for muscles in a thousand new ways. A human brain is greatly hampered in its usefulness if it has only two hands of a man to do its bidding. There are machines each of which can do the work of a multitude of hands, when directed by one brain. That is efficiency.

Anything which tends to slow work down is waste. Every effort should be made to speed work up. Increased production means enlarged lives for mankind. Human hands alone can do no more than they did long ago by way of fast production. Only machines, not nerves and muscles, can increase men's output. We have scarcely seen the start of the mechanical age, and after it is under way we shall discover that it is also a mental age as never has been known before. One of the reasons it will be notably mental will be that it will be notably mechanical. It requires a surprising amount of complexity to displace the mechanical effort of the man. The difference between the automatic and the semi-automatic machine is very great. Its significance in industry is immense. But once the fully automatic has been achieved, the output and quality of the product will be greatly increased. All fully automatics, on account of their very complexity, require attendants of mental capacity greatly increased over that of men who are merely parts of semi-automatics.

There could be no greater waste than keeping good brains at work directing the hands of the bodies they control in the hand-execution of mechanical tasks because of the mere failure to invent and develop machines to execute those tasks better and faster than hand work can execute them under good brain direction. Man will progress in intellectual things according to his release from the mere motor-tasks.

A human brain is greatly hampered in its usefulness if it has only two hands of a man to do its bidding.

The history of slavery is full of illustrations of the value of machinery. Slavery, the use of men as beasts of burden and as motors, was mental bondage for the men who thought they benefited by it, as well as physical bondage for the men they held in thrall. While slave labor was available, the brains of men in general were not stimulated to the creation of machinery. This was more disastrous in its general effects than was realized by the majority, even of those opposed to slavery. It meant that human beings all along the line, not only the enslaved but the enslavers, could not be released by machinery for efforts better and more elevating than those to which they had been habituated in the past. Progress of mind became impossible.

That is the reason why I call machinery the greatest of emancipators. I will go farther and say that human slavery will not have been fully abolished until every task now accomplished by human hands is turned out by some machine, if it can be done as well or better by a machine. Why chain a man, thus wasting him, to laborious work which a machine could do? All men cannot walk out of the shadow into the light until all men understand the foolishness of such procedure.

. . . human slavery will not have been fully abolished until every task now accomplished by human hands is turned out by some machine . . . Why chain a man, thus wasting him, to laborious work which a machine could do?

The shoe factory of today requires better employees than were required by the old processes of laborious, slow, hand work. Some of the old time cobblers were fine fellows who could think, but they would have thought far more and better if their ignorance of machinery had not shackled them to the awl and hand–hammer-driven peg, to the bristle-tipped waxed-end. These things did nothing then which now are not far better done by our machines. I have said that men's brains are bettered by machinery, if it is of the right sort. That with which we now make boots and shoes develops brains far more fully than work with the old tools did or could. This is proved by the fact that when, by working at machines, men's brains are improved sufficiently, the men who have shown ability to run the first machines are promoted to the operation of those which are now more complicated and run still faster, requiring of their operators increased alertness and mentality.

There is no common-sense in the cry that machine work is monotonous. On the other hand it creates a good product, uniform and universally dependable, which is something hand-work never could do. Machine work robs the product of the ill-effects of man's changing physical and mental conditions. The hand worker's product is uneven. Far too much of it is too bad to enable it to compete successfully with the output of the machine.

There is no common-sense in the cry that machine work is monotonous.

Americans use more machinery than anybody else. I am told that American workers each can run six looms of a certain kind, Germans five, Frenchmen five, Englishmen (whose workers never have ceased agitating against machinery) five—and Chinese one, the quality being the same when the cloth is inspected. If the Chinese should begin suddenly to use machinery extensively, it would be only a matter of time when they could run more machines than they can now. Their indicator numeral would go up in the scale. But at the start, one Chinese could run but one machine. The workers of the so-called "machinized" nations can operate the larger numbers I have stated because working with machines has much increased their mental development.

If we continue to increase machine production and the number of machines engaged at it, the next generation will be far beyond where we are now in its intelligence as well as in the possession of facilities for getting the good things out of life.

One of the most foolish things men say, and one which they often repeat, is that too much substitution of machine-work for hand-work will bring over-production. The idea is complete nonsense. There cannot be over-production of anything which men and women want, and their wants are unlimited except insofar as they are limited by the size of their stomachs. The stomach is the only part of man which can be fully satisfied. The yearning of man's brain for new knowledge and experience and for pleasanter and more comfortable surroundings never can be completely met. It is an appetite which cannot be appeased. Talk of over-production is a bugaboo.

A general benefit ensues inevitably from the increasing use of machinery. Not only do the workers benefit through the development enforced on them by the machines, but, in exact proportion as the machines enable the manufacturers to turn out more and better work, the sale of their manufacturers is permitted at a decreased price. If the manufacturer can sell at a decreased price then, automatically, it becomes possible for the man of average income to have more things than theretofore. That man of average income has gained tremendously through the creation of machines. There is no doubt in my mind that in quantity production, so called, lies the greatest hope which now exists to cheer the human race. Quantity production cannot possibly occur without machinery. Therefore no man should rail against machine-power. It is application of good fertilizer to industry.

One of the most foolish things men say . . . is that too much substitution of machine-work for hand-work will bring over-production. The idea is complete nonsense.

We use every known device of science, and continually seek for new ones, in our efforts to enlarge the production of our grain fields, our fruit orchards, and our vegetable gardens. What is that but striving to stimulate our plants and trees to quantity production? Are not the productive powers of men as worthy of good fertilizer? Machinery is the influence which enables men to do what stimulated plant life does to increase this year's output as compared with last year's to make certain for next year of more than this year's yields. It is as worthy an ambition to make two pairs of shoes where one was made before, that is, with the same human effort, as it is to devise agricultural means of making two blades of grass grow this year where only one grew last.

When objection to machinery has occurred among the workers it has been as foolish as is the refusal of men to accept any other opportunity for progress. Time was when printers all over New York City, and, indeed, the nation, struck or threatened to strike against typesetting machines, fearing that if they should come into general use fewer printers would be hired and at lower wages. The machine won, of course. And there are far more printers working now than were working then, and wages are higher. The economic status of the printer has much improved. So has his intelligence. So has his self-respect. He does not have to do things with his brains and muscles which a machine without brains can do better and faster. The printers of today would strike if you should try to take machines away from them.

The history of the typesetting machine is like that of every other machine which has been introduced to perform work previously done by hand, laboriously, slowly, expensively, and less perfectly. The sewing machine, for instance, has increased by fiftyfold the employment in the fields which it affects.

Wherever something has compelled us to put in machinery to do work theretofore done by men's hands and muscles while brains have remained comparatively idle, all of us, and especially the men directly involved, have gained. If labor everywhere would strike against the use of men as animals instead of protesting against their use as human beings, it would show superior wisdom. Such a strike would have an unprecedentedly good effect on human life, for in very many of our most important activities the possibilities of machine development as an accessory to human intelligence and productiveness are, even yet, not fully understood.

David Sarnoff
1891 – 1971

David Sarnoff ruled over RCA for forty years. This renowned visionary was instrumental in bringing both radio and television to a mass audience and in founding NBC in 1926. The Russian native took many chances as he introduced new technology to the public, but as he once reflected, "All of life is a risk, and I learned it earlier than most." He was referring to his immigration to New York City. It was a hazardous journey spent in the bowels of a ship, where he and his fellow Russians were packed in like sardines. Once in America, he eventually found a job as a telegraph operator. The *Titanic* disaster in 1912 propelled wireless technology to the forefront and Sarnoff along with it—he was one of the first to report the disaster from his New York station post.

In 1919 General Electric (GE) bought American Marconi and changed the name to RCA. Under GE, Sarnoff realized his first great vision, moving radio from a point-to-point application between designated operators to a point-to-mass audience, or commercial radio. He sold the idea to GE management and was charged with its development. In selling it to America, his vision was matched by his rhetoric: "The day is coming when a man will be ashamed to admit that his home is not equipped with a radio broadcasting device, just as a man today would be ashamed to admit that his home is not equipped with a bathtub. I regard radio broadcasting as a sort of cleansing instrument for the mind, just as the bathtub is for the body."

Radio went nationwide in 1923. That same year, Sarnoff declared that television would be the "ultimate and greatest step in mass communications." But it was not until 1939 that a regular broadcast program was launched. Sarnoff announced the birth of this new art, television programming, with the same gusto he had radio: "It is a creative force which we must learn to utilize for the benefit of all mankind." Not everyone agreed, and in *The Fabulous Future* Sarnoff answers his 1950s critics who believed technology would be man's undoing. Like Edison, he believed technology is liberating and will bring humans closer to each other.

The Fabulous Future

David Sarnoff

What is likely to be the special character of the quarter century ahead of us? Personally, I am convinced that it will be a period of drastic decision. It will be filled with events that, taken together, may well determine the direction and even the duration of man's destiny on this planet.

That an avalanche of advances will be forthcoming in the sphere of science and technology is not a matter of surmise. The new types of energy released by the atom and controlled by the electron have already proved highly effective. The features of vital technical growths can be discerned in numberless embryos in the womb of science: our amazing network of research laboratories.

But these features will be matched by even more significant developments in the political, social, and moral spheres. Indeed, the pressures of technical changes will themselves intensify problems of adjustment, forcing us to seek solutions in line with our ideals of a good society.

Long-stagnant races and continents have awakened to an awareness of their rights, needs, and latent strengths. Long-accepted ways of life and codes of conduct are being menaced by a new barbarism that already dominates a third of the human race. A hunger for faith and salvation, for age-old values beyond the material and the temporal, gnaws at the mind and spirit of man.

This means that the coming quarter-century will be crowded with crises and climaxes. Forces that have been gathering impetus since the turn of the century will find vigorous and perhaps explosive expression. The tensions built up in our own generation are too great to be indefinitely contained. We will be confronted with great challenges that will call for dramatic commitments on our part.

If the destinies were already written in the stars and beyond mortal control, there would be little point in talking about them. But I am convinced, as are most people, that our destinies are, in large part, subject to our own volition. It is understandable that at times we have been frightened and bewildered. But we do have a choice: we can grovel in terror before the mighty forces of science and historic adjustment, even as savage man groveled before lightning and other natural phenomena. Or we can face those forces with courage, determination, and calm intelligence. We do have such a choice because we are not the passive objects but the active manipulators of those forces. . . .

Progress, a Chain Reaction

The most futile intellectual exercise is the discussion as to whether an industrialized society is "desirable." We might as reasonably argue whether the tides and the seasons are desirable. The genie of science could not be stuffed back into the bottle even if we so wished.

In theory, backward countries might still choose the simple life, but in practice they are clamoring for the devices and living standards of the West. The strongest appeal of Communist propaganda to retarded populations is in its promises of power dams, factories, mechanized farming, and the like. Much of the revolutionary leadership in Asia and Africa is provided by natives who have been educated in the West and have tasted its technological comforts and advantages.

The genie of science could not be stuffed back into the bottle even if we so wished.

Disparagement of the age of science and mass production, a nostalgia for the supposedly idyllic prescientific past, are familiar themes in twentieth-century literature. Only a few months ago a book titled *Tomorrow Is Already Here,* by Robert Jungk, warned that Americans are hell-bent for a soulless, mechanized tomorrow, populated by dehumanized cogs in runaway machines.

I doubt whether those who denounce our world would, in the showdown, permanently exchange the material amenities of England, France, or America for those of darkest Africa. At the very least, I assume, they might spare the typewriters and printing presses with which they make themselves heard.

Nostalgia for What?

As a cure for hatred of science, I recommend a protracted visit to some really primitive region of open sewers and open sores, cruel rates of infant mortality and decrepit old age at forty. Nostalgia for the simple past romanticizes drudgery, disease, and ignorance. It glosses over the poverty, social injustice, and feudal despotism that usually go along with a primitive economy.

The claim that there is an inherent conflict between science and our immortal souls—that science is the natural enemy of the soul—does not stand up under examination. The man in an airplane is not necessarily less devoted to truth, justice, and charity than his forefathers in oxcarts. Virtue does not necessarily go with primitive plumbing, and human dignity can be nurtured in a skyscraper no less than in a log cabin.

Nostalgia for the simple past romanticizes drudgery, disease, and ignorance.

True, the marvels of technology have come upon us so suddenly that they have created problems of adjustment. Age-old inertias have been disturbed. But on the whole the adjustment has been remarkably good; the human problems caused by applied science are serious, but no more so than those it has solved. The crux of the matter is not in evils inseparable from technology but in the time lag in the assimilation of what technology has to offer.

Marx and Prometheus

The industrial revolution touched off by the steam engine brought trouble in its train: vile slums, child labor, brutal work hours and work conditions. But the time lag was bridged, slowly and surely. As capitalism matured, its fruits were spread to more and more people in goods, health, social security, and a new dignity of labor. Huge middle classes, not foreseen by Karl Marx, have arisen. The distance between rich and poor, as measured by living standards, has steadily shrunk. The scientists who sparked the industrial revolution can rest in peace, their consciences assuaged.

The same, I believe, holds true of inventiveness in our own time, including the splitting of the atom. Every achievement on the physical plane packs danger as well as opportunity. It is the ancient dilemma posed when Prometheus gave man the fire that both warms and consumes. The inventive urge that brought us motor cars also made possible Panzer divisions. Pyromaniacs, however, cannot be blamed upon Prometheus, nor saturation bombing upon the Wright brothers.

It is well to recall that the twentieth century has also won victories, great and small, on the political, cultural, and moral levels. They are in evidence all around us, saturating our existence. They are spelled out in universal suffrage, civil freedoms, more widespread education, easier access to and greater appreciation of the products of genius in the arts; in society's growing acceptance of responsibility for the old, the widowed, the orphaned, and the helpless.

Technology and the Spirit

In my own lifetime I have seen the liberation of multitudes from overwork, exploitation, and ravaging diseases to which they had seemed forever condemned when I was a boy. It is not a worse but an immeasurably better society that we live in. The same decades that witnessed the control of the electron and the birth of nuclear energy also saw a substantial improvement in race and class relations and the enactment of vital social legislation. Along with the assembly line and automation has also come the rise of trade unions and a more equitable sharing of the products of labor and management.

America, the classic land of technology, enjoys the largest freedom from destitution, ignorance, and dissent along with political rights and social improvements unique in history. In average citizen is not the common man but the uncommon man, for he has an amplitude of well-being and opportunity that pre-scientific societies reserved for a small and arrogant elite. Moreover—and this needs emphasis—the most magnificent flowering of science and technology has always occurred in countries where liberty prevailed. The close affinity between freedom and material abundance should give pause to those who derogate material progress.

"The figures show," Dr. Arthur H. Compton said recently, "that where technology has been used for the service of man, there is in broad total a healthy growth not only in man's biological life but also in his intellectual and spiritual life."

A society geared to technology is *compelled,* in order to remain viable, continually to lift the levels of human welfare. Greater purchasing power, more leisure, expanded relish for the end products of factories, communications, and entertainment—these are the very conditions of its survival. It draws its vitality from free men with an ever larger direct stake in the society, as totalitarians who would combine technology with slavery soon learn to their distress.

The Final Link

Science, far from nurturing pride, encourages humility. Its every victory reveals more clearly a Divine design in nature, a remarkable conformity in all things, from the infinitesimal to the infinite, that surpasses mortal understanding.

In its early stages, modern science seemed at odds with religion: but this was merely a token of its immaturity. The more familiar story, in our time, is that of scientists who become increasingly aware of the mystery of the universe and come to religion, in its fundamental sense, through knowledge of the limitations of science. And, indeed, how can those who play with the building blocks of the universe, its atoms and electrons and genes, fail to be touched by awe? More than ever, man's soul is involved in the equations of our lives.

Also the physical closeness engendered by science is promoting ever closer social and intellectual relations between peoples. Generations ago essential isolation of countries was taken for granted: It was a function of distance and difference. Today a dictatorship that would isolate its subjects must erect Iron Curtains and walls of electronic jamming. With worldwide television, which I regard as a certainty before 1980, the sense of our common humanity will deepen. It is the strange, the unknown, that frightens—but the strangeness will be removed by visual contact, to reveal the familiar physiognomy of our neighbors.

We know in our hearts that modern war can cause such overwhelming devastation to life and property as to become a species of suicide. The atom and the electron have made it almost as disastrous for the winner as for the loser. This decisive fact must, in the long run, cancel out war as an instrument of national policy. We cannot know when or what form the coming "one world" will take, but world law enforceed by world police seems inherent in the age of science and technology.

The physical closeness engendered by science is promoting ever closer social and intellectual relations between peoples.

The forces I have discussed appear to me to cause a chain reaction. First, science and technology create material abundance. Second, this produces new conditions and demands that compel adjustments with resulting social advances. Third, the interdependence of people in a world shrunk by science inevitably requires broader mental concepts, which lead to greater ethical and moral stature—which in turn stimulate man's spiritual growth.

It seems to me unqualifiedly good that more and more of the weight of arduous toil will be unloaded onto the backs of machines; that the sum total of pain and agony will be further reduced by the progress of healing; that modern communications will bring peoples and nations into closer contact, leading to better understanding of one another.

Robert N. Noyce
1927 – 1990

Robert N. Noyce, the cofounder of Fairchild Semiconductor (1959) and of Intel (1968), is considered the inventor of the silicon microchip. Noyce was born in Iowa, where his father was a Congregational minister. His good Protestant upbringing included learning the value of hard work. In contrast to his early rural life, he chose to study physical electronics at the Massachusetts Institute of Technology, earning a Ph.D. in 1953. Although Noyce was not a churchgoer as an adult, his father influenced the way he managed at Fairchild and Intel. Instead of a corporate hierarchy, he chose an-everyone-is-equal approach to management. For example, even parking was on a first-come, first-served basis, with no reserved spots for the executives.

Noyce's idea of a corporate organization was to set up strategic units that were autonomous and answered only to themselves. Even newly hired engineers were allowed to purchase what they wanted for a project, no matter the cost, without going through a bunch of red tape. Also, councils were held for problem-solving. No one council or individual was given real power; the councils were more like discussion groups made up of peers, and solutions involved a democratic process. They were not unlike problem-solving groups within a church.

Noyce thrust young engineers into positions of responsibility and put them in charge of major projects. If they came to Noyce for advice, his typical response was: "Look, here are your guidelines. You've got to consider A, you've got to consider B, and you've got to consider C. But if you think I'm going to make your decision for you, you're mistaken. Hey, it's *your* ass." Noyce wanted his people to be self-reliant but was equally concerned with rewarding their innovations. For him, innovation was crucial to the success of a nation. Toward that end, Noyce left Intel in 1987 to form Sematech, a consortium of chip makers whose sole purpose was to develop semiconductor technology and meet Japanese competition head on. Noyce's message concerning the need to encourage risk-taking and innovation for civilization's sake is all too clear in *Innovation: The Fruit of Success.*

Innovation: The Fruit of Success

Robert N. Noyce

A panel of industrial managers on which I was recently a participant was asked about the ability of the U.S. to maintain a lead over the rest of the world in the highly competitive business of technological innovation. A leading German industrialist who was a member of the panel volunteered an observation: it's true that other nations are spending large amounts to subsidize research and development in new technology, he said. But in doing so Germany has "a major disadvantage." He pointed out several individuals around the room who had left major companies to start their own firms with a new idea or a new approach. "That just doesn't happen in Germany," he said. "And I doubt that we'll ever catch up." He meant it.

I am not consciously a student of innovation or its management. I have been closely involved in two highly innovative enterprises and can offer some observations, but I've made no statistical studies. When interviewed by students of innovation, I usually respond by saying "But I was only doing what I wanted to do. Sometimes I had to change certain things so I could continue to do what I wanted to do."

The Risk of Not Meeting One's Goals

What are the sources of innovation? There's an old saying that necessity is the mother of invention. That's my answer: the motivation for innovation is the necessity for change. In the semiconductor industry, where no product has lasted more than five years, there is no chance to rest on your laurels and not go on with the battle.

People have often asked me if I felt I was taking a great risk. The answer is that I never felt there was any great risk in starting new ventures. The greater risk was missing an opportunity and therefore not meeting my own goals. I always knew I could go out and get another job, so I wouldn't starve. And the jobs I left were not so challenging to me as the new prospect.

Risk-taking is a question of confidence in the outcome.

Though I had worked since I was 12 years old, my total experience in business at the time we started Fairchild was about four years. So I didn't know that failure could occur. That was a major advantage: though observations of failure may lead us to avoid obvious mistakes, they may also discourage us from innovation, which must be approached with confidence in success.

I never felt there was any great risk in starting new ventures. The greater risk was missing an opportunity . . .

Looking at some of the motivations and some of the changes I went through in the early, formative years will, I think, be instructive. After finishing at M.I.T. in 1953 I went to work for Philco. I had offers from R.C.A., General Electric, I.B.M., and Bell Labs. When I went through those laboratories, I decided that they all knew what they were doing.

But Philco needed me: I would be a necessary cog in that machine. I don't mean to run down the other organizations. It's just that I felt that in those larger, better-founded research organizations I wasn't going to have an essential role.

. . . an innovative scientist must be recognized as necessary and vital to the future of the organization.

Then Philco did something which was, I suppose, in the end the cause of my leaving. They told me, in effect, that I could continue to work on what I was doing if I could get the government to pay for it. I decided that Philco wasn't really interested in my research; it was just another way to collect money from the government. I have since compared doing cost-plus research for an industry to putting your venture capital in a savings account. You're not going to lose much, but you're certainly not going to gain much, either.

The moral of that story is that an innovative scientist must be recognized as necessary and vital to the future of the organization. Cost-plus research communicates the opposite message.

"Am I Really Needed Here?"

I joined Bill Shockley at his new company primarily because I wanted to play in the big leagues. He clearly was the father of the industry; he shared a Nobel Prize for the invention of the transistor a year after I went to join him.

I recall one episode at Shockley Transistor that may be instructive in how not to motivate your people. One morning I came to talk to Bill about some new results I'd just found in the laboratory to check if my interpretation was right. And he called some friends back at Bell Labs to ask them that question. Suddenly an uncertainty came to my mind: Am I really needed here? If he can call friends at Bell Labs and gets answers to the same questions that I was trying to answer in the laboratory, my presence here isn't that important. If other people agree with what you do, then you can go ahead.

There's another story with the same moral which I haven't told very often because it seems like sour grapes. I have in my notebooks from those years a complete description of the tunnel diode. When I showed it to the boss, he showed no interest in the idea, so we went on to other projects. (Not that I missed anything; the work had been done elsewhere and was published shortly thereafter.) The message of "no interest" is certainly a demotivator.

Finally we got down to the question of whether to work on transistors or four-layer diodes. I frankly was more interested in transistors. There was an immediate market for transistors, but there seemed to be a problem in developing a market for the diode.

That was in 1957, and it was then that a group of us started what is now the Fairchild Semiconductor Division, to make transistors. Individual venture capital had not really become popular. Most of the places where we were directed to look for capital turned out to be corporate sources. Fairchild responded immediately. They said, "We've looked at that field. It's a fertile field. You've got a good approach to it. You've got adequate capability in your people." So they went ahead and funded our venture, offering what was for me at that time a phenomenally high reward: if you succeed at this, we'll pay you several years' salary all in one chunk. That deal left no question about the objective, and there was no question about what really got me interested. The criterion was earnings. There was no interest in research papers, no interest in professional pride. There was only one goal: to make the profit-and-loss statement come out right.

That organization was the start of what is now called "Silicon Valley," the beginning of all the semiconductor companies in the Santa Clara Valley—Rheem which later went to Raytheon, Signetics which later went to Phillips, General Microelectronics which later went broke, National, Intel—the source of the planar transistor, the integrated circuit, the MOS circuit, and many more.

The reward system in all of these ventures was based on success, and the motivations were extremely high. Not too long ago I was in Russia, and I found that academicians in that society are really very well rewarded. I asked them about getting their technology into Russian factories somewhere, and they said it was very difficult.

After I came back I characterized it this way: In America, when you get your new technology into a profit-and-loss statement they make you a millionaire. In Russia it's quite different: if you go out and manage a factory and you miss the quota, they make you a miner in Siberia.

A Power Struggle Between "Yes" and "No"

One advantage in start-up situations is that the technical staff is also the sales force. In the early days, the technology people have to be out talking to the customers almost on a continuous basis so they have feedback on the direction in which to go. The motivation to look very closely at the profit-and-loss statement keeps you very sensitive to market needs and costs.

As Fairchild grew we lost some of that original flexibility, so I left to try again to do it better. I can see some of the mistakes we made at Fairchild; let me mention some of those that I think are important.

Most important, I think, is the fact that, because Fairchild Semiconductor was extremely profitable, the corporation drew money out of it to put into other entrepreneurial start-ups. In a sense, we were hurt by our own example of success; the parent company's management apparently concluded that if you simply support a group of people and give them some money, they will soon come back with more money than you gave them. In the case of Fairchild Semiconductors this happened after only two years, which is very short. As management drew down our resources, we gradually lost significant amounts of our total capability. At the same time, corporate management failed to give major attention to the semiconductor organization, and this made us feel no longer important.

And I have to take responsibility for some very counter-productive policies and practices, too.

One is what I call group-think. As we built up capabilities, we collected many experts in applications, finance, marketing, etc. Any decision to go along with a new product innovation had to pass through a very narrow gate. A single negative vote could kill a project, and one positive vote was worth approximately zero. I wondered if we should have done it the other way, so that a single yes vote could initiate action.

I did do that with my requisition system in the organization. When an engineer filled out a requisition, a buyer placed the order. Anyone who wanted to stop the order had to call the purchasing agent and direct him to cancel. That worked well; it was far better than waiting six weeks for the president to sign the requisition.

On the other hand, our incentive pay policy for the product managers in the factory turned out to be counterproductive. We developed a simple system of rewarding managers on the basis of the gross profit on their lines, which sounds just grand. But this reward turned out to be a very short-term motivator. It was absolutely impossible to add a new product on any manager's line. Each manager wanted to shove it off on somebody else, because each manager knew that new products lose money for at least the first three to six months; any new product that he had to launch was going to cost the manager money out of his own pocket.

I began to feel during this time that big is bad. The spirit of the small group is much better. Everyone works much harder. They cooperate more, because each can see the total impact of his or her activities.

Entrepreneurs Aren't Much Interested in Retirement

By the time I left Fairchild to try to do it again, the competition was really entrenched. At the time Fairchild started, the largest semiconductor company was less than $50 million in annual volume; by the time we started Intel, the largest company was about $500 million—and it was a powerful company that had learned how to do the business. So our new strategy was to avoid that competition by doing something new.

After looking back and examining the advantages Fairchild had, we decided to emphasize young, eager people at Intel. We wanted to find people who had the motivation and stamina to put in the long, dedicated hours necessary to make a new company succeed.

Once more we set up very high rewards. We gave options—and we still do—to every professional employee of the company. But we have no retirement plan. We've found that—compared with more immediate rewards—there's not much interest in retirement plans among people with an entrepreneurial spirit.

The person we hired was typically going to a much smaller responsibility than he previously had, as measured by title, the number of employees we had, or the salary that we paid him. We wanted him to come with us because he was interested in the project and was willing to take a risk. I don't like the idea of hiring a salesman who wants a salary instead of a commission. I want him to be confident that he will do better on commission. We tried to get experienced people so we were at least starting even with the state-of-the-art.

We pioneered the electronic watch; as you know, the pioneer is the one with the arrow sticking out of his back. The watch business has been good, but it has also been very painful.

We had a much happier experience with the microcomputer, which Intel also pioneered; it was introduced by Intel only five years ago and is already making major changes in the way people think about the use of the computer in the future. With an 80-percent certainty, you'll have a microcomputer in your automobile by 1980. You'll have one attached to your television set to play games with—probably within the next couple of years. Building your own microcomputer is becoming as popular among hobbyists as building a hi-fi set was in an earlier era.

Intel is making it tougher for others to compete with us. This is a typical big-company attitude. We're taking on some longer-range projects to widen the areas of our application; I feel that you can plan as far ahead as you can look back on success. And we're doing a lot of rear-guard action to be sure that somebody doesn't come along and hurt us. We want to force new entrants into our territory to find new areas of activity and new innovations for success; we don't want them to make their success at our expense.

A Coming Crisis in Innovation

I am convinced that there are still enormous opportunities for innovation, that we still have huge changes coming in our life-style. But I also feel that we are approaching a crisis in innovation. I fear that we as a country are growing closer to the Russian reward system, as I call it, in which there is no incentive for small organizations to succeed. I remember the Germans' feeling that they'll always be a step behind because they don't have the small independent organizations to innovate.

I also believe that corporate management has done a poor job of convincing the general populace that "what's good for General Motors is good for the country." People laugh at that statement, but it isn't all that laughable. What it means is that we have not convinced enough Americans that the success of its industry is in fact crucial to the success of the nation and all its people. We're not attracting our best young people to industry. We're killing the goose that lays golden eggs.

Finally, it seems to me that the overall attitude of our society is quite different from that of a decade ago; there isn't the same "can-do" attitude that we had in the 1960s. Any time we try to solve a problem we seem increasingly to turn to subsidy, thus weakening or driving out private enterprise; business can't compete with the false economics of government. I think there are enormous dangers in continuing such counterproductive actions.

Yet I'm optimistic, and I guess that's one of the basic characteristics of the entrepreneur. Our nation's downhill trend can be changed if we can really clarify our goals as a country and if we take great care to strengthen rather than weaken our corporate structures and their individual managers. And I see the confidence returning. There's no question in my mind but that the U.S. is absolutely the best place in the world to promote innovation. Our society is better organized to promote and take advantage of it, and our spirit is really undaunted. We haven't gone nearly as far as we can go, and there's a great deal of opportunity out there to do it all over again.

Charles B. Wang
1944 –

Charles B. Wang is cofounder, chairman, and CEO of Computer Associates International (CA), the largest software maker after Microsoft and Oracle. To achieve success in this unruly industry, he had to be tough, a characteristic he brought from youth. To begin with, Wang and his family were forced to flee their home in Shanghai, China, after the Communist revolution in 1949. They immigrated to Queens, New York, and found themselves living in a housing project. Eventually life got better and he attended Queens College, earning degrees in mathematics and physics. Then, while looking through the help-wanted ads, he noticed plenty of work for computer programmers and decided to enter the flourishing industry.

It didn't take Wang long to realize that clients' real needs often were ignored as new technology was forced on them. So when the chance came in the mid-1970s to buy the software division of the company he was working for, he and CA cofounder Russell Artzt went for it, hoping to bring a more customer-focused strategy to their work. Artzt, more of the R&D guy, fondly remembers Wang's sales tactics when it came to selling their software. "He'd pick twenty pages out of the yellow pages," Artzt said, "drink three cups of coffee, and not go to the bathroom until he'd cold-called every potential customer."

They went public in 1981 and have used the proceeds to ultimately make some sixty acquisitions. Wang targets struggling competitors that have key software products, buys them out, and then guts the operation. The acquired employees are ranked, their profiles entered into CA's merger acquisition program system (MAPS), and within seven days of the deal's closing cuts are made. When attacked for the harsh process, Wang retorts, "We tell them the truth, so they can get on with their lives." He also wants the truth about his own everyday operations. He worries that CEOs are too disconnected from their information technology people, often separated by different vocabularies, nothing more. In the following selection Wang explains his vision of a world in which information technology is as accepted as a utility like electricity.

Techno Vision

Charles B. Wang

Articulate a Vision That Is Germane to the Business

Without a bold vision of business, clearly articulated and effectively implemented, well-aligned information technology is irrelevant. However, the technology is the necessary base and business enabler. If that base is not conspicuously in place or does not work reliably, there is little if anything to enable. The vision must have hooks at every level. It must be broad enough to inspire buy-in from everyone in the organization, leaving no one out, yet specific enough to inspire information technology initiatives at the grass-roots level.

There Is a Fine Line Between Vision and Hallucination

Steve Jobs, originally of Apple and now of NeXT, has a forceful, visionary outlook that changed the face of the computer industry and perhaps the world. His was a vision that was well defended against inconvenient facts. He pressed everyone, especially doubters, to align with his vision. Sometimes Jobs's persistence paid off. More often, it failed. While his place in history is assured, it's not as a CEO. Jobs' leadership didn't allow for collaboration; his colleagues eventually suspended their own judgment when they entered what was termed Jobs' reality distortion field.

My point is that CEOs of the connected organization need all the help they can get. Teamwork cannot be sustained in an environment that shouts down naysayers. If your vision cannot survive attack, it may not be worth defending. There can be no assistance from colleagues whose best judgment is suspended in deference to your vision.

An Ounce of Application Is Worth a Ton of Abstraction

I have a bias for action. Do something and see if it works. I admire one company with a creative program for getting executives and computers together. This company invites the teenage sons and daughters of executives to come into the office on weekends where they are trained on the various office information systems. At that point, the company sends the systems home with the teenagers so that the kids can train the executives in the comfort of their homes. The systems are already loaded with relevant corporate data. As the executives learn the system, they work with real corporate data so that they can immediately see the value of analyzing data.

There Is No Such Thing as a Technology-Neutral Decision

The information technology element of business is becoming dominant and transparent. Information technology per se can no longer be divorced from the myriad decisions CEOs have to make. Organizations are pure information processing machines. Their job is to capture, massage, and channel information. The information-processing infrastructure you enable (for it won't be enabled otherwise) will increasingly differentiate your company from the competition. Only information technology will create the connections between your product or service and the customer. Because every decision you make has an information-technology implication, it is vital for you to be informed and comfortable with the strategic issues. The quality and quantity of information comprehended per unit of time may now determine who wins or loses, whether the issue is a customer order or a national war.

Information Technology Doesn't Support the Business; It Is the Business

I cannot be clearer than this: Give up any idea you may have about how information technology can support your business. Your business is information and information is your business.

Information technology changes everything you have ever learned about business management. It has changed the very meaning of management and the skills needed to do it well. Information technology flattens management. It has already flattened millions of managers who have failed to accommodate themselves to the inevitable. Forces like this make no exceptions. Even for you—maybe especially for you.

Please don't feel that you're being singled out. You're in good company. Everyone—your colleagues, your competitors, even your customers—is reeling. Thanks to the transformation inspired by information technology, every economic activity is up for renegotiation.

So deeply embedded in every process that it is all but invisible, information technology will underlie every business activity in the connected organization. Information technology will not be considered a tool or even a way to leverage human knowledge. It will become an expected utility, much like electricity, noticeable only in the rare event it is withdrawn.

Bill Gates
1955 –

The year was 1968. Bill Gates was in eighth grade when his school purchased an ASR-33 Teletype (a.k.a. computer). The moment Gates sat down at the terminal, the prototypical nerd was created. However, this was no ordinary nerd, because Gates clearly understood how to turn software into hard cash. From the beginning, he equated computer programming with power. As Gates once recalled, programming provided him with an opportunity "to control everything. There's no compromise. Every line is yours and you feel good about every line. It's kind of selfish. . . ." This feeling soon gave way to a greater vision. As early as 1974 Gates and Paul Allen (cofounder of Microsoft) anticipated the impending invasion of the personal computer.

Their first big coup was latching on to IBM in 1980 and winning a contract to develop an operating system, which came to be known as MS-DOS. As Microsoft grew, Gates instituted a top-notch recruiting program that lured the smartest people by promising to make them rich with stock options—today there are hundreds of Microsoft millionaires. As far as leading the company, Gates said, "I sort of know where we are going long term. I've got to make sure people are coming up with messages consistent with that future." And as for Gates's continued success, H. Ross Perot once said, "Most corporate executives in the United States don't understand their product at all. Guys running huge companies don't understand their product: They're financial men, they're lawyers, you name it. Bill Gates is a guy who knows his product. He can get right down there on the floor with his best programmers and mix it up."

As the octopuslike Microsoft ventures aggressively into the Internet and the media, it has sparred repeatedly with the U.S. Justice Department. Worried that their innovation will be stifled, Gates is not afraid to counterattack. Like David Sarnoff, he also has had to deal with critics who raise ethical questions about the advances in technology. In *A View from Olympus,* Gates deals with the moral issue as well as explains why he thinks computers and the Internet will enrich our lives.

A View from Olympus

Bill Gates

The Decline of Middlemen

The key mechanism of capitalism is matching buyers and sellers. Who has something that you are interested in? What is the quality, the price? Are any others bidding on it? This is information. More and more, information about goods and services, buyers and sellers, will migrate to the network. Once that happens, then the people who have been profiting as middlemen passing that information along—well, their world becomes very different. Buyers and sellers will go direct. It doesn't take a genius to figure out that the percentage of middlemen will go down quite a bit.

The Rise of Micromarkets

Today if you want to send information to one person, you send an email or call them up. To send to a million or more people, you create a TV show or a newspaper. But try reaching a few thousand people—that's a problem. The economics are sticky. The cost of locating people who might be interested in your content and reaching them through distribution channels favors scale. But once you are in the electronic world, that distribution bottleneck goes away. In the future you'll see lots of content that is aimed at a few thousand people. Media distribution channels will be radically redefined.

Wildly Disruptive to Your Business Model

Every business has to think about how it adds value to the supply chain. With electronic networks and the decline of middlemen, the key is figuring out your new role. The people who should be thinking about this the most are retailers. That's an area where electronic networks could be wildly disruptive, and nobody really knows the answer.

At a kiosk in a small storefront, you should be able to order clothes custom-made, and you should be able to examine a wide selection and even see what you would look like in [an outfit], with the right sort of digital database available for that.

Book buying on the Web is going at a pretty good rate. This is significant. I like to buy videos, older videos, obscure videos—and that's very difficult to do right now. I'd love to have somebody set up in doing that. There are many types of merchandise where breadth and choice matter a lot.

How to Play the Future

Computers evolve at the pace of Moore's Law.* Digging ditches doesn't. There are some things here that take time. Fiber doesn't just grow toward the home. So to make intelligent bets on the future, you have to understand what will be going on in the next ten years. Most people *overestimate* what is going to happen in the next two or three years and *underestimate* what is going to happen in the next decade. Take

*Moore's Law is named after Gordon Moore, cofounder of Intel, who once predicted that the capacity of the computer chip would double every year.

high-speed communications. Once you get the infrastructure in place, then people will expect everything to work that way. Once I tell my lawyer he's got to work that way, then he converts and he starts working that way, and it just sort of pulls everybody in because everybody interrelates to everyone else. With that kind of phenomena, things can be very dramatic. But not in two or three years. The work of conditioning twisted pairs to run ADSL, the cost of upgrading the cable infrastructure to carry two-way data, the time waiting for regulatory things to clear—this doesn't happen in two or three years.

Every business has to think about how it adds value to the supply chain. With electronic networks and the decline of middlemen, the key is figuring out your new role.

But in Ten Years?

In ten years it gets wild. Three groups of things interest me. One is the very predictable result Moore's Law has on computer capability. PC power in absolute terms gets so large that your ability to do rich things—like keeping your entire personal photo collection on your PC—will be a piece of cake. That's very predictable, and still it's a very cool thing. That's an application people would be interested in.

Then there are breakthrough things that are certain to come between now and 2006. Extremely cheap flat-panel display. . . . On the surface of my desk and on a lot of my walls, I'll have displays with project status, sales data—all there. I'll just walk up and touch it and instantly dive in and see different views of information. That will be pervasive. Input will be done with pointing devices or by talking to the computer. The computer will be talking to us, and it will see. It will see when we walk into a room.

Surely You're Joking, Mr. Gates

People have been saying I'm too optimistic. These are things that I'm investing in doing. I have lots of people working on all of these things. When the computer can see you, recognize you, respond to your speech and gestures and things like that, then it becomes much more pervasive in how it fits into your environment and how you can use it as an information tool. People just grossly underestimate this.

> *Most people* overestimate *what is going to happen in the next two or three years and* underestimate *what is going to happen in the next decade.*

Screens will have much better resolution than they do today. Sometimes you want to work on a screen close up and sometimes on a screen faraway. You'll have multiple computers and screens connected through wired or wireless infrastructure. With wall-size screens and lots of bandwidth, you can say, "Hey, I want to see that camera on the roof at that Club Med near Puerto Vallarta! I want to see what it's like down there on the beach right now!"

Computer Haves and Have-Nots

This is a serious issue. If this tool is as great as we think it is, you want it to be broadly available. We once had a problem like that with books, but over a period of literally decades, society adopted the notion that everybody should have access to books. Lots of local money was raised for libraries. Lots of philanthropists, most notably Carnegie, got involved to make sure that happened. Today nobody can really say to you "Geez, I was screwed because I didn't have any books." You would say to him, "Hey, go to the public library. They've got more than I've got in my house—even my house!"

Maybe in 1900 it was cool to go to the library. Today it's not. But if you can get public terminals in there, and get kids in there talking about how they use it and the cool things they find, then you would increase availability. Maybe kids of a certain age or people of a certain income should get to access intellectual property royalty free or royalty reduced. Why not? There is no marginal cost.

IQ Level Shouldn't Make a Difference

I don't think of IQ as a static thing. Sure, at any point in time that's the case [that people of less than average intelligence are shut out], but I'll bet if you took a group that tested-average, and you gave them access to tools like these over a period of years, they would test above average. The tools [computers, etc.] accelerate people's intellectual progress. It's like saying before libraries everybody had an average IQ of 100 and after libraries everybody had an average IQ of 100. Who could dispute that life is richer today when you can go and read Charles Dickens and you can go and read biographies of people whom you can relate to and who are inspiring to you? That's better than being a field hand who never learned how to read. I think the world is progressing and resources are becoming more abundant. . . . I'd rather go into a grocery store today than to a king's banquet a hundred years ago.

Is the Net a Force for Moral Good?

The morality thing is a little confusing to me. It's a very broad term. We have somebody like Lee Kuan Yew [architect of modern Singapore] who has created a society basically without drug use and with extremely low levels of crime, and you compare that to the U.S. His choice of how he creates community values—a form of semiauthoritarianism—is something that most people in the U.S. would disagree with. A Singaporean would look at the U.S. and say Americans love the guns, they love the crime, they love the disparity in income levels. I think you're going to get disagreements about even what is good.

I think the world is progressing and resources are becoming more abundant. . . . I'd rather go into a grocery store today than to a king's banquet a hundred years ago.

The U.S. is the place where the Internet is happening. Let's say it makes the whole world like the U.S. Some people would say that's good. Some people would say that's bad. The morality thing is way too judgmental. It's a tool of communication. It's a tool for people to achieve more of their potential.

PART IV

Evolving Perspectives on Labor

Often conflict is necessary to provoke change. Disputes between employer and employee have played an important role in the evolution of business leadership, and Part IV is organized chronologically to provide some context to the changing relationship between capital and labor, between executive and employee, between leader and follower. What is learned is that it takes more than a paycheck to win cooperation. Frederick Coolidge Crawford, who was famous for busting labor unions, explains what happens when he waves the magic wand over a factory to improve production. Harry Bullis, once chairman of General Mills, uses a snake charmer to explain why labor must be educated on how they fit into the big picture. And Frederick W. Smith, founder of Federal Express, provides some very practical programs for winning loyalty. All of the authors offer insights into how better to involve employees in day-to-day business affairs. Reading through the selections, it becomes apparent how much more enlightened business leaders are today than a hundred years ago.

William Randolph Hearst
1863 – 1951

Orson Welles produced a thinly veiled takeoff on William Randolph Hearst in his 1941 movie *Citizen Kane,* in which Hearst (a.k.a. Kane) is portrayed as a wealthy, tyrannical megalomaniac who loses his soul in the pursuit of power. The family vehemently refuted this depiction, and with good reason. Granted, Hearst was born into money, built an even greater empire, and lived in a castle; however, after graduating from Harvard, he refused to go into his father's prosperous mining business and instead elected to join Joseph Pulitzer's *New York World* as a staff reporter. He chose the more difficult path and learned the media business from the ground up.

Hearst left *The World* to purchase his father's old newspaper, the *San Francisco Examiner,* in 1893. Two years later he made his first big move by acquiring the *New York Journal* and going head to head with Joseph Pulitzer, his one-time mentor. Their battle for New York spawned "yellow journalism." Hearst quickly earned the reputation as a muckraking sensationalist, his inflammatory headlines even played a role in instigating the Spanish-American War. In addition, his repeated attacks on President William McKinley caused many to believe he was behind the 1901 assassination. As a result, Hearst was forced to hire armed guards to protect himself. He survived and eventually owned newspapers in most major cities across the country; his stable of magazines included *Good Housekeeping, Harper's Bazaar, Cosmopolitan,* and *Popular Mechanic*; and later the company added radio and television stations to its holdings.

Welles's "Citizen Kane" undoubtedly had his faults as a newspaper man, but Hearst devoutly believed in the American ideal and did much to protect the underprivileged and raise the level of social conscience through his headlines. The following selection is a medley of three editorials, in which he addresses the conflict between laborer and captain of industry. While the capitalist deserves his profit, Hearst argues that he cannot suppress the common man to get it and urges tolerance when it comes to unions. Unions, he says, made America and Hearst pleads with his audience to move forward and end the violence.

Labor Relations: The Division of Wealth

William Randolph Hearst

In this country labor is universally honored and is universal and appreciated. In this country there is no working class, but every man worthy of the name is a working man. In this country there is no class of men that work with their hands while another class work with their brains. In America all men work with their brains, and when we say that American laborers are the most efficient on earth, we do not mean that their hands are different from those of other men, but that their minds are clearer, quicker and more effective than those of other men.

In this country the mechanics work, the farmers work, the clerks work, the business men work, the professional men work, and even the millionaires work. We have no aristocracy save that of intellect and industry, and the proudest title of our most successful millionaire is "Captain of Industry." In a country where all men are working men, there should be greater community interest, better mutual understanding and sympathy. It is in behalf of this better understanding that I speak today. I have no patience with the prejudices which exist between alleged classes when the classes themselves do not really exist.

There is no reason for hostility between employer and employee, between capitalist and wage-earner. Capital is but the accumulation of wealth which employer and employee create together. Wages are but the division of profits. Both employer and employee are entitled to their share of the profits, and as long as the division is just and equitable there is no occasion for conflict. If the division is not just, it can always be made so by arbitration, and there is still no occasion for conflict.

We have no aristocracy save that of intellect and industry, and the proudest title of our most successful millionaire is "Captain of Industry."

Let us all regard one another as fellow working men and treat one another with consideration and tolerance. Let us all labor harmoniously to create wealth in order that there may be the greatest possible amount to be justly divided. . . . Therefore, I say, there should be no prejudice entertained by the capitalists toward the laborer, and there should be no prejudice by the laborer toward the capitalist. There should be an appreciation of the essential part which each plays in the creation of wealth.

The working man is worthy of his hire, the business man of his profit. The man who digs the precious metal from the earth is worth his wage. The man who tells him where to find the gold deserves his profit, too. The great financial promoters, organizers, executives of America are worthy of recognition and reward.

They work as hard as any of us, and their work is absolutely necessary to the full production of the riches out of which are paid here in America the highest wages in the world. Through many an anxious day and many a wakeful night these men have planned and prosecuted the great enterprises which have developed the wealth of the Nation and have given employment to millions of men. Let them have a liberal share of that wealth as long as that is the incentive which stimulates them to useful activities. Let them have wealth as long as it is honestly acquired through enterprises that benefit the whole community. The riches they amass and call their own are seldom spent in extravagance and luxury upon themselves, but are put back into new industries to produce more wealth and give employment to more men. The true captain of industry is the general of our industrial army. He cannot do without soldiers, and yet, no matter how well the soldiers fight, the victory depends very largely on the general's skillful conduct of the campaign.

The great business man is the manager of the enterprise in which we are all embarked. He is as necessary to us as we are to him, for, no matter how well we work, the success of the enterprise and the profit of it depend very largely on the ability of his management.

To achieve the most complete success for all there should be the greatest harmony between promoter and wage-earner and an ungrudging appreciation of each other's value. To win the fullest victory there should be confidence and concerted action between the commander and the men behind the guns. And now, my friends, in the creation of wealth and in the equable distribution of wealth not only is co-operation necessary but organization is necessary. Organization in unions, organization of capital, all organizations which tend to make human effort more effective, to increase and not to curtail the production of wealth are of advantage to mankind.

The great financial promoters, organizers, executives of America are worthy of recognition and reward.

Labor unions are valuable not only to their own members but to the whole community. Farmers' unions are valuable not only to their own members but to the whole community. And honest, law-abiding organizations of capital are valuable not only to their own stockholders but to the whole community. . . . I plead for equal laws for all, for equal rights for all, for equal justice for all. I plead for opportunity for all honest men, and for harmony and co-operation between all honest men. I plead for unprejudiced recognition of the advantage of organization and combination, and for intelligent discrimination between what is good and what is bad. I assert the multiplied value of united action and declare for the principle of union.

A hundred and a quarter years ago a little band of patriots united to secure better and freer conditions, to protect themselves from the exactions of their so-called superiors. They protested, struck, rebelled—call it what you will—against tyranny and oppression. They fought a long and gallant fight. They deprived themselves and their families, they struggled and endured and died that they might win a righteous cause. They established the United States of America, with independence, equality, and opportunity for all men.

Since then, it seems to me, it little behooves a free and favored citizen of this liberal land to be opposed to unions. What is our government but a union? What is our motto? "In union there is strength." If there are faults in our Government, let us correct them, but not condemn all government. When there are faults in our unions and combinations, let us correct them, but not deny the value of united effort.

My friends, we have come out of and up from a dark and dreary past, where there was the weariness of effort without system or organization, the discouragement of great labor with little result. We have come into the light of higher civilization, and in it we see plainly the advantage of organization and co-operation, the enormously increased product of united effort.

Let us go forward and not back; let us organize, since the faculty of organization is the measure of intellectual development, but let us proceed with due regard for each other's rights, with consideration of each other's services, with appreciation of each other's value. Let us organize unions of labor, unions of farmers, unions of capital, and let us conduct them, not narrowly and selfishly, but broadly and liberally, for our own best interests and for the public interest as well.

Let us combat organization that operates for evil with organization that operates for good. Let us fight the trusts and oppressive monopolies, not with the slings and arrows of an age that is past, but with a modern armament—with the twelve inch batteries and disciplined battalions of an age of organization.

Let us organize a union of all good citizens to preserve our government as patriots founded it, to conduct it impartially for the benefit of all and to perpetuate for our children the independence, equality and opportunity which our fathers with devotion, sacrifice and heroism won for us.

Good Wages for Good Work

In industry good wages and good work are equally important. Good work makes a good product. Good wages make a good market. A high standard of wages means a high purchasing power and it should be one of the business objects of employers to maintain a general high standard of wages in order to maintain a general market for their products. On the other hand, it should be the intelligent purpose of the labor unions to meet any depressed situation in business by increasing productivity, and removing hampering union rules which interfere with productivity and profits.

The first requisite for the payment of good wages is that the employers make enough money to be able to pay good wages. Wealth cannot be distributed until it is created, and whatever interferes with the creation of wealth interferes with the distribution of wealth in wages as well as in profits.

When union rules interfere with the creation of wealth they interfere with the welfare of labor as much as they interfere with the welfare of capital. As a matter of mathematical fact, they interfere with the welfare of labor a great deal more than they interfere with the welfare of capital, because about ninety per cent of the wealth created is distributed in wages, and capital is well content with anything like ten per cent of the wealth created.

Wealth is production. There may be prospective wealth, putative wealth, potential wealth, in the soil, in the ore veins, in various latent forms—but actual wealth is only that which has been produced into the things that men require. The more there is of production, therefore, the more there is of wealth.

And everything from human skill to labor-saving machinery which increases production increases wealth and increases the welfare of the entire human race. The greater comforts, luxuries, conveniences and advantages that modern man possesses over men of former ages are due directly to increased productivity, which puts many of these comforts and advantages within the reach of all. Still greater skill, still greater mechanical ingenuity and productive machinery will provide still greater comforts, conveniences and advantages, and place them at the disposal of absolutely all.

Whenever labor by restrictive rules, or capital by curtailing production, interferes with the creation of wealth, it interferes with the material development of the race and with the common possession of the advantages of modern productivity as far as each restrictive act is operative. There are two fundamental facts to be recognized: First, that productivity is necessary for permanently high wages; and second, that high wages are essential to general prosperity. The less the productivity, the less there is to be distributed in profits and wages. That is reasonably obvious.

And since the vast majority of the people of this or any other country are wage-earners, and general prosperity depends upon the prosperity of the mass, it is equally obvious that only liberal wages will create general prosperity and the general purchasing power, which in turn, means the prosperity of every individual and of every individual business. Let us, therefore, pay good wages for good work and give good work for good wages. For only by such cooperative effort can we create the fullest productivity, the greatest purchasing power and the greatest prosperity.

Compensation of Executives

The object of society, like the object of any individual employer, should be to get the best work out of its employees. Everyone needs a stimulus to do his best work. These stimuli are generally wealth, position, distinction.

Few—very few—work merely for the love of achievement. Everyone must feel the urge of desire and the realization of being able to accomplish through his work the satisfaction of his desire.

In organized society no man should loaf on his job. In an army it is just as important for the generals to strive as for the soldiers to strive. In the social organizations it is just as important for the executives to work as for the laborers to work. Therefore, human society must be liberal with its gold braid, must hang up in front of its ablest executives baubles of wealth and position and distinction for them to work for.

It pays to pay well. It pays to pay workingmen well and it pays to pay big executives well. Society wants the best work that is in them.

DANIEL GUGGENHEIM
1856 – 1930

Daniel Guggenheim, whose family made its astounding fortune in mining, was considered to be as powerful as J. P. Morgan in the early twentieth century. Like so many others at the time, the family's rise to power followed the typical Horatio Alger story. Guggenheim's father, Meyer, came to America with nothing and started out as a door-to-door peddler of household goods. Soon he opened his own shop and started making good money as a manufacturer and importer of fine embroidery. Old Meyer was intent on creating a dynasty, and he told his sons, "You see, my boys, singly the sticks are easily broken, together they cannot be broken. So it is with you. Together you are invincible." When the patriarch realized his own mortality and died in 1905, Daniel took the reins.

The family had stumbled upon mining when they bought a one-third interest in two Colorado mines. The innocent speculation turned into a bonanza and fueled their desire to expand their mining interests. Under Guggenheim's leadership they soon pushed into Alaska and South America. One of Guggenheim's strategies was to use cheap labor and mine raw materials in undeveloped countries to force domestic costs down. Having more money itself was not what interested him. In a letter to his son he wrote, "Money, to me, for the luxury that it will give me has very little value. But money is power, and the power is the thing to use, not to abuse." For example, he contributed a great deal of money to the development of aeronautics and is considered the foster father of U.S. aviation.

The real secret to his success was, Guggenheim said, "A combination of tenacity and tact. You see, roasted pigeons won't fly." While Guggenheim exploited resources, he treated foreign dignitaries and those around him very well, making few enemies. And while his labor policies were at times harsh, he acknowledged that the industrial organization must be democratized. In *Some Thoughts on Industrial Unrest,* written in 1915, he presents some ideas on how to reconcile with labor. Guggenheim begins to offer practical solutions to the issues that William Randolph Hearst raised.

Some Thoughts on Industrial Unrest

Daniel Guggenheim

Chiefly because of the advancing cost of living, but largely at the same time on account of the ever-growing inequality in the division of the wealth of the nation, there has been for many years a steady increase of discontent among the laboring people of the United States. This discontent is bound to keep on growing unless radical steps are taken to alleviate the present condition of the laboring classes. A great many things have been done during the past few years to benefit the laboring man but more must be done, and more will be done, because employers of labor and managers of business are commencing to realize to a greater extent than ever before the nature of their obligations toward their toiling employees. Just as the business man of today no longer believes that in order to get on in business he must roll his competitor in the dust, so no longer does he follow the practice of grinding his laborers down, paying them the lowest wages possible and utilizing them for his own interests and nothing beyond that.

Whatever may be the temporary expedients adopted to tide over present difficulties with which the laboring population is confronted, the ultimate solution of the entire labor problem must come through governmental action after careful and nonpartisan scientific study. Private philanthropy has done a great deal toward reducing industrial discontent. The people could not live that are not employed if it were not for the philanthropic work that is now being carried on. But no matter how much is done, enough is never done because the people themselves do not realize what the situation is and there are so many thousands of people who do not like to part with the money they have made, money which often they do not need and which is of no advantage to them. Furthermore, private philanthropy is confronted always by two great obstacles. It has a tendency to pauperize the people whom it is intended to benefit and it cannot reach many people who are deserving of help because of their aversion toward accepting charity. These obstacles can be surmounted only through state action. Unemployment, sickness, old age and similar problems of labor can be solved only through some system of social insurance managed and applied by state authority. If a man is out of employment, it is the duty of the state through some agency to help him obtain work. If a man is physically unfit for labor either on account of injuries, sickness, or age, provision should be made by the state for his care.

Just as the business man of today no longer believes that in order to get on in business he must roll his competitor in the dust, so no longer does he follow the practice of grinding his laborers down . . .

Our industrial organization must be democratized. It must be transformed so that the laborer himself may have a voice in the determination of all the conditions by which his interests are affected, the length of his working hours, the amount of his wages, and the surroundings amid which he labors.

As indicated before, the attainment of industrial democracy must come in the main through scientific legislation. Through the action of the federal and state governments, employers and laborers must be brought together by a system of laws in the making of which all members of each class shall have an opportunity to participate. A great deal has been done in the way of legislation in this country but we are still years behind many foreign countries in providing for the welfare of workmen. Although many people are of the opinion that too much legislation is being enacted, I do not agree with that idea, nor do I think that we have begun to legislate to the extent that we shall in the future for the welfare of the workmen. I think the difference between the rich man and the poor man is very much too great, and it is only by taking steps to bridge the gulf that exists between them that we shall be able to get away from the unrest now prevailing among the working classes.

Our industrial organization must be democratized. It must be transformed so that the laborer himself may have a voice in the determination of all the conditions by which his interests are affected . . .

An important feature of the industrial democracy should be the establishment of a system through which the laborers may be permitted to share in the profits of industry. It should be provided, however, that the share due the laboring man may be given him in bulk at the end of a certain period and deposited in some bank or savings institution. The laborer usually does not know how to save and if he gets his money by the week he spends it; his expenses constantly keeping pace with his receipts. A few men learn how to save but it is a difficult matter for a poor man to learn. Therefore, if he has an extra bonus at the end of a certain period, no matter how small it is, it should be deposited in bulk at some savings bank. As soon as a man has something of his own which he puts aside he feels differently, having acquired the pride of ownership and the knowledge of how to save. The cultivation of thrift will be of benefit not only to the individuals who save but to the people at large.

. . . the difference between the rich man and the poor man is very much too great, and it is only by taking steps to bridge the gulf that exists between them that we shall be able to get away from the unrest now prevailing among the working classes.

Industrial reforms can be brought about only by collective action and the first step toward securing the legislation necessary to the establishment of industrial democracy must be the organization of the workers who are to be benefited. The fact must not be overlooked that we have at the present time good organizations and bad organizations among laborers, just as we have "good trusts" and "bad trusts." The quality of leadership decides the quality of the organization. But good labor organizations, of which we have a great many in this country, can get together, analyze their difficulties and dispose of them. Such organizations deserve the fullest measure of coöperation from all employers, and it is through their united action that proper laws may be passed for the improvement of the economic condition of the people. We have already made a start in this country toward the establishment of industrial democracy through the enactment of laws regulating the hours of labor, laws fixing compensation for injuries, and laws regulating the conditions of employment. Progress in the future will be more rapid than in the past. WIth a proper organization of the forces of labor and capital and the cultivation of a mutual regard for the rights and obligations of both it will be possible to bring about any desirable change in our industrial system.

William Cooper Procter

William Cooper Procter's grandfather William and William's brother-in-law, James Gamble, founded Procter & Gamble in 1837. Their first products were soap and candles; their first big hit was Ivory Soap, because it floated—a result of too much steam getting into a batch of soap as it was being made. Housewives loved the soap, and two generations later Procter walked the floor personally inspecting each valuable kettle of Ivory Soap. Some of the kettle operators were even known to taste the soap to determine if it was done or not. By 1878 the company was producing twenty-four different kinds of soap, a reflection of its pioneering marketing strategy to make its own products compete against each other. Each was to eventually find its own market segment.

While Procter may have enjoyed his soap, he found dealing with the press and sharing internal information dirty. In fact, the New York Stock Exchange delisted the company from 1903 to 1929 because it wouldn't provide enough information. (This cult of silence supposedly continues today in the world of Proctoids.) One problem Procter couldn't ignore was labor upheaval. In 1886 and 1887 the company suffered through fourteen strikes and 50 percent turnover. Procter understood the employees' grievances about working conditions because he had held every job in the factory on his way to the helm. So for his entire tenure he focused on labor relations.

In 1887 Procter & Gamble was the very first to start a profit-sharing program. Procter's other initiatives included giving the employees Saturday afternoons off with pay and introducing comprehensive insurance benefits that covered health, disability, and death. His good relations with labor reached an apex in 1903, when employees were offered a stock ownership program. Interestingly, profit-sharing and stock ownership were not immediate successes; the employees had to be educated on exactly what they stood to earn. *How We Divide with Our Men* provides a great case study for how labor relations began to emerge from the dark ages, and Procter's ideas remain just as relevant today.

How We Divide with Our Men

William Cooper Procter

"Is your firm afraid of Bolshevism among its employees?" a friend asked me the other day. "No," I answered, "not at all." The question sent a series of pictures flashing through my mind. One of these, which would have been far more effective than my denial, throws an interesting light on the mental attitude that thirty-three years of profit-sharing have given our workmen.

In February, 1918, we told the Employees' Conference Committee, our men's parliament, that we were going to give them the eight-hour working day as soon as possible. "War demands are so heavy," we explained, "that the ten- and eleven-hour day must be continued for the present, although we recognize the eight-hour day as a base, and we'll pay you time-and-a-half for all overtime."

Two months after the signing of the armistice we were able to announce that we would go ahead to the standard eight-hour day and would stop the overtime work.

"You are going to make considerably less money," I said to the men, "unless your wages are raised. I want you to call meetings in all the departments, and thresh this out. Decide what wages you think you ought to receive if the eight-hour day goes into effect, and report your decision in ten days."

In each of the thirty-five departments at Ivorydale (our Cincinnati plant) the workers got together and talked out the situation. They then compared results at a general meeting of the conference committee. Promptly at the end of ten days the decision of the general meeting was brought back in the shape of a report—a report which shows there is no breeding ground for Bolshevist bacilli at the Ivorydale plant.

"We want the eight-hour day," the report ran; "but it is our unanimous decision that we don't want to say what you shall pay us. You know as well as we that the cost of living has gone up, and you'll take that into account. You have always treated us right, and we know you are going to keep on doing it."

Soon after we received this report the company was able to announce a new scale of wages, under which the lowest paid able-bodied man in the plant would get fifty cents an hour, and the average worker would receive as much for eight hours' work as ten hours had been bringing him before. I was pleased to learn later that this scale was above that set by any department in their informal discussions.

Our employees have been called "working capitalists."

Perhaps the title is not too far afield. But to me it is of more significance to know that they are contented and happy.

Many of our innovations were born more of the earnest desire to foster this spirit of content, and to give our workers freer opportunity to express themselves, than of the mere wish to improve their finances.

The Employees' Conference plan was, I believe, the first move of its kind in business history. Certainly it was one of the first. Together with the profit-sharing, group insurance, and pension and benefit plans, it is simply in line with our conception of the square deal.

Early last year we worked out the idea of having the employees elect by secret ballot a conference committee to meet monthly with the management, in order to bring to our attention matters that seemed to need correction, or to make any suggestions for the general betterment. Each department with not more than fifty workers chooses a representative, and there is one representative for every fifty persons in the larger departments.

Many of our innovations were born more of the earnest desire to foster this spirit of content, and to give our workers freer opportunity to express themselves, than of the mere wish to improve their finances.

Up to the present no suggestion by the employees, and they have made many, has been turned down unless we were able to show them that it was impracticable. I always feel that if I talk with our men and cannot convince them that they are wrong, the chances are they are right.

Business men know that wages are higher and working conditions better in a large manufacturing plant than in a small one. Yet the men in the smaller plant—working longer hours, paid less, and not so well looked after—are usually more contented. The reason lies largely in the fact that men feel a more intimate personal interest in the smaller organization, and therefore a greater loyalty to it.

The chief problem of "big business" today is to shape its policies so that each worker, whether in office or factory, will feel he is a vital part of his company, with a personal responsibility for its success, and a chance to share in that success. To bring this about, an employer must take the men into his confidence. They should know why they are doing things, the relation of their work to other departments, and, so far as practicable, to the business as a whole; they should be told those elements of cost of production affected by their work, or they cannot put intelligent effort into what they are doing. What is more, I believe that the workman should have some means through which he can give expression to his ideas as to the general policy of the business, in accordance with his position and ability, and especially as it relates to his own work.

On March 1st, 1919, at the "Dividend Day" meeting, I announced to the men that we had decided to ask them to elect three of their number to sit on the board of directors of the company—the body that has the authority to discharge me, or the general superintendent, or the general manager, or any other officer of the company.

I told the men that this meant that their influence and voice would run through the whole organization more fully than ever before; and that this influence, these rights, placed upon them a corresponding obligation.

"The only real test of the plan's success," I explained, "is contentment and the greater production that comes from contentment, based on the realization that you are assured, in accordance with your position and ability, a free and full voice in the conduct of the industry to which you are giving your lives."

Steps such as these may seem iconoclastic to many businessmen, but they are the logical sequence of the distribution of profits carried on by this company for more than three decades.

"Tell me how your profit-sharing plan works," other employers sometimes say to me. "I want to start something of the sort myself. I believe it will pay in the long run."

The chief problem of "big business" today is to shape its policies so that each worker, whether in office or factory, will feel he is a vital part of his company . . .

"If that is your object, don't do it," I always answer. "No one can build a sound profit-sharing plan on the desire to make money. You must be possessed of the conviction, not only that a fair share of the profit existing without the profit-sharing plan belongs to the worker, but that under the profit-sharing plan the worker will produce enough additional to pay his profit-sharing dividend. Your interests must be primarily in the men and seeing that they have the opportunity of earning, through increased interest, the additional money; and, above all, you must realize that it is more than money that the men want, it is a sense of ownership, that can be, in part at least, developed through profit-sharing. Without this unselfish motive on the part of the employer, profit-sharing will never be a success, for both he and the men, in the end, will distrust each other and be dissatisfied with any distribution made.

. . . it is more than money that the men want, it is a sense of ownership . . .

Our profit-sharing program started back in 1886, when the Knights of Labor movement was agitating American workmen. In one year we had no fewer than fourteen strikes, and men were quitting daily for trivial causes.

I was just out of college, with rather radical ideas, for those times, on business problems. The situation distressed me. Day in and day out I was working beside these men, nearly all of whom I could call by their first names.

One of my earliest adventures in industrial discontent was the discovery of the fact that these men were working too long hours. I talked the matter over with my father, who was then at the head of the firm, and persuaded him to give the men Saturday half-holiday. So far as I know, we were the first firm in the country to take this step.

The next move in order was to make the men feel that their own interests and the interests of the firm were identical. So we worked out our first profit-sharing plan. To build the framework for this plan was no slight job, for we were pioneers and had to blaze our own trail.

We finally decided that net profits should be divided between the firm and its employees in the proportion that the men's wages bore to the total cost of production. To illustrate: Assume that we paid $20,000 a year in wages, spent another $70,000 in additional manufacturing costs, and had a total sales for the year of $100,000. Then the $10,000 difference between our costs and our sales would be net profit, and would be divided two-ninths to the men and seven-ninths to the firm.

This system was crude, but it was a far reach forward for those days. The men received it rather half-heartedly; but when at the end of the first six months they were paid a dividend of eleven per cent of their wages, signs of interest began to be shown.

The first year this plan was in operation we had three strikes. Since then we have had only one strike in our history, and that was forced at a branch plant by I. W. W. pressure from the outside.

From 1887 to 1903 we made numerous changes in the plan, one of which was to give up the system of costs and profits, and to pay every worker in the plant, twice a year, a dividend of twelve per cent of his wages.

All these plans had one serious defect in common—the workers looked on their semi-annual "Dividend Day" checks as merely extra wages, and spent them as such. Very little of this money was going into their savings accounts.

For a time this situation baffled us. Then I decided that we could place a premium on thrift by requiring the men to save a certain fraction of their wages before they would receive any extra money from the firm. Through the plan that went into effect in 1903 we said, in substance, to each workman, male and female, in our employ:

"To every dollar you save we will add four dollars, until as much money as you make in a year has been accumulated. This money is then yours. Our only stipulation is that it must be invested in the common stock of the company. We expect our stock to increase greatly in value. That increase, too, will be yours. However, we will protect you against depreciation. If you should ever decide to leave the company, and your stock should then be below the market price at which you obtained it, we promise to return to you in cash that full market price."

Profit-sharing has many attendant advantages. For one thing, it inclines a man to stay on the job by giving him a vital interest in the business. Fifty-six men at the Ivorydale plant have been with us from twenty-five to forty years. Nearly half of the more than 2,700 workers are employees of from one to forty years standing. The average annual turnover shown in industrial plants is 120 percent, twice the annual turnover shown at Ivorydale. Our records show that if a man stays with the company one month, long enough to get fairly acquainted, he is likely to remain here indefinitely.

I believe that the spirit of thrift and the sense of responsibility that have come to our men through the profit-sharing plan have had much to do with the rapid development of leaders among them.

All but one of the men in places of power with this company today have come up through the ranks, and most of them started at not more than a day laborer's or a clerk's salary. Our general superintendent began work as a boy in the box factory at $2 a week. The superintendent of the plant at Port Ivory, New York, entered our employ sixteen years ago as a $45 a month bill-of-lading clerk. Our chief engineer at Cincinnati started at $5 a week. It is only fifteen years since our general sales manager was a $60 a month clerk in the treasurer's department. The Central and Western sales managers broke in as office boys; and so the list might be carried on.

Our experience, however, has proved to us the great value of a college education, and I cannot urge young men too strongly upon this point. While all but one of the men in places of power in this company today have come up through the ranks, over eighty per cent of those men drawing salaries in excess of three thousand dollars a year are college graduates. They start with the crowd, but the trained mind demonstrates its value as truly as the skilled laborer stands out over the unskilled.

All but one of the men in places of power with this company today have come up through the ranks . . .

Remembering how these men came out of the crowd and forced recognition of their merits, I have slight sympathy with the theory that luck plays a controlling part in business success. Luck exists, of course, and some folk seem to get more than their share of it, but to every man comes enough luck so that he will be able to make his mark if he has the native ability, ambition, and vision to measure up to his opportunities.

. . . I have slight sympathy with the theory that luck plays a controlling part in business success. . . . to every man comes enough luck so that he will be able to make his mark if he has the native ability, ambition, and vision . . .

The first promotion, that which lifts a man from the crowd is the hardest to get. It is like the private's promotion to corporal. But once the workman has become a foreman, or is given any position with authority over other men, he has risen where he can be seen. He *will* be seen, too, for every employer is sweeping his organization with a spyglass to seek out ability.

Looking back over the lives of the men whom I have watched as they won their way to leadership, I find five marked characteristics: they have been aggressive, truthful, unselfish, and courageous, with the power of decision and determination to carry decision through. Lacking any one of these, and especially the latter, a man's success is very doubtful; granted the five, it is assured.

Aggressiveness and good health usually lodge together; that is why I am always preaching the gospel of physical fitness. Look over the world's leaders and you will find, for the most part, men of tireless physical vigor. Some great men have been frail, a few have been invalids; but each case is an exception to the rule. Most great men have been charged with the physical vigor out of which is born much of the dynamic force that drives them through to success. Men who work their minds for sixteen hours a day and slight their bodies are violating the laws of the very success they seek. I firmly believe that fifty per cent of whatever I have been able to accomplish has been due to strength and endurance.

From twenty to twenty-five, or the first few years out of school, is the most important period in a man's life. If he has not found himself, if he has failed to make some definite impression by the time he is twenty-seven or twenty-eight, barriers will have been built up in front of him which only the very exceptional men can scale.

I firmly believe that fifty per cent of whatever I have been able to accomplish has been due to strength and endurance.

Sometimes one will hear a young man remark, "I can afford to take things easy until I am thirty or thirty-five. Then I will make up for lost time." This is the most foolish of fallacies. Men who make their mark in middle age almost invariably have established an outstanding reputation for ability, aggressiveness, and ambition in the first years of their business life.

Real genius may be handicapped, but never permanently held down, by being misplaced. Yet each employer has a great responsibility to make sure that he is helping his men to develop themselves by giving them jobs that "fit" them and that measure up to their abilities. We put 100-horse-power loads on 50-horse-power men and break them. We put 50-horse-power loads on 100-horse-power men and there is unused energy running to waste. The most successful employer is the one who can most closely match the load to the man.

I have already mentioned my belief that no man can handle his job with full efficiency and economy unless he knows why he is doing it, and what it costs. The next step this company is going to take will be based on these facts. We are going to let each department share in the lessened cost of production. Our books will be thrown open to the men; they can see for themselves the costs of production in their departments for a given period. We hope so to arrange matters that each department that is able to obtain the same results more cheaply will divide the savings with the firm.

This is simply another adventure in common sense and justice. The laboring man wants no one to become hysterical or sentimental over him. He resents it. All he wants is to be treated fairly.

. . . no man can handle his job with full efficiency and economy unless he knows why he is doing it, and what it costs.

One thing we have continually tried to avoid is any interference with the private life of our workers. I have always felt that the employer who follows up his direction of a workman's job by telling him what he should do at home is unduly impertinent to a man's soul.

Any system of rewarding labor must be predicated on the fact that every man shall return value received for what he gets, otherwise the system is unsound and cannot continue.

My greatest pride in our profit-sharing plan comes from the knowledge that it reaches the minds of our workers as well as their pocketbooks. Out of thrift has come independence; out of independence has come freedom and happiness. We have not only given our men additional money—we have helped them to find additional ideals.

Frederick Coolidge Crawford

Frederick Coolidge Crawford made a name for himself by battling labor unions during a period of renewed labor upheaval in the 1930s and 1940s. After earning a civil engineering degree from Harvard in 1914, Crawford joined Thompson Products, an auto parts manufacturer. The company branched out into supplying aircraft manufacturers during World War I, and not long after became the largest manufacturer of airplane engine components. When the founder of the company, Charles E. Thompson, died in 1933, he had his ashes spread over the city of Cleveland via airplane. That same maverick spirit imbued the company. As Crawford said, "We try to create an atmosphere in which the brain takes wing. A man here can feel free to propose crazy things. We stimulate dreaming."

When he took over the company after Thompson died, Crawford focused on maintaining the company's spirit. He encouraged and rewarded suggestions for improving operations and never hesitated to promote those with potential. To keep employees informed and to hear their gripes, Crawford constantly visited the factories. In his speeches to workers he often referred to the company as "an Ol' Brown Hen" that would keep everyone warm if they kept her fat and feathered. His message worked; in the first twenty years of Crawford's leadership, company sales grew 8,900 percent.

The one thing Crawford despised was unions. In the 1930s he crushed attempts by the CIO and AFL to organize his workers. "The unions call me a fascist," Crawford said, "but I have nothing against unions per se. But if a union merely wants our people just to increase its membership, it has no place here. But if a union leader can show me how to improve production, resulting in better wages, and increase workers' enthusiasm, I'll love him." Crawford considered himself a liberal who distrusted those who intruded upon other's freedom. In the following selection from 1943, he argues that labor relations are at a critical turning point, and there is a need to address again the opportunities available for individual enterprise, a notion that he felt was being taken for granted.

Good Human Relations: The Solution of Labor Problems

Frederick Coolidge Crawford

There is something significant in such a large group of busy industrialists coming together in weather like this and leaving their businesses to consider the problems of industrial relations. Meetings of this kind are far more important than we realize. In the solution of the problem of industrial relations, we will find the solution of many other problems that look very serious to us today. We are passing through very critical years, and a new order of some kind seems to be shaping up. Whatever lies ahead, the relationship between those who manage capital and labor is going to play an important part.

Periods in American Industrial Life

As one views the progress of American industry, there seems to be four distinct periods. The main characteristic of each of these reflects the dominant note of contemporary life in America. First, there was the period of the pioneer, when the country and industry were both young. The pioneer was the old fellow who relied on ingenuity and hard work to build the business. Then came the time when the banker who provided the capital for growth was dominant. This was followed by a period when the sales manager, with his merchandising techniques, took precedence over the other members of the organization.

Today, we have come into a new age in which human relations will be a dominant factor in all divisions of the business. I look for the coming of a vice president of human relations, who will rank as an equal with the treasurer, the secretary, the sales manager, and the engineer in the operation of the enterprise.

The present period is one of emotional emphasis. We have lived in a world of make-believe for the past ten or twelve years. Things today are not called what they really are, but what people want to believe they are. We have even changed the names of things. We don't talk about the union; we talk about maintenance. Now to me, maintenance has always meant keeping up the plant, and I used to think a directive was something to do with control. We use the same old terms, but we don't mean the same things.

We wanted a more abundant life, so we killed all of our little pigs and started restricting agricultural output. Few people stopped to think that only in more and better production could we secure the things we sought. We even turned to magic in this country. We changed the value of gold, and then sat back like King Canute to watch the tide of depression roll out—but it didn't roll.

Politicians are quick to capitalize on the emotions of the people. We are living in an age of illusions. Hitler went to war on a great illusion. He told his people he was superman and could steal what they wanted, and they wouldn't have to work for it. In my relations with some of our government agencies, I find that there is a kind of make-believe going on there, too. I have trouble in reconciling the reasoning of some of our politicians with their conclusions. Now, we're going to win this war—Americans always come through—but this make-believe background of illusion isn't very good preparation for tackling the hard job of war production, much less the industrial relations problem of the period that is coming after the war is over.

The American worker today is ready to fall in behind any parade that goes by if he thinks he can improve his lot, and he isn't very much interested in logic or facts.

Human Relations Is the Key to Production

The industrial worker in America is a good fellow and a loyal American, but he is the victim of bad leadership. He will fight and die for his country. He doesn't want a fundamental change of things in America, but he has one great weakness, which we all share in this make-believe age in which we live: He is far too susceptible to leadership, good or bad. He has been rather badly misled by labor racketeers and political demagogues. He thinks he's smart. He'll jump on any bandwagon that promises big things. If he gets burned, he'll jump off. The American worker today is ready to fall in behind any parade that goes by if he thinks he can improve his lot, and he isn't very much interested in logic or facts. It is pretty much an emotional weakness. He needs facts, and he needs the truth. He needs understanding. He needs instruction and persuasion by good leadership.

Most misconceptions of industry are due to ignorance on the part of the working man, but many of them have been the result of bad labor or bad political leadership. Whether through ignorance or misrepresentation, they are basic misunderstandings, and they must be removed. Until they are cleared away—no matter what the workers are paid nor how fine the working conditions may be in our plants—we won't get very far with good industrial relations.

Many of these misunderstandings are so obvious that we have overlooked them or haven't even thought them worth considering. To correct them, we must go to our men and tell them the facts in simple, understandable words. We must use parables and try to dramatize the story of industry until we rid their minds of their "bugaboos."

One of the most deeply rooted fallacies in the mind of the working man is the idea that to produce less per hour will benefit him, because it will make his work last longer. This is a complete misconception of the fundamental truth that the source of all wealth lies in increased production. The worker fails to understand that the raise in wages, the better job, the continued employment he wants, and the high standard of living he enjoys, all depend upon increasing the rate of production.

It is inconceivable how anybody could have missed that truth in America, a country that has grown great and prosperous through improved production methods. Our people receive the highest wages in the world and are able to purchase the best goods at the lowest prices. We have practiced successful production techniques, but we haven't explained to the worker how free enterprise works. We haven't told him that when he increases his rate of production, costs go down, orders pour in, business increases, and jobs are made more secure.

The worker knows that he wants better food, clothing and shelter, that he wants more money and a higher standard of living, generally, but what have we done to tell him how these things can be secured? The worker believes that if he stretches out production and does less work, he gains by it in the long run. To correct this misapprehension, management must sell the American worker the basic idea that the raises he wants, and the bargains his wife wants, can come only from increased production.

Industry has been crucified for ten years on the statement that wages alone determine purchasing power. The fact is that only increased production means increased purchasing power, because it provides higher wages, lower prices, and better dividends. This truth must be sold to the worker and to the American public.

Another misconception in the mind of the average worker is that income is not fairly divided in America. I have asked thousands of workmen how much labor gets and how much the owners get, and I have never known one to reply that labor received more than 30 percent of the available income. Workers think that the stockholder gets the cream and the working man gets the skimmed milk. The truth is exactly the opposite.

The most astounding fact in all American industrial life is that the distribution of the available dollar is about 90 cents to labor and 10 cents to capital. These figures must be dramatized to interest the average worker. Does the worker know that $6,000 has been invested for every job in the plant? Does he know how small the dividends are and how great is the risk of loss? Comparatively few workers want to purchase stock once they realize these facts. They prefer to put their savings in the bank.

Workers think that the stockholder gets the cream and the working man gets the skimmed milk. The truth is exactly the opposite.

Management must keep the workers sold on free enterprise. How many of you have ever told your workers what the stockholders' loyalty to the company means to them? How many of you have figured out the comparative returns received by owners and workers? In a recent meeting of our men, I emphasized the loyalty of the stockholders and told how they came through with more capital to make more jobs, and a workman in the rear of the room yelled, "Hurrah for the stockholders!" I said, "How many of you fellows would like to give three cheers for our stockholders," and the rafters rang with cheers. That was something new in industrial relations! But good labor relations are so easy and so effective when we come down from the front office and meet with the workers and approach our problems in a simple, straightforward human way.

I have told our folks about the old prospector who said he knew where there was a gold mine, and the barkeeper who agreed to provide the "grubstake" he needed. The prospector said he had to have a donkey, a slab of bacon, a sack of flour, a pick and a shovel, and $500. The barkeeper "grubstaked" him. When I asked our men what they considered a fair division of the profits of the venture—the division between ownership and labor—everybody said, "fifty/fifty."

I explained to them what is meant by available income. How we must subtract from total sales the cost of materials, operating expenses, and taxes. The money that is left, which can go to either labor or ownership, is available income. Then, when I told them that our available dollar was divided 90 cents to those who work and 10 cents to those who own the business, they were astounded. They told me that they thought the stockholders were suckers to leave their money in any enterprise for such a small return.

We cleared up another worker fallacy by graphically showing our workers the facts regarding executive salaries. Management has often kept these salaries a secret. Perhaps it has been a little ashamed of the boss's salary, because to the worker, 50, 60, or 70 thousand dollars looks like Rockefeller's millions. We tried a new approach, and I would suggest that industry generally give some thought to it. To a group of workers who inquired about officers' salaries, we said: "Appraise the value of the president of the company in terms of so many laborers. There are a group of landscapers out there working on the grounds; how many of them do you think the boss's services are worth?"

They appraised the value of the boss at one hundred and fifty laborers, and then I said, "Fellows, do you realize that you are putting the president's salary at $400,000, for each one of these laborers, with his overtime, receives from $2,500 to $3,000 a year? As a matter of fact, the president of the company has a salary of $100,000, by the time he has paid his taxes, his net income is about equal to that of 30 laborers." They were astonished, and since that time, there have been no disputes over salary at all.

We should approach the subject realistically, and frankly state the fact that the boss's salary is neither unfair nor antisocial. Figure out the net income of the head of your company and interpret it in terms of the number of laborers it equals. In most companies, executive salaries amount to less than a penny an hour for each worker whom they employ. You will find that almost everybody in the plant will say that the boss isn't receiving too much pay, after all, for the hard work he must do and the heavy responsibilities he must carry.

Some Interesting Experiments in Better Understanding

The interests of owners and workers are identical, but the workers are bewildered. They have heard the erroneous statement that 2 percent of the people own 80 percent of the nation's wealth. Ownership and income are completely confused in their minds. We should try to straighten them out by explaining that ownership must be controlled by those who are competent and able to secure maximum production.

It is the distribution of income in America that makes our democracy the best way of life the world has ever known. To illustrate, let me tell you the story of Tony and his wheelbarrow. It seems that Tony was a smart laborer who came to this country because he wanted to get in on the great opportunities that America offers. He wanted an abundant life for himself and his family. He decided that he, too, would be a capitalist and work for himself.

A school house had been built in the town in which he

lived, and it was decided to grade the lawn, so the School Board advertised for bids. When Tony presented his bid, he was told that he must have a wheelbarrow and a shovel before he could bid on the job. But he reasoned that it was not essential that he own the wheelbarrow. He could rent one, make one, or get somebody to give him one. The essential thing was to have it as a tool with which he could go to work. So Tony rented a wheelbarrow and got the job. Each day he earned ten dollars for himself in income because he had possession of capital. The wheelbarrow was worth only five dollars, yet every day he earned twice that amount. Thus, Tony learned that industry must first have capital before it can start operations and earn income.

Your factories and mine are just wheelbarrows. If our workers only knew that the facilities they have are simply the tools with which to work and secure their share of American income, their ideas would change. It challenged our boys the other day, when we told them that during the ten depression years we had paid out a hundred million in wages and salaries, and that at no time in those years was the whole company worth as much as ten million dollars.

The responsibilities of management and workers are different. Another of labor's "bugaboos" involves the misunderstanding of this difference.

This is even more striking. The wages we pay out every year equal the entire value of our plant. If our workers understood these facts, they would not be concerned about ownership at all. I say to our workers, "Men, go ahead, put on a revolution. Shoot the stockholders and take over the plant. Have one grand blowout, and you won't get anything like as much money as you are going to get every year if you will just use this wheelbarrow and pay yourself income."

Ownership in itself isn't particularly important. It is much more profitable to all concerned for Henry Ford to own and operate his property and lie awake nights figuring out how to get out a new model car, so that there will be income to distribute, than to have his workers own the property. Henry Ford once said to his men, "If I gave you this company, it wouldn't be a gift of cash. I'd have to say, 'Joe, you take some bricks; Bill, you take a wheel off the machine; John, you carry away a door.' " The workers would have been taking the handles and wheels off the wheelbarrow and wouldn't have been able to produce anything at all. Ownership is relatively unimportant; income distribution is the thing that counts.

The responsibilities of management and workers are different. Another of labor's "bugaboos" involves the misunderstanding of this difference. Both are workers—whether at the machine in the plant or at the desk in the office. In practically every large American industry, management is made up of executives who came up through the ranks. They work every day. Many of them ring time cards. Most of them get a pay envelope and run home to pay their bills, just as you and I. The important difference is that upon management falls the added responsibility of perpetuating the business. American industry has a wonderful story to tell, yet how poorly it tells it.

On one occasion, I said to a group of our workers, "What do you boys want more than anything else? Another raise? All right, fellows, I want a raise, too. Let's rob the cash drawer. Let's divide its contents. But wait a minute. I'm going to tell you something that you and I need more than a raise, and I bet you'll agree with me. We need assurance of a good job next year—a job like the one we have today. You and I want a job tomorrow, and on me rests the responsibility of maintaining the financial strength of this company, so that we are sure of our jobs." There wasn't a man among them who didn't agree that management has that responsibility and who didn't want us to carry it out and see that his job was secure. Job security looms high in the worker's mind, and it is a fundamental part of the company, just like its money, assets, and equipment.

The growth of the company is also necessary to job security. If the worker asks why we want the company to grow, the answer is that if there are a hundred men in the plant, and he is No. 100, when business gets slack, he will be the first fellow to lose out. If, however, it grows to one thousand workers, and he is No. 100 in seniority, 90 percent of the personnel must go before his job security is affected. Now, if we ask him, "Do you want this business to grow and give you that protection?" The answer is invariably, "Yes."

I visited a company in 1922 that had 600 workers. I visited them a year ago and found it employed 10,000. Of the original 600 workers, one had become president, three, vice presidents, five, factory managers, over 500 supervisors—nearly all had become part of management. Is the workman interested in seeing the business grow when you can demonstrate facts like these that affect his future? How often have we used such potent examples with our workers?

Labor and management together own a magic wand. Let me tell you a simple story that I told to a group of 1,500 men recently. They liked it, and it might serve as an example of a new approach in industrial relations. I asked a roomful of men to imagine that they went to work in the morning and did exactly what they had been doing for the past six months. They got the same pay for the same production; the stockholder had the same investment in the company, and the customer paid the same prices for the products. Then I asked them to imagine that on a certain Monday morning I came to work and waved a magic wand over the plant, without anybody knowing it, and during that week every machine delivered twice as many pieces as before.

I asked them to imagine again what would happen at the end of the week, if we had been shipping a million dollars worth of products formerly, and now had twice as many pieces to ship—two million dollars worth. Then, when the money came in and we paid our wages and bills and expenses and dividends, there would be a million dollars left.

I asked them to picture that million dollars in paper money piled up on the receiving room floor. Where did it come from? A million dollars in wealth had been created that didn't exist before. So we called in the workers and stockholders and customers and said, "Boys, look at that—a million dollars, and all the bills are paid. What will we do with it? Well, the worker has been loyal; let's give him a third of it. Mother won't object to that. The customer has been loyal; let's give him a third. He'll be happy to have a cut in prices. The stockholder has been loyal; let's give him a third. He'll be glad to get an increased dividend. Now, everybody's happy!"

This is the secret of what we all want—a more abundant life with greater income. What is this magic wand? It is cooperation between management and men to increase production and reduce waste. It is the cutting out of wasted time around the noon hour and at the rest period. It is in keeping the machines in order and in not making unnecessary scrap. It is workers and engineers getting better tools and better methods, and in management performing its duties with wholehearted participation. This simple story brought a rousing response.

Conclusion

The direct, frank, human approach is necessary. Industrial relations are very vital to our present war production, and they all play an important part in the solution of our postwar problems. In better industrial relations may lie the secret of preserving free enterprise in America. Industries in the future will be judged by their human relations as well as by their products. The president of the company himself will do well to change his hobby from engineering or sales or finance or golf to that of human relations—not because he wants to, but because of the kind of age in which we live.

Management has all the advantages. Management has the brains, the money and the time. Our men work with us eight hours a day, and we pay them money. A crackpot leader gets them for ten minutes on the way home and tries to take money away from them. Who has the advantage?

I don't think management has always been smart in tackling its problems. We haven't analyzed the kind of world we live in and realized the amount of money a man gets has comparatively little to do with whether he is happy in his job or not. Don't too many of us say, "I pay him well and give him a locker to put his clothes in. Why isn't he happy?" What people think of us and our motives is so much more important than the pay.

I am convinced that what the working man thinks about his boss and his company is the key to satisfactory industrial relations. It calls for a sales job in which the workers are regarded as the customers and in which we are competing with other salesmen who have other things to sell. Now, how do we go about a sales job? The American manager is capable of selling any kind of good product to anybody. How does he do it? He goes out and looks around at the housewife's wants and studies her likes and dislikes. Then he wraps up a package of merchandise that will appeal to her. Why haven't we done that with our workers? In this emotional age, that is what counts. Have we tried to see things through their eyes and hear things through their ears? Have we met them as customers and sought their goodwill, and are we selling an honest product?

The importance of the human factor must be recognized. It isn't only the money we pay our workers that counts today. It is what they think about us that is important. It is clearing away the misconceptions about industry that have kept them alienated from us. That is probably where management has fallen down badly—in not seeing the misunderstandings and destroying them, in not getting behind the eyes of the worker to see what he sees, in not trying to understand the worker better and feel what he feels.

The human voice is still the greatest medium of exchange of ideas the world has ever known.

Don't work through a lawyer or any number two man. Try the direct approach, and keep trying it. You'll be amazed at the reception you'll get and the results you'll finally achieve. If it can't be done this way today, it just can't be done at all. The human voice is still the greatest medium of exchange of ideas the world has ever known.

There is a great job ahead, and it is a most fascinating one. Human relations is one of the most interesting things in the world. Dabble in human relations and human reactions in your business, and you will have a lot of fun.

May I repeat in closing that the time has come for every forward-looking industry to appoint a Vice President of Human Relations of equal rank with the treasurer, the engineer, and other top executives. The time has come for the big boss himself to make human relations his hobby—not because he wants to, but because it is the kind of age in which we live, and we can't change it. It is going to be that kind of an age for many years to come—an age of emotional emphasis.

In tackling the problems which lie ahead, I call for the courage that overcomes fear and for the resourcefulness that overcomes want. We need a rebirth of the third old freedom—the freedom of opportunity and individual enterprise. Gentlemen, only in this will we find the solution to our postwar problems and the secret of building the kind of America we want!

Harry A. Bullis

Harry A. Bullis served as president and chairman of General Mills in the 1940s and 1950s, and was one of the few business leaders willing to butt heads with Senator Joseph E. McCarthy. The brash self-confidence necessary for taking on the formidable senator was a trait Bullis developed in his youth; as a teenager he stammered, but overcame the handicap. Bullis also learned humility, something he did not forget as a leader. In a speech to other captains of industry, he said, "Let's not sell ourselves down the river by getting too self-interested. We are not the main economic factors of the country." Instead he pointed to the working man as being the country's dynamic economic unit and vital strength.

Bullis could identify closely with the common man, for after serving in World War I, he joined one of General Mills' predecessor companies as a simple mill hand. In 1928, the year General Mills was officially formed by consolidating a number of firms and creating the largest flour-milling company in the world, Bullis became secretary and controller. When he became president in 1942, he pushed the company hard into prepared foods, because on-the-go consumers had begun to desire less time in the kitchen and to prefer prepackaged convenience. Today General Mills is best known for its cereals and Betty Crocker cake mixes.

Growth was dramatic under Bullis, and as a leader he forced decision making down onto the line managers. His advice to the troops was to avoid playing it safe, don't be afraid of yourself or your responsibilities, take risks, and be tough-minded. Bullis also set his sights on world trade. As he pointed out, "The word 'neighbor' has taken on a new dimension in the world of today, and a greater significance through instant communication, through economic interdependence, and through the need to close ranks against the threats to our way of life." One of those threats involved an issue close to home: the constant conflict between management and labor. In *Business and Labor,* it's clear that the struggle to define the relationship between management and labor continued in 1952.

Business and Labor

Harry A. Bullis

The subject of business and labor is as vast as the United States itself. In fact, if you stop to think about it, it is our modern industrial United States. Practically everyone, in one way or another, is in on the act, including the politicians.

Ours is a cooperative system where millions of men daily carry on labor-management cooperation. That is why we all get along most of the time so extraordinarily well. But we always put our troubled areas of infection under the microscope. One area at times goes a little explosive. It is our labor-management relations.

I would like to emphasize just one phase of that explosive subject. It is a very human phase and it can be understood easily by any man or woman who wants to live securely, raise and educate a family and get his scoopful of cream. In other words, it can be understood by practically everyone. I am talking about human relations in our industrial life. Human relations I will define as the relationship between the sons of Adam, all endowed with a reasonable quota of human cussedness, in their daily striving for the same thing. That same thing is a good life, or the good things of life.

Unfortunately, agreement on the same objective does not always assure peace. Once a somewhat disreputable man and his wife were hauled into court because the neighbors complained their constant fighting disturbed the peace. When the judge asked if they couldn't agree on something and stop fighting, the boisterous couple replied, "Oh we do agree, your honor, on one thing. We both want the whiskey bottle at the same time."

But we always put our troubled areas of infection under the microscope. One area at times goes a little explosive. It is our labor-management relations.

It is impossible to overstress the importance of human relations in our modern industrial life. We are in a state of semi-war and if we, meaning labor and industry, cannot get along with each other in our free society, we face two threats:

1. If harmony between management and labor cannot be achieved through free exercise of their rights, then more and more, government will take over in order to keep things going. That would slowly paralyze our free enterprise system and bring us nearer to socialism, or statism.
2. If industrial strife slows down our production and technological advance, the Soviets may decide that it is the proper time to start an all-out war.

As an industrialist, and one of the team of management that has developed in our company a reputation for human relations we are proud of, and which has been a large factor in our successful operations, I have learned a few things about getting along with people. Until industry, as a whole, learns these basic facts of life, there cannot be much industrial teamwork.

Management must recognize that every man on its payroll, every member of its labor force, is first, last, and always a human being. He is not a machine. He is not a commodity. He *is* an individual.

Management must cease to think of a human individual as something composed of two separate and distinct parts, one part muscle that carries on physical activity, and one part brain, that does the thinking. The individual, whether he is a laborer in the mill or a clerk in the office, is a unit, which both acts and thinks at the same time.

It is always difficult to predict what individuals will do. And we do know that each person is different from every other person. However, we can be sure that all individuals on the payroll are as alike as peas in a pod in these personal aspirations:

1. He wants to get ahead.
2. He wants assurance of security for himself and his family.
3. He wants to be recognized as an individual and to feel he belongs in the organization.

Management must cease to think of a human individual as something composed of two separate and distinct parts, one part muscle that carries on physical activity, and one part brain, that does the thinking.

The most obvious form of the desire to get ahead is the desire for good wages or salary. In some cases—but not as many as you might think—there is also the desire to advance. For those who want to climb up, management must keep an "open door" policy of advancement. For those content to stay in the ranks, management must prove that they have a future in the business, too. In other words, convince them that their opportunities will be in direct ratio to the success of the business that employs them. And what helps business will in turn help them.

The desire for security is today probably stronger than at any other time in our industrial history. It is the cause of much labor-management strife. An employee's security is related to the security of his company. That seems like simple high school economics. Nevertheless, management must never forget for a minute that the desire of employees for security for their families and themselves is so deep-rooted and defensive, that if business fails to provide at least reasonable security, employees will turn to government and politics to give them that security.

Of course, there are limits beyond which business cannot go to provide steady jobs for its labor force. But it's a safe bet that business in general can do more than it has been doing.

If labor is forced to look toward politicians and government for security, we can expect more centralized government—that would mean bigger taxes and less liberty of operation for business.

The desire for security is today probably stronger than at any other time in our industrial history. It is the cause of much labor-management strife. An employee's security is related to the security of his company.

Even if you give an employee a decent income and a reasonable degree of security, he wants something more. He wants satisfaction in his work, the respect of his fellows and the knowledge that he belongs. These wants are less definite than wages, hours of work, pensions and insurance. But they are equally important. Deny them and you'll have a threatening sense of frustration and restlessness in your company.

It is one thing to say business and labor are a team. But unless management gives its employees a complete financial picture of its operation—and in terms labor can understand—labor cannot be expected to act like members of a team. If management spells out in facts and figures not only its earnings but also payroll totals, earnings reinvested to create more jobs and services, taxes and all other costs of doing business, labor, being in the know, is far more likely to accept economic factors than if kept in the dark.

Management is slowly awakening to the fact that its employees have only a meager understanding of the economic forces under which they work and earn their living. Business is a little like the woman who had neglected to tell her husband she had at an earlier time been a snake charmer. When he upbraided her for not telling him, she replied, "But you never asked me."

It is industry's duty to its labor force—as well as to protect itself from unnecessary government controls—to explain clearly the part business plays in modern American society.

An economic system which has produced the highest standard of living in the world does not have to apologize for its success. For its mistakes, yes, but not for its success. Yet unless business is willing to invest time and money to explain to its employees honestly and in terms of their personal interest, what the combination of capital, management and labor has done to produce more goods and more services than any other combination ever dreamed of, business may be forced to apologize for its success.

Labor's stake in the expansion of our free enterprise system is vital—if they do not realize what the free market means to them in terms of wages, security and individual freedom, then it is industry's first duty in human relations to begin to educate them.

We must not be afraid of controversy between capital and labor. The only way to avoid controversy is to shackle our freedom. Without freedom there would be no controversy—and there would be no free labor unions or free businesses as we know them today.

A strike should not be called lightly by labor. A strike should not be courted lightly by capital. A strike should be a last resort. A strike is like shooting in self-defense. Used prudently, the strike is a device that has its proper place in the American economy. But if this weapon is abused, it may threaten the very freedom that makes strikes possible.

The rise in wages in the United States since the end of the war has been about ten times the rate of rise in the European countries. In Europe, there are governments which profess to be "Labor." Yet they succeed in doing very little for labor. That is not because their hearts and objectives are not in the right place. It is rather that their system just doesn't work well.

A strike should not be called lightly by labor. A strike should not be courted lightly by capital. A strike should be a last resort. A strike is like shooting in self-defense.

Though workers sometimes erroneously think over here that the hearts of management are not in the right place and that their emotions and methods are screwy, there is no question but that this modern capitalist system of ours does produce by far the best gains for the workers.

Management and labor must cooperate together and work as a team and thus attain their common objective of a Good Life. In General Mills we have a slogan: The Best Is Yet To Come, If We All Keep Working Together.

I believe people do not advance in business because:

1. They are not willing to pay the price in intelligent hard work; they are not willing to go the second mile, when they are paid for going only the first mile.
2. Many individuals do not exercise their "bump of curiosity" by trying to find out what makes the business click and what part they must play to make theirs the winning team.
3. Some people do not advance because they are afraid to pull down the Flag of Safety First and run up the Flag of Adventure First. There are always some individuals who are playing it safe and doing what they think the "Boss" wants rather than doing those things that are for the best interests of the company.
4. Some people do not advance because they do not know how to get along with other people. They want to be stars, but they have not learned how to play ball with the team. No one gets anywhere in business without cooperation. I have learned that the other fellow will cooperate with you if he thinks that by working with you he will get ahead.

Many people, whether they are classified as management or labor, accomplish worthwhile results and achieve great things in large measure because they wish to repay the United States of America for all of the advantages and opportunities which have been given to them. One way to repay the debt which we all owe to the United States is to work for unification among all classes and to give other people hope and courage and help them to develop their self-confidence and self-respect.

Frederick W. Smith

1944 –

The founder of Federal Express and the father of the express-transportation industry, Frederick W. Smith, is a born entrepreneur—it is in his blood. His father founded the Dixie Greyhound Bus line among other ventures, was a multimillionaire by the 1930s, and partied with the likes of Howard Hughes in Hollywood. After Smith attended Yale University, he went to Vietnam in 1967 a commissioned lieutenant. He led search-and-destroy missions, and was awarded two Purple Hearts and a Silver Star as well as other commendations. While there, he learned some of his most important business lessons. A marine sergeant, for example, told him that, to survive, "There's only three things you gotta remember: shoot, move, and communicate." The advice translated well into the business world.

After the war, Smith said he was determined "to do something productive after blowing so many things up." For his first venture, he bought an airplane brokering business, but sold it because he didn't like dealing with all the shady characters in the industry. It was in airplane hangers, however, that the idea of Federal Express was hatched. In 1971 Smith spent $3.6 million on two Falcon jets. Buying the planes was the easy part; he then had to convert them to hold cargo, apply for government approval, fight for industry reform, find investors, and sell his idea to customers. Before Federal Express turned into an overnight sensation, Smith and the Smith family trust would end up in debt for more than $20 million.

The phenomenal growth that followed frightened Smith. He worried not only about delivering the deluge of packages but about losing what he called the esprit de corps. He didn't want to lose the loyalty that had kept the company together in tough times, the sort of loyalty he learned in Vietnam. So Smith introduced a variety of policies that included in part, no layoffs, a guarantee of fair treatment, promotion from within, and generous profit-sharing. In *Creating an Empowering Environment for All Employees,* Smith's policies exemplify how far corporations have come in offering their employees incentives, benefits, and a stake in the business.

Creating an Empowering Environment for All Employees

Frederick W. Smith

Improved quality, reduced inventories and rapid response have become the keys to economic survival in this increasingly competitive global market. In the new math of productivity, time is a successful competitor's most precious commodity.

The need to use time as a customer satisfaction tool has never been greater. And while we at Federal are time merchants to a world in search of quality, we have found that the use of time *within* our organization bears equal consideration. I suggest that premise pertains to most companies.

Getting a new product or product information to global markets first is often the sole criterion for success or failure. But between inception and production there is a whole lot of room for delays—ideas sidetracked in the chain of command, development thwarted by turf battles, fear of failure or confusion over "Who's on first?" Meanwhile, the competition introduces its product and its sales are off and running.

In a service company, like ours, the perception of quality is influenced every time an employee interacts with a customer. If an employee can't answer a question or resolve a problem, or at least know where to go to get a problem solved expeditiously, the moment as well as the customer is easily lost.

Quality and Empowering Employees—A Must

Most certainly, people are the key to quality. Organizations that recognize human potential and empower their people to act will be empowering their companies to excellence.

Empowering people is the most important element in managing time within the organization. Empowered people have the necessary information to make decisions and act; they don't have to wait for multiple levels of approval. Empowered people identify problems and fix them. They'll do what it takes to keep customers happy. Empowered people don't have time for turf battles because, when everyone shares power and a common goal, turf becomes irrelevant; and teamwork, an imperative. At least, that is what it says in all the books.

And I believe it, because I've seen it work at Federal Express. We may not be the consummate role model for empowerment; but we're trying to be—because we must.

Defining and Infusing Empowerment into Daily Work Experience

Although many companies now recognize the potential impact of empowerment, they are stymied by the drastic cultural change it may require. How do you take a buzzword like empower, infuse it with life, and make it a reality in everyone's daily work experience?

How can you take power off the members only list and get those very people to see that sharing power means gaining power? More and more companies are therefore asking, how do you turn a company upside down—invert the pyramid—and get the focus where it should be?

Because of Federal Express's reputation as a people-first

company, we are often asked these questions. While we don't have all the answers, I can share what's worked best for us.

How do you take a buzzword like empower, infuse it with life, and make it a reality in everyone's daily work experience?

First, we believe the central value upon which we were founded is just as viable today and will continue to be the benchmark for the future: 100 percent customer satisfaction.

In the name of customer service, we relentlessly pursue the total elimination of errors. We have no choice when you consider that a 99.2 success rate in our business today translates into 2.75 million failures per year.

The Curtain Goes Up Every Night

Our business is like a Broadway play. The curtain goes up every night—and we cannot postpone the last act. This imperative is supported by 85,000 people who perform according to a finely-tuned scenario in which timing is everything.

A late plane out of Brussels will affect operations in New York, Anchorage, and the Far East. Mechanics must therefore maintain each plane in top condition so that pilots can deliver the customers' shipments on time to our stations where couriers must sort and deliver those packages and documents *on time* to customers around the globe. Every day, customer service agents on five continents, moreover, must be able to help our customers with their first shipment or their bulk shipment or their overdue shipment. Every day.

Meeting the Daily Challenge

To add to that daily challenge are always elements beyond our immediate control—a hurricane in England, of all places, volcanic eruptions in Alaska, an earthquake in San Francisco; all in addition, of course, to the less cataclysmic rain, sleet, and snow to be encountered—somewhere—every day. The search for root causes is moot in these situations. These are the times when we have to rely on contingency plans and backup contingency plans and human ingenuity to make the right decision, on the spot, and to act expediently. Every time.

Getting the job done . . . Take, for example, the experience of Hal Hileman, one of our telecommunications specialists. A Rocky Mountain blizzard had knocked out a mountaintop radio relay, cutting off phone service at several Federal Express offices. The phone company would not be able to repair the connection for five days. So Hal chartered a helicopter. When the pilot couldn't land, Hal jumped out, slogged through waist-deep snow, and reconnected the cables. He didn't go through layers of approval. He just acted. He knew that what he had to do was right and absolutely in line with our 100 percent customer satisfaction goal.

There are hundreds of examples of our people going above and beyond to do whatever was necessary to meet or exceed our customers' expectations. And they have been doing this from our first day of operation in 1973—before the word "empowerment" entered our business lexicon.

Creating a Positive Workplace Environment

Of all the questions we get asked, the one we hear most often is how do you motivate your people to give their best so consistently?

To begin with, I am convinced that *we* don't *motivate* anybody to do anything. I believe our job as managers is to provide a workplace in which the highly motivated people who come to us—stay that way.

Essentially then, the challenge lies in creating, or possibly recreating, a workplace in which people can be the best they can be. Realistically, there is no simple answer, no single program, no one policy that covers "all of the above."

Our experience is that the gestalt of an actionable corporate philosophy—goals that grow out of it and management systems and programs that are consistent with it—provides the basis for what we might call a "power environment." I'm convinced that well-meaning quality circles or quality action teams or any other single attempt to elicit employee power will be useless in the absence of such an environment.

We at Federal Express have worked from the beginning to create a workplace that fosters respect for human dignity, ingenuity and potential. It all revolves around a simple philosophy: People, Service, Profit. That statement drives every action of every manager in our company. We believe that when people are treated with dignity and respect, they will carry that message throughout their daily work experience and directly to our customers. Profit is a natural by-product.

Federal Express's People Philosophy

At the base of our people philosophy is a commitment to no layoffs which we've observed, even in the face of our decision to discontinue our ZAPmail service several years ago. Over 1,300 people were affected by that decision, yet no one lost his job. From what I have seen, a job-secure environment stimulates risk-taking and innovation. People are not afraid to fail.

We've learned that you've got to let people make a mistake or two once in a while. Well-intentioned efforts that don't work out are just as important as successes. And if you hang the people who try to do something that doesn't quite work, you'll get people who don't do anything.

People Systems

Employee Surveys

We have several systems in place that encourage risk-taking by providing opportunity for employee input and opportunity for management to listen and respond. For example, the *action* phase of our annual employee attitude survey—called *Survey Feedback Action*—is a vital tool for helping managers surface potential work-group problems: Managers must meet with their staffs within six weeks after the survey results are distributed and develop an action plan for dealing with every concern.

If you hang the people who try to do something that doesn't quite work, you'll get people who don't do anything.

Such plans have resulted in programs that have been implemented companywide. We added an incentive compensation program for professional employees, for example, to our established management incentive program and have made broad changes in the way we select and prepare our managers.

Guaranteed Fair Treatment Process

Our Guaranteed Fair Treatment Process, our in-house avenue for airing grievances, is another way we listen to our people. While most of our cases are settled in the first stage of this three-step process, quite a few get to the top level, the Appeals Board.

Every Tuesday morning our chief operating officer, chief personnel officer and I meet to review grievances. In some cases, we delegate adjudication to a Board of Review composed of the employee's peers. Both of these boards may overturn management decisions. Taking advantage of this process, our people have helped us see that some policies need revision, or perhaps need to be re-thought altogether.

Time and time again, the fair treatment process lets us hear the concerns of our people, and we've done our utmost to respond with workable solutions.

We've changed our attendance policy, our ground operations accident prevention policy, and have modified the fair treatment process itself from a five-step to a three-step process. And those are just a few examples.

Open Door

A third channel for surfacing people's concerns is our Open Door process, which directs employees' questions to the persons in the company best qualified to answer them. Most companies have a stated open door philosophy but ours differs from many because the process is monitored to ensure that each question is answered within fourteen working days.

We have exported our Survey Feedback Action, Guaranteed Fair Treatment Procedure, and Open Door processes, with some modifications, to most of the countries we serve and have found that the central idea of our people philosophy—treat others as you want to be treated—translates well in our off-shore locations. Culture and language may differ but human nature is universal.

Setting Goals, Reinforcing Them and Empowerment

It's important to share with every employee how important we believe people issues are. One of our three corporate objectives, for example, is a people objective specifically directed at improving our manager's leadership scores, as measured in our annual Survey Feedback Action program, by certain percentage points over the prior year.

Setting goals and reinforcing them in word and action is at the heart of empowerment. Our experience tells us that people who understand goals and how their job relates to them are much more inclined to exert their best effort.

Pay-for-Performance

We put teeth in our goal-setting by tying management bonuses directly to our reaching corporate goals. If goals are not met, no manager, no matter how high, gets a bonus. Pay-for-performance is actually incorporated into every person's job description and performance appraisal.

Couriers who maintain excellent levels of customer service and superior ratings on other performance indicators, for example, receive bonuses every six months.

The pay-for-performance message is also reinforced by our profit sharing programs in which both mid-year and year-end distributions are based on performance criteria.

Rewarding Quality Efforts

Also, we seek ways to reward individual and team quality efforts. Just as we emphasize doing the right thing right the first time, we try to reward the right behaviors because we've found that what gets rewarded gets done. The *Circle of Excellence* award, presented monthly to the best performing Federal Express station, underscores teamwork. Our *Golden Falcon* is awarded to employees who go above and beyond to serve their customers.

The *Bravo Zulu* (Navy talk for "well done") program gives managers the prerogative of awarding a dinner, theater tickets or cash, for example, to any employee who's done a particular outstanding job. Our highest award, presented annually, is our *Quality Achievement Award*.

Those who earn these awards have one thing in common: They are living proof that people who understand what is expected of them and are given autonomy to do it, will do that and more—they'll go beyond our expectations and probably their own. And that is the real payoff of empowerment.

Quality and Career Advancement

The reward-performance connection helps create a power environment that is further enhanced when quality performance leads to career advancement. So, we strongly adhere to a career opportunities policy that encourages promotion from within. The policy is activated through weekly job postings followed by a thorough search for a qualified person from within the company before we look outside.

Building Power into the Job

Of course, not everyone can or wants to move up the corporate ladder. Power for most of us is in the job itself. Assuming an organization supports risk and tolerates failure, and the people in it understand their role and how it affects the corporate goals, the task then becomes one of finding ways to build power into each job.

Obviously, people must be given the training and information necessary to meet customers' expectations—be that customer internal or external. Beyond that, people must be given responsibility and autonomy, a voice in decisions affecting their job, and the encouragement to innovate. That's quite a challenge for any organization and ours is no exception.

Any job requiring repetitive routines presents particular challenges. In our company, over 2,500 customer service agents have such jobs. They take telephone requests from customers regarding package pick-ups and provide information about shipments already in progress. Most agents report that by the time they've been on the job six to nine months, they are becoming bored. In a year's time, as many as 25 percent have left their positions for others within the company.

These same people are usually the first Federal Express employees to come in contact with customers. Their task is critical to each customer's perception of quality, so we researched opportunities for job redesign and found that *redesign* boiled down to increased power. We automated the more routine calls to free agents to handle more complicated situations that called for individual and on-the-spot decision making by the agents.

Involving People and Teams in the Total Quality Process

Another way of enhancing agents power was to involve them in the total quality process. All customer service management was trained in establishing quality teams for their department. Over a third of the customer service agents are now involved in quality teams and have identified opportunities for improving their jobs and their organization.

The Zinger-Johnson-Durant Solution

We're reminded every day that the person closest to the job is, indeed, in the best position to know how to improve it. Take, for example, the contribution of three of our Phoenix couriers who used quality improvement techniques to make the station sorting process more efficient. Dan Zinger came up with an idea for redesigning the process and building a new sort table. Paul Johnson and Joseph Durant helped Dan with the design layout, construction and installation.

The results were astounding. Training time was reduced, the workload was distributed more evenly and teamwork increased noticeably. The sort time was reduced from two hours to one hour and fifteen minutes, lost revenue from mis-sorts decreased, and the total annual savings to the Phoenix station was over $32,000 a year.

We're reminded every day that the person closest to the job is, indeed, in the best position to know how to improve it.

Formalizing and Tracking Service Quality

Another method of diffusing power and enhancing employee involvement has been in formalizing our quality processes.

In doing so, we are putting tremendous emphasis on reducing and preventing errors. We came up with a list of 12 things that could go wrong in delivering a package or document, assigned values based upon how strongly customers felt about any one of these errors, multiplied that by the number of times it happened in a week, and created a weekly service quality indicator (SQI). The lower our SQI score, the better we did our job that week.

Such a program requires constant support. Since our operations managers' position is the critical pivot for ensuring quality services, we designated a first-line manager in each of our 35 operating districts as full-time coordinator of the SQI programs. This person became the liaison with the three SQI service teams in each of our field stations who were actually working the issues. The coordinator led the program and was responsible for the outcomes. The impact has been incredible. What had been extra work for the manager now became a passionate mission for employees involved.

Grass-roots Quality and Access to Information

Grass roots quality efforts are scattered across our global operations; but our goal is that every person feel empowered with or without the outlet of a formal program or quality action team, and that, quite frankly is still coming.

One way we can encourage the requisite self management is to maintain our flat organizational structure which pushes responsibility down by its very nature. There are just five levels of management between our couriers on the road and the executive floor. As a result, day to day decisions *have* to be made by our front line employees who must be very well informed.

Surveys reveal that people's preferred information source is their immediate manager. So, we've focused our communications effort on these front-line managers. As we've expanded across international boarders, that strategy has made very good sense.

Federal Express TV
Global dispersion and rapid expansion place stress on corporate culture by complicating communications. So we've launched a live television network that reaches our people throughout the United States, Canada and Europe.

There are just five levels of management between our couriers on the road and the executive floor.

FedEX Overnight airs live every morning and is taped locally to play throughout the day. It tells everybody how we did the night before. Recapping operations worldwide, the report helps our people respond to problems our customers may be experiencing.

This network, FXTV, has proven invaluable to our managing of major changes. We announced the merger of FedEx and Flying Tigers, for example, to our employees within an hour of informing Wall Street and *before* we released the news to the media. Then, throughout the merger process, we used the network for live phone-in question and answer sessions between senior management and employees. Our people didn't mince words; they had a lot of hard-hitting questions and we gave them straight answers. I truly believe this broadcast significantly reduced the anxieties about the merger.

The way I see it, leadership does not begin with power but rather, with a compelling vision or goal of excellence.

When videos of these sessions were shown to a company considering their own television network, they were thun-

derstruck by the candor of exchanges between emp
and senior management.

Frankly, I don't think any of us considered this n
We just took it for granted because that's the way we do things at Federal Express. The way I see it, leadership does not begin with power but rather, with a compelling vision or goal of excellence. One becomes a leader when he or she is able to communicate that vision in such a way that others feel empowered to achieve excellence. We must create organizations with a shared vision of excellence.

Federal Express has no secret formula for success. The secret is in all of the management books. The difference is that we really try very hard to do what they say.

PART V

Company Culture

The quality of a workplace goes a long way in motivating the employee. But does company culture mean artwork hanging in the hallways and fancy coffee blends in the cafeteria? No. It's about values and treating employees right. For David Packard, it's not having to lock the tools and parts bins to prevent theft; for An Wang, founder of Wang Laboratories, it's judging corporate behavior by the same standards as personal behavior; for Robert Haas, chief at Levi Strauss, it's risking profits for doing the right thing. The real secret, of course, is figuring out how to take an abstract notion such as ethics or employee empowerment and making it a concrete reality instead of a topic of conversation. Toward this end, Part V provides concrete examples and usable advice.

David Packard
1912 – 1996

Growing up in Pueblo, Colorado, a rough-and-tumble town of brothels and saloons, street fights and shootings, David Packard was anything but a prototypical electronics nerd. He loved to fish, ride horseback, and play sports. But then, at the age of twelve, he bought a radio kit and built his own vacuum tube receiver. Packard went on to study electrical engineering at Stanford University, where he met his future partner, Bill Hewlett. After graduating in 1935, Packard took a job with General Electric in New York. Three years later he returned west and the two college buddies started their business in a Palo Alto, California, garage—now the official historical landmark of the birthplace of Silicon Valley.

The garage was a modest beginning, but their dreams were lofty; Packard reflected, "We wanted to direct our efforts toward making important technical contributions to the advancement of science, industry, and human welfare . . . we didn't want to be a 'me-too' company merely copying products already on the market." In 1947 they incorporated, and the company went public in 1957. It wasn't until the late 1950s, when their product lines had diversified from just audio oscillators to all sorts of electronic and medical equipment, that Packard gave any thought to organizational structure.

It was time to decentralize, but Packard was worried the personal elements of the "HP Way" might disappear. He always believed that the best form of management was MBWA, Management by Walking Around. In addition, he knew, "little details often make the difference between a quality product and one that isn't as good." Individual employees were an integral part of those details, and he didn't want to lose his people in what he feared would become a bureaucracy. So he was very adamant about the goals of the reorganization. "A primary goal in setting up these divisions was to give each one considerable autonomy," he said, "creating an environment that fostered individual motivation, initiative, and creativity, and that gave a wide latitude of freedom in working toward common goals and objectives." Such ideal aspirations can be difficult to achieve, but Packard shows the way in *Trust in People.*

Trust in People

David Packard

If an organization is to maximize its efficiency and success, a number of requirements must be met. One is that the most capable people available should be selected for each assignment within the organization. Especially in a technical business where the rate of progress is rapid, a continuing program of education must be undertaken and maintained. Techniques that are relevant today will be outdated in the future, and every person in the organization must be continually looking for new and better ways to do his or her work.

Another requirement is that a high degree of enthusiasm should be encouraged at all levels; in particular, the people in high management positions must not only be enthusiastic themselves, they must be able to engender enthusiasm among their associates. There can be no place for halfhearted interest or halfhearted effort.

From the beginning, Bill Hewlett and I have had a strong belief in people. We believe that people *want* to do a good job and that it is important for them to enjoy their work at Hewlett-Packard. We try to make it possible for our people to feel a real sense of accomplishment in their work.

Closely coupled with this is our strong belief that individuals be treated with consideration and respect and that their achievements be recognized. It has always been important to Bill and me to create an environment in which people have a chance to be their best, to realize their potential, and to be recognized for their achievements.

. . . the people in high management positions must not only be enthusiastic themselves, they must be able to engender enthusiasm among their associates.

Each person in our company is important, and every job is important. In the highly technical fields in which we operate, little details often make the difference between a quality product and one that isn't as good. So what we've tried to engender among all our people is the attitude that it is each individual's business to do the best job he or she can. I recall the time, many years ago, when I was walking around a machine shop, accompanied by the shop's manager. We stopped briefly to watch a machinist making a polished plastic mold die. He had spent a long time polishing it and was taking a final cut at it. Without thinking, I reached down and wiped it with my finger. The machinist said, "Get your finger off my die!" The manager quickly asked him, "Do you know who this is?" To which the machinist replied, "I don't care!" He was right and I told him so. He had an important job and was proud of his work.

The way an organization is structured affects individual motivation and performance. There are military-type organizations in which the person at the top issues an order and it is passed on down the line until the person at the bottom does as he or she is told without question or reason. This is precisely the type of organization we at HP did not want . . . and do not want. We feel our objectives can best be achieved by people who understand and support them and who are allowed flexibility in working toward common goals in ways that they help determine are best for their operation and their organization.

The close relationships among HP people encouraged a form of participatory management that supported individual freedom and initiative while emphasizing commonness of purpose and teamwork. In the early years we were all working on the same problems. We solicited and used ideas from wherever we could get them. The net result was that each employee felt that he or she was a member of the team.

Profit Sharing for All

As the company grew, we could no longer take teamwork for granted. We had to try to emphasize and strengthen it. That's one of the reasons we didn't single out divisions or groups that were doing particularly well. And why benefits such as profit sharing are provided not to selected individuals or groups but to all eligible employees. It's imperative that there be a strong spirit of helpfulness and cooperation among all elements of the company and that this spirit be recognized and respected as a cornerstone of the HP Way.

When we were small and insignificant and had to hire the best people we could find, we had to train them and then hope they would work out. We wanted our people to share our goals of making a profit and a contribution. We in turn felt a responsibility to provide them with opportunity and job security to the best of our ability. Thus, we made an early and important decision: We did not want to be a "hire and fire"—a company that would seek large, short-term contracts, employ a great many people for the duration of the contract, and at its completion let those people go. This type of operation is often the quickest and most efficient way to get a big job accomplished. But Bill and I didn't want to operate that way. We wanted to be in business for the long haul, to have a company built around a stable and dedicated workforce.

We were very close to our employees. We understood their jobs and shared much of their lives with them. We also were learning which of our people had management potential, although sometimes we learned the hard way. Once we promoted a man, a good worker, to be the manager of our machine shop. A few days later he came to see me. He said he was having a tough time managing and wanted me to come out to the shop and tell his people that he was their boss. "If I have to do that," I said, "you don't deserve to be their boss."

When Trust Is Missing

Going all the way back to the beginning of the company, Bill and I have placed great faith and trust in HP people. We expect them to be open and honest in their dealings with others, and we trust they will readily accept responsibility.

We did not want to be a "hire and fire"— a company that would seek large, short-term contracts, employ a great many people for the duration of the contract, and at its completion let those people go.

I learned, early in my career, of some of the problems that can be caused by a company's lack of trust in its people. In the late 1930s, when I was working for General Electric in Schenectady, the company was making a big thing of plant security. I'm sure others were, too. GE was especially zealous about guarding its tool and parts bins to make sure employees didn't steal anything. Faced with this obvious display of distrust, many employees set out to prove it justified, walking off with tools or parts whenever they could. Eventually, GE tools and parts were scattered all around town, including the attic of the house in which a number of us were living. In fact, we had so much equipment up there that when we threw the switch, the lights on the entire street would dim.

The irony in all of this is that many of the tools and parts were being used by their GE "owners" to work on either job-related projects or skill-enhancing hobbies—activities that would likely improve their performance on the job.

When HP got under way, the GE memories were still strong and I determined that our parts bins and storerooms should always be open. Sometimes not everyone gets the word, however, which accounts for an incident that occurred some years later. Coming into the plant one weekend to do some work, Bill Hewlett stopped off at a company storeroom to pick up a microscope. Finding the equipment cage locked, he broke open the latch and left a note insisting that the room not be locked again.

Keeping storerooms and parts bins open was advantageous to HP in two important ways. From a practical standpoint, the easy access to parts and tools helped product designers and others who wanted to work out new ideas at home or on weekends. A second reason, less tangible but important, is that the open bins and storerooms were a symbol of trust, a trust that is central to the way HP does business.

ROBERT D. HAAS
1942 –

Some call the Levi Strauss company culture visionary in its approach, others call it flaky. The leader behind the vision, Robert D. Haas, is the first to say "The notion of the CEO as hero, as all-wise, as having all the answers" is obsolete. His philosophy includes a mix of liberal idealism and practical management principles. It reflects the man who was a Peace Corps volunteer and a Harvard MBA. He strives to make diversity, empowerment, communication, recognition, and ethics a reality rather than a topic of conversation. Haas explains, "We are not doing this because it makes us feel good—although it does. We are not doing this because it is politically correct. We are doing this because we believe in the interconnection between liberating the talents of our people and business success."

Haas's liberation of employees and ideas on teamwork in the factory have, in some instances, resulted in cutting the turnaround time from order to shipment in half. In other words, Haas's value-based system of management has proven to be both a cultural and a financial success. And yet a certain toughness lurks. When he took over the company in 1984, he cut 3,500 jobs and led a leveraged buyout in 1985. In 1997 the company announced 6,400 U.S. layoffs, forced on them by competition from companies that manufacture their clothing in the cheap-labor countries of Central America and Asia. Haas learned that liberal vision and financial realities sometimes clash; however, those seamstresses laid off reportedly were given severance packages as generous as those given to management.

Layoffs notwithstanding, Haas has been accused of letting values get in the way of management realities, and he concedes that sometimes the firm's soft practices have given competitors the edge; but ultimately he doesn't believe you have to be "a macho company" to achieve "responsible commercial success." In *Ethics: A Global Business Challenge,* Haas discusses how to take ethics from being an abstract concept to a concrete part of strategic planning. He talks about setting goals, taking action, and empowering the employee to bring about change.

Ethics: A Global Business Challenge

Robert D. Haas

What is most puzzling about most instances of business wrongdoing is that they clearly contradict both the values that are held by most of us as individuals and the collective standards we have established for appropriate business behavior.

In his famous essay on civil disobedience, Henry David Thoreau wrote that a corporation "has no conscience, but a corporation of conscientious men is a corporation with a conscience." I'd like to think that if Thoreau were writing today he would have spoken of both men *and women* with a conscience, though regrettably the corporate world remains more of a male enclave than it should be.

If Thoreau is correct, and I believe he is, how do we help honorable men and women confront and address the ethical challenges they face in the everyday world of work? This is the puzzle all of us must work to solve.

I'd like to conduct a brief quiz. By the way, these are the same questions I raise with my associates at Levi Strauss & Co. when I lead one of our ethics training programs. Do you:

- Consider yourself to be an ethical person?
- Believe that it's important for business to function in an ethical manner?

- Believe that you know an ethical dilemma when you see it?
- Feel there are clear answers to ethical problems?
- Believe that you always know an ethical dilemma when it arises and always know how to resolve it?

Clearly, all of us feel strongly about ethics in the abstract. But at the same time, each of us is keenly aware of the struggle we face as ethical dilemmas arise. It is a common struggle between our own desire to be ethical and the competing pressures of business performance. Like so many, we at Levi Strauss & Co. struggle every day with how to create a business culture that promotes ethical behavior.

RISKY BEHAVIOR

When examining the ethics programs of companies it is useful to bear in mind the three very different approaches to dealing with ethical dilemmas. These are:

- Neglect—or the absence of any formal ethical programs;
- Compliance-based programs; and
- Values-oriented programs.

It is hard to imagine that any large company could rationally ignore the importance of ethics or fail to develop management policies and programs, given the effect ethical breaches can have on financial performance, sales, and corporate reputation. But some companies clearly don't get the message.

According to the Institute for Crisis Management, more than half of the news crisis stories filed in 1993 were crises brought on by the questionable judgment of management—firings, white-collar crime, government investigations, and discrimination suits. Coverage of these types of corporate misdeeds has risen 55% since 1989, while coverage of "operational" crises—chemical spills, product tamperings—has declined 4%.

Obviously, there are grave consequences for ignoring ethical problems. There is also increasing evidence from academic studies that shows positive correlations between responsible business behavior and return on investment, stock price, consumer preferences, and employee loyalty.

Do you . . . Believe that you always know an ethical dilemma when it arises and always know how to resolve it?

The companies that ignore ethics do so on the basis of assumptions that are false and never challenged. They seem to view ethics either as unimportant or as a costly and inconvenient luxury.

I think they're wrong on both accounts.

I believe—and our company's experience demonstrates—that a company cannot sustain success unless it develops ways to anticipate and address ethical issues as they arise. Doing the right thing from day one helps avoid future setbacks and regrets. Addressing dilemmas when they arise may save your business from serious financial or reputational harm.

Many companies share this view, and a number of them have chosen a second approach to ethics—what Lynn Sharp Paine, an associate professor at Harvard, refers to as compliance-based programs. These ethics programs are most often designed by corporate counsel. They are based on rules and regulations, with the goal of preventing, detecting, and punishing legal violations.

Until recently, we were among the companies that took this approach. The centerpiece of our efforts was a comprehensive collection of regulations that spelled out our worldwide code of business ethics. In it, we laid out rules for hiring practices, travel and entertainment expenses, political contributions, compliance with local laws, improper payments, gifts, and favors. We addressed topics ranging from accounting practices to potential conflicts of interest. As you might guess, it was a long and weighty list of dos and don'ts for our people to follow.

This approach didn't serve us well. First, rules beget rules. And regulations beget regulations. We became buried in paperwork, and any time we faced a unique ethical issue, another rule or regulation was born. Second, our compliance-based program sent a disturbing message to our people: "We don't respect your intelligence or trust you!" Finally, one of the most compelling reasons for shedding this approach was that it didn't keep managers or employees from exercising poor judgment and making questionable decisions.

The Values Approach

Today at Levi Strauss & Co. we base our approach to ethics on a values orientation that includes six ethical principles: honesty, promise-keeping, fairness, respect for others, compassion, and integrity. Using this approach, we address ethical issues by first identifying which of these ethical principles applies to the particular business decision. Then we determine which internal and which external stakeholders' ethical concerns should influence our business decisions. Information on stakeholder issues is gathered and possible recommendations are discussed with "high-influence" stakeholder groups, such as shareholders, employees, customers, members of local communities, public interest groups, our business partners, and so forth.

This principle-based approach balances the ethical concerns of these stakeholders with the values of our organization. It is a process that extends trust to an individual's knowledge of the situation. It examines the complexity of issues that must be considered in each decision, and it defines the role each person's judgment plays in carrying out his or her responsibilities in an ethical manner. We're integrating ethics with our other corporate values, which include diversity, open communications, empowerment, recognition, teamwork, and honesty, into every aspect of our business—from our human resource practices to our relationships with our business partners.

Ethical Global Contracting

I'd like to illustrate how we're linking ethics and business conduct with an area of increasing importance to many global corporations—the contract manufacturing of products in developing countries.

Because Levi Strauss & Co. operates in many countries and diverse cultures, we take special care in selecting contractors and those countries where our goods are produced. We do this to ensure that our products are being made in a manner that is consistent with our values and that protects our brand image and corporate reputation. So, in 1991, we developed a set of Global Sourcing Guidelines.

Our guidelines describe the business conduct we require of our contractors. For instance, the guidelines ban the use of child or prison labor. They stipulate certain environmental requirements. They limit working hours and mandate regularly scheduled days off. Workers must have the right of free association and may not be exploited. At a minimum, wages must comply with the law and match prevailing local practice, and working conditions must be safe and healthy. We also expect our business partners to be law abiding and to conduct all of their business affairs in an ethical way.

In developing our guidelines, we also recognized that there are certain issues beyond the control of our contractors, so we produced a list of "country selection" criteria. For example, we will not source in countries where conditions, such as the human rights climate, would run counter to our values and have an adverse effect on our global brand image or damage our corporate reputation. Similarly, we will not source in countries where circumstances threaten our employees while traveling, where the legal climate makes it difficult or jeopardizes our trademarks, and where political or social turmoil threatens our commercial interest.

Since adopting our guidelines, we've terminated our business relationships with about 5% of our contractors and required workplace improvements of another 25%. Likewise, we announced a phased withdrawal from contracting in China and exited Burma because of human rights concerns, although we remain hopeful that the human rights climate in these countries will improve and we can alter these decisions.

In the process of creating guidelines, we formed a working group of 15 employees from a broad cross-section of the company. The working group spent nine months formulating the guidelines, using our principle-based decision-making model to guide their deliberations. Drafting these guidelines was difficult. Applying them has proven even more challenging.

From Goals to Actions

When we were rolling out our guidelines—which included extensive on-site audits of each of our 700 contractors worldwide—we discovered that two of our manufacturing contractors in Bangladesh and one in Turkey employed underage workers. This was a clear violation. At the outset, it appeared that we had two options:

- Instruct our contractors to fire these children, knowing that many are the sole wage earners for their families and that if they lost their jobs, their families would face extreme hardships.

Or we could:

- Continue to employ underage children, ignoring our stance against the use of child labor.

By referencing our ethical guidelines to decision-making we came up with a different approach, one that we believe helped to minimize adverse ethical consequences.

We will not source in countries where conditions, such as the human rights climate, would run counter to our values . . .

The contractors agreed to pay the underage children their salaries and benefits while they went to school full-time. We agreed to pay for books, tuition, and uniforms. When the children reach legal working age, they are offered jobs in the plant. Thanks to these efforts, thirty-five children have attended school in Bangladesh; another six are currently in school in Turkey.

And how did we benefit from this situation? We were able to retain quality contractors that play an important role in our worldwide sourcing strategy. At the same time, we were able to honor our values and protect our brands.

Ethics Cost Money?

Applying our sourcing guidelines has forced us to find creative solutions to vexing ethical dilemmas. Clearly, at times, adhering to these standards has added costs. To continue working for us, some contractors have added emergency exits and staircases, increased ventilation, reduced crowding, improved bathroom facilities, and invested in water-treatment systems. The costs of these requirements have been passed on to us—at least in part—in the form of higher product prices. In other cases, we have foregone less expensive sources of production because of unsatisfactory working conditions or other concerns about the country of origin.

In today's world, a television exposé on working conditions can undo years of effort to build brand loyalty.

Conventional wisdom holds that these added costs put us at a competitive disadvantage. Yes, they limit our options somewhat and squeeze profit margins in the near-term. But over the years, we've found that decisions that emphasize cost to the exclusion of all other factors don't serve a company's and its shareholders' long-term interests.

Moreover, as a company that invests hundreds of millions of advertising dollars each year to create consumer preference for our products, we have a huge stake in protecting that investment. In today's world, a television exposé on working conditions can undo years of effort to build brand loyalty. Why squander your investment when, with foresight and commitment, reputational problems can be prevented?

Ethics as Strategy

But you don't have to take my word for it. There is a growing body of evidence that shows a positive correlation between good corporate citizenship and financial performance. Studies by leading research groups such as Opinion

Personal Responsibility

We learned that you can't force ethical conduct into an organization. Ethics is a function of the collective attitudes of our people. And these attitudes are cultivated and supported by at least seven factors:

- commitment to responsible business conduct;
- management's leadership;
- trust in employees;
- programs and policies that provide people with clarity about the organization's ethical expectations;
- open, honest, and timely communications;
- tools to help employees resolve ethical problems, and
- reward and recognition systems that reinforce the importance of ethics.

Ultimately, high ethical standards can be maintained only if they are modeled by management and woven into the fabric of the company. Knowing this, the challenge is to cultivate the kind of environment where people do the right thing.

Research Corporation and Yankelovich Partners, respected scholars, and socially responsible investment firms underscore the correlation. Companies that look beyond maximizing wealth and profits and are driven by values and a sense of purpose outperform those companies that focus only on short-term gain.

Companies with strong corporate reputations have been shown to out-perform the S&P 500, have higher sales, sustain greater profits, and have stocks that outperform the market. These are results that no bottom-line-fixated manager can afford to ignore.

Similarly, a recent study suggests that how a company conducts itself affects consumer purchasing decisions and customer loyalty. A vast majority—84 percent—of the American public agrees that a company's reputation can well be the deciding factor in terms of what product or service they buy.

These findings mirror our own experience. Our values-driven approach has helped us in many ways. We have identified contractors who want to work for Levi Strauss & Co. to achieve our "blue ribbon" certification, enhancing their own business stature. We have gained retailer and consumer loyalty. Retailers feel good about having us as business partners because of our commitment to ethical practices. Today's consumer has more products to choose from and more information about those products. A company's reputation forms a part of the consumer's perceptions of the product and influences purchasing decisions.

Companies with strong corporate reputations have been shown to outperform the S&P 500, have higher sales, sustain greater profits, and have stocks that outperform the market.

At the same time, we're better able to attract, retain, and motivate the most talented employees, because the company's values more closely mirror their own personal values. Because government and community leaders view us as a responsible corporate citizen we have been welcomed to do business in established and emerging markets.

Long-term Interests

We are living in an environment in which ethical standards and behaviors are being increasingly challenged. Addressing these dilemmas becomes even more difficult when one overlays the complexities of different cultures and value systems that exist throughout the world. For example, in some cultures honesty will take precedence over caring—"tell the truth even if it hurts"—whereas other cultures find caring, or "saving face," the predominant value.

As you grapple with some fictitious ethical quandaries, I encourage you to ask yourself these questions:

"How much am I willing to compromise my principles?"

"Are there times when I'm willing to risk something I value for doing the right thing?"

For me and my associates at Levi Strauss & Co. I think the answers have become clear: Ethics must trump all other considerations. Ultimately, there are important commercial benefits to be gained from managing your business in a responsible and ethical way that best serves your enterprise's long-term interests. The opposite seems equally clear: The dangers of not doing so are profound.

Michael Josephson, a noted ethics expert, defined ethics this way: "Ethics is about character and courage and how we meet the challenge when doing the right thing will cost more than we want to pay."

The good news is that courage carries with it a great reward—the prospect of sustained responsible commercial success. I think that's what each of us wants our legacy to be. And I believe ultimately our key stakeholders—all of them—will accept nothing less.

Sir Adrian Cadbury

Sir Adrian Cadbury, who was chief at Cadbury Schweppes PLC, one of the world's largest food and beverage companies, was knighted in 1977 for his services to country and people. His English ancestors who founded the company, however, were less fortunate. They were Quaker commoners who had to overcome religious prejudices. Learning from their hardships, when brothers Richard and George Cadbury opened their chocolate works in 1861, they immediately established a company culture that put the employees first. Their factory boasted a gymnasium, playgrounds, and cricket fields, among other amenities. This heritage was continued by Sir Adrian, who once reflected, "Quakers have always had a belief in achieving, as far as one can, agreement by consensus and also a very strong belief in the worth of the individual."

Before joining the company in 1952, Sir Adrian also learned a great deal about teamwork when he competed in that summer's Olympics in rowing and his team finished a respectable fourth. "The beauty of racing in a crew is that you learn any victory is the combined effort of everyone. In the same way, company results reflect the performance of the whole firm." Another racing lesson that has translated to business: Know when to make your move and pounce. For example, Sir Adrian was one of the driving forces in the merger between Cadbury and Schweppes in 1969.

When it comes to leadership, Sir Adrian believes you must be quick on your feet not only to meet changes in the marketplace but to adapt to your people's expectations. He said, "You need flexibility in responding to the heightened desire of individuals to live their own kind of life." While some might fear anarchy, Sir Adrian welcomes individualism as long as his employees remain self-motivated and results-oriented, because "then you won't have to supervise what they do in detail. You can spend your time thinking where the business ought to be going and what these people ought to be applying themselves to." In *Ethical Managers Make Their Own Rules,* Sir Adrian grapples with individualism and dissects the complex nature of decision making.

Ethical Managers Make Their Own Rules

Sir Adrian Cadbury

In 1900 Queen Victoria sent a decorative tin with a bar of chocolate inside to all of her soldiers who were serving in South Africa. These tins still turn up today; often complete with their contents, a tribute to the collecting instinct. At the time, the order faced my grandfather with an ethical dilemma. He owned and ran the second-largest chocolate company in Britain, so he was trying harder and the order meant additional work for the factory. Yet he was deeply and publicly opposed to the Anglo-Boer War. He resolved the dilemma by accepting the order but carrying it out at cost. He therefore made no profit out of what he saw as an unjust war, his employees benefited from the additional work, the soldiers received their royal present, and I am still sent the tins.

My grandfather was able to resolve the conflict between the decision best for his business and his personal code of ethics because he and his family owned the firm which bore their name. Certainly his dilemma would have been more acute if he had had to take into account the interests of outside shareholders, many of whom would no doubt have been in favor both of the war and of profiting from it. But even so, not all my grandfather's ethical dilemmas could be as straight-forwardly resolved.

So strongly did my grandfather feel about the South African War that he acquired and financed the only British newspaper which opposed it. He was also against gambling, however, and so he tried to run the paper without any references to horse racing. The effect on the newspaper's circulation was such that he had to choose between his ethical beliefs. He decided, in the end, that it was more important that the paper's voice be heard as widely as possible than that gambling should thereby receive some mild encouragement. The decision was doubtless a relief to those working on the paper and to its readers.

The way my grandfather settled these two clashes of principle brings out some practical points about ethics and business decisions. In the first place, the possibility that ethical and commercial considerations will conflict has always faced those who run companies. It is not a new problem. The difference now is that a more widespread and critical interest is being taken in our decisions and in the ethical judgments which lie behind them.

Most business decisions involve some degree of ethical judgment: few can be taken solely on the basis of arithmetic.

Secondly, as the newspaper example demonstrates, ethical signposts do not always point in the same direction. My grandfather had to choose between opposing a war and condoning gambling. The rule that it is best to tell the truth often runs up against the rule that we should not hurt people's feelings unnecessarily. There is no simple, universal formula for solving ethical problems. We have to choose from our own codes of conduct whichever rules are appropriate to the case in hand; the outcome of those choices makes us who we are.

Lastly, while it is hard enough to resolve dilemmas when our personal rules of conduct conflict, the real difficulties arise when we have to make decisions which affect the interests of others. We can work out what weighting to give to our own rules through trial and error. But business decisions require us to do the same for others by allocating weights to all the conflicting interests which may be involved. Frequently, for example, we must balance the interests of employees against those of shareholders. But even that sounds more straightforward than it really is, because there may well be differing views among the shareholders, and the interests of past, present, and future employees are unlikely to be identical.

Eliminating ethical considerations from business decisions would simplify the management task, and Milton Friedman has urged something of the kind in arguing that the interaction between business and society should be left to the political process. "Few trends could so thoroughly undermine the very foundation of our free society," he writes in *Capitalism and Freedom,* "as the acceptance by corporate officials of a social responsibility other than to make as much money for their shareholders as possible."

But the simplicity of this approach is deceptive. Business is part of the social system, and we cannot isolate the economic elements of major decisions from their social consequences. So there are no simple rules. Those who make business decisions have to assess the economic and social consequences of their actions as best as they can and come to their conclusions on limited information and in a limited time.

We Judge Companies—and Managers—by Their Actions, Not Their Pious Statements of Intent.

As will already be apparent, I use the word ethics to mean the guidelines or rules of conduct by which we aim to live. It is, of course, foolhardy to write about ethics at all, because you lay yourself open to the charge of taking up a position of moral superiority, of failing to practice what you preach, or both. I am not in a position to preach nor am I promoting a specific code of conduct. I believe, however, that it is useful to all of us who are responsible for business decisions to acknowledge the part which ethics plays in those decisions and to encourage discussion of how best to combine commercial and ethical judgments. Most business decisions involve some degree of ethical judgment: few can be taken solely on the basis of arithmetic.

While we refer to a company as having a set of standards, that is a convenient shorthand. The people who make up the company are responsible for its conduct and it is their collective actions which determine the company's standards. The ethical standards of a company are judged by its actions not by pious statements of intent put out in its name. This does not mean that those who head companies should not set down what they believe their companies stand for—hard though that is to do. The character of a company is a matter of importance to those in it, to those who do business with it, and to those who are considering joining it.

What matters most, however, is where we stand as individual managers and how we behave when faced with decisions which require us to combine ethical and commercial judgments. In approaching such decisions, I believe it is helpful to go through two steps. The first is to determine, as precisely as we can, what our personal rules of conduct are. This does not mean drawing up a list of virtuous notions, which will probably end up as a watered-down version of the Scriptures without their literary merit. It does mean looking back at decisions we have made and working out from there what our rules actually are. The aim is to avoid confusing ourselves and everyone else by declaring one set of principles and acting on another. Our ethics are expressed in our actions, which is why they are usually clearer to others than to ourselves.

Once we know where we stand personally we can move on to the second step, which is to think through who else will be affected by the decision and how we should weight their interest in it. Some interests will be represented by well-organized groups; others will have no one to put their case. If a factory manager is negotiating a wage claim with employee representatives, their remit is to look after the interests of those who are already employed. Yet the effect of the wage settlement on the factory's costs may well determine whether new employees are likely to be taken on. So the manager cannot ignore the interest of potential employees in the outcome of the negotiation, even though that interest is not represented at the bargaining table.

BLACK AND WHITE ALTERNATIVES ARE A REGRETTABLE SIGN OF THE TIMES.

The rise of organized interest groups makes it doubly important that managers consider the arguments of everyone with a legitimate interest in a decision's outcome. Interest groups seek publicity to promote their causes and they have the advantage of being single-minded: they are against building an airport on a certain site, for example, but take no responsibility for finding a better alternative. This narrow focus gives pressure groups a debating advantage against managements, which cannot evade the responsibility for taking decisions in the same way.

In *The Hard Problems of Management,* Mark Pastin has perceptively referred to this phenomenon as the ethical superiority of the uninvolved, and there is a good deal of it about. Pressure groups are skilled at seizing the high moral ground and arguing that our judgment as managers is at best biased and at worst influenced solely by private gain because we have a direct commercial interest in the outcome of our decisions. But as managers we are also responsible for arriving at business decisions which take account of all the interests concerned; the uninvolved are not.

The ethical standards of a company are judged by its actions not by pious statements of intent put out in its name.

At times the campaign to persuade companies to divest themselves of their South African subsidiaries has exemplified this kind of ethical high-handedness. Apartheid is abhorrent politically, socially, and morally. Those who argue that they can exert some influence on the direction of change by staying put believe this as sincerely as those who favor divestment. Yet many antiapartheid campaigners reject the proposition that both sides have the same end in view. From their perspective it is self-evident that the only ethical course of action is for companies to wash their hands of the problems of South Africa by selling out.

Managers cannot be so self-assured. In deciding what weight to give to the arguments for and against divestment, we must consider who has what at stake in the outcome of the decision. The employees of a South African subsidiary have the most direct stake, as the decision affects their future; they are also the group whose voice is least likely to be heard outside South Africa. The shareholders have at stake any loss on divestment, against which must be balanced any gain in the value of their shares through severing the South African connection. The divestment lobby is the one group for whom the decision is costless either way.

What is clear even from this limited analysis is that there is no general answer to the question of whether companies should sell their South African subsidiaries or not. Pressure to reduce complicated issues to straightforward alternatives, one of which is right and the other wrong, is a regrettable sign of the times. But boards are rarely presented with two clearly opposed alternatives. Companies faced with the same issues will therefore properly come to different conclusions and their decisions may alter over time.

A less contentious divestment decision faced my own company when we decided to sell our foods division. Because the division was mainly a U.K. business with regional brands, it did not fit the company's strategy, which called for concentrating resources behind our confectionery and soft drinks brands internationally. But it was an attractive business in its own right, and the decision to sell prompted both a management bid and external offers.

Employees working in the division strongly supported the management bid and made their views felt. In this instance, they were the best organized interest group and they had more information available to them to back their case than any of the other parties involved. What they had at stake was also very clear.

Our ethics are expressed in our actions, which is why they are usually clearer to others than to ourselves.

From the shareholders' point of view, the premium over asset value offered by the various bidders was a key aspect of the decision. They also had an interest in seeing the deal completed without regulatory delays and without diverting too much management attention from the ongoing business. In addition, the way in which the successful bidder would guard the brand name had to be considered, since the division would take with it products carrying the parent company's name.

In weighing the advantages and disadvantages of the various offers, the board considered all the groups, consumers among them, who would be affected by the sale. But our main task was to reconcile the interests of the employees and of the shareholders. (The more, of course, we can encourage employees to become shareholders, the closer together the interests of these two stakeholders will be brought.) The division's management upped its bid in the face of outside competition, and after due deliberation we decided to sell to the management team, believing that this choice best balanced the diverse interests at stake.

Actions Are Unethical if They Won't Stand Scrutiny.

Companies whose activities are international face an additional complication in taking their decisions. They aim to work to the same standards of business conduct wherever they are and to behave as good corporate citizens of the countries in which they trade. But the two aims are not always compatible: Promotion on merit may be the rule of the company and promotion by seniority the custom of the country. In addition, while the financial arithmetic on which companies base their decisions is generally accepted, what is considered ethical varies among cultures.

If what would be considered corruption in the company's home territory is an accepted business practice elsewhere, how are local managers expected to act? Companies could do business only in countries in which they feel ethically at home, provided always that their shareholders take the same view. But this approach could prove unduly restrictive, and there is also a certain arrogance in dismissing foreign codes of conduct without considering why they may be different. If companies find, for example, that they have to pay customs officers in another country just to do their job, it may be that the state is simply transferring its responsibilities to the private sector as an alternative to using taxation less efficiently to the same end.

Nevertheless, this example brings us to one of the most common ethical issues companies face—how far to go in buying business? What payments are legitimate for companies to make to win orders and, the reverse side of that coin, when do gifts to employees become bribes? I use two rules of thumb to test whether a payment is acceptable from the company's point of view: Is the payment on the face of the invoice? Would it embarrass the recipient to have the gift mentioned in the company newspaper?

If what would be considered corruption in the company's home territory is an accepted business practice elsewhere, how are local managers expected to act?

The first test ensures that all payments, however unusual they may seem, are recorded and go through the books. The second is aimed at distinguishing bribes from gifts, a definition which depends on the size of the gift and the influence it is likely to have on the recipient. The value of a case of whiskey to me would be limited, because I only take it as medicine. We know ourselves whether a gift is acceptable or not and we know that others will know if they are aware of the nature of the gift.

As for payment on the face of the invoice, I have found it a useful general rule precisely because codes of conduct do vary round the world. It has legitimized some otherwise unlikely company payments, to the police in one country, for example, and to the official planning authorities in another, but all went through the books and were audited. Listing a payment on the face of the invoice may not be a sufficient ethical test, but it is a necessary one; payments outside the company's system are corrupt and corrupting.

The logic behind these rules of thumb is that openness and ethics go together and that actions are unethical if they will not stand scrutiny. Openness in arriving at decisions reflects the same logic. It gives those with an interest in a particular decision the chance to make their views known and opens to argument the basis on which the decision is finally taken. This in turn enables the decision makers to learn from experience and to improve their powers of judgment.

I use two rules of thumb to test whether a payment is acceptable from the company's point of view: Is the payment on the face of the invoice? Would it embarrass the recipient to have the gift mentioned in the company newspaper?

Openness is also, I believe, the best way to disarm outside suspicion of companies' motives and actions. Disclosure is not a panacea for improving the relations between business and society, but the willingness to operate an open system is the foundation of those relations. Business needs to be open to the views of society and open in return about its own activities; this is essential for the establishment of trust.

For the same reasons, as managers we need to be candid when making decisions about other people. Dr. Johnson reminds us that when it comes to lapidary inscriptions, "no man is upon oath." But what should be disclosed in references, in fairness to those looking for work and to those who are considering employing them?

The simplest rule would seem to be that we should write the kind of reference we would wish to read. Yet "do as you would be done by" says nothing about ethics. The actions which result from applying it could be ethical or unethical, depending on the standards of the initiator. The rule could be adapted to help managers determine their ethical standards, however, by reframing it as a question: If you did business with yourself, how ethical would you think you were?

Anonymous letters accusing an employee of doing something discreditable create another context in which candor is the wisest course. Such letters cannot by definition be answered, but they convey a message to those who receive them, however warped or unfair the message may be. I normally destroy these letters, but tell the person concerned what has been said. This conveys the disregard I attach to nameless allegation, but preserves the rule of openness. From a practical point of view, it serves as a warning if there is anything in the allegations; from an ethical point of view, the degree to which my judgment of the person may now be prejudiced is known between us.

Shelving Hard Decisions Is the Least Ethical Course.

The last aspect of ethics in business decisions I want to discuss concerns our responsibility for the level of employment; what can or should companies do about the provision of jobs? This issue is of immediate concern to European managers because unemployment is higher in Europe than it is in the United States and the net number of new jobs created has been much lower. It comes to the fore whenever companies face decisions which require a tradeoff between increasing efficiency and reducing numbers employed.

If you believe, as I do, that the primary purpose of a company is to satisfy the needs of its customers and to do so profitably, the creation of jobs cannot be the company's goal as well. Satisfying customers requires companies to compete in the marketplace, and so we cannot opt out of introducing new technology, for example, to preserve jobs. To do so would be to deny consumers the benefits of progress, to short-change the shareholders, and in the longer run to put the jobs of everyone in the company at risk. What destroys jobs certainly and permanently is the failure to be competitive.

Experience says that the introduction of new technology creates more jobs than it eliminates, in ways which cannot be forecast. It may do so, however, only after a time lag, and those displaced may not, through lack of skills, be able to take advantage of the new opportunities when they arise. Nevertheless, the company's prime responsibility to everyone who has a stake in it is to retain its competitive edge, even if this means a loss of jobs in the short run.

Where companies do have a social responsibility, however, is in how we manage that situation, how we smooth the path of technological change. Companies are responsible for the timing of such changes, and we are in a position to involve those who will be affected by the way in which those changes are introduced. We also have a vital resource in our capacity to provide training, so that continuing employees can take advantage of change and those who may lose their jobs can more readily find new ones.

The company which takes drastic action in order to survive is more likely to be criticized publicly than the one which fails to grasp the nettle and gradually but inexorably declines.

In the United Kingdom, an organization called Business in the Community has been established to encourage the formation of new enterprises. Companies have backed it with cash and with secondments. The secondment of able managers to worthwhile institutions is a particularly effective expression of concern, because the ability to manage is such a scarce resource. Through Business in the Community we can create jobs collectively, even if we cannot do so individually, and it is clearly in our interest to improve the economic and social climate in this way.

Throughout, I have been writing about the responsibilities of those who head companies and my emphasis has been on taking decisions, because that is what directors and managers are appointed to do. What concerns me is that too often the public pressures which are put on companies in the name of ethics encourage their boards to put off decisions or to wash their hands of problems. There may well be commercial reasons for those choices, but there are rarely ethical ones. The ethical bases on which decisions are arrived at will vary among companies, but shelving those decisions is likely to be the least ethical course.

The company which takes drastic action in order to survive is more likely to be criticized publicly than the one which fails to grasp the nettle and gradually but inexorably declines. There is always a temptation to postpone difficult decisions, but it is not in society's interests that hard choices should be evaded because of public clamor or the possibility of legal action. Companies need to be encouraged to take the decisions which face them; the responsibility for providing that encouragement rests with society as a whole.

Society sets the ethical framework within which those who run companies have to work out their own codes of conduct. Responsibility for decisions, therefore, runs both ways. Business has to take account of its responsibilities to society in coming to its decisions, but society has to accept its responsibilities for setting the standards against which those decisions are made.

An Wang
1920 –

An Wang, electronics genius and son of a Shanghai English teacher, lived his youth in a politically tumultuous China. Somehow Wang managed to survive both the Chinese civil war in the 1930s and Japan's brutal World War II occupation. He did, however, suffer through the deaths of his parents and elder sister, all victims of the fighting. Of this embittered early life, Wang said, "I learned to negotiate my way in unfamiliar territory. I became a loner by circumstance, not by choice, but the discovery that I could survive and even thrive on my own gave me confidence." By the time he arrived in the United States in 1945, as a university student in a two-year fellowship program, he was certain he could accomplish anything.

After receiving a Ph.D. in physics at Harvard, Wang took a research position in Harvard's computation laboratory. He immediately forged a breakthrough in the problem of mass information storage, which he patented. The 1940s was the most creative period in computer development, according to Wang, because the industry was not yet of commercial importance and developments in this critical industry were openly discussed. Times certainly have changed. Wang himself soon entered the commercial war zone, making the leap from researcher to entrepreneur when he founded Wang Laboratories in 1951. Soon thereafter he began negotiations to sell his memory core patent for mass storage to IBM, which he likened to a high-stakes poker game. With an eventual $500,000 payoff, he felt like a winner. Wang went on to introduce the first desktop calculators in 1965, word processors in the 1970s (which propelled the company into the Fortune 500), and computers in the 1980s.

Throughout Wang Laboratories' astounding growth, Wang never forgot his guiding principles, which were based on the Confucian philosophy of simplicity, moderation, balance, and responsibility. He believes that a company culture is determined largely during its early years through close personal contact between the leader and the employees. Wang discusses the standards a CEO must set and how they effect a company in *Responsibility.*

Responsibility

An Wang

I think that corporate behavior should be judged by the same standards as personal behavior. I also think that both individuals and corporations have the responsibility to make some positive contribution to the world.

As the founder and CEO of a major corporation, I have a responsibility to the customers, employees, vendors, shareholders, and communities that Wang deals with. As an individual, I have a direct responsibility to return to the institutions and communities that nurtured and educated me a portion of the benefits I have derived from them. For this reason, in both my corporate and individual activities, I have taken pains to pay the greatest attention to the concerns and needs of those closest to home, which in my case is Boston and its surrounding towns.

At their root, my feelings about corporate and individual responsibility originate in a strong sense of loyalty I have always felt toward the people, communities, and institutions in my life. These feelings were strengthened when I witnessed what happens when people in power have no sense of social responsibility. I am referring to the abuses in the interior of China during World War II. In the absence of a strong central government, the local generals acted only to protect their power and enhance their fortunes, and the immediate result was anarchy and suffering among the peasants. The long-term result was a revolution and a Communist regime that brought its own form of oppression. The corrupt generals ultimately brought about their own downfall, but not before they had inflicted great damage and suffering.

I think that corporate behavior should be judged by the same standards as personal behavior.

The lesson in this is that it is not enough to rely on outside authority to enforce moral or legal behavior. The compass of values has to be within a person or a corporation. Often one hears the contrary; that a corporation should be an amoral instrument, a money machine that maximizes its profits within rules set by the community. This argument holds that corporations that get distracted from this goal by social and community responsibilities end up making less money, which decreases consumer spending and increases unemployment and hurts those same communities as a result. My own belief is that just the opposite is true.

For one thing, no community can police an institution as well as the institution itself, and if a company places profits above ethics, then that organization will violate community standards no matter how stringently laws and codes are written. And those violations will produce demoralization of the workforce, ill will in the community, and perhaps lawsuits that will have a long-term negative impact on the bottom line anyway. On the other hand, the company that orients itself toward serving both its community and its customers will reap long-term rewards in the form of loyal customers, peaceful labor relations, and positive community relations.

There is, in fact, evidence in support of this. A study conducted by Johnson & Johnson showed that over a period of thirty years, a group of companies selected exclusively because of their reputation for social responsibility outperformed both the Dow Jones Industrial Average and the S&P stock averages by an extremely large margin.

. . . it is not enough to rely on outside authority to enforce moral or legal behavior. The compass of values has to be within a person or a corporation.

A number of American companies have consciously chosen to hold themselves to a higher standard of social responsibility than the law requires. Johnson & Johnson, for instance, asks its employees to read, study, and sign a written code of ethics. The company hopes that by doing so, its employees will adopt those values for themselves. I do things differently, but I endorse the spirit behind Johnson & Johnson's policy. My approach is to try to convey by example the ethical standards I expect the company to adhere to.

The very nature of business makes it all the more important that a sense of social responsibility be deeply rooted in a corporation. I have written about the relativity of events, and about the importance of adaptability in both individual and corporate behavior. Markets change, tastes change, so the companies and individuals that choose to compete in those markets must change. The abilities that help one to compete in these changing markets change, as well. There are times that call for decisive action, and there are other times when it is wiser to be more moderate. This continual flux makes it all the more important that two things remain constant. The company should never lose sight of the reason it is in business, and the people who run the company should never compromise their values for the sake of expediency. Without these, both a company and the people who work for it are in danger of losing their identity given the continually changing landscape they must negotiate.

The company should never lose sight of the reason it is in business, and the people who run the company should never compromise their values for the sake of expediency.

This is not a simple matter, as anyone who has been in business knows. As a company becomes larger, the pressures of maintaining growth can begin to obscure the original mission of the company. Not everybody plays fair in the marketplace, and there is the continual temptation to respond in kind to dirty tricks, or to play at the level of the competition. For instance, as a multinational, we have the option of competing in a number of Third World markets where corruption and bribery are considered business as usual. Many companies accept the situation, however reluctantly, and let their employees know that they will not disapprove of surreptitious bribes if they result in increased orders. That is not the approach I have taken. So far, we have not established a Wang office in the markets where this is the most prevalent.

Because the company bears my name, I cannot accept a lesser standard of behavior for the corporation than I demand of myself.

Then there are situations where the moral issues do not involve corruption, but rather questions of injustice. About ten years ago, I became uncomfortable with our owning a subsidiary in South Africa. As someone from a race which has suffered its share of discrimination, I could hardly ignore the abuses of apartheid. On the other hand, I felt an obligation not to abandon our customers or the people who worked for us, and for whom Wang was their livelihood. So we took the step of selling the subsidiary to the man who was managing it for us. This reduced our direct presence, although we still sold equipment through this distributor. We maintained this relationship until last year. I had hoped that things in South Africa would change over this period. But they didn't, and I began to feel that they never would unless people like myself made stronger statements. So I severed our last remaining connection to South Africa. Finally I decided that we had no choice but to do so.

Because the company bears my name, I cannot accept a lesser standard of behavior for the corporation than I demand of myself. My purpose in founding Wang Laboratories was to devise equipment and services that would increase worker productivity and make jobs easier. However, if in pursuit of this goal, my company exploited its own employees or its surrounding community, or pursued business in an unethical manner, this would negate whatever positive contributions the company made through its products. It has been said that ultimately all a person has is his reputation. In my case, that reputation is shaped not just by my actions as an individual but also by the reputation of Wang Laboratories.

Ben Cohen and Jerry Greenfield
1951 –   1951 –

Ice cream's most famous and creative duo, Ben Cohen and Jerry Greenfield, met in seventh-grade gym class. The two kids shared a joy for eating and remained friends right through high school. In 1969 they went their separate ways to college. Ben dropped out of Colgate University to become a potter's apprentice, but ended up going through a series of jobs, from short-order cook to hospital admissions clerk. Finally he called Jerry to see if he wanted to go into business. Their plan was ambiguous at best: "We wanted to pick a product that was becoming popular in big cities and move it to a rural college town, because we wanted to live in that kind of environment." They kicked around the idea of bagels, then pizza, before settling on ice cream.

Ben and Jerry's next step was to look at areas in the United States with the highest average temperatures, but they discovered plenty of competition already established there, so they turned north, namely Vermont, where there was no competition. Ben and Jerry rented an abandoned gas station and lived off Saltine crackers and sardines while they renovated it. When they opened in 1978 their ice cream was a hit, but after three years they were just breaking even. It took Ben's dad to inject some sense into their somewhat liberal business minds and to convince them to raise prices for their premium product.

By 1982 business was really rolling and they thought it might be a good time to sell the company. But they didn't. Instead, the thought of letting go refocused their energy and mission. Ben and Jerry said they decided "to see whether a business could survive while being a force for progressive social change." Their crusades are well documented. Management of the business, however, continued to be a struggle because they themselves never liked to be managed. Recently they have stepped back from day-to-day operations, preferring to act as cheerleaders and caretakers. Ben and Jerry also continue to develop a values-driven strategy and culture that can be defined and implemented. As they admit, "Integrating a social mission into the everyday actions of a business is new, uncharted territory." In the following selection they provide their vision of a values-driven company.

Lead with Your Values

Ben Cohen and Jerry Greenfield

When we started making ice cream in 1978 we had simple goals. We wanted to have fun, we wanted to earn a living, and we wanted to give something back to the community. Only we didn't really know what that last item meant.

Then, as the business grew, our aspirations grew as well. We wanted to create a company we could be proud of. In order to do that, we—and the like-minded companies we connected with along the way—had to find an alternative to the traditional business model. What evolved from that search is what Anita Roddick, founder of the Body Shop, called "values-led business."

Values-led business is based on the idea that business has a responsibility to the people and the society that make its existence possible. More all-encompassing and therefore more effective than philanthropy alone, values-led business seeks to maximize its impact by integrating socially beneficial actions into as many of its day-to-day activities as possible. In order to do that, values must lead and be right up there in a company's mission statement, strategy, and operating plan.

Let's say, for example, that we're looking at three possible new ice cream flavors. Being values-led means choosing the flavor that gives us the best opportunity to integrate our commitment to social change with the need to return reasonable profits to our shareholders. Assuming all three flavors are profitable, if we find out that we can make one of them using nuts from the rain forest (in order to increase economic demand for the living rain forest) and we can put the ice cream in a rain forest–themed container that raises awareness about the problem of rain forest deforestation, we would choose that flavor. (That's exactly what happened with the development of our Rainforest Crunch flavor.) This is as opposed to making the decision based on what would be *most* profitable from a purely short-term financial perspective.

By incorporating concern for the community—local, national, and global—into its strategic and operating plans, the values-led business can make everyday business decisions that actualize the company's social and financial goals at the same time. Instead of choosing areas of activity based solely on its own short-term self-profitability, the values-led business recognizes that by addressing social problems along with financial concerns, a company can earn a respected place in the community, a special place in customers' hearts, and healthy profits, too.

Consumers are accustomed to buying products despite how they feel about the companies that sell them. But a values-led company earns the kind of customer loyalty most corporations only dream of—because it appeals to its customers on the basis of more than a product. It offers them a way to connect with kindred spirits, to express their most deeply held values when they spend their money. Unlike most commercial transactions, buying a product from a company you believe in transcends the purchase. It touches your soul. Our customers don't like just our ice cream—they like what our company stands for. They like how doing business with us makes them feel. And that's really what companies that spend huge amounts of money on advertising are trying to do—make their customers feel good about them. But they do it on a superficial level, with sexy women and cool cars.

Our experience has shown that you don't have to sacrifice social involvement on the altar of maximized profits.

Unlike most commercial transactions, buying a product from a company you believe in transcends the purchase. It touches your soul.

One builds on the other. The more we actualize our commitment to social change through our business activities, the more loyal customers we attract and the more profitable we become.

Cause-Related or Values-Led?

Over the past fifteen years, the success of Ben & Jerry's and other values-led companies has proved that there are plenty of customers who, when given a choice between products of equal quality, prefer to spend their money with companies whose values they share. Consequently, the idea that business should give back to the community started to seem less bizarre, and a lot more appealing, than it did when we were getting started. During the mid-eighties, the concept of "cause-related marketing" entered the mainstream corporate world.

Consultants started selling cause-related marketing campaigns to big corporations. Hershey's put Treats for Treatment coupons in Sunday newspapers and gave money to children's hospitals in exchange for each coupon redeemed. MasterCard started donating money with each transaction to anti–child-abuse organizations. Geo gave a fleet of fuel-efficient cars to TreePeople, a tree-planting group in Los Angeles, and planted a tree for each new car sold.

Cause-related marketing is a positive step. But it doesn't challenge the basic paradigms of conventional business and conventional marketing. It acknowledges that business has a responsibility to give back to the community, but it doesn't take advantage of the fact that the real power of business lies in its day-to-day activities. So a company that's doing cause-related marketing operates from a traditional, exclusively profit-maximizing motivation—then adds a charitable component almost as an afterthought. Instead of giving products a boost using a half-naked woman in a multimillion-dollar advertising campaign, cause-related marketing gives products a boost by associating them with compelling causes.

Our experience has shown that you don't have to sacrifice social involvement on the altar of maximized profits.

The basic premise of values-led business is to integrate social values into day-to-day business activities—into the very fabric of the business and its products. By contrast, the basic premise of cause-related marketing is to tack social values onto the marketing campaigns of a business that does not take social values into account in its other business activities.

At its best, cause-related marketing is helpful in that it uses marketing dollars to help fund social programs and raise awareness of social ills. At its worst, it's "greenwashing"—using philanthropy to convince customers the company is aligned with good causes, so the company will be seen as good, too, whether it is or not. Corporations know if they create the perception that they care about their consumers and the community, that's likely to increase sales. They understand that if they dress themselves in that clothing, slap that image on, that's going to move product.

But instead of just slapping the image on, wouldn't it be better if the company actually *did* care about its consumers and the community? Wouldn't it be better actually to *do* things that benefit people and society? That will also sell product—as well as motivate customers, employees, and investors. In most cases doing that doesn't cost any more. As a matter of fact, it may cost less.

Values-led business recognizes that the greatest potential a business has for benefiting society is in its operations—not in donating a small percentage of profits from its bottom line to charitable organizations.

Business has now become the most powerful force in society. We cannot solve social problems unless business accepts a leadership role. That in turn requires business to act in the interests of the common good. This is a very new role for business—one it is not used to or prepared for. The norm has been for business to be a special interest, and adversarial to the rest of society.

WHICH VALUES LEAD?

For the purpose of this book, the values we're talking about are what are often referred to as "progressive social values." We see our business, and values-led business in general, as promoting social progress for the common good: advocating for the many people in our society whose needs are not served by the status quo; giving a voice to the people who normally aren't heard; helping to address the root causes of poverty. That's why we've partnered with the Children's Defense Fund, whose purpose is to advocate the needs of children, and why we buy our brownies from a bakery that employs economically disenfranchised people, and why we're participating in the campaign to redirect a portion of the military budget to fund human services.

One of the most moving customer letters we ever got was about our Peace Pops and our involvement with One Percent for Peace. . . . The guy who sent the letter, a peace activist, wrote, "People who are out there working for peace are always viewed as being lefty hippies or bleeding hearts. They aren't taken seriously. They don't have much credibility. But when a company the size of Ben & Jerry's takes a stand for peace it legitimizes that stand in the public eye."

The central role business plays in our society means that business can give credibility to progressive causes in ways that social movements alone can't—much as the corporate world has lent credibility to conservative causes. Business is just a tool. It can be used to improve the quality of life in general or just to benefit business's narrow self-interest, that of maximizing profits.

Usually, when corporations are motivated strictly by financial self-interest, in order to meet their corporate goals they make decisions that don't serve the majority of the people. Tobacco companies oppose antismoking legislation. Manufacturing companies oppose antipollution legislation. Coal companies profit from strip-mining. Banks benefit from redlining in the inner city.

Business is just a tool. It can be used to improve the quality of life in general or just to benefit business's narrow self-interest, that of maximizing profits.

Those businesses are led by the values of short-term profit maximization.

The thing is, most corporations don't make their values, their beliefs, or their political activities public. They don't put their politics on their packaging. Instead, they might pay lobbyists to oppose environmental legislation or to support corporate tax loopholes. They might make donations or fund politicians' campaigns.

Most corporations do what's become normal for businesses to do: They express their values covertly—using their customers' money to achieve political ends that many of their customers would probably disagree with if they knew where their money was going.

In 1776 the Scottish economist Adam Smith wrote in his book *An Inquiry into the Nature and Causes of the Wealth of Nations* that if individuals and organizations acted in their own interests, an "unseen hand" would guide them to the right moral choices, and benefits would flow indirectly to others in society. We seem to forget, however, that an integral part of Adam Smith's theory was free access to information, because he believed that if consumers and other actors in the economy had access to full information about the products and services they were purchasing, they would make the right choices.

Most corporations do what's become normal for businesses to do: They express their values covertly—using their customers' money to achieve political ends that many of their customers would probably disagree with if they knew where their money was going.

Consumers can affect our collective quality of life by influencing one force that strongly controls it. And that force is business. We can influence business by "voting with our dollars": supporting companies that reflect our values. When we buy from the Body Shop, we oppose animal testing and support international human rights. When we spend our money with Patagonia, we help fund environmental initiatives. When we shop at local stores that support the community, we encourage other consumers and businesses to do the same.

That's why values-led businesses need to be public about their social activities. How can people know which companies to "vote" for if companies are secretive about their social stands and activities? When business acts covertly, it locks people out of the process. It deprives consumers of the opportunity to use their purchasing power to support social goals they believe in.

Most of the methodologies we'll talk about . . . would also work for implementing conservative values—except for one thing: If you're out front with what you stand for and your beliefs are unpopular, you could end up turning off a whole lot of customers. We believe customers are more likely to support a company with progressive values because, as we've said, our definition of progressive values is that they serve people's desire to alleviate social problems. If you take the average person and put him in a room with both a starving child and a gun, and you give him $5 and say, "With this money you can either buy this gun, because someone may attack you, or you can feed this starving child," we believe most people would feed the child.

In the same way, most customers would rather do business with a company that shares those values.

WHOSE VALUES LEAD?

In the case of Ben & Jerry's, the drive to make the company a vehicle for social change came mainly from the top—specifically, from Ben. That's often the case in small entrepreneurial companies. But in large corporations it's as likely to be the employees who push for social and environmental improvements.

Maybe an employee of the phone company goes to her division manager and says, "You know, I'm a member of Greenpeace, and they sent me this information about chlorine and how it creates dioxins, one of the most toxic chemicals known to humankind. And our Yellow Pages are printed on chlorine-bleached paper; and we go through five hundred thousand tons a year. What if we switched to chlorine-free?" Initially the manager says, "Sorry, no way we can do that." So the employee does a little research on her own, keeps the conversation going. Finally she convinces the manager to give unbleached paper a try. Sure enough—the company gets letters of praise from customers, and an award from an environmental group, and great press. And the customers feel good about the formerly anonymous phone company. The next time they get a call from the competitor offering them $50 to switch, they say, "No—I like my phone company."

So then the division manager tells another manager, "I've been able to source chlorine-free paper, and I'm psyched. We're reducing dioxins by five percent. We have the only Yellow Pages out there that's chlorine-free. The environmental community loves us. The general community loves us. Everybody loves us all of a sudden, and they used to hate us." Then the second division manager starts thinking about how he can incorporate social concerns into his business decisions. It goes on from there.

Once it's demonstrated that these changes can be made, and that they're having a positive effect on consumers, and that they're having a positive effect on employees (and therefore keeping them with the company), it becomes clear that integrating social concerns is good for business on many levels. But whether the impetus comes from the top, the bottom, or the middle—and no matter how big or small the company is—the social mission needs to be sold throughout the ranks if it's going to be brought to its full potential.

Let's say Joe, the purchasing guy, finds an unbleached cover stock for the same price, a little less, or even a little more than bleached stock. Joe then has to sell the idea to Sam, the marketing guy, because the cover stock's going to be tan now, not white. Then Sam's got to convince Mary, the creative director.

This doesn't happen just on environmental or social issues. In order for any change to be made inside a corporation, it has to be sold internally. The extent to which a company can be values-led depends on how completely the people in the organization have embraced, or bought into, the company's social mission.

Akio Morita

1921 –

Akio Morita, a physicist, was having lunch when news came of the Hiroshima bombing toward the end of World War II. Understanding the devastating results of the atomic bomb, he announced to his colleagues, "We might as well give up our research right now. If the Americans can build an atomic bomb, we must be too far behind in every field to catch up." Yet, in war-devastated 1946 Tokyo, he and a friend founded the company that would become Sony. Their mission: to be "an innovator, a clever company that would make new high-technology products in ingenious ways" and help rebuild Japan's economy.

Their first innovative product was a tape recorder, but no one in postwar Japan was interested in spending scarce money on a toy. Morita realized that "having a unique technology and being able to make unique products are not enough to keep a business going. You have to sell the products, and to do that you have to show the potential buyer the real value of what you are selling." The man of science had to become a merchandiser. Morita took his tape recorder to the Japanese court system. At the time it was overwhelmed with postwar problems, and stenographers were few; the tape recorder became an invaluable replacement. The innovations continued with the first transistorized television set in 1959 and later the fabulously popular Walkman.

Morita moved to New York City in the 1960s, where he experienced a far more permissive culture than Japan's. While he didn't enjoy everything in wild New York, Morita learned from his experience and later wrote, "the exposure to other cultures teaches an insular Japanese that . . . he must fit into the world, and not the other way around." It opened his mind to different political systems, religions, and ideas in general. He brought what he learned to his leadership at Sony. Traditionally, many Japanese executives acted like gods in a regimented environment, but Morita did not. While America offered many insights into business, Morita believes the United States could learn much from Japanese culture. In *American and Japanese Styles* he dissects the two countries' business philosophies and searches for a middle ground.

American and Japanese Styles

Akio Morita

Generally, in the United States, management's attitude toward the labor force and even the lower-level executives is very hierarchical, much more so than in Japan, an Oriental country where Westerners always expect to see such hierarchies. When I visited the Illinois television assembly plant of Motorola, one of the first things I noticed was that the offices were air-conditioned, but out on the shop floor it was stifling, people were dripping with sweat, and big noisy fans were blowing the hot air around. The workers were plainly uncomfortable, and I thought, "How can you get quality work from people laboring under such conditions? And what kind of loyalty can they be expected to show to the big bosses in their cool offices!" In Japan people often used to say that the shop floor where the goods were made was always more comfortable than the workers' homes. That has changed as the Japanese workers have become more affluent, and air-conditioning has become more common at home. By the middle of 1984, more than half of Japan's homes and apartments had it. But back in the late fifties, we air-conditioned our factories before the offices.

Amenities are not of great concern to management in Japan. The struggle for an office with a carpet, a water carafe, and an original oil painting on the wall is not common. Just recently a U.S. company, the maker of highly complex computerized graphics equipment, formed a joint venture with a Japanese company and the Japanese partner said to his foreign associate: "We would like you to design the showroom, but please allow us to design the office space upstairs." It seemed reasonable enough. The showroom was beautifully appointed, with soft lighting and comfortable chairs for visitors and clients. The equipment was highlighted using modern display techniques, and there were video demonstrations and elegant four-color brochures on the company and its equipment. Upstairs, the entire office staff was housed in one big open room without partitions, just a grid of desks with telephones, filing cabinets, and other necessary furniture in a simple, very Spartan arrangement. The U.S. partner raised his eyebrows, and his Japanese colleague explained, "If Japanese clients come into the office of a new and struggling company and see plush carpet and private offices and too much comfort, they become suspicious that this company is not serious, that it is devoting too much thought and company resources to management's comfort, and perhaps not enough to the product or to potential customers. If we are successful after one year, we might put up low partitions. After two or three years, we might give the top executive a closed office. But for now we have to all be reminded that we are struggling together to make this company a success."

Exactly my sentiments. We want everybody to have the best facilities in which to work, but we do not believe in posh and impressive private offices. Or perhaps I should say we do not give such things priority. At Sony we have comfortable offices everywhere and some new and impressive buildings, but our headquarters in Tokyo is nothing more than a converted factory building. We have made it comfortable and functional, but it still bothers me a bit that visitors have to climb two short flights of stairs to get to the reception desk. Generally, in Japanese industry, the investment goes into those things that relate directly to the product. And often the building that houses a factory site will look very much like a warehouse. But inside it will have all the essentials. Too often I have found in dealing with foreign companies that such superfluous things as the physical structure and office decor take up a lot more time and attention and money than they are worth. Obviously, in some businesses it is important to put on a show for the clients, but people in the hardware business rarely need to do this. We like to give thought to the atmosphere within our plants, to provide a comfortable, simple, and pleasant work environment, which we believe has a direct effect on product quality.

When we started the company, clothing was scarce and expensive on the black market. People came to work in an odd assortment of gear; returning soldiers wore bits of their uniform or old-fashioned suits that had been saved for many years. If a person was fortunate enough to have a good suit, he didn't want to wear it to the office where he might risk burning a hole in it with acid or soiling it. Some of our employees just didn't have the money to invest in a work jacket. So with company money we bought a jacket for everyone to wear in the office. Pretty soon these jackets became a symbol of our company family. As the company prospered, we could have done away with the jackets—we used to have a summer jacket and a winter one—because we were all being better paid and could afford our own, but everybody seemed to like the idea, and so we just decided to continue to provide them. In the beginning, we executives had a different colored name tag from the others, but we eventually adopted the same kind worn by everyone else. Today these jackets and tags are being used everywhere, even where class distinctions made people hesitant to wear them at first. Many of us liked our blue jackets, and I still wear mine occasionally.

But in the early seventies, when diplomatic relations were restored with the People's Republic of China and contacts increased and news coverage picked up, the papers often had pictures of large groups of Chinese in their Mao jackets all looking alike, and some people around Sony began to joke that when a group of us gathered for a meeting we looked like the people in the pictures from China.

Too often I have found in dealing with foreign companies that such superfluous things as the physical structure and office decor take up a lot more time and attention and money than they are worth.

I wanted a change. And so on Sony's thirty-fifth anniversary I asked the design departments of several Tokyo department stores to compete for the contract to design and supply the entire company with new jackets. They came up with some very good designs, I thought, and some of our people wore the jackets to see how they worked out on the job. There was no clear favorite. Finally, I took the problem to my friend, the fashion designer Issey Miyake. He came to the company and watched how the people worked. He went into the plants, the labs, and the offices to observe the kinds of movements they must make, and about a year later he came up with a simple and ingeniously designed gray jacket with red piping that has sleeves that can be removed, turning the jacket into a kind of vest that can be worn all year around. That ended the complaints; I figured correctly that even if people were not too pleased with the jackets, they couldn't very well complain when they were wearing something created by one of the world's top fashion designers. So nobody could doubt it, I made it a point to insist that Miyake put his label in every garment. Today one of those jackets on a Sony employee is as good as a credit card in business establishments near our facilities. The wearing of that jacket makes a person feel that he is part of our team effort, and merchants in the neighborhood will often give credit to someone who asks for it just on the strength of the jacket and the person's name card.

Japanese attitudes toward work seem to be critically different from American attitudes. Japanese people tend to be much better adjusted to the notion of work, any kind of work, as honorable. Nobody would look down on a man who retires at age fifty-five or sixty and then to keep earning money takes a more menial job than the one he left. I should mention that top-level executives usually have no mandatory retirement age, and many stay on into their seventies and even their eighties.

At Sony we have mandatory retirement from the presidency at sixty-five, but to utilize their experience and knowledge we keep former executives who have retired as consultants. We provide them with office space and staff, so that they can work apart from the day-to-day affairs of the company, at Ibuka Hall, a building located five minutes away from the headquarters building. From time to time, we ask them for advice and they attend conferences and other events as representatives of Sony. Many of those people who retire from managerial jobs find executive positions in smaller companies or subsidiary companies of Sony where their managerial experience and skill are needed and valued.

Workers generally are willing to learn new skills. Japan has never devised a system like the American, in which a person is trained to do one thing and then refuses to take a job doing anything else—and is even supported by government funds while he looks for a job that suits his specific tastes. Because of Japan's special situation, our people do not have that luxury. And our unemployment rate lately has not reached 3 percent.

One old style of management that is still being practiced by many companies in the United States and by some in Japan is based on the idea that the company that is successful is the one that can produce the conventional product most efficiently at cheaper cost. Efficiency, in this system, becomes a god. Ultimately, it means that machinery is everything, and the ideal factory is a perfectly automated one, perhaps one that is unmanned. This machinelike management is a management of dehumanization.

Japanese attitudes toward work seem to be critically different from American attitudes. Japanese people tend to be much better adjusted to the notion of work, any kind of work, as honorable.

But technology has accelerated at an unparalleled pace in the past few decades, and it has entailed digesting new knowledge, new information, and different technologies. Today, management must be able to establish new business ahead of its competitors, rather than pursue higher efficiency in manufacturing conventional products. In the U.S. and Europe today, old-fashioned low-level jobs are being protected while the new technologies are being neglected.

More important, an employee today is no longer a slave to machinery who is expected to repeat simple mechanical operations like Charlie Chaplin in the film *Modern Times.* He is no longer a beast of burden who works under the carrot-and-stick rule and sells his labor. After all, manual labor can be taken over by machine or computer. Modern industry has to be brain-intensive and so does the employee. Neither machinery nor animals can carry out brain-intensive tasks. In the late sixties, when integrated circuits had to be assembled by hand, the deft fingers of Asian women were greatly in demand by U.S. companies. As the design of these devices became more and more complicated, along came more sophisticated machinery, such as laser trimmers, which required not deft fingers but agile minds and intelligence. And so this upgrading of the workers is something that every country will have to be concerned about, and the idea of preserving old-fashioned jobs in the modern era does not make sense.

This means educating new employees and reeducating older employees for new challenges.

That is not all. At Sony we at times have scientists' participate in sales for a while because we don't want our scientists to live in ivory towers. I have always felt they should know that we are in a very competitive business and should have some experience in the front lines of the business. Part of the training program for graduates who enter Sony as recruits fresh out of university includes a program where nontechnical persons undergo a month of training at a factory and technical persons work as salespeople in a Sony shop or department store, selling our products.

Japanese labor practices are often called old-fashioned in today's world, and some say the old work ethic is eroding in Japan as it has elsewhere, but I do not think this is inevitable. As I see it, the desire to work and to perform well is not something unnatural that has to be imposed on people. I think all people get a sense of satisfaction from accomplishing work that is challenging, when their work and role in the company are being recognized. Managers abroad seem to overlook this. People in America, for example, have been conditioned to a system in which a person sells his labor for a price. In a way, that's good because people cannot coast; they know they have to work to earn their money or be fired. (I also think the way Americans make their children do work to earn their allowance is a fine idea; in Japan we often just give the money without requiring anything of our children.) In Japan we do take the risk of promising people job security, and then we have to keep motivating them. Yet I believe it is a big mistake to think that money is the only way to compensate a person for his work.

People need money, but they also want to be happy in their work and proud of it. So if we give a lot of responsibility to a younger man, even if he doesn't have a title, he will believe he has a good future and will be happy to work hard. In the United States, title and job and monetary incentives are all tied together. That is why, if a young person has a big job, management thinks he has to have a big salary. But in Japan we customarily give raises each year as employees get older and more experienced in the company. If we give an unusually high salary to one person, we cannot continue to give him annual increases indefinitely. At some point, his salary will have to level off, and at that point, he is likely to get discouraged. So we like to give the same sort of raise to all. I think this keeps our people well motivated. This may be a Japanese trait, but I do not think so.

At Sony we at times have scientists' participate in sales for a while because we don't want our scientists to live in ivory towers.

I believe people work for satisfaction. I know that advertisements and commercials in the U.S. seem to hold up leisure as the most satisfying goal in life, but it is not that way in Japan yet. I really believe there is such a thing as company patriotism and job satisfaction—and that it is as important as money. It goes without saying that you must pay good wages. But that also means, of course, that the company must not throw money away on huge bonuses for executives or other frivolities but must share its fate with the workers. Japanese workers seem to feel better about themselves if they get raises as they age, on an expectable curve. We have tried other ways.

When we started our research laboratory, we had to go out and find researchers, and because these people had more education and were, naturally, older than our normal new employees we decided they should have higher wages, equivalent to U.S. salary levels. One suggested plan was to put them under short-term contract, say three years, after which we would decide whether to renew or not. But before we decided on this new pay scheme, I asked the new employees whether they would prefer the more common system of lower pay to start, but with yearly increases, or the three-year contract at a much higher wage.

People need money, but they also want to be happy in their work and proud of it. So if we give a lot of responsibility to a younger man, even if he doesn't have a title, he will believe he has a good future and will be happy to work hard.

Not one of them asked for the American-level salary. Everyone opted for long-range security. That is why I tell the Americans I meet that people don't work only for money. But often when I say it, they respond, "Yes, I see, but how much do you pay the ones who really work hard?" Now this is an important point. When a worker knows he will be getting a raise each year, he can feel so secure that he thinks there is no need to work hard. Workers must be motivated to want to do a good job. We Japanese are, after all, human beings, with much in common with people everywhere. Our evaluation system is complex and is designed to find really capable persons, give them challenging jobs, and let them excel. It isn't the pay we give that makes the difference—it is the challenge and the recognition they get on the job. . . .

In the late sixties a European Commission internal memo on Japan was leaked, and a great stir was created because it referred to the Japanese as "workaholics" who live in "rabbit hutches." There is no doubt that inadequate housing is a major problem in Japan, and nobody could deny that the Japanese are probably the hardest-working people in the world. We have many holidays in Japan, but only about the same number as the United States. We do not give long summer vacations, even to our schoolchildren.

At Sony we were one of the first Japanese companies to close down our factory for one week in the summer, so that everybody could take off at the same time. And we long ago instituted the five-day, forty-hour week. The Japan Labor Standards Act still provides for a maximum forty-eight-hour work week though it is soon to be revised downward, and the average work week in manufacturing is now forty-three hours. But even with up to twenty days of paid vacation a year, Japanese workers managed to take fewer days off and spend more days on the job than workers in the United States and Europe.

It was only in 1983 that banks and financial institutions began to experiment with the five-day week, closing one Saturday a month, and eventually the whole nation will move closer to the five-day week. Still, International Labor Organization data show that Japanese work longer weeks and have fewer labor disputes than workers in the U.S., the U.K., France, or West Germany. What I think this shows is that the Japanese worker appears to be satisfied with a system that is not designed only to reward people with high pay and leisure.

At Sony we learned that the problem with an employee who is accustomed to work only for the sake of money is that he often forgets that he is expected to work for the group entity, and this self-centered attitude of working for himself and his family to the exclusion of the goals of his coworkers and the company is not healthy. It is management's responsibility to keep challenging each employee to do important work that he will find satisfying and to work within the family. To do this, we often reorganize the work at Sony to suit the talents and abilities of the workers.

I have sometimes referred to American companies as being structures like brick walls while Japanese companies are more like stone walls. By that I mean that in an American company, the company's plans are all made up in advance, and the framework for each job is decided upon. Then, as a glance at the classified section of any American newspaper will show, the company sets out to find a person to fit each job. When an applicant is examined, if he is found to be oversized or undersized for the framework, he will usually be rejected. So this structure is like a wall built of bricks: the shape of each employee must fit in perfectly, or not at all.

In Japan recruits are hired, and then we have to learn how to make use of them. They are a highly educated but irregular lot. The manager takes a good long look at these rough stones, and he has to build a wall by combining them in the best possible way, just as a master mason builds a stone wall. The stones are sometimes round, sometimes square, long, large, or small, but somehow the management must figure out how to put them together. People also mature, and Japanese managers must also think of the shapes of these stones as changing from time to time. As the business changes, it becomes necessary to refit the stones into different places. I do not want to carry this analogy too far, but it is a fact that adaptability of workers and managements has become a hallmark of Japanese enterprise.

When Japanese companies in declining or sunset industries change their line of business or add to it, workers are offered retraining and, for the most part, they accept it eagerly. This sometimes requires a family move to the new job, and Japanese families are, again, generally disposed to do this.

Who owns a company anyway? Is it the managers, the shareholders, or the workers? The question is not as simple as it sounds. In Japan we feel that the company must be as much concerned with the workers as with the shareholders. I understand very well the importance of stockholders. We have many of them, and more than 40 percent are non-Japanese. The duty of management is to use their funds effectively and to give them a return on their investment greater than they could have realized if they had used it themselves in some other way. But this does not always mean dividends. It could also mean growth in the value of the stock they hold, which is considered more important than dividends in Japan, since the tax rates on growth of the value of the stock are lower than rates on dividends. A company that reinvests in itself instead of paying out dividends will in the long run be returning more to the shareholders, and certainly more than many companies in the United States and Europe that pay dividends out of fictitious profits.

Sometimes fights between companies, especially in takeover attempts, can lead to some strange battles that drain the vitality from companies. The unfriendly takeover hasn't yet happened in Japan, though one major case was pending at the beginning of 1986 but failed by midyear, and many businessmen think this tactic, common in America, may one day take hold here.

In Japan we believe one of the most important things in a company is the workers' morale; if the workers lose their enthusiasm for the company the company may not survive.

My argument with the American system in this regard can be illustrated by the case of a joint venture company founded with only four million dollars more than fifteen years ago in Japan. The company became phenomenally profitable very quickly and began paying handsome dividends, yet retained plenty of earnings. In fact, by 1985 the company had built two new plants completely out of retained earnings, without resorting to any loans, and there was still over one hundred million dollars in retained earnings in the bank. Then the American partner's parent company came under attack by a corporate raider, and to fend off the raider the company had to buy its own stock at a very high price. To do this they needed cash, and their eyes fell on the joint venture company in Japan and its earnings. They told their partner in Japan that they wanted an immediate dividend declared, taking more than three-fourths of the retained earnings, so they could fight the takeover. The Japanese partner didn't want to sacrifice the earnings, but the pressure was so intense he could not resist.

In Japan we believe one of the most important things in a company is the workers' morale; if the workers lose their enthusiasm for the company the company may not survive. The employees view loss of retained earnings as a threat to their job security. We feel a company that sells its assets has no future. It seems to be difficult for some Westerners to understand this idea we have in Japan that the company belongs not only to the shareholders and the managers. The shareholders can take their money out any time they wish. In America the managers can leave when their contracts expire, and the workers can drift in and out. But I believe in most cases workers want job security, even in the United States and Europe. The workers are the people least able to defend themselves and yet they are indispensable to both management and shareholders. . . .

Once a decision is reached, whether it originally came up from the shop floor or down from the front office, it is the Japanese way for everyone to devote every effort to implementing it without the sniping and backbiting and obstructionism that is sometimes seen in some Western companies.

If I have written a lot about top management and workers so far, I have not meant to exclude middle management, which is so important and in Japan differs from the Western model. Many Japanese companies operate on the "proposal" system, in which middle management is expected to come up with ideas and concepts to be proposed to top management for judgment. This of course differs from the concept of one-man or small-team management that is so common in the

West, and especially in America, where it may be a legacy of the frontier or pioneer spirit. (In Japan we have been exposed to American movies since before the war, and we have come to assess the American spirit in those terms, which is probably not altogether a good or accurate thing. But we like the idea of "fighting spirit," and sometimes in sports and even business we admire the player with the best spirit, even if he loses.) It may sound like a contradiction to say that Japanese companies, as opposed to Western companies, are run by consensus in light of what I have already written about the individuality we prize at Sony and other Japanese companies such as Honda, Matsushita, and some others, where a strong central figure traditionally makes bold decisions, seemingly all by himself. But it is not a contradiction.

The concept of consensus is natural to the Japanese, but it does not necessarily mean that every decision comes out of a spontaneous group impulse. Gaining consensus in a Japanese company often means spending time preparing the groundwork for it, and very often the consensus is formed from the top down, not from the bottom up, as some observers of Japan have written. While an idea may arise from middle management, for example, top management may accept it whole or revise it and seek approval and cooperation all down the line. When I pulled my bluff on the Walkman, threatening to resign, my colleagues knew that I was ahead of them, that I was using all of my experience and knowledge of marketing and consumer psychology in making my decision. And because of it they committed themselves 100 percent to helping make the project a success. If we had failed with the Walkman, I could not have pointed to any market research as the cause of the fiasco.

Once a decision is reached, whether it originally came up from the shop floor or down from the front office, it is the Japanese way for everyone to devote every effort to implementing it without the sniping and backbiting and obstructionism that is sometimes seen in some Western companies.

It is a fine situation to be in, because everybody is doing his share of the work, but getting there can be difficult.

My second son, Masao, worked for Morgan Guaranty Trust in New York and London for two and a half years after he graduated from Georgetown University, and he finds the Japanese way of reaching consensus and planning tedious. His viewpoint is very interesting to me, and very Western. "In a Japanese company they like to have meetings," he complains. "They spend hours and hours at it, and I am always frustrated because I want to know exactly why we are meeting and what we are going to decide. I have trouble keeping my eyes open after the first five minutes. At Morgan I worked in foreign exchange trading, and time was so precious that we didn't waste it in meetings. If we had to make a presentation, we would always give the conclusion first, and if anybody wanted to know how I arrived at the conclusion they would ask. In Japan they like to explain first and they don't tell what they have decided until the very end. But sometimes it is difficult to understand all the explanation without knowing where it is headed."

This is a problem that seems to bother foreigners who are exposed to the system. A journalist who came to Japan to do a lot of interviews of Japanese businessmen visited me near the end of his trip. I asked him what his impression was and he was very frank. He said that after several weeks he had finally figured out how to understand the Japanese: "I don't have to listen to the first part of what they say. I only have to begin to pay attention when they say 'however . . .' because up to then they are expressing everybody else's ideas. After that they are expressing their own ideas." You have to be very patient in dealing with the Japanese. It takes most Japanese a long time to tell people what is really on their minds.

The group management system of Japan, where decisions often are made based on proposals from younger management, can be an advantage for a company. Young managers can be expected to remain with the same company for twenty or thirty years, and in ten years or so they will move into top management jobs. Because of this the young managers are always looking ahead to what they want the company to be when they take it over. If top management looks down at middle and lower management and is always pressing them to show profits this year or next, as is common in the West, and fires these managers for not producing profits, it is killing the company. If a middle manager says his plan or program may not break even now, but will make big profits ten years from now, nobody will listen to him, and he may even be fired.

Our encouragement of long-range plans from up-and-coming employees is a big advantage for our system, despite all the meetings and the time spent in discussing and formulating plans. It enables us to create and maintain something that is rare in business in the West: a company philosophy. Since our employees stay with us a long time, they can maintain a consistent outlook. Company ideals do not change. When I leave the company, the Sony philosophy will continue to exist. In the United States it is rare for any company to have its own philosophy, because whenever top management changes, the new person imposes his own very strong views. In fact very often boards of directors will go far out of the field of business of their company to bring in a new top officer to "clean house" and change everything in the company.

If top management looks down at middle and lower management and is always pressing them to show profits this year or next, as is common in the West, and fires these managers for not producing profits, it is killing the company.

Recently, one of these outsiders came into an American company, closed down several factories, laid off thousands of employees—and was hailed by other executives in articles in *The Wall Street Journal* as a great manager. In Japan such a performance would be considered a disgrace. Closing factories and firing employees and changing corporate direction in a business slump may be the expedient and convenient thing to do and may make the balance sheet look better at the end of the next quarter, but it destroys the company spirit. And when the business rebounds, where will the company go to get experienced workers who will produce quality goods and work hard and loyally for the company?

I think one of the main advantages of the Japanese system of management over the American or the Western system in general is this sense of corporate philosophy. Even if a new executive takes over he cannot change that. In Japan the long-range planning system and the junior management proposal system guarantee that the relationship between top management and junior management remains very close and that over the years they can formulate a specific program of action that will maintain the philosophy of the company. It also may explain why in the initial stages progress is very slow in a Japanese company. But once the company communicates its philosophy to all employees, the company has great strength and flexibility.

When crises hit various industries, such as after the oil shocks of 1973 and 1979, Japanese companies showed this flexibility. Shipbuilding companies began to manufacture antipollution equipment, computer software, even dishwashers. A mining company began to make bowling machines. A textile company, Kanebo, started making cosmetics and is now a major factor in the local market. When movie attendance declined, a Japanese studio started a leisure industry using its movie theater properties.

More recently, with the fall in world demand for steel, steel makers, already the most efficient in the world, have begun to sell their byproduct gases, such as carbon monoxide and hydrogen, to chemical companies as feedstock, which also lessened the chemical companies' reliance on petroleum. Now there is lively competition among Japanese steel makers in marketing these gases.

In another recent example, a Japanese steel company joined with an American semiconductor maker to produce silicon wafers for making masterslices for semiconductor gate arrays and very large-scale integrations for telecommunications circuits. This was the first case of a steel maker entering the market for semicustom logic chips. The steel company's experience as an efficient producer of small-batch customized steel products, using computerized production control and quality assurance systems, seems to make a fine fit with the American manufacturer. Both companies will learn from this experience, and especially the employees of the Japanese firm, who will be looking into the future having had the experience of working in a shrinking industry.

Such corporate moves make more sense to me, as a Japanese manager, than some I have seen in the United States. Americans pride themselves on being rational in their business judgments: the total logic of the American business schools seems to be cold, deemphasizing the human element. We in Japan see the bases for success in business and industry differently. We believe that if you want high efficiency and productivity, a close cordial relationship with your employees, which leads to high morale, is necessary. Sometimes it is more important to generate a sense of affinity than anything else, and sometimes you must make decisions that are, technically, irrational. You can be totally rational with a machine. But if you work with people, sometimes logic often has to take a backseat to understanding.

PART VI

Habits and Idiosyncracies

How should you answer the telephone? Why make appointments? Have you eliminated certain words from your vocabulary? Many great leaders have been taught or have cultivated particular habits to strengthen their character and enhance their performance. A. P. Giannini, founder and chairman of BankAmerica, always answered the telephone himself—it was one his routines to keep in personal touch with customers, employees, and any troublesome issues. Part VI explores these seemingly minor habits, from the eccentric to the strategically logical, that can go a long way in making a great leader. As Ray Kroc, founder of McDonald's, said about personal discipline, "He who wants it may have it! He who wants it may have it! But you've got to want it! Now how much do you want it? What will you pay to get it?" Every leader must sacrifice something to gain something.

JOHN H. JOHNSON
1918 –

John H. Johnson, the most powerful African American businessman in America, was born to abject poverty in rural Arkansas. Fortunately, while the country was in the depths of the Great Depression, he was able to secure his first job through the National Youth Administration, an arm of President Roosevelt's New Deal. In 1942 he seized his destiny by founding *Negro Digest* magazine with $500 he borrowed using his mom's furniture as collateral. Three years later he started *Ebony,* which would become the cornerstone of his empire. In order to succeed in publishing, he knew he had to reverse the prejudice against advertising in African American magazines. Johnson emphatically argued "that Blacks were brand-conscious consumers who wanted to be treated like everyone else—not better, not worse."

Johnson literally had to create the black consumer market in every aspect. When advertisers did come on board, they insisted on using white models. Johnson convinced them to use light-skinned blacks at the very least, and eventually in the 1960s real "Blackness." Johnson helped open whole new professions for African Americans, from modeling agencies to marketing firms. But as a pioneer, Johnson had to deal with other companies poaching his employees. To stop the brain drain he made a list of thirty key employees he needed to keep growing and then gave them whatever they wanted. Not one left him, except for retirement or death.

Over the years, he became what he called an ambassador to white America. One of his primary messages was a call for equal opportunity, but with a different spin. In his autobiography, he reflected, "Enlightened self-interest; that was my theme. I asked corporate leaders to act not for Blacks, not for civil rights, but for their corporations and themselves." As blacks were given more opportunity to earn more money, they in turn bought more goods and services from corporate America. Everyone profited. Although faced with so many overwhelming business and social issues, Johnson refused to give up as he fought for his company and his race. His early persistence became an addictive habit. Both the pain of failure and his immutable drive are exemplified in *Failure Is a Word I Don't Accept.*

Failure Is a Word I Don't Accept

John H. Johnson

We were a legend after only six months of publication. And it seemed on the surface that everything was going my way.

I was turning deals left and right, I had two hot magazines, and I was selling 400,000 copies a month.

I had it made.

Right?

Wrong.

Success was killing me.

The more *Ebony*s I sold, the more money I lost.

And bills were piling up.

I owed the printer and the engraver and suppliers all over town.

They were singing my praises in Harlem and Hollywood, and I was hiding in my office to avoid my creditors.

The problem was obvious to anyone who could read a balance sheet.

I was selling too many magazines without a supporting advertising foundation, and I was confronted with three interlocking problems.

The first was the economics of slick paper. Which cost money. Big money.

The second problem was the economics of printing a magazine with quality reproduction on million-dollar presses.

Again money.

Big money.

The third problem was the economics of numbers.

Two hundred thousand magazines with slick paper and good reproduction require more trees, ink, and postage stamps than 100,000 magazines.

Three hundred thousand cost more than 200,000.

And so on.

I remember firing a young man for using the word failure.

The situation would have been funny if it hadn't been so serious. The glamorous *Ebony* was getting all the attention, and all the praise, but the steady, undramatic *Negro Digest*, 100,000 to 150,000 copies monthly with relatively small production costs, was paying the bills. But there was a limit to the debt structure *Negro Digest* could carry. The runaway success of *Ebony* was stretching the *Negro Digest* corset to its breaking point. And if *Negro Digest* collapsed, John H. Johnson and the whole structure were going down with it.

Why didn't I rein in *Ebony* and cut back on its growth?

I couldn't. It was a simple matter of arithmetic. The more *Ebony* readers, the more potential advertisers.

Why didn't I walk away from the *Ebony* sweepstakes?

You've got to be kidding.

Walk away from a potential gold mine that dwarfed anything I'd ever dreamed of?

No way.

There was no way I was going to give up a publication which had grown in a short time from 25,000 to nearly half a million. I wasn't confused. I knew what I was doing. The only question was: Could I find continuous advertising support before the new magazine wrecked me and my company?

And so, as we headed into the backstretch of 1946—the most dangerous and difficult year in my personal and corporate life—my position was roughly this: I had a tiger by the tail and I couldn't afford to hang on or let it go.

For the moment—for a *brief* moment—I considered the possibility of failure. But the mere thought of the word made my body shake and my heart pound, and I banished it once and for all from my life and vocabulary.

I remember firing a young man for using the word *failure.*

"Nothing personal," I said, "but I'm too insecure myself to have people around me who believe that failure is a possibility. Failure is a word that I don't accept."

I dismissed another associate who kept trying to tell me that I couldn't make it.

"I've got to fire you," I said. "I'm not sure I can make it myself. The last thing I need is someone telling me that I can't make it."

The energy I sought, then and now, was the energy that comes from focusing all your powers, like a beam, on a single point.

Failure: I was at war with the word and all its variations.

The word I wanted to hear, then and now, was *success.* The energy I sought, then and now, was the energy that comes from focusing all your powers, like a beam, on a single point. I used to lock myself up in my office and say the word *success* out loud, over and over, like a Buddhist monk chanting his mantra. I used to say to myself, "John Johnson, you can make it. John Johnson, you can make it. John Johnson, you can make it, John Johnson, *you can and must make it.*"

When things got real tough, I'd call my mother and she would say, "You can make it."

I told her one day in perhaps the worst week of my life, "Mother, it looks like I'm going to fail."

"Son," she said, "are you trying hard?"

"Yes."

"*Real* hard?"

"Yes."

"Well," she said, closing the conversation, "whenever you're trying hard, you're never failing. The only failure is failing to try."

I also called Mary McLeod Bethune, the former National Youth Administration executive who headed Bethune-Cookman College. Mrs. Bethune, who was another one of the most unforgettable characters I've known, was short and black as polished ebony. She was not what the world considers beautiful, but she had so much soul force and authority that when she walked into a room all eyes were pulled to her, as if to a magnet. I was a graduate of her NYA program, and she considered me one of her boys. It was only natural for me to turn to her when the difficulties mounted.

"Hang on," she told me. "Have faith, keep trying." She paused and added:

"The project is too good to end, the Lord wouldn't want it to end."

I'm convinced that the only way to get ahead in this world is to live and sell dangerously.

Years later, when I met W. Clement Stone for the first time, I told him, "I've been practicing PMA—Positive Mental Attitude—since I started my first business. I didn't know what to call it, and I didn't know how to define it, but I was doing it—and it helped me survive."

The reason I survived is that I refused to believe the signs that said I was defeated. And I dared to do things I couldn't afford to do.

And I'm convinced that the only way to get ahead in this world is to live and sell dangerously. You've got to live beyond your means. You've got to commit yourself to an act or a vision that pulls you further than you want to go and forces you to use your hidden strengths.

For you're stronger than you think you are. And what you need—what all men and women need—is an irrevocable act that forces you, on pain of disgrace, jail, or death, to be the best you that you can be.

Kemmons Wilson
1913 –

Kemmons Wilson not only founded Holiday Inns but is considered the father of the modern motel. His success story typifies the American dream. His father died when he was only nine months old, and his mother struggled to keep food on the table. Starting at the age of seven, Wilson held part-time jobs to help out. In 1930 he dropped out of high school to join the workforce permanently, making $12 a week with a Memphis cotton broker. A couple of jobs later he had saved up enough money to build his mother a house, which he did. Wilson liked construction so much that he started his own business. During the post–World War II home construction boom, he found himself in the right place at the right time and became a millionaire which gave birth to one of his favorite axioms: "Remember that success requires half luck and half brains."

The idea for a motel chain came about when Wilson took his family by car to Washington, D.C., in 1951. Motels near the highway were scarce and not always particularly clean or hospitable. When he returned home he decided to build his own motel chain, and hired an architect to draft plans for a truly family-oriented motel. Beginning in 1952, the first four motels were built around Memphis just off the highways to cater to travelers, which was a key to early success. Another one of Wilson's successful innovations was setting up a chain-wide reservation system in 1965, so that the customer could call one number and make reservations anywhere.

Early expansion stalled, however, so Wilson decided to franchise. The company went public in 1957, and by 1960 there were more than 100 hotels. Wilson remained active with the company until he suffered a heart attack in 1979 and decided to retire. At that time there were 1,759 Holiday Inns in fifty countries. Even though he was already a multimillionaire, he had worked incessantly to build his chain. Hard work is his number-one tip for success. He said, "Work only half a day; it makes no difference which half—it can be either the first 12 hours or the last 12 hours." Wilson divulges some of his other habits in *Take Your Idea and See It Through.*

Take Your Idea and See It Through

Kemmons Wilson

Sometimes, the first step is the hardest—coming up with an idea. Getting an idea should be like sitting on a pin. It should make you jump up and do something. I've had a great many ideas in my life. And some were good, some were great, and some I'd prefer to forget about.

The important thing is to take your idea and see it through. Not all of your ideas are going to be good ones. But just remember, "A man who wins may have been counted out several times, but he didn't hear the referee."

Of course, my rise was not without some failures. But it's a mistake to worry too much about making mistakes. A man who never makes mistakes is also the man who never does anything.

I guess I've made as many or more mistakes than anyone in the world. But I try to learn from my mistakes and profit from my failures. And of course, it is stupid to make the same mistake twice. However, I've done that too.

My good friend, who is now deceased, Norman Vincent Peale, wrote a book: *Enthusiasm Makes the Difference.* This is so very true. Also the lack of enthusiasm makes all the difference in the world in a person's life. It has been said that enthusiasm is the most contagious thing in all of the world.

Personally, I think the lack of it is. Both are like the measles—highly contagious. Very little has been achieved without enthusiasm. And any individual is very old if he has outlived enthusiasm. All we need to be really and truly happy is to have something to be enthusiastic about.

Getting an idea should be like sitting on a pin. It should make you jump up and do something.

Attitude towards life determines life's attitude towards us. Many games have been won or lost simply by the attitude of the players and the participants. Many lives have failed because of the wrong attitude of the individual. As long as the people of this great land are willing to work, then we can know that the American dream is very much alive and there's still hope for us.

I firmly believe that attitude is one of the most important things in a person's life. Attitude is a magic word in every language. Learn to smile and be happy. Make the most of whatever comes to you in your life. Whenever there's a smile in your heart, you just can't keep it a secret, for your face and your actions will reveal it.

In fact, the smile on your face is the light in the window that tells people that you are at home. Although there are hundreds of languages in the world, a smile speaks all of them. In fact, a smile is a curve that can set a lot of things straight. It is not necessary to know a person's name to greet him with a smile.

You know, success is built by doing everything the best possible way. If you really want to be happy in your life, you must learn to enjoy and even love your work. If you can't, then it's high time for you to be looking for another job.

Success may not be yours just for the asking. It can certainly be yours if you are willing to work hard enough for it. Decide now that you're going to be successful, and then put every ounce of physical and mental energy into the effort of making that prediction come true.

A 40-hour week has no charm for me.
I'm looking for a 40-hour day.

I've always been a firm believer in hard work. I believe the freedom to work is second only to our religious freedom. Work is the master key that opens the door to all opportunities.

If a person truly knows what he wants out of life and is willing to work hard, then he can rest and be sure that life will pay its richest dividends to the person.

I believe that work is not a man's doom, but a man's blessing.

A 40-hour week has no charm for me. I'm looking for a 40-hour day.

"I have worked in boom times and in recessions, in the Great Depression and in time of war. Our government has had Republicans and Democrats and conservatives and liberals. Through all of this I have seen our free enterprise system survive and provide the economic means to build the greatest society in the history of the world.

My feeling is that the free-enterprise system is in good shape for the 1990s. And this is because the system provides rewards for the entrepreneur who recognizes opportunities and acts on them.

I've seen a lot of changes over the span of my business career and I guess the only perfect science is hindsight.

There's no question that either you take charge of change, or change will take charge of you.

Ray Kroc
1902 – 1984

"It's dog-eat-dog, and if someone tries to get me I'll get them first. It's the American way of survival of the fittest." This quote comes from the man who built the McDonald's fast-food chain and gave us the congenial Ronald McDonald. Ray Kroc was also a fighter who at fifteen lied about his age so he could join the army during World War I. Perseverance, in particular, was his trademark, and a quality he needed when he became a salesman after the war. Kroc was selling milkshake machines when he first met the McDonald brothers in California. Of this first encounter, he said, "I was amazed. This little drive-in having people standing in line. . . . If they could have 100 stores like that one, I could sell them 800 multimixers."

Instead of selling them 800 mixers, Kroc sold them on the idea that he could sell franchises based on their setup and that everyone would make lots of money. From the start, Kroc set strict guidelines for franchisees, who were allowed only one store until they proved themselves worthy. His dedication was all-consuming; he wrote in his autobiography, "I believe in God, family, and McDonald's—and in the office, that order is reversed." In 1961, Kroc built Hamburger University, the first full-time training facility in the industry, so he could spread his gospel effectively.

Another major contributor to McDonald's success was that Kroc demanded complete conformity, from hamburger size, to employee uniforms, to store design. McDonald's industry leadership in this area was an extension of Kroc's mind: "I don't think in that 'grand design' pattern. I work from the part to the whole, and I don't move on to the large-scale ideas until I have perfected the small details." While control was critical, Kroc encouraged grass-roots entrepreneurship among the franchises because he knew that he was not blessed with a new product touch. The Big Mac and the Egg McMuffin, among other top sellers, were invented by individual franchisees and fueled the company's growth. While Kroc respected creative talent, as a leader he forever relied on rigid self-discipline to succeed, which he explains in the following selection.

Self-Discipline Called Key to Success

Ray Kroc

The longer I live, the more importance I attach to a man's ability to manage and discipline himself. The longer I live, the more firmly convinced I become that the essential factor that lifts one man above his fellows in terms of achievement and success is his greater capacity for self-discipline. Talent plays its part, but talent or aptitude is not *the* difference. Every day in every field of endeavor, we see talented men whose special abilities are wasting away, contributing little to the success of the individual or the good of mankind. And every day we observe others who are less gifted but who have accomplished more.

Education is a priceless aide to success, but education is not the difference. The educated derelict is a common sight, and so is the man who has achieved resounding success without the opportunity for, or the advantage of, a formal education. I can only conclude that, while formal schooling is an important advantage, it is not a guarantor of success—nor is its absence a fatal handicap. Is the difference a matter of differing levels of intelligence? I don't believe so—even though a person with a superior intellect is fortunate and thus possesses a running start toward success. But the relationship between intelligence and accomplishment is something less than constant, and we frequently encounter both the brilliant ne'er-do-well and his opposite number—the man of average intelligence, but superior achievements.

For my part, I have concluded that the quality which sets one man apart from another, the factor which lifts one man to every achievement to which he reasonably aspires—while the other is caught in a slough of mediocrity for all the years of his life—is not talent, nor formal education, nor luck, nor intellectual brilliance. It is talent coupled with industry and personal efficiency that will produce high levels of achievement. Education without self-discipline is of limited and academic value, but, combined with diligence and strong will and properly directed, it becomes productive and practical. Yes, I'm totally convinced that the essential difference between one man and the next—one of whom becomes a man of achievement and distinction, while the other remains one of the crowd—is the former's greater capacity to manage himself. The man with the capacity for self-discipline can tell himself to do the truly important things first. Therefore, if there is not enough time to go around and something must be neglected, it will be the less essential tasks. It is this man that can carry out his own instructions to do what he says he will do and make himself finish the job which he starts.

The longer I live, the more firmly convinced I become that the essential factor that lifts one man above his fellows in terms of achievement and success is his greater capacity for self-discipline.

Here is the most interesting thing about the capacity for self-discipline. He who wants it may have it! He who wants it may have it! But you've got to want it! Now how much do you want it? What will you pay to get it? He who wants it may have it! The capacity for self-discipline is something we can and must generate within ourselves. The one ingredient we most need for success is our for the asking, for the wanting, if we only want it enough.

I'm reminded of a story about the great pianist who gave a marvelous concert and at the end a lady rushed up to him and said, "I'd give anything in this world if I could play like that!" And he said, "No you wouldn't." She could have, if she wanted to; anybody could. I know, as a piano player, that piano playing is mechanical to a great extent. But it's the dedication, the disciplining to practice that makes the difference. And when you're talking about a concert pianist, somebody who's along in years, he has been practicing for years—years of practice by the hours, several hours a day every single day. Practice, practice, practice, practice. Sacrifice and discipline—that's what it gets down to. And so he said, "No you wouldn't," meaning that what she said she wanted to attain she wouldn't pay the price to get it—to discipline herself to do the studying and practicing required to be a concert pianist.

Here is the most interesting thing about the capacity for self-discipline. He who wants it may have it! . . . But you've got to want it!

So here's what I'm saying; you've got to find out what it is that you want and then pay the price in self-discipline to get it, and you'll love it. And you'll be the happiest person that ever lived.

Dave Thomas
1932 –

Who can forget the Wendy's TV commercial, "Where's the Beef?" Since then the founder of the Wendy's restaurant chain is known for appearing in his own commercials that display his dry sense of humor and hefty girth. Back in his youth, Thomas ate many a meal in cheap restaurants with his dad, and it was then that he decided to be a restauranteur. He liked to eat, period. During the Korean War, he volunteered and attended the army's Cook and Baker School. According to Thomas, feeding 2,000 hungry soldiers a day taught him "some important skills about the big picture of feeding a lot of people."

After the army, he worked as a short-order cook for a man who also happened to own four Kentucky Fried Chicken franchises. Luckily for Thomas, the franchises were failing, so his boss offered him a deal: If Thomas could turn around the KFCs, he would receive 45 percent ownership. Thomas made good, then cashed out for $1 million in 1968 and started Wendy's with his proceeds. He emphasized a homey feeling in his restaurants and fresh burgers that didn't sit under heat lamps. Both quality and image were key, for as Thomas explained in his autobiography, "Food is a personal thing, and it's tied closely to family life. People want to know the values of the person ladling it out." The way those values are communicated are important, which is why he became a highly visible spokesman for Wendy's.

As an adopted child who moved a dozen times in fifteen years, Thomas knew work to be a "constant companion" and recognized that through hard work he couldn't help but succeed. But with success came mistakes, too, and he admits that one of his biggest was resting on his laurels after Wendy's initial success. Instead, he should have been planning for the future and looking for ways to improve. He said, "Not looking for problems is a problem itself." But he concluded that mistakes make the woman or the man, and he rededicated himself. One way to prevent mistakes, he believes, is to develop routines. For example, every month Wendy's polls customers because Thomas believes it's critical "to keep checking to make sure the customer understands who you are." Thomas delves further into the need for routines in the following selection.

The Wonder of Routine

Dave Thomas

Wendy's president Gordon Teter may be the most routine guy I've ever met, and I mean that as a compliment. He comes from a deeply religious family. At Purdue University, he was a great scholar, quite a football player, and a campus leader. Gordon's really smart. Even better, he has a strong streak of common sense. I think he can handle any job at Wendy's. One of the great things that Gordon taught us in running the Wendy's business was to keep it focused and keep it balanced.

For a while, Wendy's was what I would call promotion-crazy. One month we would promote our single hamburgers at 99¢ and the average restaurant would sell thousands of them. The next month we'd promote chicken sandwiches at a special price, and most of our restaurants would sell a couple thousand of those. All this commotion brought in tons of customers, so you would think that it was a great idea.

Honestly, it was a lousy idea, because a restaurant that sells thousands of hamburgers one month is a different restaurant from one that sells a thousand chicken sandwiches. Because of our advertising, we were basically changing what kind of restaurant we were every thirty days. That's what Gordon told us.

One of the things that made Wendy's a better restaurant was actually putting a limit on the number of good ideas that we had—or at least the number that we decided to *act on* at any one time. Instead of having fifty good ideas a month and doing them all hit-or-miss, we decided we would have only two or three good ideas and execute the heck out of them. We slowed ourselves down and learned our routine. A lot of people try to do and be everything—too many things—at once. Just do what you can and be who you are.

One of the things that made Wendy's a better restaurant was actually putting a limit on the number of good ideas that we had—or at least the number that we decided to act on at any one time.

It's not easy to be disciplined, and that brings me back to Gordon Teter. Not because he's a Wendy's guy, but because he is who he is. Let's look a little bit closer at Gordon's background to see how he got such a knack for discipline.

You don't have to outfox people. Mostly, you just have to do the basics well, time and again.

Gordon's father, Fred, was an executive with the drug company Eli Lilly out of Indianapolis. Gordon's grandfather owned a farm, but it was really Gordon's father and his brother Jim who ran it. And Gordon, too. The farm was a good-sized operation with corn and soybeans, cows and pigs. Gordon pulled his weight on the farm, which meant tending to the animals at five in the morning and in the evening, too. It also spelled an extra push from everybody during planting and at harvest time.

Gordon's mother, Bonnie, was a substitute teacher. She came out of a foster home and really appreciated the value of a family and an education. So you can understand why Gordon hit the books as hard as he did. Gordon's home was steeped in strong Christian values.

This all explains a lot about Gordon. But where did he learn all this great stuff about disciplining yourself to keep things simple? Maybe it was when he was playing high-school football at Lawrence Central in the small town of Lawrence, Indiana. His team won a lot of games. What was their secret? Seventy-five percent of their offense was just four different plays. The other 25 percent were little "wrinkles" on those four plays. You don't have to outfox people. Mostly, you just have to do the basics well, time and again.

A lot of folks today don't like routine. Not me. I'm all for it. . . . It can cure the most unexpected things.

Gordon did a lot as a kid, but he didn't try to do too many different things—just as his football team was disciplined and didn't try to do too many fancy maneuvers. I think that most American families are too busy trying to do too many good things for themselves and for their kids—ballet class, swimming team, soccer tryouts. No kid has to play five sports, and no parent has to belong to five church committees. When you take on that big a load, how much can you really do well? Can your life ever really follow a sensible routine—the kind of routine that lets you get things done well, day in and day out?

A lot of folks today don't like routine. Not me. I'm all for it. Take clean restaurants, for instance. If there ever was a routine that needed following it's getting a restaurant ready to open for customers every day. As I travel around the country visiting Wendy's restaurants, the managers always know I'm coming. Not surprisingly, a lot of extra effort goes on before I get there to make the restaurants sparkling clean. I'm glad they do it, but I wish I could get every manager to act like I was going to visit their restaurant every day of the year.

Routine can help in lots of other ways, too. It can cure the most unexpected things. Being short in the cash register is a problem in many restaurants. Sometimes it's internal theft. Often it's making change carelessly, especially when there are a lot of customers. Retailers and restaurants have all kinds of ways of fighting shorts in the register. Video cameras, surprise inspections, even undercover spies. But do you know what the single best weapon against register shortages is? None of the above. It's simply the discipline of routine reporting. Having people call in the shortages for their restaurant to the home office every day. The shortages could be low. They could be high. Whatever they are, you don't beat people up over the phone for what they report. But the simple fact that they have to report their shortages makes people pay more attention to what they're doing and helps keep a handle on the problem.

Can your life ever really follow a sensible routine—the kind of routine that lets you get things done well, day in and day out?

Families have routine disciplines. Or at least they should:

- Homework is a routine, and there should also be routine reporting of how things are going in the different classes.
- Chores are a routine, and the reporting about what got done and what didn't should be pretty clear.

- Church, praying, or spending some time with a sick or lonely relative—those are good routines.
- Eating together and talking a few nights a week is a good routine for a family to fall into. (Heck, what did you expect a restaurant guy to say?)

Sandra L. Kurtzig

All she wanted was a decent job and to start a family—little did Sandra L. Kurtzig know that one day *Business Week* would name her one of America's most influential business leaders. After earning a master's degree in aeronautical engineering at Stanford University, Kurtzig decided she wasn't cut out for hard-core engineering. Instead she was attracted to the nuances of selling. In 1971 Kurtzig was selling computer time-sharing for a division of General Electric when a potential customer in Silicon Valley told her she should quit and start her own company. Later she reflected, "The hardest part of going into business for myself was simply the idea of it: leaving the security of a large corporation like GE to become a contract programmer, a gypsy, wandering from company to company, living off my wits."

Kurtzig did go into business for herself, writing software programs for manufacturing companies that tracked inventory, sales, shipping, and the like. In 1973 her company, ASK Computer Systems, had two employees and a gross income of only $50,000. But Kurtzig had resolve and boldness going for her. When it came to deal making, she said, "You need good sense to know what to ask for, guts to ask for what you want, diplomacy to know how to ask for it, and leverage to get it." Her break came when she convinced Hewlett-Packard to put her software into some of their commercial minicomputers.

Kurtzig took her company public in 1981 and four years later she left day-to-day operations to spend time with her children. But then the firm stumbled and fell, so in 1989 she initiated a leveraged buyout and retook control. Kurtzig made a list of priorities, the most important one being that the company had to regain its entrepreneurial vision. "I'm an entrepreneur," she said, "and my style is aggressive, risk-taking, persistent, and demanding. I believe, as entrepreneurs must, in the survival of the fittest." Part of that survival depended on how Kurtzig was viewed by Wall Street analysts. For example, back in 1982 when she wanted a divorce, she was advised to wait a year because Wall Street might react badly and beat up ASK's stock. In the following selection Kurtzig provides some poignant tips on how to deal with the Street and being *In the Public Eye.*

In the Public Eye

Sandra L. Kurtzig

I had explained a bit about the stock market to Andy, my nine-year-old, and when ASK went public, he saved his allowance and did some odd jobs to buy a single eleven-dollar share. He had his eye on an eighteen-dollar model airplane. Every day he checked the paper to see how the stock was doing, and at the end of the first week, when it was only at thirteen, he was disappointed. I told him that things usually didn't happen so fast but that if I worked hard, pretty soon, maybe, he'd have his eighteen dollars. This seemed to satisfy him, but a few weeks later, when the stock was up two more points, he came back to me and said, "Mommy, the stock's only at fifteen dollars. You must not be working hard enough."

Andy was no different from anyone else who bought ASK stock, whether an institutional investor or a personal friend. They all were impatient, hoping for a quick return on their investments. When they got it—and over the years many made millions on ASK stock—everything was hunky-dory. But if they lost money, many were bitter and angry and, in some cases, let me know about it. Wanting to do a good job, wanting to please, I knew as long as they held the stock, they had power over me. They could check on ASK's value and tell whether I worked hard enough every day. Everyone could, including Andy, my parents, and my parents' friends. Paul Ely

[Kurtzig's financial adviser] was right. As a public company you were in the public eye, constantly judged, like it or not.

As for ASK's past successes, they were just that—history. Stockholders weren't paying eleven dollars a share for what ASK had already accomplished. They were betting on what it would accomplish in the future.

So aside from the excitement of running a public business, of reading about myself and ASK in nearly every newspaper and magazine in the country, of being on talk shows, being asked to sit on boards, being invited to hotsy-totsy social events, and getting far, far more attention than I deserved, I spent my first year as CEO of a public company scared to death. Maybe we did just have a tiger by the tail with MANMAN?* Maybe our success was just dumb luck? Maybe our competitors who'd never really made a convincing grab for the pie were getting smarter? Maybe, maybe. And everywhere there were analysts watching for that first misstep, that flat quarter, the new product that bombs. It was a fearful situation to be in, and though I had a very supportive board of directors and excellent vice-presidents, I felt as if I were facing it alone.

That's it for the complaining. The fact is, I wanted ASK to be a public company, and for the most part I thrived on our new, higher profile. I particularly liked working on the quarter system. I enjoyed having to prepare a report card to my stockholders every three months and the challenge of improving quarter by quarter. It suited my goal-oriented personality perfectly. I've always felt more comfortable when problems are broken down into manageable chunks, and that is precisely what making the quarter is all about. It's like cramming for a test. You turn all your attention to the obstacle ahead—your financial goal for that quarter. And when you surmount it, you tool up for the next. At the same time the trick is not to fall into the trap so many U.S. companies do of living quarter to quarter. You've got to balance quarterly performance with long-term goals.

*MANMAN was the name for Kurtzig's franchise software program used by small to medium-sized manufacturers to manage their business.

After we went public, about 10 percent of my time went into talking with and appearing before the financial community. This was a restless, fickle crowd, these analysts, brokers, and fund managers, and demanded a lot of attention, mostly at a never-ending stream of financial conferences. If you didn't show up, you were conspicuous by your absence. "What's going on at ASK? Are they being acquired? Are they having problems?" So I showed up.

Rather than just make an appearance to pitch my stock, I used the conferences to generate sales. Given a forum, I never failed to say "Hey, I know you guys are looking real seriously at buying stock in such and such company, but do you realize it's thinking of buying an ASK system? If it does, it'll be a better company for you to invest in."

Traveling from conference to conference, I created a perception in the marketplace that if a company was using MANMAN, it was probably managing its manufacturing operation better than if it used a competitor's system. It even got to a point where almost every manufacturing company presenting at a conference was asked if it was using an ASK system. All this attention was not lost on the venture capitalists in attendance, who encouraged the start-up companies they were investing in to adopt MANMAN.

I also developed a scheme for getting analysts to provide us with sales leads. I passed out cards headlined GIVE ASK THE BUSINESS, with space for their names and the names of two manufacturing companies that could benefit from ASK's software. We also inserted the cards in our company newsletter, annual reports, press kits, and the promotional brochures we sent to brokers, analysts, customers, prospects, and shareholders. The response wasn't enormous, but with our product costing more than $200,000 we didn't need thousands of leads—just a handful that panned out.

We also did some advertising, including a combined TV and *Wall Street Journal* print campaign that won our agency, Chiat-Day, a Clio—the Oscar of advertising—and recognition at the London International Advertising Awards for the best print trade campaign of the year. In the end, however,

I'm convinced it was ASK's continued appearances at trade shows and seminars that really sold our systems.

Whatever we were doing, we must have been doing it right. By 1982 ASK was the eighth-fastest-growing public company in the United States and the nation's fastest-growing software company. Venture capitalists were scouring the countryside looking for another ASK to invest in, whereas just a few years back VCs who heard I was "in software" often thought I was manufacturing women's lingerie.

In a poll of analysts conducted by the *Wall Street Transcript* I was selected one of the top three CEOs in the computer software industry. *Working Woman* hailed me as the "Queen of Silicon Valley." A local radio station asked me to be its guest weather reporter! I was getting invited to the social events and dinners of people I'd never met before, sometimes even reading the next day about my appearance at a dinner or party I hadn't attended. And everyone wanted my opinion. On September 30, 1981, most people didn't know my name. On October 1, whatever I thought about any topic was newsworthy.

In just a few years more than ten thousand articles about ASK appeared in magazines and newspapers around the world, usually focusing on me. A private person, I was uncomfortable with all the scrutiny. I also felt guilty that I was getting all the attention and that the others in the company weren't. One day I mentioned my concern in a meeting with Marty, Tom, Ken, and Bob. They'd just returned from a management development session put on by our accounting firm, Arthur Young, at which they'd been asked to write out their own job descriptions, and mine as well. For mine everyone had written "To attract the press." Good publicity, they told me, regardless of whether it was centered on me or not, was good for the whole company. It boosted the value of the stock, helped sales, and improved morale. By then more than half the company was in sales offices scattered throughout the United States, and it was important for everyone to read about ASK and see ASK's name on television and in the papers. So I said okay, I'd go along with it.

One day, following a two-week climb of ASK stock for no apparent reason, I got a call from New York, from one of ASK's largest investors. He was planning a trip out west and was wondering if we could have dinner. Halfway through the meal I realized that our dinner was the *only* reason he'd flown from New York to California. I had no idea what was up, but I was my usual chatty self. When we were finished with coffee and about to leave, he suddenly leaned over and held my wrist gingerly.

"I have a very touchy question to ask you," he said. I liked him and wanted to put him at ease.

"Ask anything," I reassured.

"I just don't know how to go about asking you this but, but—"

At this point I was getting nervous. "But what?"

"Well, there's a rumor going around—"

"A rumor?" I couldn't imagine what it was.

Suddenly he blurted out, "A rumor that you have a terminal illness."

It's funny how you react to something like that. My first impulse was to laugh if only to release the tension. I tried, but the laugh wouldn't come. Oddly enough, my next thought was that maybe the rumor was true and I hadn't been told. I quickly realized it couldn't be; I hadn't been to a doctor in years. Again I tried to muster a laugh but couldn't. Instead, I flashed back to the dinner and replayed our entire conversation. Obviously uncomfortable, he repeated what he'd come three thousand miles to say. "There's a rumor on the Street that you have a terminal illness."

So I said, "Well, if it's true, I haven't been told yet."

"I'm glad to hear it," he said. "I'm truly glad to hear it."

As it turned out, with ASK's stock climbing and climbing, a large brokerage house had sold short thousands of shares of ASK stock, betting, in other words, that the stock price would go down. When it continued to climb and they had to cover their short, millions of dollars were at stake. So they started the rumor about my imminent demise, hoping it would send the stock on a nosedive. It didn't work.

WILLARD F. ROCKWELL, JR.
1914 –

Willard F. Rockwell, Jr., the man who brought us the first space shuttles, also brought his company a long way from the days when it was a modest truck axle manufacturer. Rockwell's father founded what was to become Rockwell International back in 1919. Not long after, the company moved into producing a full line of vehicle and aviation parts. Before the elder Rockwell brought his son on board, he insisted on a solid education and encouraged him to study both engineering and accounting at Penn State. He said to his son, "It's the safest training you can get. When business is good, the bosses want engineers. When it's bad, engineers are the first people they fire, but then they begin looking for accountants to figure out what's wrong."

When the younger Rockwell became president of the company in 1963, he needed those accounting skills and more—in 1967 the firm merged with struggling North American Aviation and was soon losing $1 million a day. And the purpose of the merger with the country's largest aerospace contractor was to create synergy! As a Rockwell executive explained, "Those scientific longhairs throw away ideas every day that should be useful to us. We're going to get out there and go through their wastebaskets." Unfortunately, layoffs were necessary as operations were streamlined. Eventually the company found solid footing. It won a string of government contracts to build the Saturn V rocket engines for the Apollo missions, the fleet of space shuttles, and the B-1 bomber.

Rockwell left the company in 1979 to start a venture that was dedicated to the commercialization of space. "Space," he said, "is where the future is." His grand scheme included buying NASA's space shuttles for launching satellites and carrying out independently funded research. Rockwell was certain that because of government budget constraints, what were traditionally military projects would be spun off to civilians. Rockwell scrapped the space shuttle project when the *Challenger* blew up in 1986. With all his high-flying schemes and experiences, Rockwell made sure he grounded himself in reality from time to time. He explains how he did so in *Reviewing Yourself.*

Reviewing Yourself

Willard F. Rockwell, Jr.

Level with Yourself

William Wordsworth called self-inspection the best cure for self-esteem. But for most executives, objective self-appraisal takes an ample dose of self-discipline. The key role of ego drive in achieving executive success has been too well covered by the management press for me to labor it here. Still, it does take on a special significance for the manager who is seriously interested in identifying his weaknesses and shoring them up. Such an individual finds himself faced with the delicate task of balancing his healthy egoism against a compelling desire for self-improvement.

It's not easy. As a wit points out, "There are two kinds of egotists: Those who admit it, and the rest of us." But another student of business observes on a more sober note: "When a man is really important, the worst adviser he can have is a flatterer."

One fact of high executive life is certain. If flattery is your dish, you can get all you want. For one thing, the average executive *is* much above average in intelligence and capability. Moreover, however humble you may strive to be, you are well aware of your superiority, and you would be less than human if it did not make you just a little smug on occasion.

Adding fuel to the boss's smugness is the respect—sometimes bordering on reverence—of his subordinates. The executive who thinks he's "the greatest" usually finds ample support for his conviction. Particularly if he lets his people know that such support meets with his approval.

The problem then is to retain the ego drive you need to lead men and make crucial decisions, and, at the same time, to assess your performance in an honest and meaningful way. The trick, in my experience, is to keep each of your two identities in its proper perspective. First there is the "you" you would like to be. That's the one that gets flattery. Then there is the real "you," the executive with many powerful strengths, but with a sprinkling of weaknesses mixed in. Recognizing the weaknesses that exist is an essential ingredient of successful self-appraisal. From what I have seen, the executive who believes himself totally lacking in weaknesses is usually the weakest of all.

One might also argue that no executive would deliberately take an action that he knows to be weak. And there you have the hub of the problem. To pinpoint your weaknesses and take steps to correct them, you are going to need help. And the way to get help is to slap down subservience on the one hand and gain skill in identifying objectivity on the other.

Just as you will need backup evidence in your support appraisals of subordinates, so you will need backup evidence in assessing your own abilities. But in this case it will be less easy to come by. You cannot always tell a subordinate: "Skip the flattery, Bill. Tell me what you really think." You may be able to say this to a close associate at times, but rarely to a lower echelon employee.

Still, there are ways of getting around the dilemma. For one thing, you are as good as your program and ideas. Agreement with what you do constitutes an endorsement of your performance. Disagreement, if you take positive steps to discourage blind endorsement, can serve as a powerful appraisal tool. The idea is to get the whys and wherefores and to clamp down on the "yes men" in your organization. If a subordinate claims that his views coincide with yours, find out why. Where possible, explore his thinking before you reveal your own decision. Require him to come up with specific arguments to either support or refute your thinking. And mold your heroes of the men who show enough courage to intelligently oppose the boss.

Place a Premium on Courage

It is not always easy to listen to the sound of other drummers when the one you want to hear beats loudly in your ears.

Several months ago, a company I know developed an exciting new product line. The marketing people boiled over with enthusiasm. The president, a strongly growth-oriented executive, was swept along by the tide of this fervor. He painted a glowing picture of the potential to the financial vice-president, an astute executive whose views always had been carefully weighed by the president in formulating his own decisions. Privately, the man was not so sure the product line was ready for market. He had heard rumblings and grumblings from Manufacturing and Engineering regarding problems they were running into. But, reluctant to buck such formidable opposition as Marketing and the chief executive, he said nothing. The line was introduced to the marketplace.

As it turned out, the introduction was premature. The technical and production segments were unable to keep pace with Marketing's go-go enthusiasm. Not all items were fully developed. Not all bugs were completely eradicated. Almost from the first day, customer complaints started pouring in. The company's excellent quality image was seriously undermined.

The president, crestfallen, called in a consultant to determine why and how the blunder had been made. His findings, emerging mainly from a series of soul-searching interviews, were blunt and revealing. The financial executive, manufacturing and engineering managers, and others bared their true feelings which in the main had been squelched by the Marketing-president combine.

"The devil's advocates were never given a chance to air their views," the consultant said simply.

As a result of the consulting experience, meaningful changes were made. The promotion and compensation machinery was altered so that automatic increases and advancement for top and middle management were discontinued. Performance was more closely and systematically appraised, with an eye on specific contributions. An "executive sorting" system was installed whereby the status quo advocates and bandwagon hoppers, comfortably ensconced in their ruts, were distinguished from the company's courageous climbers.

The president learned, in seeking counsel, to call on the climbers and sidestep the "yes men." He also learned to cloak his own opinions so as to get the free and unbiased independent judgment of others. "I found out, too," he told me recently, "that if you want the truth, you have to convince people of your willingness to accept it."

Single Out Your Lesser Strengths

From what I have seen, successful top executives in general have considerable vision and widespread experience. On the whole they are intelligent people, widely read, intellectually curious. Yet there are but few men who, like Winston Churchill, possess the brand of genius which communicates itself to everything they touch. Though generalists in the main, most executives have talents that center strongly about a specific area of administration—law, finance, marketing, engineering—depending on their business background and training.

My point is this. Though top executive responsibilities cover a wide scope of company activities, traditionally the high-level manager possesses maximum strength and confidence in some areas, a measure of uncertainty in others. The executive with a heavy technical background, for example, may find himself a trifle testy when called upon to make judgments in accounting or marketing areas. The executive who comes up via the marketing route may feel even more uncomfortable in dealing with manufacturing requirements.

Writing for *Nation's Business,* Research Institute of America editor Auren Uris asks: "Are you a four-way expert?" He divides the executive's people. The paperwork aspect, according to the author, requires the accountant's keen eye for detail. Planning calls for imagination and creativity. To excel procedurally, one needs financial talents and ability to "think technical." Handling people skillfully requires a sensitivity to individual feelings and attitudes, the ability to "think human."

As Uris points out, few of us are flexible enough to master all of these diverse qualities. The ideal in self-appraisal is to recognize our greater strengths, our lesser strengths, our outright weaknesses for what they are.

Once these are accurately defined and solidly ingrained, we can concentrate on applying weaknesses and strengths to the improvement of our personal productivity. An executive can ask: Am I cashing in on my financial acumen to the maximum? Is my superficial understanding of chemical processing hindering my performance in any way? Should I devote more effort to studying certain aspects of the operation? Should I be shoring up a specific weakness, or should I compensate for it by delegating the responsibility?

The idea, of course, is to relate such questions to your own operation. A by-product of self-appraisal that I find particularly fruitful is the pinpointing of areas where weaknesses block or delay profit objectives. Once the situation has been spotlighted, remedying the problem becomes merely a matter of course.

WILLIAM WRIGLEY, JR.
1861 – 1932

Always a free-wheeling spirit, William Wrigley, Jr., the future gum magnate, ran away from home at the age of eleven to escape working in the family's soap manufacturing business. He went to New York, where he sold newspapers, but soon was back home. In 1891 he left for good, going to Chicago with $32 in his pocket, determined to make his fortune. In the beginning Wrigley continued to sell soap, offering a free can of baking powder as an incentive to his buyers. Soon the baking powder proved more popular, so he started selling it exclusively while now offering two pieces of gum as incentive. In a continuing twist of fate, the gum became more popular, so Wrigley went into the gum business.

Wrigley said that his rules of business included using good judgment, thinking hard, and acting quickly. But his number-one principle: Appeal to the consumer either through incentives or advertising. He was fanatical about it, once stating "Babies who never heard about you are being born every day, and people who once knew you forget you if you don't keep them reminded constantly." On at least two occasions he sent chewing gum to every person listed in every phone book in the United States. And who can forget the simple yet enduring slogan plastered on billboards for almost a hundred years: "The Flavor Lasts." But not all promotions worked. In 1902 Wrigley blew $100,000 on advertising in New York and didn't make a dent. He cracked the market $350,000 later. Wrigley willingly acknowledged, "A fellow can't always guess right, but the balance in the end is on the right side."

By 1922 Wrigley had factories in Chicago, Brooklyn, Toronto, and Sidney, making 10 billion sticks of gum a year. He bought the Chicago Cubs baseball team and took them from the bottom of their division to the World Series. When they won the National League pennant in 1929, he told the team to go party and "no expense account under $50 would be honored." While a free spirit who loved a good time, Wrigley was also a practical businessman. Both traits are evident in *I Never Make an Appointment,* which is about dealing with people problems, managing precious time, and making it to baseball games.

I Never Make an Appointment

William Wrigley, Jr.

Most business men with large interests and heavy demands on their time will see callers only by appointment. I never make an appointment. I see a good many people in the course of an average business day—but none of them have come by appointment. They have dropped into the office, asked for me, and if I was not overbusy I have seen them.

The only entries on my calendar pad nowadays are directors' meetings. Except for directors' meetings of my own company, I pay very little attention to these. I used to take interest in any affairs—of my company or of any other company—that came before me.

It used to be that the day's appointments started with my arrival at the office. The callers lined up in the outer office, and one by one I saw them on schedule. Frequently it was 11 o'clock or later before I even got a chance to look at my morning's mail. The afternoons were like that, too.

It was all right during the earlier days of the business, when I had a great deal to see to personally. And then, when the war [World War I] came along, I did not begrudge a minute of the weeks spent in service, "drives," and all that sort of thing. It was needed, and hence there was no use worrying about it.

But after the war, when the continual drag showed few signs of easing up, I began to feel the strain.

When I analyzed it, hardly a one of all my callers wanted to see me about my business. It was all about their business. If a proposal had really to do with the actual operation of our business, the man who made it generally knew enough to go straight to the executive in charge of that end of our business, instead of coming to me.

So I made an "about face." I decided I would have no more appointments. If any one wanted to see me, he could gamble his time on the chance of catching me at leisure. If I was not busy, I would see him—I will see anyone about almost anything if I have not something else taking up my time when he calls.

But if a caller came at a time inconvenient to me, he would simply have to try again. The decision was made with all consideration due other people's time and comfort. I have no wish to be inconsiderate or discourteous. But I found I simply could not afford the time that appointments take.

It leaves my day so much more flexible. If I want to spend the whole morning going over with one of our executives a plan which is tremendously important to our business, I do not have to take 15 minutes out of the middle of it, and break my whole trend of thought, to keep an appointment with a 10:30 caller.

. . . there are a lot of people calling on business men who place a high value on their own time—a higher value than they place on the time of the business men on whom they call.

The man who calls by appointment quite naturally feels that he is entitled to a reasonable length of time. Fifteen minutes is perhaps the least he expects. I do not blame him for feeling that way, for he knows that on a day's schedule appointments can hardly be placed closer together than every 15 minutes.

But the man who drops in, and is ushered into my office immediately or after a short wait, has no feeling that a section of time has been marked off for his exclusive use. Without even going through the formality of thinking about it, he realizes that if I work on that basis then I must work at other things in between visitors. Moreover, he feels moderately surprised—agreeably surprised—at getting in so easily. So he states his business briefly, we get it over with, and out he goes.

Then, too, there are a lot of people calling on business men who place a high value on their own time—a higher value than they place on the time of the business men on whom they call. They are perfectly willing to have me stay in my office to await the time of their appointments—but they will not risk their own time on calling without advance appointments. When this is true, the call missed is no loss to me. The time saving on this one class of callers alone amounts to a good vacation every year.

It all nets down to this: Varied as my business interests are, I could handle them comfortably in four hours a day. Courtesy and consideration of others lengthens out my day considerably, by the time I give to other folk's business.

But the saving in my time since I have refused to make appointments is very real, and in some ways measurable. For one thing, all my life I have loved to go to baseball games. I have, moreover, something above $3,000,000 invested in baseball.

So now, every afternoon during baseball season, I am out at the ball park. Afterward, to be sure, I come back to the office. But that afternoon at the ball game is one benefit I can trace back to refusing to make appointments.

A. P. GIANNINI
1870 – 1949

A. P. Giannini made his mark by founding the Bank of Italy in San Francisco, which would become the largest commercial bank in the United States forty years later. By then it was known as BankAmerica and was one of many companies under Giannini's umbrella creation, TransAmerica. Giannini learned about business by working for his stepfather on the San Francisco docks, buying and selling fruits. The family business flourished and Giannini actually retired at thirty-one to live off his investments. But then he was invited to sit on the board of a local savings and loan. Other board members' indiscretions angered him, so he quit to start his own bank in 1904.

Giannini democraticized banking the way Henry Ford democraticized cars; in other words, he made it affordable and useful for the average person. His first big break came with the great 1906 San Francisco earthquake. The city was in a state of anarchy, but while some bankers closed indefinitely, Giannini opened the very next day, sitting at a borrowed desk on a pier. He emerged a hero with a rapidly growing legion of loyal customers. As Giannini built his empire, he developed a grand vision for nationwide banking: "The bank of tomorrow is going to be a sort of department store, handling every service the people may want in the way of banking, investment, and trust services." And he was right on the mark.

Giannini started buying banks first in California, then moved east. He preferred to buy rather than to build so he could keep the old staff and maintain ties to the community, having learned the importance of community support from the 1906 earthquake. Characterized as a "regular knockout for personality with a titanic head, a face like a rock, and a voice like a howitzer," Giannini made quite an impression on both customers and employees. He didn't sit in a private office, explaining "That's the trouble with bankers. They shut themselves off away from people and don't know what's going on." He also liked to wander through the bank and look employees in the eye. His desire to stay in touch with employees, customers, and reality is exemplified in *I Answer the Telephone Myself.*

I Answer the Telephone Myself

A. P. Giannini

At the age of 56 and after 44 years in harness I have yet to have anyone to answer the telephone for me. I have had very little use for a private office. I have hardly had an assistant who might, in the accepted sense of the term, be called a private secretary.

I have found it quite possible to dispense with most of the trappings which many executives find necessary. Perhaps I do not impress people as much as I might. But of this I am convinced—I can accomplish more work without the trappings.

As president of the Bank of Italy I had my desk on an unpartitioned floor which is entirely given over to the major executives and their assistants.

One advantage was that I could see those who were waiting to interview me. Frequently if I was engaged in a long interview and knew some one waiting would require only a moment I would beckon to him, taking the necessary time to attend to him from the longer interview.

When I had a letter to dictate, instead of pressing a button for a stenographer whose sole duty was to take my dictation, it was my custom to look about the floor for any stenographer who appeared to be available, step over to her desk, thereby saving three or four minutes of her time, and not sacrificing any of my own, dictate my letter, and return.

Frequently, too, I would act as my own messenger boy, taking papers to another officer's desk rather than sending them. This practice gave me valuable contact, not only with the other officers, but often incidentally with those they might happen at the time to be doing business with.

To use a figure of speech, I am no longer subjected to a cross-fire, between meeting the public and keeping directly in touch with the operation problems of a rather extensive business organization. But I still have a great many people to see during the course of a business day and a great many decisions to make. I find that cutting away the trappings helps—just as it always has.

I have found it quite possible to dispense with most of the trappings which many executives find necessary.

There is no anteroom connected with my present office. My visitors can see me the moment they open the door; and I can see them. That is the way I like to have things. In the center of the room, which is rather larger than the average private office, is a table with chairs drawn up about it, and reading matter. Here visitors may wait if they see I am occupied when they come in.

As I have said, I have no assistant who could be called a private secretary in the ordinary sense. To be sure, I have assistants who attend to various matters. But their tasks are more their own tasks than mine. I do not need the services of a private secretary to look after my appointments, for the very good reason that I have none to amount to anything. I tell anyone who wants to see me to come in at any time, and I try to see him without keeping him waiting unduly.

I find that by answering the telephone myself I can often settle a matter definitely which might otherwise require a personal interview.

I have often noticed that knotty problems often seemingly solve themselves if the subconscious mind is given an opportunity to work on them.

I attend to correspondence as opportunity permits. It is not often that I find a problem so knotty that I must concentrate on it undisturbed. In fact I have often noticed that knotty problems often seemingly solve themselves if the subconscious mind is given an opportunity to work on them. I find that by just going ahead with less important tasks—seeing those who want to see me—difficult decisions often work themselves out, and to better advantage, perhaps, than if I had made a more conscious effort.

PART VII

Motivators and Mentors

Money is the greatest motivator. It alone, however, will not go far when it comes to rallying the troops and extolling them onward. The motivational techniques offered in Part VII run the full spectrum, from the subtle to open confrontation. Ralph Lazarus, who once ruled over the Federated Stores empire, motivated his executives and managers by not giving orders and allowing them complete freedom to do their job. Louis F. Swift, on the other hand, writes about using sarcasm and discipline to get workers hopping. But Swift offered other incentives to his employees to create a balance between negative and positive reinforcement—and that is just one of the secrets discovered in the following essays. Some of the mentoring lessons include the intriguing idea of teaching through the eye and how to judge someone's strengths and weaknesses.

Ralph Lazarus

Ralph Lazarus was once chairman and CEO of the largest retailing operation in the country—Federated Department Stores. Included in this holding company were premier stores, such as Bloomingdale's, The Bon Marche, Abraham & Straus, and Filene's. The group was originally put together in 1929 by Lazarus's father. Within ten years the founder wielded enough power to convince President Roosevelt to move Thanksgiving from the last Thursday in November to the fourth, which resulted in extending Christmas shopping a few critical days. (Roosevelt hesitated initially, thinking Thanksgiving was a religious holiday.)

When Ralph Lazarus took the helm in 1968, Federated had just about reached a saturation point in the industry, so to fuel growth he led the company into supermarkets and mass merchandizing. Sales tripled during the 1970s, driven both by Lazarus's shopping spree and by the fortunate fact that his stores' upper-class clientele was mostly impervious to the economic downturns of the time. During his tenure, Lazarus was attacked occasionally for being more concerned with pomp than profits. For example, he championed fancy displays in Bloomingdale's windows and once brought several alligators north to display in stores. While sometimes flamboyant, Lazarus was a hard worker. In a 1963 speech he suggested that the misuse of leisure time should be treated like a plague.

Lazarus was also very concerned with social issues and was chairman of the Committee for Economic Development, whose purpose included financially assisting public schools and studying ways to improve urban areas. Lazarus understood all too well that the city was the department store's meat. Education became his primary cause. He said, "The speed of change and the growing complexity of both knowledge and the world will force us to extend formal education throughout life in order to keep up with the demands of new and old occupations. . . ." That statement certainly holds true today; however, Lazarus also makes it clear in *The Case of the Oriental Rug* that running a company takes much more than having an MBA. You still have to be willing to listen to outrageous ideas that make no business sense and to appreciate the intangible role people play in a company's success.

The Case of the Oriental Rug

Ralph Lazarus

Just about a year ago a good friend of mine (I'll call him Joe) came to my home one weekend to tell me a sad but all-too-familiar story.

At age 42, he said, he had just been asked to resign from a vice-presidency in one of the nation's leading corporations. Worse, this was the third consecutive time, he confessed, that he had been forcibly separated from gainful employment. "What," he asked plaintively, "is the matter with me?"

Together we ran over the facts: Top graduate of a top business school. Good family background. Good appearance. Sound personal habits. No visible clue that could reasonably explain his failures.

A week or so later I met the president who had fired him. "What happened to Joe?" I asked.

"Listen," the President replied. "Three years ago we thought Joe was a real find. I even visualized him as my successor. He knew how to smell out a problem. He knew how to get the facts. He knew how to make a decision. But we learned to our sorrow that that's all he knew. It never occurred to him that the best decision in the world is no good until somebody does something about it. He never learned that an executive has to be effective through other people—and that you make a decision not just on the facts but in terms of who will do what you think needs to be done."

"PEOPLE-BLINDNESS"

Hidden in this single unhappy incident is, I believe, a fundamental truth about today's class of rising young executives. Many of them will fail to reach their goals. They will fail not for lack of competence, but because they have a "people-blindness" that, time after time, traps them into making a technically good decision that just won't work in practice. They haven't learned that an executive succeeds or fails not so much because of what *he* does, but because of what he is able to get someone else to accomplish.

Graduates of our business schools, I regret to say, seem to me to be particularly susceptible to this malady—and in its most virulent form. That is true even though today's MBAs are, on average, the best-trained prospective employees that we have ever interviewed. Knowledgeable. Competent. Aggressive. The problem is that these graduates are frequently even more impressed with their qualifications than we are. They seem to feel that their teachers have taught them everything they need to know and that their classroom training assures them success. In short, their heads are full to overflowing with the knowledge from which good decisions spring. Their hearts, unhappily, have not yet developed that human sensibility that would permit them to understand that *what* should be done can often be learned as a classroom exercise, but *how* it should be done and getting it done involve people—and people experience is seldom to be had under campus or laboratory conditions.

TODAY'S "PRACTICAL EXPERIENCE"

Let me hasten to make the point that my objective here is to do more than to repeat that hoary, old executive cliché about the difference between "book learning" and "practical experience." I know that today's "book learning" is far superior to yesterday's. I know that today's student is harangued endlessly to "weigh the human factor." It is also true, however, that today's "practical experience" involves far more than was encompassed by the old saw about learning the business from "the bottom up."

. . . an executive succeeds or fails not so much because of what he *does, but because of what he is able to get someone else to accomplish.*

Practical experience, by my definition, means these things:

1. A thorough understanding of how a particular organization works, what its principles are, how and why they were developed;
2. A thorough knowledge of and respect for the people who were smart enough to invent these principles and make them successful;
3. A realization that an individual can succeed in a particular organization only when he discovers how to contribute within a previously established framework and only when he has learned that he is writing a song that someone else must sing.

Ideas and Implementation

All this adds up to people-experience—the development of a set of antennae that will be sensitive to the intricate relationships of the modern corporation. And that's precisely where so many promising young men fall off the sled. Their educations have taught them to pick, in the abstract, an academically right answer. At that point, they think the job is done—never realizing that *what* you decide to do is dependent on *how* you plan to do it. And, beyond that, that you can only know the *how* when you have visualized it in terms of *who*. Bluntly stated, it all comes down to this: Good ideas are easier to come by than good implementation. A brilliant idea poorly implemented is almost always less successful than a mediocre idea enthusiastically executed. And when you use those polysyllables—implement and execute—you really mean who is going to do it and how will he get it done.

The Rug Buyer

I had my first lesson on this subject many years ago when I was getting my lumps as a novice in our family store in Columbus, Ohio—F. & R. Lazarus & Company. We had a rug buyer there who became a legend—and for good reason.

Like all of our buyers, he prepared a written plan for the upcoming selling season prior to going to market to buy his merchandise. The plan, in the case I am describing, was approved by management. The only difficulty was that, when he returned from his buying trip, he had bought—not what he had outlined—but the biggest assortment of Oriental rugs that any of us had ever seen. Pressed for an explanation he said: "I liked them."

Now, management had a problem. A survey of customers would have proved, I feel sure, that there was no burning desire on the part of Columbus housewives to carpet their floors with the bounty of the East. The prices were far beyond the store's normal range. There was, in short, no conceivable reason why our store should put perhaps 75 percent of its floor-covering investment in a product that Columbus obviously did not want. No reason, that is, except the one that my father instantly understood.

That reason was the buyer himself. My father knew he was an enthusiast—a man who, if backed in his convictions, could translate an unsupportable idea into a cash-register success. We kept the rugs. The buyer sold them—using every wile in his considerable experience. Even today Columbus may be unique for at least one thing. It probably has more square feet of Oriental rugs than most cities twice its size. And all because the store was smart enough to look harder at the man than at the facts.

A brilliant idea poorly implemented is almost always less successful than a mediocre idea enthusiastically executed.

The Branch Store

There is a modern counterpart of this same story. Not long ago we sat around the conference table in our Cincinnati headquarters discussing the question of opening a branch store for one of our twelve divisions. Our central office staff was on one side of the table; the divisional management on the other. We were agreed that the growth potential of the trading area served by this division justified branch expansion. The question was what kind of store should the new branch be. We had surveyed the area. We knew all about income levels, population trends, traffic patterns, shopping habits, customer preferences. The facts seemed to substantiate the central office position. The new branch should be a smaller version of the successful downtown store—catering, in price lines and assortments of merchandise, to the kind of people who already though so well of us.

That's what *we thought*. The man who had the responsibility for the building and the profitable operation of the new branch had the exact opposite idea. He argued for a totally different store. He didn't want what we call an "image" branch; he wanted a convenience store stocked with major emphasis on budget merchandise. There were very few facts to support his position. He was asking us, in effect, to invest millions of dollars in a store that was in precise contradiction to his successful downtown operation. He really had only one argument on his side: He was convinced he could make *his* idea succeed. We were pretty sure that, feeling as he did, he could not summon the enthusiasm to make *our* idea pay out.

But it is equally true that you can't earn your keep in top management if all you can do is to bludgeon your subordinates into accepting your solutions . . .

We built the store his way. I don't like it very well. Customers sometimes complain that it doesn't stack up with the downtown store. The hard fact is, however, that that branch store is one of the most profitable in our company.

Another Branch Store

There is an encore to that incident that does not have so happy an ending. The basic facts are the same. Another division of our company likewise was in a position, in our opinion, to add a branch store. The difference was that that store management did not want to expand, even though admitting that the opportunity was clearly theirs. We debated the question endlessly. Finally, the store reluctantly agreed to build. The resulting branch was handsome in design, sound in policy, efficient in operation—and disappointing in results. It had everything but the enthusiastic backing of the people who didn't want to build it but now had to operate it. The right decision had produced the wrong result. People were the difference.

In reciting these stories I do not want to create the impression that I think that a good executive can be defined as a man who merely accepts other people's ideas because they happen to be enthusiastic about them. That would be nonsense. But it is equally true that you can't earn your keep in top management if all you can do is to bludgeon your subordinates into accepting your solutions—even when you're right. Perhaps I can illustrate the difference in terms of our business.

Management Supervision

Our company, Federated Department Stores, Inc., consists of 12 divisions operating 61 department stores. These divisions are largely autonomous. Financial control is maintained at headquarters but, beyond that, each division is pretty much its own master and each is held accountable for its sales, growth, and profit performance.

We exercise management supervision through the device of twice-yearly planning meetings and irregular store visits where we learn to know the organization and see what they are doing on their home grounds. Prior to the planning meetings the central office makes a detailed study of the division's performance, its forecast of sales for the year ahead and for as much as ten years ahead. Our statistical analysis covers each of the some 250 departments in the store—men's wear, shoes, dresses, infant's wear, home furnishings and so on. We compare the results of the preceding period and the plans for the future with those of our eleven other divisions. This preliminary analysis then goes to the division for comment and review. Together we agree on an agenda for the upcoming meeting. Before division and central office actually sit down to talk, we have drawn a kind of portrait of the problems and opportunities that we may have with that particular division. We can jointly see its strengths and weaknesses in relationship to its trading area and in comparison to our other operations. And we can weigh its current operating results against the well-defined framework of long-term objectives which we have together developed as the basis of operating policy.

Managing by Influence

The simplest thing to do when we sit down with our store principals face-to-face would be to say, for example: "You're doing a lousy job in furniture. Go to division Z where the profits are four times yours. Find out how they do it and run your store accordingly." That would be the easy way—the easy way to disaster.

The direct order approach wouldn't work in our business for a variety of reasons. Good as division Z's furniture idea is, it was designed for a different city and designed to be effective in the hands of a different organization. It wouldn't work in another division because it is human nature to resent being forced to accept another man's idea. Most important, it wouldn't work because we hold each division accountable for growth and profit. We can't make them accountable unless we also give them the freedom, the authority, to run the show as they see fit.

That does not mean that we ignore the problems—or leave them in limbo for sometime solution. We don't. We wouldn't last long in the brutally competitive world of retailing if we did. It does mean that we have had to abandon authoritarianism as a management method—and we have had to learn how to manage by influence, by suasion, by example.

Management Strategy

What I am saying, of course, is simply this: Federated has a sales plan for each of its divisions. That plan, in every instance, is designed to isolate the essentials of success in the immediate future; it is tailored to fit the people who must implement it. But we also have a second plan—our own management strategy for convincing divisional executives that the objectives we have jointly agreed to are both desirable and attainable. We are deadly serious about our responsibility to persuade—so serious, in fact, that, when our plans go awry, we charge the failure to *our* lack of salesmanship, not the division's lack of implementation.

Our divisional chief executives are superior men. We want the full force of their superiority to be felt in our business. We want the flavor of their varied personalities, the flower of their individual creativeness reflected in our enterprise.

Take, for instance, the case of the sickly furniture department. We would do these things. We would first discuss the problem generally—in terms of the kind of store we have agreed we want to run. We would fit the specific problem into that general agreement. We would suggest a half-dozen possible causes of that problem—such things as merchandise suitability to the market, physical presentation of the items for sale, capability of the buying and selling organization. We would name a store or stores which have solved the same problem. We would urge study of those successful stores. But there would be no table-thumping and no "you-do-it" directives.

Rather, we would probably wind up the discussion by saying something like this to our division president: "Obviously, you need to do something about furniture. But don't make the mistake of *adopting* anybody's idea, including ours. Look at the successful ideas and then *adapt* them to your situation. Just let us know what you're going to do, and when you're going to do it." In short, we would try to illuminate the problem—and give it a sense of urgency—but we would not dictate the solution.

The Gains from Freedom

While no principle is universally applicable, this kind of management works best for us—and for what seem to me to be obvious reasons. Our divisional chief executives are superior men. We want the full force of their superiority to be felt in our business. We want the flavor of their varied personalities, the flower of their individual creativeness reflected in our enterprise. It can be only if we give them freedom and authority to run their own shows.

And there's another thing. By guaranteeing to our top executives this kind of freedom and responsibility we encourage them to do likewise with their subordinates. The end result is that planning, decision-making, responsibility for profit are pushed farther and farther down in our organization. Down, for example, to the man who runs that ailing furniture department and who, ultimately, must make it work.

Human Wisdom

Many a young man steeped in the right-and-wrong, black-and-white textbook method of problem-solving finds this kind of theory of management hard to take. He is the "computer-executive" who reads the tape and knows the answer to anything. Some others, by contrast, have the flexibility of mind and spirit, the intellectual humility to keep on learning. These men succeed. The tragedies are the Joes of the business world—men who spend their acknowledged brilliance devising ideal solutions which can be executed only by those ideal men who do not exist. The result is that today, in almost any company, you'll find at least one might-have-been president who has been quietly sealed off from further promotion because his people-blindness will not permit him to bend his own definition of a good decision to fit the people who have to execute it.

The best top executives today are the men who add the qualities of human wisdom and effective salesmanship to the findings of the slide rule.

The fact is that the best top executives today are the men who add the qualities of human wisdom and effective salesmanship to the findings of the slide rule. They know that it doesn't make much difference nowadays whether you produce shoes, steel, or toothpaste—or sell real estate or insurance. They know that we're all in the people business. We sell to people or buy from people. And as executives we look to people to do those things which make us succeed or fail.

The Executive's Ear

There is an interesting corollary to this point. Not long ago, I spent an evening with a veteran magazine editor of national reputation. I asked him this question:

"How can you possibly cram into your head all the things you need to know to judge the hundreds of different stories you publish each year? Politics. Atomic energy. Sports. Medicine. Taxes. Marriage. Foreign relations with Latin America, India, and the Common Market. Are you really expert in all those fields?"

The ear that hears people, that hears what they feel as well as what they say—this is the key to success in any business today.

His answer, in my opinion, might well be reproduced in our business textbooks. He grinned and said:

"I'm a fraud. I appear to know so much and I really know so little. The complexities of the modern world are totally beyond the grasp of any single man. I don't just judge ideas. I try to fit those ideas into a total picture I have developed of the kind of magazine I want to edit. Most particularly, I judge the people who submit those ideas. Over the years, I've developed an ear that distinguishes the sound of truth from the sound of exaggeration and falsehood. In every issue that I publish I bet my job that my ear has told me right."

That editor is doing exactly what most chief executives have to do. Surrounded by experts on finance, law, research, real estate, and marketing—each a labyrinth of special knowledge—the boss must depend on his ear, too.

The ear that hears people, that hears what they feel as well as what they say—this is the key to success in any business today. It takes a lot of listening to develop that kind of ear. Listening to customers who do or don't buy what you have to sell. Listening to outrageous ideas that somebody believes in. Listening *to* gripes and listening *for* that sound of excitement that spells success.

This kind of sensitivity is what management is so earnestly seeking in the young men it hires today. Business can't use men at the top whose college training has made them rigid with scholastic arrogance. But there are big opportunities waiting for those who will bring us two things: the fine intellectual tool-kits they have assembled in college; a modest acceptance of the fact that they still have to learn how to put them to use through other human hands.

JOHN H. PATTERSON
1844 – 1922

John H. Patterson is considered the father of modern salesmanship and one of the greatest motivators of men. Before Patterson made his mark with the National Cash Register Company (NCR), he went to Dartmouth University, where he claims he acquired a lot of useless knowledge. One of his subsequent jobs was managing a coal yard and a store for the employees, which was always in the red because the clerks were skimming. It was then that Patterson read about a contraption that tabulated sales called Ritty's Incorruptible Cashier. He bought two registers in 1882. In 1884 he bought the entire Dayton, Ohio, company and changed the name to the National Cash Register Company.

As the father of salesmanship, his innovations ranged from establishing an equitable sales quota system, to codifying sales talk, to producing the first sales manual that incorporated his favorite mantras, including "Visualize! Analyze! Dramatize!" Patterson was also a pioneer in how he treated factory workers. The walls of his first plant were made 80 percent with glass for healthful lighting, had lockers and showers, swimming pools, hot food and medical care, and well-landscaped grounds—all to stimulate the employees.

Many believed Patterson was an eccentric, beginning with the sign outside his office door: BE BRIEF: OMIT ALL COMPLIMENTS ABOUT WELFARE WORK. On occasion, he was known to burn the contents of his executives' desks—to give them a fresh start, he said. Eccentric or not, by 1910 Patterson's company sold 90 percent of the cash registers in the United States, a fact that attracted the interest of the U.S. Department of Justice. In 1913 Patterson was indicted for violating the Sherman Antitrust Act. He was facing a year in jail when the great Dayton flood hit and 90,000 were made homeless. Patterson came to the rescue and offered victims shelter, food, drinking water, medicine, and was declared an instrument of God by the Salvation Army. Coincidentally, his indictment was thrown out on appeal shortly thereafter. Patterson was a genius at getting others to see things his way, and his motivational power is clearly evident in *How I Get My Ideas Across.*

How I Get My Ideas Across

John H. Patterson

One day years ago, in the Dayton high school, the school board paid us a visit. It was an occasion when we were all expected to make our best showing. The teacher told me to explain a rather involved calculation. I asked if I might use the blackboard—my first teacher had taught me from the blackboard. Instead of merely putting down the figures, I drew a diagram and from it explained how the results came. In effect I dramatized the problem. It was all very simple and I adopted the graphic method only because I had found that I could understand things better and talk about them more clearly if I had something concrete before me. My demonstration was the hit of the day.

Later I taught school in the White Mountains. I found that the pupils understood even the most difficult problems if I drew both the right and the wrong way side by side on the blackboard and then told why the one was correct and the other was not. They did not forget the two contrasting pictures.

Those incidents are at the base of my whole system of business teaching; they are the foundation of its main principles:

1. Teach through the eye.
2. Contrast the right with the wrong way.

Business is only a form of teaching. You teach people to desire your product; that is selling. You teach workmen how to make the right product; that is manufacturing. You teach others to cooperate with you; that is organization. To succeed in business, it is necessary to make the other man see things as you see them. I say "as you see them"—which means that you yourself must first see and believe before you can tell another. I have been trying all of my life, first to see for myself, and then to get other people to see with me. The measure in which I have succeeded is the measure of the progress of my company. The methods which I shall set down here are those which have proved best with me—and I have tried many ways.

One of the many advantages of teaching through the eye is its exactness. Accuracy comes to me as a heritage from my parents and grandparents; one of them was a surveyor and all were brought up in the school of Scotch precision. I like to be definite. I have often heard a speaker ask, "Do you see my point?" He wants to know if the hearer actually has the point in eye as well as mind, that he understands it well enough to make a mental picture. Well then, why not draw the picture? Instead of asking if the point is seen, why not draw the point so that it cannot help being seen?

An argument is good according to the amount of the dramatic which it contains. Of course the particular situation limits the dramatization, but I have found that words, whether written or spoken, without some kind of drawing on which to center attention, are not effective.

The very first advertising that we put out after starting the N.C.R. taught me this lesson. I had some five thousand circulars printed describing the new machine and what it would do. I told what it had done for me and how it could prevent business leaks. It was a good circular, but it did not contain a picture of the cash register. Having put the envelope into the mails, we hurriedly hired two extra men to answer inquiries. We waited and we might be waiting still, for we did not get a single inquiry! Nobody knew what we were talking about!

Business is only a form of teaching. You teach people to desire your product; that is selling. You teach workmen how to make the right product; that is manufacturing. You teach others to cooperate with you; that is organization.

Then I started to canvass for the machine with one of our agents. We had a little model made with three keys—the regular machine then was a very big affair—and this model we carried about with us into cafes and grocery stores. We met opposition everywhere. The idea got around that we were selling thief catchers, and the clerks—the proprietors, also, in many instances—resented the very idea of dishonesty. But I knew that the actual receipts in any unchecked business were usually more than what remained in the till. However, no argument, no selling talk, could prove that point. Only a use of the machine could convince. We put registers in on trial. Even then we had to circulate about to make sure that the clerks pressed the keys. No one who did not live through those days can imagine what opposition we had. They would not see that it was fair neither to the clerk nor to the owner to be without a check on the cash—that it protected the first from unjust accusation and the second against mistakes; that the register was a business adjunct.

That register merely punched holes in strips of paper and the proprietor at the end of the day had to count the holes, multiply by the 5 cents, 10 cents, or whatever amounts each hole represented, and thus gain the total for the day. We could not present the many points of today, for our machine was but in its infancy; we had to sell on the straight talk that it checked the cash. We sold exclusively on money saved by its use and we did not sell until the machine had shown in practice that it saved money for the prospective purchaser—for what we now call the "P.P." From the registers in operation we gathered facts for future sales talks.

The first agent that we hired outside of our immediate family was a man named Crawford. He would not carry a miniature machine; he said that not only would carrying a machine take him out of the high-class salesman list, but that also he would not be able to see the proprietor; the clerks would spot him by the machine that he carried. I had a life-size picture of the register drawn and asked him to take that with him. Again he objected; he said that it would stuff out his pocket if rolled and if folded the creases would spoil the effect. I told him to roll it on a stick. He replied that he could not carry a stick. Then I suggested rolling it around his umbrella, but that would not do because then the cover would not fit on the umbrella.

"Well," I said, "why don't you get a new umbrella cover?"

"No, that was too expensive."

I drew for him a pair of scales; on one side I put "No Sales—Loss $25 a Day," on the other side I put "New Umbrella and Cover $5—Make $25 a Day."

"Now," I asked, "which do you want to do?"

He bought the new umbrella and cover and founded a large income. I have learned—and I have used it thousands of times—that drawing a beam scale and listing on one side the advantages and on the other the objections to any certain plan will quickly show the objections in their true proportions just as it showed Crawford when he was hesitating about spending $5 to make $25 a day. He had gotten that extra $5 out of its true setting. The scales brought it back. We had not been talking about the same thing. I was talking about making more money and he was talking about not spending $5.

It should be self-evident that you cannot convince a man if he does not know what point you are trying to make—if he is thinking of something different from what you want him to think about. And it is right here that the spoken word fails, for not only is it not enough in itself to hold attention, but there is no certainty that your hearer takes the same meaning from the words that you intend to convey. Very few people understand words. The uneducated man, for instance, may have only a local and limited meaning for a word which brings up dozens of ideas to the more educated man. Take a very simple instance. Food to a baby means milk or, at the most, two or three articles; food to a laboring man has a somewhat broader meaning because he is accustomed to a wider variety than an infant; but "food" to a chef calls up thousands of delicacies prepared in many different ways and as something primarily to prepare rather than something for himself to eat.

How a Simple Diagram Puts the Idea Across

In order to confine the subject, to make sure of what is under discussion and to nail down the points as made, I evolved the pyramid form of diagram. Here is how it works. First I draw a triangle and label its apex with the point I intend to make. I start with the conclusion so that there can be no mistake as to what I am about. The conclusion is the result of certain other secondary conclusions or facts. I find that most ideas divide themselves into five parts, which is a particularly convenient number, because in speaking of the parts it is possible also to use the five fingers of the hand to check off the points as made. Therefore I divide the base of the triangle or pyramid into five divisions and at the head of each division write its name. The sum of the divisions is the main conclusion which is to be proved. Naturally each of the five sectional conclusions is composed of certain facts or leading-up arguments. I list them in columns under the subheads. The result is a structure of five pillars of elemental facts each supporting its capital fact. On the capitals rest the pyramid, at the apex of which is the conclusion. It is all a simple process of analysis.

How does this pyramid help a talk? Take a concrete case. Suppose you want to have your employees take better advantage of their opportunities. I make a pyramid headed "Ways I Can Improve Myself," "I Am a Member of the Double-Up Club," or give it some other title that states the object which is to be attained. The end is to be reached through the man bettering himself simultaneously in a number of ways. These ways are the natural divisions of life and are five: Physical, Mental, Moral, Financial, and Social. Under each of these five columns I list the things to be done; that is, if a man improves on all of the points listed he is greatly helped in striving to attain the object set out at the head of the table. I simply put down in black and white in a logical diagram the various things to do for self-improvement and to attain the very desirable end which heads the diagram as an object. I take out all speculation as to right or wrong and show the man what he may gain by absorbing the principles. The conclusion also answers the eternal question: "Where do I come in?"

You can convince yourself by these methods and you can convince others so thoroughly that they will go out and convince the public.

It also has many other uses. For instance, you can diagram the functions of a department or an individual. Any subject is the better for being set out in this kind of half geometry and every element of doubt removed. In each department we have cabinets containing charts showing the scope and the duties of the department, the head, and his assistants. Every report is thus pyramided and, if it is of a permanent nature it is printed on cardboard and swung into the cabinet. The entire information concerning the activities of any department hangs in its meeting room and one has but to swing out the proper panel to know in a moment what has been done and what is under way. We reduce everything to its important facts and put it up on the wall.

How We Practice What We Preach

One of the first articles of furniture that I bought was a blackboard on which to make these demonstrations; eight or nine years ago we substituted great pads of paper mounted on artist's easels, and now every discussion on every subject goes forward pictorially as well as orally. When we decide on anything we post it up as settled and go on to something else.

The pyramid is only one of the various ways of putting over the idea or of holding attention. Another is the caricature. Little grotesque drawings are wonderfully effective. I have mentioned the scales; that was one of the first. Now I have a whole system of cartooning or "chart talks." A circle with a dollar mark means a piece of money, a bag marked with a dollar is a lot of money. Many good effects can be had with moon faces. Draw a circle, put in a few dashes for the eyes, nose, mouth, and ears. Twisting these lines gives the expressions; the out-of-date man has the corners of his mouth down; the chipper, up-to-date fellow has the curves up. The drawings are homely, but the most effective cartoonists are not the men who make the prettiest pictures; the thing is to express the idea and the contrast.

The big bag and the little bag of money, side by side, are the natural heads for the right way as opposed to the wrong way; the one brings much money, the other little money. If you sketch these rapidly as you talk, there is no danger of people letting their minds wander; they are bound to look at what you are doing and thus to go with you through the successive stages to the point you want to make. And again the funny figures put people in good humor.

I hold that one cannot rely on speech alone to make himself understood or to gain and hold attention. A dramatic supplement is needed. It is better to supplement whenever possible with pictures which show the right and wrong way; diagrams are more convincing than mere words and pictures are more convincing than diagrams. The ideal presentation of a subject is one in which every subdivision is pictured and the words are used only to connect them. I early found that in dealing with men, a picture was worth more than anything I could say. I used to employ an artist to hang around in the shops with me and quietly make sketches of things that were not being done right. Then the sketches were made into drawings and I called the men together and showed them exactly what they were doing. When I heard of the stereopticon I immediately bought one and projected the drawings on the screen, which of course made them even more effective than on paper. Then came the moving picture. I think that I had one of the first machines ever made, and now we have a big department and many motion picture films and more than 60,000 colored stereopticon slides.

I have spoken of dramatic effects. They are not the result of chance but of study and must be either lifelike or caricatures. There is no betwixt and between, for that will not hold attention. I have often acted through the parts in a regular drama—a real play composed to bring out some point—with the other executive officers of the company taking leading parts. When I want to teach a group of salesmen the proper approach and the demonstration, I have a grocery store or some other kind of store fitted out in detail. The grocery has real goods on its shelves, the shoe store contains real shoes. A grocer gets a better idea of what you are doing if he finds that the can of tomatoes on the shelf is one such as might be found in his store and not a mere dummy. A playlet given two years ago in which I took part as a salesman gave the approach, demonstration, sale, and installation of our then latest model cash register. I played it because I had discovered that the agents were getting away from the fundamentals of salesmanship. It started with the evolution of a store, the call of the assistant to the sales agent, the visit of the sales agent, the demonstration, the call of the merchant and his wife with the agent on the banker and then on the endorser of the note with which he proposed to borrow the money to pay for the register, of their visit to the landlord for improvements and so on through every event which would be apt to happen in the sale and installation of a register. That was so effective that we had it made into a film for teaching purposes.

Let me go outside of my own affairs for some illustrations. Not long since I heard a noted Russian lecture on his country and its hopes. I presume that he sought to teach people to help Russia. But whatever his object was he did not achieve it because he did not know how to convince. He first told us of Russia, its size, divisions, and population; but he did not have a map, nor did he give anything with which we could print the facts on our minds. Suppose he had shown a large map and then put the United States inside of Russia; the audience would have had an idea of its area. A million square miles does not bring up a mental picture. He spoke of the great population; the figures meant nothing. If he had given a diagram with the population of Russia as eight times bigger than that of the United States we should have understood him. The trouble was that he put himself ahead of his subject. He was not content merely to act as a presenter. Therefore, if he did have anything to say, we did not get it. He had not planned, he had not set his stage, and thus had not made the most of the dramatic. Therefore he failed.

The dramatic points do not come by accident. If every man trying to put over an idea to one man or to 10,000 would study his setting, he could achieve the interest-holding moments.

Once when I found an audience of agents getting away from me, I held up a $10 bill before them, tore it to bits and threw it on the floor. The people sat up and then I said:

"Did you think that I was going to waste that bill? I was only trying to show you what you were wasting by not giving attention." Turning to an assistant, I continued: "Just pick up the pieces of that bill and paste them together."

Making a Group of Men Change Their Minds

I had the attention of that crowd for as long as I wanted it. A long while ago the question was up in one organization of making interchangeable parts on the registers. I had all the foremen and superintendents in a meeting. I told them that all of the parts had to be interchangeable and standardized; the plan seems simple enough now, but at that time standardization was practically unknown—our mechanics were not used to close work and the machinery was not as accurate as it is today. The "practical men" opposed me.

I asked for opinions until finally nearly everyone in the room had spoken. I waited—I always like to have the other fellow bring up all the objections first. When they had done, I said:

"Those who feel that we cannot make to a standard, step to this side of the room."

All but three of the men took their places in the opposition. Then I spoke to the three:

"You have made one machine that works right, then go ahead and make another. If you made one, you can make more. Anything that can be made by hand can be made by machinery. As for you fellows," speaking now to the insurgents, "you find out how to do it or look for other jobs."

That was 25 years ago; without interchangeable parts the cash register business would have broken down.

Since the war began, it became necessary to raise the prices of the machines. The agents and sales managers protested; they said that our business would go, that prices had to be kept where they were. I called them all in to Dayton and we had a meeting. I staged the affair. Back of me on the platform I had a great sheet of paper and a sign painter.

I asked the people to state their objections to the increasing of prices. The objections came ripping out from the audience like shots from a machine gun. As fast as they came, I had the sign man post them on the big sheet. We spent all of the first day, gathering objections. I did nothing but exhort. When the meeting closed we had a list of at least a hundred different reasons why the prices should not be raised. Every possible reason was up there before the men and it seemed conclusively settled in the minds of the audience that no change should be made. Then the meeting adjourned.

On the next morning, I took up the objections one by one and explained by diagrams and words exactly why each was unsound. The people were convinced. Why? Everything that could be said contra was up in black and white and the discussion centered. No loose ends were left. We settled everything on the spot.

But in a case such as this one it would not have been enough, in my mind, merely to have settled the point in dispute. A meeting of agents should break up with all of the audience filled with a new lot of enthusiasm; perhaps the points of the register itself might have been a little blurred in the discussion. That would never do. We had to have a dramatic climax. I had arranged for that and just before the close of the conference. I had a hundred men march, one by one across the stage; each bore a banner and on that banner was a picture of a part of the latest model register and just what it did. Then when the last man had passed across, they all came back into a kind of grand finale—the complete machine. The meeting ended with the agents on their feet and cheering wildly.

After a meeting I always try to have the audience write what they got out of the talks and demonstrations. This lets one know the points they gained and whether they got the points it was intended they should get. It is always a good scheme to discover in some way what impression you have made—to test your methods. Thus you find your weak spots and can strengthen them.

These are the methods by which we taught our agents how to sell our machines and which they also used to the public with the product. And the cash register was not easily sold to the public; it was hard to educate them, for, essentially the machine acted as a monitor and no one likes to be told about the mistakes he has made. We have found all of these devices serve to get the points over in quicker and better fashion than by mere words. Our whole force uses them not only with the public but in all company discussions of policies. They have been used with the workmen and they have been used in public affairs.

How We Proved Our Plan in Outside Affairs

After the Dayton flood, when the people wanted to abandon the town to its ruins, we staged a meeting—we like to do things in meetings. We had a great red heart on the platform with contrasts of what Dayton had been, what it was then, and what it might be.

We showed stereopticon views of the pioneers who had made Dayton and of the big, individual things that those stalwart men had done. We did that because in the audience were many descendants of those very men and if the descendants were won over, there would be enough leaven through the whole audience to raise it.

The nerves from the eyes to the brain are many times larger than those from the ears to the brain. Therefore, when possible to use a picture *instead of words, use one and make the words mere connectives for the pictures.*

And we did raise that audience! At the beginning of the meeting, not one-tenth of the people wanted to bother further with Dayton. Then they began to be interested—they warmed up, bit by bit, until finally you could not have kept their money in their pockets. When the meeting closed, we had $2,000,000 subscribed. The last dollars were rung up on an enormous cash register standing on the steps of the court house, amid the wildest enthusiasm I have ever known. The same methods brought the city manager form of government to the city. I think they pay.

If I should reduce my principles of idea-conveying to a creed, it would run something in this fashion:

1. The nerves from the eyes to the brain are many times larger than those from the ears to the brain. Therefore, when possible to *use a picture* instead of words, use one and make the words mere connectives for the pictures.
2. Confine the attention to the exact subject by drawing outlines and putting in the divisions; then we make certain that we are all talking about the same thing.

Before you try to convince anyone else, make sure that you are convinced, and if you cannot convince yourself, drop the subject. Do not try to "put over anything."

---

3. Aim for dramatic effects either in speaking or writing—study them out beforehand. This holds the attention.
4. Red is the best color to attract and hold attention, therefore use plenty of it.
5. Few words—short sentences—small words—big ideas.
6. Tell why as well as how.
7. Do not be afraid of big type and do not put too much on a page.
8. Do not crowd ideas in speaking or writing. No advertisement is big enough for two ideas.
9. Before you try to convince anyone else, make sure that you are convinced, and if you cannot convince yourself, drop the subject. Do not try to "put over anything."
10. Tell the truth.

Louis F. Swift

Louis F. Swift, the leader of one of the world's greatest meatpacking houses, Swift and Company, had quite a legacy to live up to. Louis Swift could trace his descendants to the *Mayflower,* and his father, originally a butcher from Massachusetts, was the one who had built the Chicago-based food empire that included establishments from London, to Tokyo, to Shanghai. Swift had every intention of growing the already vast business, and to keep his finger on operations he relied on timely and pertinent weekly reports. Too many executives, he believed, felt that reviewing reports was merely routine. Swift, on the other hand, made sure his managers provided useful information.

While mastery over facts was critical to Swift, he despised useless meetings that were supposed to be for information sharing. "No businessman of experience will deny that meetings are the champion expedient of the buck-passer and of the time-waster," he said. Swift used facts to standardize the operation of the company's various facilities, which gave the firm the upper hand at running a clean slaughterhouse and minimizing spoilage. And it was not Swift and Company but a competitor, Armour, that was attacked by Upton Sinclair in *The Jungle,* a scathing, fact-based novel about the Chicago meatpacker.

The Swifts were pioneers in other aspects, too. They contributed to the development of refrigeration cars for shipping meat back East, which proved much cheaper than moving live cattle. As for the employees, as early as 1900 Swift encouraged them to buy stock in the company. While motivating men was critical to the firm's success, Swift never believed in overpraising a man or conferring titles—traits he inherited from his father. However, while his father once said, "Swift and Company can get along without any man, myself included," the son disagreed. The *Mayflower* descendant understood the importance of a company's heritage and of the standards the leader set. In the following selection, Louis Swift provides insight into his father's capacity for leadership and a sense of what it's like to succeed such a man.

G. F. Swift: I Can Raise Better Men Than I Can Hire

Louis F. Swift

All his life G. F. Swift was developing at a prodigious pace, developing in mind and skill and knowledge. Quite as naturally as a boy attaining manhood loses his awe toward many unremarkable adults who a few years before towered above him, so father found his standards always changing.

First and last a good many of his men, most of them a deal younger than their employer, left him because they had failed to keep within hailing distance as he progressed. Not that he expected every man to keep up with him. But the man in a key position—that man kept step or stepped out.

Only a good man could suit him for long. Father was sizing his people up all of the time. He compared their performances. He watched their present performances in the light of what he knew about their past abilities.

"The best a man ever did shouldn't be his yardstick for the rest of his life," was the maxim and the working rule by which he managed his men.

Even more than in developing executives—and he excelled at it—G. F. Swift's knack of dealing with human beings appeared in his contact with the rank and file of employees.

To people in Swift and Company who did not know him well, or who had not worked with us long enough to understand what was at the bottom of his relationship with employees, the head of the business sometimes seemed an unpleasant, hot-tempered boss. He was unquestionably sarcastic. Sarcasm was his tool for keeping his subordinates alert and free from mistakes which should not be repeated.

But his irritability (as it seemed to some employees) arose out of disappointment. He was really disappointed, with a sense of personal error, when he found a weakness in an employee who he had not expected would have that particular failing.

One plan he followed constantly to minimize expensive errors was to get reports on all claims allowed our customers. These reports came to him on large sheets with brief particulars of each claim. Each summary described the error behind the claim, and told who had made it.

Whenever he found a few unoccupied minutes in the day, he sent his office boy for a claim-sheet offender. Into his office would march some clerk he had never seen before. The culprit always knew, from the time the claim was allowed, that eventually he would be personally called to account for the error involved by his chief.

Father would sit there for a moment sizing up the man responsible for the loss. To the clerk it unquestionably looked as if his employer was racking his brain for a refinement of ingenious punishment. Actually, the boss was looking him over to see whether he seemed like a man who would habitually make mistakes, or whether he was worth trying to save. His tendency was to err on the side of charity and to give the employee a chance to make good.

After a moment he would speak. "So you're the young fellow who ordered out 500 pounds of leaf lard and 250 pounds of compound when a customer had bought 250 of lard and 500 of compound."

"Yes, Mr. Swift."

"I suppose you know the customer claimed he used it up just the same way as if he'd got what he ordered, and we had to bill it to him the way he ordered instead of the way we shipped?"

"Yes, sir."

"I suppose you think it doesn't make any difference if you make mistakes like that. Doesn't make any difference to a big rich company like Swift's if it has to allow a customer a claim for $13.47. We'd be in a fine fix if everybody made that kind of a mistake once a month, wouldn't we?"

The employee who emerged from the encounter with the least damage and still on the payroll was the one who did not try to excuse the error. He was a wise workman who acknowledged his mistake and showed by his demeanor that he recognized it as a serious offense which he would guard against carefully in the future.

Father did not consider that any mistakes were allowable in a well-managed business. That was his base on which he built the whole structure. He knew that errors would continue to be made. But none were allowable.

This is one of the really sound principles of business management. No mistakes are allowable, and every mistake must be regarded as a serious lapse. If any other attitude is taken toward errors, then there is no controlling them.

Twenty or thirty years ago it was no doubt easier to hold employees to a strict accountability. Discipline in the office and in the packinghouse was almost as strict as discipline in the family. And back in the '80's and the '90s the head of the family was obeyed or there was real trouble!

Father was a strict disciplinarian. Not always did his disciplinary measures bring about the results he had counted on. But he kept right on working along the same sound lines nevertheless.

He was walking through the cellars at one of our western plants one day with the superintendent of the plant when a negro trucker passed by, whistling loudly. "Stop that man whistling, stop him!" the chief directed. So the superintendent called, "Hey, Sam, no whistling on the job"—which was the first ever heard of this in the plant in question. And the chief added, as explanation to the surprised trucker, "If every one whistles we'll have no order in the plant."

A few minutes later they went to the hog killing floor. The hog house was small for the plant and everything was still being done by hand.

The gang was composed of stalwarts every one . . . The day's schedule was 6,000 hogs, a big day's work. Someone had started the negroes singing when the whistle blew that morning, and the work had been turned out 600 hogs an hour, 10 a minute, right from the start.

"Here! Here! Stop it!" the astounded visitor had to shout to make himself heard over the ringing chorus of "Down in Mobile." So the superintendent called the foreman, who immediately silenced the singers.

"That will slow up the work, Mr. Swift," the superintendent told him. "We want to get out 6,000 hogs today, and we'll never do it without the singing. It helps those boys work."

"Never mind," directed his employer. "I think we can kill the hogs without any musical accompaniment. Yes sir, we turn out a lot of pork at Chicago without singing."

"You have conveyor chains, rolling tables, all the other facilities at Chicago for speeding up the work. If you need to turn out a little more than the usual production, you speed up the conveyors a little and the men speed up to keep pace."

"I think we don't need the singing. It's bad for discipline" was the final word on the subject.

But later in the day, as the visitor and the plant manager entered the superintendent's office, that practical soul took from his desk the production reports which had been accumulating during the day. They showed that, from the moment the singing had stopped, hogs had been killed at the rate of 400 an hour instead of 600 as before. He handed the sheet to his chief without comment.

"Hm," came the decision after a considerable pause. "Hm. I guess maybe there's a little something in what you say. Maybe you might let those boys sing when they've got an extra lot of work to do. But"—regretfully—"singing is mighty hard on discipline."

One of his cardinal principles which enabled him to raise better men than he could hire was his sparing use of compliments. He believed in seldom praising. His creed held that if a man does good work, that deserves no praise. It is exactly what he is paid to do. If his work is exceptionally fine, still do not praise him. Give him a raise, and at the first chance a better job with more responsibility. Thus you give the man the benefit he has earned by his ability. You have, as an employer, advantaged yourself of the employee's capacity. And you have not spoiled him by telling him he is good.

He tried his best to hold his managers to the same point of view. He did not want them upsetting the applecart by giving out praise. Once at Saint Joseph he was going over the plant with the manager when they encountered a negro janitor engaged in some job which, while it had to be done, was outside a janitor's regular duties. The manager praised him for his alertness in seeing the need and pitching into the job on his own hook. As they walked away he said to his chief, "There's one of the best men in this plant. He's always surprising me by doing better than I can expect any one to do."

They walked on for a minute or two in silence. Then from the depths of his experience the older man offered his tart comment: "You're going to spoil a good boy—spoil a good boy, Mr. Donovan."

At another of our plants he was going through with a younger man, a foreman who has since become a plant superintendent. As they were standing by a long zinc table where they were doing the scraping by hand he inquired, "Mr. Pratt, where do you think these hogs should be cleaned?"

"Right here where they are now being cleaned," answered the foreman.

"We don't do it that way at Chicago," retorted father—this was the reply he used to squelch anyone at any of our other plants who stood up for an inferior way of doing. Chicago was at that time supposed to include all of the packinghouse virtues developed to date.

"There are a lot of things you don't do at Chicago," replied Pratt. "We're scraping them while they're still hot from the scalding water. At Chicago they scrape the hogs on the rail. I think this is better than the Chicago way."

. . . if a man does good work, that deserves no praise. It is exactly what he is paid to do. If his work is exceptionally fine, still do not praise him. Give him a raise . . .

"Young man, you're right," his employer admitted—the highest praise he could bring himself to administer.

The veteran who went through this experience laughed about it many years later. And he commented, "I believe this is the only time Mr. Swift ever agreed with me about anything we discussed! Next time I was in Chicago I observed that he had them handling their hogs by our method."

It is noteworthy that the chief did not tell the man his idea had been adopted. He knew the originator would see it sometime at Chicago. Meanwhile there was no use acting as if the man had done something to make a fuss over.

But if G. F. Swift was sparing of praise, he was lavish with advice about better ways to do things. He never overlooked an opportunity to instruct.

"How do you think these hogs are dressed?" he inquired of a plant man on another trip.

"I think the day's killing is well dressed," the employee told him.

"I beg to differ with you. That's all"—and he waved the younger man back to his work.

Next day the plant man received a letter from the plant superintendent with the president's criticism attached. Busy as he was, father had gone into it in great detail. It was a constructive set of instructions on one operation of pork packing. Giving instructions took up a much larger part of his usual day than did praise.

One thing he insisted on was absolute honesty. Time and again he came to my desk or called me to his and pointed out some slip-up in shipping dates, or a let-down in quality, or something else which had the appearance of a sharp corner having been cut to get an advantage for Swift and Company. He would lecture me on the specific mistake. But always he would end up by talking about the need for being honest. "We want character to go with our goods. And 16 ounces is a Swift pound."

So it is not surprising that in the early days especially, before the spirit of fair dealing had been absorbed by all of our people, a good many men got through in a hurry. Usually it was for lies they had told, or for misrepresenting to customers. Father had no use for anyone who had any other standard than absolute honesty and 16 ounces to the pound.

I recall one man who was fired for stealing. He appealed to the front office. "I've worked for you 20 years, Mr. Swift," he pleaded.

"You stole, didn't you?"

"Yes sir."

"You worked for me 20 years too long, then," was the decision.

This kind of discipline was not inspired by any desire to be unkind. It was stern discipline, but effective.

Yet, rigid as were his ideas of discipline, he allowed them to relax for the worker who had earned special consideration, or about whom there was some reason for not holding to too high a standard of expectation.

"One of the Fairest, Squarest Bosses Anyone Ever Had"

I think it is generally agreed by the men who worked with him that Gustavus F. Swift was one of the fairest, squarest bosses anyone ever had. He treated everyone alike.

He was very much interested in the personal affairs of his people.

He wanted his people to own stock. He was a pioneer in bringing this about in a big way. His was the first large company to encourage its employees to become substantial stockholders.

Next in desirability as stockholders father rated customers. Swift stock was originally bought by eastern livestock and meat men who constituted our first body of customers, the nucleus around which our dressed-beef business was developed. When new outlets were added, either as dealers or as agents, the newcomers were given the opportunity to buy a few shares. Thus the sales organization was built up with an undivided loyalty, and a desire, founded on self-interest, that the company prosper.

I have said that sarcasm was my father's working tool in handling employees. He might be, and he generally was, very personal in his remarks, but he meant them impersonally. No matter how hard he jumped us—I got just as large a share as any one else—he left us with the feeling that it was all deserved. He left no sting, but he left us convinced. No matter how hard he might jump, no matter how wholly unpleasant he might be in the tenor and tone of his remarks, next time he saw the employee the storm had blown over.

Another of his knacks in raising better men than he could hire was his ability at cross-examination. Whether the questioning took place in his office, at home, or at the employee's desk or work-bench, the procedure had its common characteristics.

His first questions would be so unrelated that the employee would wonder what on earth he was driving at. His succeeding questions would begin to shape up into a skeleton, so that the man began to think he knew what it was all about. And then, when the conclusion seemed right ahead, father would, with one or two well-placed queries, turn an abrupt corner and convict the employee of something he had not even known he was suspected of.

But if his questionings were devious, his instructions to employees were always direct. He said absolutely what he wanted done, in as clear-cut a way as anyone could devise.

He was the driver, the dynamo of the business. He worked his men hard, and treated everyone fairly. From time to time I have heard rumors of this or that man who felt himself badly treated by father. But whenever I have been familiar with the facts, they have been all on the employer's side.

In this connection, the statement of a man who worked with my father from the start at Chicago—who came out, in fact, from the slaughter-house of Anthony, Swift and Company at Assonet to take charge of slaughtering at Chicago—is interesting. He left Swift and Company in 1897 to take a position with another company which could for the time being pay several times as much as we could for his specialized ability. Thereafter he had no connection with us, no reason for telling a good story about us.

"The Basic Explanation of Father's Oft-Repeated Assertion"

It was almost 30 years after he left us, and 15 years after he retired to live on his income, that he told a man unconnected with our business:

"I worked for G. F. Swift for 22 years. He was the squarest man I ever worked for. All that time I never asked him what he was going to pay me. I never had cause to complain. If you worked well for him, he saw that you got what you deserved in money and in every other way."

There, it seems to me, is the basic explanation of father's oft-repeated assertion: "I can raise better men than I can hire."

ANDREW CARNEGIE
1835 – 1919

The business precepts of steel tycoon Andrew Carnegie are not for the timid. To begin, Carnegie said, "The rising man must do something exceptional, and beyond the range of his special department. HE MUST ATTRACT ATTENTION." And that is exactly what he did. Back in 1854, Carnegie was a telegraph operator for the Pennsylvania Railroad Company when a serious accident occurred. Trains up and down the line were frozen. The superintendent couldn't be found, so Carnegie broke company rules and tapped out messages directing the trains on how to proceed. He audaciously signed each order with his boss's initials. Obviously, Carnegie was not without confidence and brashly advised, "Boss your boss as soon as you can; try it on early."

Carnegie also put his money where his mouth was. During a 1872 trip to England, Carnegie witnessed a new method for making steel and was convinced it was the way of the future. He returned home and invested his entire nest egg—$250,000—into building a steel plant. According to one biographer, the soon-to-be Steel King was "zealous in his careful scrutiny of every detail in the planning of the new plant." Carnegie knew that only rational planning and attention to detail would allow him to build the most efficient and advanced steel mill in the United States.

Besides coal and ore, another critical resource was men. Carnegie attributed much of his success to the men around him, and at one point he wrote an epithet for himself that read "Here lies one who knew how to get around him men cleverer than himself." But then came the 1892 Homestead strike to win better wages, during which 10 men died and scores were wounded. How could Carnegie turn so violently on the very men he claimed to cherish? One reason was that he was in Scotland at the time, so communication was poor. Another was that when it came to strikers, Carnegie preferred to "Starve them out" and "Let grass grow over [the steel] works" than reconcile any differences. Over time Carnegie learned from his own mistakes and came to have a more progressive vision of business leadership. Always a great motivator, Carnegie shares some of his wisdom in *The Secret of Business Is the Management of Men.*

The Secret of Business Is the Management of Men

Andrew Carnegie

I never see a fishing fleet set sail without pleasure, thinking this is based upon the form which is probably to prevail generally. Not a man in the boats is paid fixed wages. Each gets his share of the profits. That seems to me the ideal. It would be most interesting if we could compare the results of a fleet so manned and operated with one in which men were paid fixed wages; but I question whether such a fleet as the latter exists. From my experience, I should say a crew of employees *versus* a crew of partners would not be in the race.

The great secret of success in business of all kinds, and especially in manufacturing, where a small saving in each process means fortune, is a liberal division of profits among the men who help to make them, and the wider distribution the better. There lie latent unsuspected powers in willing men around us which only need appreciation and development to produce surprising results. Money rewards alone will not, however, insure these, for to the most sensitive and ambitious natures there must be the note of sympathy, appreciation, friendship. Genius is sensitive in all its forms, and it is unusual, not ordinary, ability that tells even in practical affairs. You must capture and keep the heart of the original and supremely able man before his brain can do its best.

One of the chief sources of whatever success may have attended the Carnegie Steel Company was undoubtedly its policy of making numerous partners from among the ablest of its men and interesting so many others of ability in results. I strongly recommend this plan to the members of the Institute* engaged in business, believing that in these days of threatened exhausting competition it will be the concerns which adopt this plan, other things being equal, which will survive and flourish.

In no field is the wise saying more amply verified than in manufacturing. "There be those who gather, yet scatter abroad, and there be those who scatter abroad, yet put into barns."

Disputes of some kind between Capital and Labor are always in evidence, but it must never be forgotten that in the wide fields of domestic service and in that of the few employees with a working master which embrace by far the greater number of wage-earners, all is, upon the whole, satisfactory; there reigns peace, with the inevitable individual exceptions.

Managing Men by Personal Touch

We see in this encouraging fact the potent and salutary influence of the personal element. The employer knows his men and the men know their employer; there is mutual respect, sympathy, kindly interest, and good feeling, hence peace. In the extensive field of domestic service we best see how true it is—"Like master, like man; like mistress, like Nan." Here we have the relation of employer and employed in its closest form, and innumerable households testify to the harmonizing effect of personal relations. The trusty servant becomes practically a member of the family, deeply attached to it; and the family reciprocates the feeling. Few householders are

* This selection is an excerpt from a speech delivered to The British Iron and Steel Institute.

without old retainers and pensioners, and to the end of their days, and even to that of the children of the household, the relationship remains unbroken. The friendship of the employers and their children for the old servants, and the affection of these for their masters and mistresses and their children, is one of the most delightful features of life.

You must capture and keep the heart of the original and supremely able man before his brain can do its best.

What has produced this reciprocal affection? Not the mere payment of stipulated wages on the one part and the bare performance of stipulated duties on the other—far from this. It is the something more done upon both sides and the knowledge each has had opportunity to gather of the other, their virtues, kindness—in short, their characters. The strict terms of the contract are drowned in the deep well of mutual regard. Labor is never fully paid by money alone.

If the managing owners and officials of great corporations could only be known to their men and, equally important, their men known to their employers, and the hearts of each exposed to the other, as well as their difficulties, we should have in that troublesome field such harmony as delights us in the domestic. It is mainly the ignorance of contending parties of each other's virtues that breeds quarrels everywhere throughout the world, between individuals, between corporations and their men—and between nations. "We only hate those we do not know" is a sound maxim which we do well ever to bear in mind.

In the progress toward more harmonious conditions between employer and employed we see that the system of payment by fixed wage has been largely supplanted by payment according to value of service rendered by workmen in positions of authority over others, and by recognition not only in money, but in position, which often counts quite as much as coin, and not seldom much more with the ablest. There remains still receiving the fixed wage the great mass of ordinary workmen; but we see in the history of the relations of employer and employed that these have not failed to rise greatly, also. The movement tending to improve the position of the worker has not passed over even the humblest, but has reached and benefited all.

Passing over the day when the capitalistic employer owned and managed his labor as slaves, it is surprising to note that even as late as last century villenage still lingered in Scotland. Miners and laborers were practically transferred with the mine when it was sold. Speaking recently to a most intelligent miner in Fife (and the Fife miners deserve their extraordinary reputation for intelligence, sobriety, and all the elements of good citizenship), I mentioned the fact that our forefathers were thus transferred, and contrasted the position now, when their committee was at that moment meeting the property owners in discussion as equal parties to a contract, both merchants—one buying, the other selling labor. To the inquiry what would be thought now if the employer desired to transfer the men with the mines, he replied:

It is mainly the ignorance of contending parties of each other's virtues that breeds quarrels everywhere throughout the world, between individuals, between corporations and their men—and between nations.

"Aw, there would be twa at that bargain, I'm thinkin'."

You have to be Scotch fully to appreciate the reply, for much lies in the accent, the twinkle of the eye and significant nod.

A Splendid Vista of Work and Capital

Thus we see that the world moves on step by step toward better conditions. Just as the mechanical world has changed and improved, so has advanced the world of labor from the slavery of the laborer to the day of his absolute independence, and now to this day when he begins to take his proper place as the capitalist partner of his employer. We may look forward with hope to the day when it shall be the rule that the workman is partner with capital, the man of affairs giving his business experience, the working man in the mill giving his mechanical skill to the company, both owners in the shares and so far equally interested in the success of their joint efforts, each indispensable, without whose cooperation success were impossible. It is a splendid vista along which we are permitted to gaze. . . .

Human society bears a charmed life. It is immortal, and was born with the inherent power or instinct, as a law of its being, to solve all problems finally in the best form and among these none more surely than that vexed question of our day, the relations between these Siamese Twins, which must mutually prosper or mutually decay, and for which separation means death—Employer and Employed—Capital and Labor.

Charles W. Patterson

Texas-born Charles W. Patterson was a legendary maverick whose favorite commands to subordinates included "Motion means money. Speed up!" and "This is no time for judicial decisions. Be quick on the trigger." Patterson was president of what was at one time the largest grocery concern in the world, Austin Nichols & Company. More recently the company was best known for its Wild Turkey bourbon, among other liquors and wines, and eventually it was bought by a French firm. Patterson was characterized as a results-oriented man of action. However, as a nineteen-year-old salesman for the H. J. Heinz Company, he almost lost his first job for lack of action. When his training manager asked Patterson if he preferred the kind of business that came to him or the kind he had to go get, the naive young man answered the former. He was fired on the spot, but then given a second chance and rehired—a lesson he never forgot.

Patterson became the company's top salesman and quickly moved up through the ranks. Eventually he took over as manager of a small division of a packing plant and subsequently increased its operations to a point where the company decided to spin it off. Suddenly Patterson found himself the head of an independent firm. While at Heinz and after, he attributed his success to not interfering with his department heads. He believed that anyone of average intelligence could be a success if empowered with the freedom to act, so he encouraged his people to run their departments as if they were their own businesses. Patterson never wanted to make the mistake of being a micromanager.

As for mistakes, Patterson said, "If you take time to think a thing over, your decision will be no better; often worse. If you make a mistake, it is not so bad, for you can turn a handspring and set it right again." He greeted all problems as if they were old comrades in an ongoing war. For him, business was a fighting game, and therefore, he believed young people should be sent to the front. In *Business Is a Young Man's Game,* Patterson offers a very poignant perspective for those who are relatively green in their career but are seeking promotion and want to be leaders.

Business Is a Young Man's Game

Charles W. Patterson

This matter of being an executive depends on a thorough knowledge of the business and the ability to decide quickly. At the present moment, world business is halting because of the difficulty men have in making up their minds. An executive must make up his mind to take the results of his mistakes, but not to let them hinder him from action. There is hardly ever anything gained by waiting; the decision is as likely to be wrong at the end of the period as it was at the beginning.

I've made as many mistakes as any man; but getting right to it and covering them up by making a decision that was *not* a mistake has saved me. In our day the most pressing need we feel, and the need we are going to feel for the next twenty years, is the need for action. That is why I believe that this day of all others is the day of the young man—he hasn't had time to grow judicial, and he isn't afraid to go ahead.

We have an unfair prejudice against young men. We wait often until they are "old" enough for certain work. The truth is they are often ready years before we let them do anything.

I had a young man once as an assistant in a department of the house of which I was in charge. He was an enterprising young fellow; he was able; he had every qualification for going ahead—except his age. He was only twenty-three years old.

At the present moment, world business is halting because of the difficulty men have in making up their minds.

I was as bad as all the rest of the fellows who get into managerial chairs, and I hesitated. For two years I held that young man back. Then at last I made him head of the department, still half afraid to promote him—he was so young. It didn't take me long to see that I had lost a good deal in the two years of holding him back. That young man was ready for his work, and had been all that time. He made a splendid head. His youth had nothing to do with it.

The truth is that most human beings grow up, in judgment, at thirty; some by the age of twenty-five; and that, after that, they are more able only because of experience and ease and dexterity in handling the job; their judgment doesn't improve much. Some few men make successes late in life, but I wonder if the delay isn't because they have been victims of circumstances, rather than late in developing.

Business is a fighting game. And when it's a question of fighting, we send our young men first. Quick decisions come easily to youth.

Anyhow, the young man should have his chance. He should be put into whatever position his ability entitles him to, no matter what his age. Age is no longer a crime in business, neither is the lack of it. And, having been put in charge, he should be left alone. This is another injustice we do our young men: we keep our hands on them for fear they will do something wrong. It is far better to let them alone. If they do something wrong, and they are worth anything, they will hurry up and do something right, quick, and make things even. And they won't stand still and deliberate and hold councils while someone else gets the business away.

Business is a fighting game. And when it's a question of fighting, we send our young men first. Quick decisions come easily to youth. I'd turn my calendar back ten years if I could: I'd be just as well fitted for my job, and I'd have that much more youth to go on.

T. Coleman du Pont
1863 – 1930

The du Pont family, one of the most potent forces in American industry, emigrated to the United States in 1799 to escape the chaos that followed the French Revolution. They first made their mark in Delaware by building a factory to make gunpowder, a product they knew was always in demand. By the end of the nineteenth century, the family had branched out into paper pulp mills, coal mines, street railway companies, and steel plants. Coleman du Pont, who stood to inherit a sizable fortune, went to the Massachusetts Institute of Technology in 1881 with one priority: to have a good time. After two years he dropped out and sought his riches in the family coal mines of Kentucky. du Pont worked his way up from mule driver, to miner, to superintendent of the company. Eventually he became involved with the electric street railway business and built it into a national concern.

As a businessman, du Pont was always willing to gamble as long as the potential reward was worth it. His biggest test came when, in 1902, his cousins Alfred and Pierre and he decided to buy out the family's ailing gunpowder business. Coleman du Pont was made CEO and president while Alfred would handle production and Pierre the finances. They personally took on millions of dollars of debt. The company had been run as if it were still 1802 so renovations began immediately and horses were replaced by machines. Between wars and construction, business boomed. For example, beginning in 1904, du Pont sold 61 million pounds of dynamite for the Panama Canal project alone. The company diversified into chemical manufacturing in 1910 and brought the world everything from nylon to atomic bombs.

Coleman du Pont's greatest contribution to the company was his development of executives. When asked how he was able to find such good men regularly, he responded that it was intuition, a sense of smell. Once he put employees in positions of responsibility, he allowed them the freedom to act. He said, "Some men make the mistake of overruling their lieutenants, of not accepting their judgment. How can you expect to develop the best that is in a man if you don't allow him to exercise his judgment . . . ?" In the following selection, du Pont elaborates on what he looks for in an employee and how to develop an executive.

Are You a Job-Holder or a Result-Getter?

T. Coleman du Pont

I haven't done much—I don't do much. I pick other men to run things for me. I'm on the lookout for the right kind of men everywhere, anywhere, and always. I've found them North and South; I've found them in factories, in banks, in steel mills, even under the ground—in coal mines. Whenever I spot a man who has made a good start I watch him, I follow his progress, I try to get a correct line on his ability. I find out all I can about the results he produces.

Ability is the thing that gets results honestly.

I never engage an executive who isn't fair.

I mean that he must deal fairly and squarely with everybody and that, in particular, he must have the right attitude toward labor. There is a lot of talk about possible trouble of a serious and widespread nature between employers and employed after the war. I personally am not alarmed, for if labor is treated as it should be treated, it will have no real occasion to kick over the traces. I have always managed to get along pleasantly with labor, and I will never select a lieutenant who is not so constituted that he cannot help but treat his workers fairly and uprightly. The man who has not learned how to get along smoothly with workers is not the type of man to place in a responsible executive position.

In addition to being fair, the man I want must, of course, have other qualities. I want a man who is fearless: courage, self-confidence, self-reliance are very important essentials. The business game cannot be played aggressively and successfully by a mollycoddle.

Then the right type of man is democratic. He must not consider himself a superior sort of personage. He must actually feel democratic; it is not enough that he try to pose as democratic—he must *be* democratic, otherwise the veneer, the sheen, would wear off, for you can't fool a body of intelligent American workmen for very long. He must ring true.

Another point: I always want a man who looks after his health. A strong, upstanding, square-shouldered fellow, whose muscles are whipcord rather than putty, is usually apt to forge ahead against all sorts of odds. The man who is of inferior physique and who doesn't look after his health properly is less likely to succeed. Good health, in a sense, is at the base of all business achievement, for the pace nowadays is too grueling for weaklings. The time a man's best effort is most needed is when a crisis has to be faced; and unless a man is thoroughly fit physically, the extra strain and stress and emotion are apt to play havoc with him at the crucial moment. Year after year I kept myself so strictly in trim that my weight did not vary five pounds from what it was when I left college.

To win in the business game—or any game, including the game of life itself—you must enjoy it. There is something wrong with a man who does not enjoy his work more and more as he gets older. This is not only my own experience, but I find it is the experience of a number of successful men with whom I have talked. A man should grow happier as he grows older, and he *can* grow happier—I don't see how he can fail to grow happier—if he is on the right terms with his work.

Here again, however, the question of health enters. To enjoy business, to enjoy life, to be fit to carry out hard or big things, a man must be in sound physical condition. Therefore, any young man who aspires to become a leader in his line should early realize the vital importance of strengthening, building up and tuning up his physical machine. I have emphasized the necessity for having ambition; but ambition is not likely to get a man anywhere unless he has a head, a body and hands capable of carrying out his ambition. Mere wishing gets a man nowhere. He must back up his wishes with action, and action is dependent in no little measure upon a man's physical stamina.

Don't misunderstand me. I am not a stickler for what is ordinarily understood by the term "hard work." Once I place a man in charge of something, I don't care a rap whether he works ten hours or only one hour a day—although I confess I have never known a man who could produce the right results by one hour's effort a day. I never try to keep tabs on his going or coming. But I do watch the results. If he produces satisfactory results, what does it matter whether he spends a lot or a little of his time in his office, or whether he plays golf often or seldom?

The higher type of man can produce the best results if given an entirely free hand. He must be allowed freedom to do things his own way. Also, the responsibility of making decisions must be left to him. I never decide things for any of my lieutenants. They must make their own decisions. How, otherwise, could I hold them responsible for results? But don't you see that under this system a man knows and feels, if success is achieved, that he is entitled to the credit, not me? This develops a man as nothing else can.

Of course, not all men are capable of filling positions which carry the responsibility of making important decisions. Some men can work wonderfully for other people; they are ideal tools, or implements, when guided by others. But they lack initiative, originality, self-courage. They are capable, faithful, valuable followers, but not leaders."

From the very start a youth begins to shape his whole future career. What he does or fails to do today governs to a large extent what he will do or fail to do tomorrow. Businessmen—at least in business matters—are sternly practical. What they want to know about a man is, What has he done? Each man writes his own answer. The sooner every young man in the country realizes this, the greater will be his chances of recognition, advancement and final success.

Theodore N. Vail
1845 – 1920

Alexander Graham Bell, who patented the telephone in February of 1876, left the actual building of the infrastructure for telephone service to men like Vail. Vail, who was working for the U.S. Railway Service and was considered the foremost expert in mail delivery, was hired by Bell Telephone in 1878. His mission was to take on Western Union and replace the telegraph with the telephone as the most important device for communication. Implicit in this mission was the job of networking the country with telephone lines, just as Vail had done with his system for mail delivery. To achieve his goals he sunk profits right back into operations, which angered shareholders looking for dividends. While on this technological frontier, he kept the numerous problems in perspective with the maxim "Real difficulties can be overcome; it is only the imaginary ones that are unconquerable."

In 1880 Vail won his battle with Western Union when he convinced it to sell out its interests, and in 1885 Bell formally became American Telephone and Telegraph. In an interesting side note, his uncle, Alfred Vail, had financed and assisted in the development of the telegraph. In fact, Uncle Alfred got Vail a job as an operator for Western Union early in his career, but Vail was fired because he "tended toward the night life and billiards." Now Vail was running the show. Two years after buying Western Union, he left AT&T a wealthy man and retired to a Vermont farm, his job accomplished.

In 1901 J. P. Morgan purchased a controlling interest in AT&T and summoned Vail to return. As per the Morgan way, the two devoured independent telephone companies and created a monopoly. Vail's primary task was to promote a natural monopoly to head off the government inquisitors. In his first letter to shareholders, he emphatically explained that the duplication of plants and services was a waste. Vail's message succeeded in holding off the government (until 1985 anyway), mainly because he brought respectability to Morgan's notoriety. In *The Making of Successful Men,* Vail's emphasis on good character is obvious; however, he also delves into how to cultivate some very practical and necessary traits for leadership.

The Making of a Successful Businessman

Theodore N. Vail

The term "business" has no narrow or restricted meaning. It is the doing of things; it is the effective use of accumulations of study, experience, and observation; it applies alike to any trade, profession, pursuit, calling, or occupation. The agriculturist, the artist, the teacher, the literary man, as well as the commercial man and the so-called "captain of industry," all are business men. Business is the byplay, the action of life; it is that which brings into high relief and prominence the pursuits, and makes available the accomplishment, of any individual.

The writer of books who, while allowing himself to be exploited and exhibited round the country, was deploring the commercialism of the American people, was doing business; he was engaged in the very commercialism that he pretended to despise.

Ordinarily the businessman is considered to be a commercial man—a trader, or collector and distributor of commodities, a banker, or dealer in exchange and securities. Usually the term is associated in our minds with more or less success.

The making of a good business man, in the narrowest sense of the term, the foundation upon which his career is to be built, must be the same in all respects as that of every good and useful man in our social organization. There is only one set of principles for every man who is to get the best out of life for himself, or to be of the greatest service to others.

Business is the byplay, the action of life; it is that which brings into high relief and prominence the pursuits, and makes available the accomplishment, of any individual.

The Pioneers of Civilization: Honesty

In certain ages and countries, a measure of opprobrium was connected with the term business, and the business man or trader held an inferior social position as the result of certain unpraiseworthy methods and acts of the traders of those days and countries; but notwithstanding this, all the pioneer paths of the civilization of the world have been staked out by those same traders, whose selfish desires led them to take great risks and open unknown regions to trade and the civilizing agencies that followed. Selfishness for personal advantage, and self-sacrifice for advantage to others, have worked together as the pioneers of all civilization.

Both exchange of commodities and exchange of thought make for the comfort, happiness, and higher enjoyment of mankind; and it is the selfish desire for gain and fame that increases business activity and brings all parts of the world into closer communication. Inter-communication and interchange are productive of civilization.

With all the higher characteristics and greater benefits of business, it has its questionable side and its questionable practices. It has been, and is, and always will be, engaged in by some persons of doubtful character; anything that tends to good can be perverted and made to pander to the selfish desires and inconsiderate greed of others. While this is to be deplored, and to be minimized as far as possible, we must never forget that the resultant good of all business activity far overshadows the evil that must be incidental to it.

If every member of society could be taught both self-respect and respect for the rights of others; if he could learn to be self-maintaining, to exercise the best that is in him, to recognize conditions that are consequent upon natural laws, and not rebel against them, to recognize conditions essential to our social organization, to shape them for their legitimate purpose, and not countenance any perversion of them for the selfish purpose or greed of others—there would soon result a state as nearly ideal as is possible in this life.

It is the character of the mass of individuals that determines the character of the social world, of which each man is a part. No great social wrong or evil can thrive in any community without the indifference, if not the acquiescence and active participation, of most of the individuals that constitute that community. *Les maisons font la ville, mais les citoyens font la cité.*

There has been too much of the idea that every boy is a possible President, that every soldier carries a general's baton in his knapsack. Every boy is far from being a possible President, and every soldier is not a possible general.

In the making of a business man the personality of the individual must be considered. There has been too much of the idea that every boy is a possible President, that every soldier carries a general's baton in his knapsack. Every boy is far from being a possible President, and every soldier is not a possible general. Men are very unevenly endowed by nature, both physically and mentally. It is upon their inherited capacity in any direction that their possibilities depend, and upon the training and education they receive that their "probabilities" depend. The result of every man's life is at best the difference between his assets and his liabilities, the balance between his favorable and unfavorable natural endowments, as affected by training, education, or preparation. All favorable qualities or natural gifts can be strengthened, and all unfavorable ones, if not minimized or completely absorbed, can be subordinated. Everything depends upon the proper appreciation, by the man himself or by others, of his possibilities, and upon the highest development of them, through proper training or education. The only limits to any man's achievements are his natural endowments as they may be developed, but fortunately for the world and for the individual, there is in the pyramid of our great social organization a place for every man, one in which he shall be at his best both for himself and for others. Each place in that pyramid is as important to the social organization as any other, and for each place the right man is essential.

Judging the Man: Accuracy

Under general conditions, all that a man receives depends upon himself. He can be helped or shoved into a position, but he must hold that position by his own efforts. If he fails, it is because the estimate made of his capacity or of his possibilities has been wrong, and the impossible has been attempted, or because those qualities that work for good have been weakened by inaction and repression, and negative qualities have become strengthened by indulgence or lack of control. Although in the individual it is easy to distinguish the extremes of good or bad, it is difficult to determine just where those extremes blend. In almost every case judgment is bound to be tempered and biased by the personal equation of both the observed and the observer. Self-recognition is the more difficult, influenced as it must be by temperament and by personal characteristics.

There are many men who have made one success—and never another. The failure to make any other has been due to personal indulgence, or neglect to employ the essential means to successful accomplishment that were employed in the earlier efforts.

SUCCESS AND FAILURE: PUNCTUALITY

In the making of a business man, it is wise to consider the meaning of success and failure. There are many failures in the eyes of the world that are far from being failures, and there are a great many successes that are not recognized.

Too much of the tendency of modern education is toward inculcating the idea that success in life is to achieve great fame, great prominence or notoriety, to accomplish great undertakings, or accumulate great riches. Unusual development and achievement in some one of these lines is the necessary accompaniment of marked progress, of great prosperity, or of a high civilization; yet it is within bounds to say that none of these in themselves bring real enjoyment, happiness, and contentment.

Under general conditions, all that a man receives depends upon himself. He can be helped or shoved into a position, but he must hold that position by his own efforts.

The strain of accomplishing large things is likely to deaden all the finer senses; the strain of holding large things is likely to preclude enjoyment through the senses that remain quick. Real enjoyment of things or conditions in life is in inverse ratio to the care, anxiety or obligations that accompany them.

Man is truly a social being. It is not in extravagant conceits, constant change, novelty, and excitement that happiness and contentment lie, but rather in the quiet simplicity of life and in the companionship that can only exist between those possessed of more or less the same average of qualities, between those who can find enjoyment in the same things.

In order to enjoy life, a man must repress inordinate ambition and cultivate contentment, but he must not sacrifice a worthy ambition to develop within proper bounds all his best capabilities and power for usefulness.

In the making of a business man, the foundation to be laid is the same, whatever the final calling or pursuit. Every pursuit or calling, with its various branches and divisions, is as many-sided as humanity itself, and offers the individual opportunities to employ his peculiar gifts to the best advantage.

The Personal Inclination: Civility

The personal inclination, so often considered as a guide to one's choice in an education or vocation, has usually little or no value. As a rule, it is the result of early environment. There is always a period in a boy's life when he wants to be a policeman or an engineer. Those historical inclinations in youth that are said to have controlled the future of so many great men are often the "recollection after the fact." The only effect of a strong personal inclination is its influence on one's industry or its excuse for lack of effort.

As pertinent to this question of inclination, it must be remembered that the underlying and governing factor in growth or development is either self-control or the subordination of one's self to others and to conditions. The measure of success is governed by capacity for self-control or capacity for subordination to conditions or to the control of others.

After self-control, the most important elements are directness of purpose and honesty, and a thorough realization of one's responsibility for every act, and of one's accountability for the result of every act.

In order to enjoy life, a man must repress inordinate ambition and cultivate contentment, but he must not sacrifice a worthy ambition to develop within proper bounds all his best capabilities and power for usefulness.

The lack of self-restraint or self-control is, in its influence on individual life, far worse than any inherited vice or taint. Nothing else is so destructive of all that goes to make success. Many of the essential lessons and good habits are best acquired at the mother's knee. Through the exercise of firmness, gentleness, and consistency from the beginning, they can be acquired unconsciously and without any of the suffering that comes through the discipline necessary to conquer settled habits. The child who is allowed to indulge his whims for this or that thing is being severely handicapped in his future struggle for success.

Give a boy an elementary education, a training and foundation, and he will do all the rest. Influence he will make for himself; the push and pull that so many depend upon, he will himself create.

In response to an article that went the round of the papers about the difficulty of finding men for positions of leadership, hundreds of letters were received. Many of the writers were serious and earnest, and showed a desire to rise above an environment that seemed to be hopeless. Others, full of conceit, desired to step into a position of leadership without experience of any kind, confident that they possessed all the necessary qualifications. Some of them offered to eat their letters or pay some absurd wager if they did not succeed. Others ranted on the theory that all employers were slave-drivers, and that no one had a chance without money and influence; still others deplored the lack of opportunity, but mentioned the numerous positions of trust they had occupied that, for some unrevealed reason, they were not able to retain. In a word, they nearly all expected to be pushed into position and kept there by brute force.

Only a few of the answers gave any indication of a capacity to appreciate what a position of leadership means, or what it requires.

Business leadership requires, first of all, natural capacity, then the training and experience that come only from a long and successful struggle with all kinds of environment and obstacles, and, lastly, some successful experience under full responsibility.

The lack of self-restraint or self-control is, in its influence on individual life, far worse than any inherited vice or taint.

In the making of a businessman, and in the course of a business life, there are practices to be cultivated, things to be learned and habits to be formed that are most helpful to success. These are the most important of them:

- Concentration upon and application to the work in hand, to the exclusion, for the time being, of all other work.
- Definiteness of purpose and thoroughness in deciding on a pursuit, and in doing and learning all that is necessary to be done or known for its accomplishment.
- Observation, or the habit of noticing little things—instinctive recognition of anything wrong, or out of place. This in incidental to orderly habits, or the result of them. General deductions from single incidents

should never be made. One incident may be accidental; many similar incidents come from a common cause.

- Foresight and precaution; there never was a successful leader who did not continue all precautions until the moment of success.
- Self-confidence, without overconfidence or offensive egotism; it should rest on a thorough knowledge of what is to be done, or on experience in the doing, or on both.
- Respect for the unknown; in every undertaking there are difficulties that only a familiar and practical acquaintance can reveal.
- Respect for the opinions of others.
- Deliberation over new ideas. Many thoughts that are seemingly wonderful lose their apparent value when slept over, or exposed to impartial criticism.
- Attention without interruption to anyone who is at all entitled to be heard. Cultivate the mind in many directions. To know intelligently about many things is always valuable to a business man.
- Reciprocity in all the affairs of life. It is only by reciprocity that permanent success can be gained. Every exchange should benefit both sides.

Those who feel discouraged by hard conditions should remember that most successful men have started under discouraging conditions.

PART VIII

Leading Revolution

Transforming, adapting, breaking down barriers, reengineering, taking risks—all are catch-words used when describing either how to keep a business growing or how to revitalize one. But they're just words. Imagine taking over the helm of a huge but struggling company whose founder has just died—and it's your father. That's what Thomas J. Watson, Jr., had to deal with as he brought IBM into the computer age. Fear of failure drove Watson. Disney's chairman Michael Eisner, on the other hand, believes that failing occasionally is the only way to keep a company vital. When it comes to leading change, Robert Galvin considers "renewal" to be the driving force. He explains what role it plays in not only energizing companies, but in creating new industries. The expertise needed for and the nuances of leading change, of leading a true revolution can never be condensed into a few phrases, as the authors prove in this section that looks to the future.

Lawrence A. Bossidy
1935 –

Before Lawrence A. Bossidy became AlliedSignal's chairman and CEO, he had risen through General Electric's ranks to become Jack Welch's number-two man. Some characterized him dryly as "Jack's Hammer" when it came to remodeling the company. Like Welch, Bossidy was an altar boy who grew up in a blue-collar town—Pittsfield, Massachusetts. From the age of twelve he worked evenings and Saturdays in the family shoe store, and when he attended Colgate University, he used his car as an office to sell white buck shoes to the preppies. Recently Bossidy reflected, "Running AlliedSignal is like running Bossidy's shoe store—only multiplied hundreds of times."

AlliedSignal was a sluggish conglomerate of aerospace and auto parts, among other products, in need of a jump-start when Bossidy came on board. Inheriting a mature company was no easy task, but he brought a positive attitude: "There's no such thing as a mature market. What we need is mature executives who can find ways to grow!" To turn AlliedSignal around, Bossidy embraced more than just cost-cutting. He said, "Restructuring is negative. You get a frightened workforce. Eventually you need to maintain or create jobs, not destroy them."

As part of his program to eliminate the old bureaucracy, make quicker decisions, and beat the competitor to market, Bossidy has pitches for new products and services presented directly to him. If someone throws out a weak idea, he'll let them know by shouting "There's an air ball!" Bossidy admits to being forthright: "For years being totally direct wasn't regarded as a plus. Then under Jack Welch, it came into vogue." Bossidy doesn't hide his feelings—nor does he hide in his office; every week he tries to visit one of the twenty businesses that make up AlliedSignal. Another of his initiatives is fostering loyalty among his employees. "I don't think there's much loyalty left in business anymore, and I don't say that as a negative. I just say that as a matter of reality." In *Reality-Based Leadership: Changes in the Workplace,* Bossidy tackles the problems of a changing world in which everyone wants to know what's in it for him.

Reality-Based Leadership: Changes in the Workplace

Lawrence A. Bossidy

Justice Oliver Wendell Holmes once boarded a train in Washington, then later realized he had lost his ticket. The conductor recognized him and said, "Don't worry about it, sir. I'm sure when you find it, you'll send it in."

Justice Holmes replied, "Young man, the question is not 'Where is my ticket?' but rather, 'Where am I supposed to be going?' "

In a few days, I will celebrate my fifth anniversary at AlliedSignal. My primary challenge during these years has been the same as the one that no doubt faces many of the companies represented here today: that is to say, creating a culture in which people focus on where they are going, instead of where they have been. A culture in which people readily embrace change.

What are some of the changes that we're seeing in the workplace of today?

- Yesterday, we held our employees accountable for effort. Today, they are accountable for results.
- Yesterday, the job market demanded loyalty to one's company. Today loyalty to the customer.

- Yesterday, we tolerated mediocrity, and one could get by with adequate job performance. Today, we demand excellence.
- Yesterday, the ideal was to work at one company for an entire career. Today we recognize that we must be ready to change employers to advance our careers.
- Yesterday, people in small companies were told to look up to the GMs and IBMs of the world and think like a big company. Today the GMs and the IBMs are telling their people to think and act like small, entrepreneurial companies.
- Yesterday, our employees had a worker's perspective on the business; keep your head down, do what you're told, don't ask questions. Today we're asking them to have an owner's perspective. We want employees to understand every aspect of the business, and not just their own function. And we're trying to get every employee to literally be an owner, to participate in an employee savings plan in which the company matches employee contributions with company stock.
- Yesterday, corporate leaders believed in avoiding risk and aimed for the day when the waters would be smooth. Problems were buried to avoid confrontation. Today, we need leaders who are willing to take prudent risks and recognize that tension and conflict are the natural state of a healthy business. People who want to surface problems early so they can be dealt with effectively.

There is considerable debate over whether these changes have been good or bad for American workers. The media and some prominent politicians certainly have their views. They've portrayed employees as miserable, helpless victims who need protection from ruthless corporate executives. While this may help sell newspapers and win some votes, I think it's an inaccurate, even insulting, representation of what's happening in today's workplace.

I'm convinced that job satisfaction is higher in this country than it was twenty years ago, not at every company, but at least in the aggregate. This is America, after all. We're a freedom-loving people. An entrepreneurial, democratic people. Americans don't like to be managed, or treated like children. They want to be asked for their ideas; they want to work in meritocracies where accountability is high and the best people get ahead; they want to be communicated with frequently about how the organization is performing; they want to broaden their skill base; they want to have a chance to own a stake in the companies for which they work. More and more companies are giving employees these opportunities, and they are responding with enthusiasm.

People want job security. But even on this explosive issue, employees are beginning to understand that it's not management who decides how many people are on the payroll, it's customers. Without a growing roster of satisfied customers, we can all turn out the lights and go home.

You didn't hear much about growth in the U.S. during the past decade.

Downsizing was all the rage. But the smoke from all the slashing and burning got so thick that some companies lost sight of a critical fact: That the only reason you downsize is to get your costs more competitive so that you can get more business. You need to grow.

Well, the smoke has started to clear, and for some companies, things look pretty much the same as they did before.

- Some haven't revamped their processes to prevent defects which increase the costs of scrap, rework, and reinspection.
- They haven't analyzed their operations to root out unnecessary work that adds no value in the eyes of the customer.
- They haven't benchmarked other companies to find a better way of doing things or even spread best practices within their own company.

- They haven't eliminated duplicative administrative functions by setting up centers of excellence which perform repetitive, high-volume, transactional functions for the entire enterprise.

In short, they used to live in a big messy house, and now they live in a small messy house.

Employees and long-term shareowners are getting restless. They're loudly asking management, "What did we go through this for? We've endured the pain of layoffs; now where's the gain?"

At long last, companies are waking up to the fact that growth is the primary goal of the corporation for employees, for shareowners and for all other shareholders. Ironically, this realization comes at a moment in history when growth has never been harder to achieve.

For the past two centuries, American business has operated in an environment in which demand outstripped supply in nearly every market. Price increases were pushed through with little resistance. Shoddy quality and slow delivery were commonplace. Manufacturing was done primarily on one continent.

Business leaders who were used to calling the shots are now being forced to dance to the customer's tune. But the dance steps are intricate, and they can't be mastered in a one-hour lesson.

Change was seen as unnecessary and, indeed, to some, illogical. The conventional wisdom at the time was "If it ain't broke, don't fix it."

This idyllic world has been shattered, first, by the rise of low-cost competitors overseas, and, secondly, by increased productivity right here at home. Today, supply exceeds demand. Price increases are hard to come by. Six-sigma quality and ten-minute delivery windows are within our grasp. We do business around the world, with people who don't look, think, or act like us.

Business leaders who were used to calling the shots are now being forced to dance to the customer's tune. But the dance steps are intricate, and they can't be mastered in a one-hour lesson. So instead of tripping the light fantastic like Tommy Tune, we sometimes trip over our own feet like Al Bundy.

I'm no Baryshnikov, but I can share with you some observations on how to grow in times of change, on how to be not only participants in the process, but rather lead it. I come at the issue from a manufacturing perspective, of course, but I trust my comments will be relevant to those of you who work in the service industries, as well.

First of all, effective leaders determine what needs to be done, and they do that by obtaining a brutal understanding of reality. In this connection, I suggest focusing on three areas:

One: What do your customers really believe about your company and your products?

Yesterday's business leaders would tell you. If there is one thing I'm sure of, I know my market. These were the people who got into trouble because their markets moved away from them, sometimes largely undetected:

- The computer manufacturer that charged ahead with mainframes when the market was moving to desktop PCs;
- The financial services company that continued on its way as competition from bank credit cards eroded its once-dominant position

It's easy to shake our heads at these examples, but are we really any different? I doubt if there is a single company in the country that will not tell you that its first priority is satisfying customers. But do they behave that way? Do they behave that way once in a while, or every day? Not many do.

Is your company organized around your product or around the service you provide? If so, some would say you're inner-directed and self-serving, because you ought to be organized around your customer.

Do you have a product design department, manufacturing department, and marketing department that don't talk much to each other, or do you have cross-functional teams which are dedicated to serving specific customers?

Do you reward your sales force and executives according to how they meet your financial goals and satisfy their superiors, or do you incentivize them according to how well they satisfy your customers?

Are your measurement systems for customer satisfaction designed by someone in your HR or compensation department, or do you ask your customers how they will measure you in terms of your success or failure in meeting their expectations?

Do you have a one-size-fits-all system for measuring customer satisfaction, or do you have a different set of metrics for each customer, recognizing that they are different, and what's important to one is trivial to another?

Is your system for measuring customer satisfaction a catch-as-catch-can, seat-of-the-pants ceremony that you rush through after a lavish dinner when your customer might be mellow? Or is it a formal, businesslike process done periodically by prior agreement with the customer as to both the criteria and frequency?

When you make hiring decisions, do you check the candidate's supervisors, or do you go to their customers to ask how they perform?

Do you hire engineers who like to sit in cubicles and design things or fix things? Or do you hire engineers who like to deal with people, who spend their time on the customer's factory floor, trying to find ways to improve your product to make the customer's life easier? Or, better yet, coming up with an idea for a new product that solves a problem you might not even have known about?

Today, leaders take nothing for granted. They know that the greater their market share and their margins, the harder other people are working to take it away from them. Their only hope is a perpetual sense of insecurity that inspires them to try to discern winds of change in the market, to come up with new and improved products and services, and to try to stay two or three steps ahead of the intense competition.

Do you have a one-size-fits-all system for measuring customer satisfaction, or do you have a different set of metrics for each customer, recognizing that they are different, and what's important to one is trivial to another?

The second reality check is: What do your employees really think of your company? I shared with you my belief that, overall, job satisfaction is higher in the U.S. today than it has been in years past. But this isn't the case everywhere.

Are your employees proud to work for your company? Do they feel that they are in control of their professional lives? Do they feel that they have it within their power to make a difference in the success or failure of the enterprise? Are they able to balance the demands of their careers with those of their personal lives?

Some companies can answer these questions more affirmatively than others, and we can all learn from some of the best practices they have established.

The third reality check is: What's your real competitive position? This includes many things: Have you identified your real market? Has it changed? What's happened to your market share over the years?

How do your margins and cost structure compare with those of your competitors, and I don't mean just your U.S. competitors.

Are your people the best in the business, or do the best people tend to migrate to your competition?

These questions are particularly important to ask if your company has been successful over the years. All too often, success breeds indifference, sloppiness and sometimes arrogance. A company that's been scratching and clawing for share in a competitive industry is almost inevitably a progressive company. A company that operates in a less competitive environment is more often a mediocre company.

I spent the first 34 years of my career with GE. Twenty years ago, this company had a reputation for being well run and it still does, deservedly so. But if you were to compare the GE of 1976 with the GE of 1996, you'd find it's not even close. It's a vastly better operation today. That didn't happen by accident. It didn't happen because of grand strategies. Rather, Jack Welch saw a freight train of foreign competition coming and didn't want to get run over by it. That was the reality GE faced, and the company dealt with it impressively.

Today, leaders take nothing for granted. They know that the greater their market share and their margins, the harder other people are working to take it away from them.

An unflinching reality check will give you a pretty good idea of where you are today.

Effective leaders then determine where they want to be tomorrow, and continually focus on the results and performance that's needed to get there.

At AlliedSignal, we decided that we wanted to become one of the world's premier companies, distinctive and successful in everything we do. We continually define for our constituencies what it means to be premier.

We agreed on a set of corporate values that serve to guide us toward the realization of our vision. Our values describe our commitment to customers, to integrity, to people and teamwork, to speed and innovation and to performance.

We are pursuing a growth strategy that goes far beyond cost control. Our plan calls for us to grow revenues by 12% per year, and we'll get there in three ways:

- One, we will grow internally by introducing a continuous stream of new products. We were proud to see our new ground proximity warning system featured on page one of *The Wall Street Journal* this morning. Being the innovation leader strengthens our bonds with customers and gives us the first to-market advantage, which enhances both our volume and our margins.
- Two, we will become a more global company. The highest rates of market growth over the next ten years will be in places like China, India and Mexico. If we're not there, we'll be boxed in by the much slower economic growth rates of the more developed world.
- Three, we will grow through acquisitions and joint ventures that fill gaps in our product offerings or extend our geographic reach. They are designed to enable us to do a better job of serving existing customers while at the same time attracting new ones.

We measure ourselves against our vision, our values, and our strategic plan every day. They aren't relegated to bulletin boards and banners and forgotten about. We know what it means to be a premier company, not because we are one, but because we are serious about becoming one.

Armed with a clear picture of where you are, a clear vision of where you want to go, and a clear strategic plan of how to get there, the only question that remains is: Can you execute? That's what differentiates one leader from another.

If I had to choose the single most important factor that determines those leaders who execute from those who don't, I'd say it's their ability to surround themselves with the best people, people who are leaders in their own right.

You all know the old maxim, "Leaders are born, not made." That's only half true. Some people are, indeed, born leaders, and you can spot them a mile away. The trouble is, there simply aren't enough of them to go around. So we need to find individuals with innate intelligence, an eagerness to learn, and a desire to work with others, and give them the tools and encouragement they need to become effective leaders, too. They may never run the company, but they can make enormous contributions to the success of your organization.

We measure ourselves against our vision, our values, and our strategic plan every day. They aren't relegated to bulletin boards and banners and forgotten about.

Avoid the trap of thinking that all leaders share the same personality traits or style of doing business. Consider the great leaders of history. Some were charismatic, some introverted. Some were jovial, some stern. Some were egotistical, some humble. There is no common cloth from which all leaders are cut.

Too many leaders make the mistake of hiring people just like themselves. People who went to the same schools or who enjoy the same hobbies. Of course, these criteria are meaningless when it comes to distinguishing those who will execute from those who won't.

Most older executives earned their stripes by completing assigned tasks competently. But the hierarchical organization of American corporations fostered a system which allowed talented lone rangers to rise through the ranks. Some said it was lonely at the top, and others complained that it was lonely in the string of corner offices that they sat in along the way. But many liked it that way, because they were able to stand out from the crowd simply by reason of their brains and hard work.

It's perfectly natural, therefore, for some leaders to want to perpetuate this type of organization in which people like them can similarly succeed.

The problem is, that type of organization in America is obsolete. American corporations have come to realize that they need to have fewer layers of management if they are to communicate daily with their organizations and if they are to become closer to the customer. The model of tomorrow's successful corporation is a flat, horizontal organization in which work is done outside the silos by cross-functional teams, teams which have leaders, not managers.

Look for people who do more than just hit their financial targets. We must no longer reward the sometimes destructive behavior of those lone rangers in the corner offices, no matter how impressive their achievements. Our people's merit increases and bonus evaluations are now based not only on making the numbers, but also on demonstrating leadership behaviors, which include communication, teamwork and an obsession with satisfying customers.

Too many leaders make the mistake of hiring people just like themselves.

Surround yourself with leaders who have strengths that are different from yours. Some executives feel threatened when they see someone come along with a tremendous amount of talent in an area that they don't understand. Worse still are their reactions to a person who has more talent in an area that they do understand.

Trying to keep talent down will drive the best people out of your organization into the hands of your competitors.

Give your people regular, honest feedback. Performance evaluations occur too infrequently these days, and when they do occur, many leaders pull their punches. Those who do hurt not only their companies but also the individuals they are evaluating. Let people know where they stand by candidly discussing their strengths and their development needs. Take ownership in helping them meet their development needs as a way to advance their careers.

Leaders also have to be ready to accept honest feedback about their own performance. And the good ones do.

Don't make the mistake of thinking you can lead with your feet up on the desk. If you're responsible for sales and marketing, you should be in the field talking to customers, not just managing the sales force from your office. If you're the head of R&D, you should be visible in the lab to see what's happening. If you're in charge of human resources, you should be on the factory floor to determine what's on the minds of your employees.

Teddy Roosevelt said long ago, "The best leader is the one who has sense enough to pick good people to do what he wants done, and the self-restraint to keep from meddling with them as they do it." He's right, but remember, sometimes in these tasks, you may be the best person for the job.

Trying to keep talent down will drive the best people out of your organization into the hands of your competitors.

In conclusion, let me briefly sum up my thoughts on what it takes to be an effective leader in an era of change.

- One, determine the task at hand by honestly assessing where you stand with customers, employees and competitors.
- Two, articulate a vision of where you want to be and values for how you want to behave. Set aggressive goals and keep everyone focused on achieving them.
- Three, fill your company with people who are bursting with energy and creativity; people with diverse talents, who nonetheless can work together in a team setting. Give people constant, candid feedback, and let them know that their highest career aspirations can be fulfilled at your company.
- And, finally, create a culture that is obsessed with customers, and build your organization and incentive systems around the interests of the customer.

Rod Kanehl, an infielder for the New York Mets back when they were losing a hundred games a year, once said, "Baseball is a lot like life. The line drives are caught. The squibbers go for base hits. It's an unfair game."

Well, business today is a lot like baseball. It's unpredictable. It's frustrating at times. And it's sometimes unfair. We'll never bat a thousand. But we take the field every day because we have a passion for the game and a hunger for success.

Robert W. Galvin
1922 –

When Robert W. Galvin's father founded Motorola in 1928, he created the unique name by combining "motor" with "victrola" (the phonograph). Why those two words? Because at the time the company was manufacturing the first commercially successful car radios. Motorola would go on to revolutionize the wireless communications industry, from developing walkie-talkies in the late 1930s for wartime purposes to making pagers and cellular phones in the 1990s for real-time information needs. Galvin started working for his father's company in 1940 as a humble stock clerk.

Once he took the helm in 1956, Galvin placed the greatest emphasis on quality, an area critical to survival when going head to head with Japanese firms. To really compete, Galvin knew that the employees would play the most crucial role; therefore, he introduced a system of communication that forced problems to the surface. For example, he created small problem-solving teams. The teams then participated in an annual tournament in which they picked a particular problem and offered a solution. The teams' recommendations were judged for their merit and winners were rewarded. Galvin said, "Communication doesn't start with what 'I' have to say. Rather, it starts with the other person. It starts with what I hear."

If, however, you were to visit Motorola's Florida pager plant, you would find no employees—it's fully automated, using twenty-seven small robots to manufacture pagers. This prototypical plant reflects Galvin's belief that a company must go through a continuous process of self-renewal and push the limits of technology. Motorola is exploring robotics as a new industry to spur growth. To determine whether a new product is worth developing, Galvin introduced an initiative that required detailed "technology road maps" from the research and development people. The maps are used to chart a product's usefulness and potential ten years into the future. At first the R&D people resisted, complaining bitterly that no one could plan the rapidly evolving future. But strategically it has made great sense. In *Real Leaders Create Industries,* Galvin explores the meaning of research and corporate renewal.

Real Leaders Create Industries

Robert W. Galvin

It is vital that we think about the "management" of technology—but management is not where things get done. Rather, allowing our engineers and scientists to accomplish the job is what lies at the root of our success.

Just as thousands of Egyptian laborers—and not their pharaohs—built the pyramids, so do the bench technologists build whatever there is for us to "manage." Conversely, failure results from holding these people back.

When I joined my dad's company in 1940, its sales were about $10 million. During my 50 years in the harness, it grew at 15 percent annually to become a $10 billion company when I gave up the chief's office in 1990. (I didn't grow it—it was those Egyptians who were *allowed* to grow it.)

At that time, it was presumed that we would continue to grow at 15 percent annually from 1990 to 1995, which we have, and that by the end of the century we would be at $30 billion. Given our remarkable technology base, I would expect us to continue growing at 15 percent and reach $100 billion by 2005. And if we reach $100 billion, why not $200 billion by 2010, then $400 billion, and eventually $10 trillion?

This is how we think in our company. The basis for it is that we expect nature, explored by scientists, to give us the solutions from which we can extrapolate particulars that will create new industries. This is what *renewal* means to Motorola: the creation of new industries.

The Meaning of Renewal

In our estimation, there is no mature technology, because there will always be something in science that will produce discontinuities of one kind or another. For instance, I saw all of the dozen or so companies that my father looked up to in the 1940s fade from the scene. And I predict that most of the competitors we have today will very likely not exist in the year 2050. We'll have a lot of competitors but they will all be new players!

Just as thousands of Egyptian laborers—and not their pharaohs—built the pyramids, so do the bench technologists build whatever there is for us to "manage."

This will occur because surprises determine what happens in high-technology businesses. Inventions that nobody thought of—the transistor, computer, satellite, etc.—came about because there were new people who adapted them, and there were a few old-timers like ourselves who believed in renewal.

Renewal is a great word. It is the driving thrust of our corporation. It comes trippingly off the tongues of our people. Renewal is a more important word than change, because if you only change it means that you have something from which to change *to*. Of course, renewal involves incremental changes (30, 50, 100 percent), but we believe that its most profound meaning is *to found anew*—to create something that was never thought of before. To that end, our most pressing objective in terms of renewal is to create new industries.

An example of this is our Iridium low-orbit communications satellite technology. It originated with two of our people in Phoenix. They presented the idea to management and we said, "Why not?" So they put the concept together for about $4 billion. But they created a market, a new industry. Motorola established the Iridium Corporation and attracted investors from all over the world. We now own 15 percent of Iridium, but it buys all of its infrastructure and most of its subscriber radios from us.

That is how you create *step functions* in technology businesses—you go out and *create* the customers. It is not just developing a product.

Training to Anticipate

How will we do this in the future? Here is a guess. I don't know whether it will succeed or not, because it's a pretty heretical idea. But I happen to think it is the only way that a large corporation is going to be able to operate successfully.

The idea is to create a process called the Anticipation Registry, accompanied by an upside-down authorization of resources. Here's what I mean:

Renewal is a great word. It is the driving thrust of our corporation. It comes trippingly off the tongues of our people.

If you are going to renew, you have to anticipate. Anticipation is really an art which I believe many more people could practice than now do. We have an objective in Motorola of, in effect, certifying the *leaders* of our company.

A leader to us is *someone who takes us elsewhere.* There are many other definitions of a leader but this is the critical one for us.

We are attempting to train people to become leaders, using role models, experience when possible, and classroom exercises. Someone who becomes a leader doesn't have to have a fancy title—he or she can be a project manager, a marketing manager, leader in personnel, or what have you. But he must leave a *legacy* of something that would never have been accomplished if he had not done it (assisted by a team, of course).

We hope to institutionalize this through an experiment we are starting, to identify people who demonstrate that they have anticipated. These people must be willing to, first, make a written commitment to doing something and then they do it.

Anyone who receives certification as a leader will have a document on their desk called the Anticipation Registry. When they demonstrate they have anticipated something, it will be recorded in the registry. Alongside this entry, they will record what they have done to provide resources for it.

All leaders who anticipate will be automatically resourced, without limit. Impossible you say? We'll get far many more ideas than we can afford? I am confident that the reciprocal will turn out to be the case. The only way we are going to be able to afford the anticipation of going from $200 billion to $400 billion in five years, and from $400 billion to $800 billion in the next five years, is to take the wraps off and let the Egyptians build the pyramids.

We will do this because we *trust* these people—we are a trusting organization with trustworthy people.

The other heretical aspect of this scheme is that once someone begins spending money to develop his idea, he will have to get permission to stop. And it is hoped that the leader at the top will ask this person, "Have you tried this, have you tried that? Why not keep trying?" At some point, he may be relieved of having to pursue his idea, but there will be no sanctions and hopefully he will go on to another idea.

This is the class of thinking we are looking at in our institution and which we believe will take us to higher levels of performance under a strategy we are calling "Growing the Growing Corporation," in which everybody grows their corporation. It won't happen immediately, of course. Initially, only a small cadre will open an Anticipation Registry, just as has been the case with our other innovations. But what about the year 2011?

A leader to us is someone who takes us elsewhere.

We don't think anybody has ever designed, philosophically and pragmatically, a basis for growing a corporation from $400 billion to $800 billion in a five-year period, and then from $800 billion to $1.6 trillion in five years, and then from $1.6 trillion to $3.2 trillion. We are designing this system.

We believe that this is the role of leadership—not management: to establish the culture and the structure that permits Egyptians to build pyramids.

Lillian Vernon
1927 –

Lillian Vernon, the most successful woman in mail order, was born in Germany, where her father had built a prosperous lingerie business. When Adolf Hitler was elected Germany's chancellor in 1933, everything changed for this Jewish family. Overnight the taunting and persecution began. After Vernon's older brother was attacked by Nazi thugs, the decision was made to emigrate to Amsterdam and then, in 1937, to New York City to escape the impending war. The moves were tough on Vernon, but she learned from her isolation and loneliness: "Now, as a businesswoman, I understand that there are advantages to being an outsider peering in. Outsiders see with a special clarity." Tragically, her brother returned to Europe as an American soldier and died from a grenade blast in 1944.

After the war, Vernon studied at New York University for two years, married in 1949, and was pregnant in 1951. The soon-to-be mother felt she had some greater purpose in the working world, but at the time it was very unfashionable for women to work. Her solution: a mail-order business run out of the house. So with $2,000 of wedding gift money, Vernon founded her mail-order business in 1951. To create an appealing image for her customers, she changed her last name from Hochberg to Vernon (after the WASPish-sounding town in Westchester County, New York) and called her company Lillian Vernon, too. In 1954 Vernon mailed out an eight-page black-and-white catalog to 125,000 potential customers. As the catalog size grew she was careful to keep her personal stamp on it.

No doubt Vernon's taste is shared by many. Sales exceeded $1 million in 1970; the company went public in 1987; and today, longtime customers number close to 20 million. Vernon considers such explosive growth as a double-edged sword; in her autobiography she wrote, "Paradoxically, it's just at the moment of explosive growth that a mail-order company teeters on the brink of disaster." Rapid growth eats cash, requires more staff, and jeopardizes timely delivery. In *Growth,* Vernon explains how she's dealt with change.

Growth

Lillian Vernon

Entrepreneurs who have founded and run companies naturally look upon their business enterprises as their own special creations, as if they were their children. You can't run a big, successful company, however, without loosening the reins, and that's not always easy to do. It feels a little like letting a beloved child go out into the world: you know you have to let go, but it's very painful.

I had always done everything and been everywhere. When a crisis threatened, I would be the one to solve the problem. I was the company firefighter and the company cop. If there was a problem in the warehouse, I was the one who called the warehouse manager, or rush over to take care of it personally. I never signed a check without reviewing the bill. Every morning I was the first in the office. And I approved every line of catalog copy, deciding that we were overusing the word *fun,* or were being precious when we described a product as *precious.* Yet I still do that. After all, with my name on the cover of the catalog, I'd better know what's inside.

Sometimes, after hours, I answered the phone and spoke directly with my customers. They were amazed to find me on the line listening to their complaints. Who, after all, can tell you more about how you're doing?

I really had nobody to teach me the ins and outs of big-company management. Most people gradually work their way up the corporate ladder, learning from other executives. But I didn't have managers who could act as guides and mentors. I had to teach myself.

If my company had continued to grow as slowly as it did through its first nineteen years, I might have had the luxury of growing slowly with it. But it didn't happen that way. In the years between 1970 and 1984, the Lillian Vernon Corporation grew from a $1 million business with a relatively small clientele to a $115 million business with customers nationwide. We went on to grow between 12 and 13 percent annually throughout the decade. That is a phenomenal expansion.

I had always done everything and been everywhere. When a crisis threatened, I would be the one to solve the problem. I was the company firefighter and the company cop.

I know it sounds wonderful, but rapid growth brings with it terrible strain. As many consultants pointed out, I had a tiger by the tail. Without warning, I suddenly had to change from being an entrepreneur to being a manager and administrator. I needed different skills. A manager's job is essentially to keep the company running smoothly day to day, to cope with crises, to keep track of information accumulating in databases. I had to learn to be a hands-off entrepreneur. My company's future growth depended on my personal capacity to grow and change.

Learning to manage was tough. I needed professional management in a hurry. Following the accepted path, I hired MBAs, "experts" in management, but what a mistake that was. In my experience, most people with MBAs are not on the same wavelength as entrepreneurs. Although I could supply the necessary entrepreneurship myself, I still wanted people in the company who could make decisions on their own. Instead, those MBAs carried analysis to the point of paralysis.

I really had nobody to teach me the ins and outs of big-company management. . . . I didn't have managers who could act as guides and mentors. I had to teach myself.

After disappointing experiences with the MBAs, I increased my involvement in finding good people. It wasn't hard to hire good managers, but I had to learn how to give them leeway and make sure that they used it. I told them, don't expect me to second-guess you. Success or failure is up to you. There's no point in hiring able people if you don't give them a chance to use their abilities. With the responsibility squarely on their shoulders, people learn to act decisively. I have always looked for another me. If I found that person, I reasoned, my company would be twice as good.

Growth brought yet another problem to the company. From the very beginning, communication among all of us was excellent. In 1972, there were eight staff managers sitting in two adjacent offices. Even if you didn't want to listen, you could not help but know what everyone else was doing. With the mail room on one side and fulfillment on the other, there were no secrets at the Lillian Vernon Corporation. By 1983, we had 650 people working in five different buildings, and keeping open lines of communication throughout the company had grown increasingly difficult, if not impossible. The staff members were becoming strangers to one another. If we wanted to project a friendly, warm image to our customers, friendship and warmth had to exist in our workplace. This was one of the knottiest problems I faced.

. . . I hired MBAs, "experts" in management, but what a mistake that was. In my experience, most people with MBAs are not on the same wavelength as entrepreneurs.

I began by holding regular meetings with the executives. We brainstormed for ideas, discussed company philosophy, and analyzed procedures. I believe that those meetings were responsible for much of our growth, for they gave the participants an overview of what was going on in the whole company. The success of the meetings depended on an informal give-and-take. As the company continued to grow and we added personnel, there were simply too many participants to maintain the old informal atmosphere. When we broke the meetings down into two separate groups, operations and marketing, we lost important feedback and communication.

In the mid-1980s, we tried a different approach. First, we asked each executive to prepare an informal but informative memo each month: How had the department fared? Had the department tested any new ideas or approaches? What plans did it have for the coming months? The memo was really a family round-robin letter of sorts, chatty and newsy. That plan did what it was supposed to do: it kept everyone in the company up-to-date.

Our second approach to the communications problem was much more radical. We decided to take a close look at a number of key positions in the company. As a company grows, there's a tendency to create new departments. The easiest solution for overworked executives is to add staff ad hoc. Such measures lead inevitably to a top-heavy organization—a situation I definitely wanted to avoid. So we made the decision to try to rely on outside resources and services whenever we urgently needed more help. I fought to keep communication free and easy, and I succeeded.

Thomas J. Watson, Jr.

1914 – 1993

The son of IBM's founder was a troublemaker and a poor student in his youth. But as an adult he was named "the greatest capitalist in history" by *Fortune* magazine. World War II aided Watson's turnaround. Commissioned a second lieutenant in the air force, he quickly learned how to manage the men under his command. He realized "that I had the force of personality to get my ideas across to others." After the war he was prepared to work as a pilot for United Air Lines; however, his commanding general said, "I always thought you'd go back and run the IBM company." It was then that Watson realized he should never sell himself or his abilities short.

Although his father had created a very respectable company, it was the younger Watson who guided it into the computer age and built a colossus. After assuming the helm in 1956, Watson surveyed the landscape of evolving technologies and likened the change from punch cards to computers as being similar to the aerospace industry advancing from DC-3s to Titan missiles. The changes were profound, and if IBM didn't adapt, it would be destroyed. He realized that technology forced a company to have "an even greater measure of adaptability and versatility." IBM, however, was stuck in the past, short on research and planning. As one journalist noted, IBM was able to continue its domination of the market only by "dumping in staggering amounts of capital" to "develop, imitate, or buy" the best technology available.

But the hefty investments did pay off because Watson reorganized the company and decentralized operations. In the old days his father had about thirty men reporting to him—an overwhelming number as far as the younger Watson was concerned. He wanted the efficiency that came with autonomy. While Watson feared tainting the company's familylike culture, he believed that when it came to problems: "Solve it, solve it quickly, solve it right or wrong. If you solved it wrong, it would come back and slap you in the face and then you could solve it right." In the following selection, Watson depicts the issues he faced in trying to solve IBM's management problems. He begins his recollections upon returning to the office just after his father's death.

Reorganization

Thomas J. Watson, Jr.

Fear of failure became the most powerful force in my life. I think anybody who gets a job like mine, unless he's stupid, must be a little bit afraid. There is such a long way to fall. Yet the fear I felt when I went back to IBM took me totally by surprise. Before Dad died I was running the business and even chafing at not getting full credit because he was around. I didn't realize how much I still needed him emotionally. I remember standing in the corridor outside my office soon after I came back from Alaska, looking dumbly up the stairs that led to his. Except for Dick's [Watson's younger brother] operation at World Trade, the weight of IBM was now all on me; if Dad hadn't died I could have been chief executive for years and never felt so burdened.

I decided it would be foolish to act as though I could totally take his place. Rather than move into his big, wood-paneled suite, I kept my own office downstairs and ran IBM from there—later we turned his office into a library. I retired his title of chairman, keeping the one he had given me: president. There was the problem of what to do with his seat on the board; I solved that by asking Mother to join. She had been at Dad's side for so long that many IBM people felt a personal loyalty toward her that I didn't want to lose.

The worst thing that can happen when a leader dies is for his followers to lose their inspiration and carry on like robots. I moved as fast as I could to prevent that. So before the year was out I called the top one hundred or so executives to a conference at Williamsburg, Virginia, and distributed power and responsibility even more broadly than before. In three days we transformed IBM so completely that almost nobody left that meeting with the same job he had when he arrived.

I think anybody who gets a job like mine,
unless he's stupid, must be a little bit afraid.
There is such a long way to fall.

I picked Williamsburg because it is a historic place and this meeting was meant to be a kind of constitutional convention for the new IBM. Almost everybody came knowing a few details of what we were about to do, and you could feel the anticipation and excitement in that rented conference room. After the tumultuous events that had already taken place that year—the settling of our antitrust case, my promotion to chief executive, and Dad's death—everybody felt that this was the takeoff point. It was the first major meeting IBM had ever held without Dad present, and we knew how far we'd come from the days of his Hundred Percent Club meetings with their circus tents and banners and songs. Of the old guard, George Phillips was the only one at Williamsburg, and he was scheduled to retire the following month. There were a lot of young men and one young woman. My age and experience were typical of the people present—I was forty-two and I'd been in management barely a decade.

What we created was not so much a reorganization as the first top-to-bottom *organization* IBM ever had. It was largely the work of Dick Bullen, the young MBA I'd named as organizational architect the previous year. Under his plan we took the product divisions that we'd already established, tightened them up so that each executive had clearly defined tasks, and then turned the units loose to operate with considerable flexibility. These were IBM's arms and legs, so to speak. At the head of the corporation, to oversee plans and major decisions, we set up a six-man corporate management committee that consisted of me, Williams, LaMotte, my brother, Miller, and Learson. I gave each man responsibility for a major piece of IBM, while leaving myself free to roam across the whole company. Finally we superimposed a corporate staff that included experts in such areas as finance, manufacturing, personnel, and communications. Their task was to work as a kind of nervous system and keep our adolescent company from tripping all over itself, as had happened a few months earlier when we had two divisions unwittingly bidding against each other on the same tract of land for a factory.

By the mid-'50s just about every big corporation had adopted this so-called staff-and-line structure. It was modeled on military organizations going back to the Prussian army in Napoleonic times. In this sort of arrangement, line managers are like field commanders—their duties are to hit production targets, beat sales quotas, and capture market share. Meanwhile the staff is the equivalent of generals' aides—they give advice to their superiors, transmit policy from headquarters to the organization, handle the intricacies of planning and coordination, and check to make sure that the divisions attack the right objectives. Du Pont and General Motors began applying this system to business as early as the 1920s, but to the IBMers at Williamsburg in 1956 it was a revolution. Everybody in that conference room had been trained under my father in exactly the same way—we'd all started out as salesmen and we'd all been molded as line managers. The phrase you heard about a successful IBM executive was "He knows how to get the donkey over the hill." We all knew how to get the donkey over the hill. But when it came to thinking about *which* hill, or whether it might be wiser to go down and around a hill rather than up and over, we tended to be as stupid as donkeys ourselves. When the meeting convened I gave a little speech saying that times had changed: "We've been a company of doers. Now we must learn to call on staff and rely on their ability to think out answers to many of our complex problems."

We then created the staff right before their eyes. There were dozens of slots to be filled, and since IBM had very few specialists on the payroll, we "made" our experts simply by naming people to the jobs. Williams and I had rejected the idea of recruiting outsiders, except in highly specialized fields such as law and science. We'd spent years weeding out Dad's yes-men and replacing them with fierce, strong-willed decision makers. If we'd hired a bunch of professors or consultants to come in and play staff against these people, the newcomers would have been eaten alive. Instead I put IBM's best executives in the new jobs, starting with Al as chief of staff. It was a huge sacrifice to move him outside the chain of command—and for Al it meant swapping a position in which he had twenty-five thousand people working for him to one in which he was boss of only eleven hundred. But by shifting our stars into the staff we enabled it to command the respect of the divisions, and that was the key to making the whole thing work.

The great strength of the Williamsburg plan was that it provided our executives with the clearest possible goals. Each operating man was judged strictly on his unit's results, and each staff man on his effort toward making IBM the world leader in his specialty. So on every operating proposal we had financial men demanding to know how it would improve profits, public relations men fighting to make sure it enhanced IBM's image, and manufacturing men insisting that we maintain the highest productivity in our plants and quality in our products. When the conference came to an end after a couple of days of workshops, there was no doubt that IBM had been totally transformed. To underline that fact we ran a special issue of the company newspaper featuring the first organization chart IBM ever had. Oddly, I had no feeling at all that we were going against Dad. I didn't think he'd have been alarmed by anything we did. If I could have asked him, "How do you want this thing run?" his answer would probably have been "I don't know, son. It was getting so big when I left that I could hardly understand it. Do whatever you think is right." That was the mandate I thought I had. Not a day went by when I didn't think about the old boy, but the only thing I really worried about was lousing the business up. . . .

The worst thing that can happen when a leader dies is for his followers to lose their inspiration and carry on like robots.

From then on I managed IBM with a team of fifteen or twenty senior executives. Some of these men were my friends, but I never hesitated to promote people I didn't like. The comfortable assistant, the nice guy you like to go on fishing trips with, is a great pitfall in management. Instead I was always looking for sharp, scratchy, harsh, almost unpleasant guys who could see and tell me about things as they really were. If you can get enough of those around you, and have patience enough to hear them out, there is no limit to where you can go. My most important contribution to the company was my ability to pick strong and intelligent men for these slots and then hold the team together by persuasion, by apologies, by speeches, by discipline, by chats with their wives, by thoughtfulness when they were sick or involved in accidents, and by using every tool at my command to make each man think I was a decent guy. I knew I couldn't match all of them intellectually, but I thought that if I used fully every capability that I had, I could stay even with them.

I was pretty harsh and scratchy myself. I wanted all the

executives of IBM to feel the urgency I felt; whatever they did, it was never enough. I was a volatile leader, perhaps even more volatile than Dad, and I justified this by telling myself that I was never harder on any of my men than he had been on me. Only gradually did I learn the virtue of restraint. We had an executive in those days named Dave Moore, a ruddy-faced, two-fisted guy I'd known growing up. Our families had been friendly. Like his father before him, Dave was manager of our International Time Recording division, which mainly sold factory time clocks and went all the way back to the company's origin. Up through the 1930s it had been one of IBM's strongest units. But after the war, when the idea of looser, more flexible factory management came along, the time clock became a symbol of the sweatshop. Not only was this bad for IBM's image, but a lot of companies simply quit using them. The division became stagnant and its profits fell because there were a lot of time clock makers and they were all competing for a smaller and smaller pie.

The best way to motivate people is to pit them against one another, and I was constantly looking for ways to stir up internal competition.

Moore did his best to turn the situation around, but year after year the results were poor. Finally Williams and I decided Moore had to be replaced. We promised him an equivalent job at the same salary, but Dave was stunned. He sought out his immediate boss, Red LaMotte, and said, "Well, I've made a success of the time division, haven't I?" Of course, if it had been a success we wouldn't have taken him out of the job, but Red equivocated, being a gentle man. When I heard of their conversation I should have just let the thing ride. But I always lost my temper when an IBM man refused to face a problem squarely. I called Moore in and said, "I don't know how the hell you can say things like that, Dave. Let's be realistic. The time equipment business is going nowhere. How can you call that a success? You can say you did as well as you could under the circumstances. But did you make money? Did your division move ahead? No, you were not a success." He left the meeting and my words festered in him. After a few months he quit, sold all his IBM stock, and took a civilian job in the Air Force. I've always regretted driving Moore out—especially since, in retrospect, it's clear he had an impossible job. His successor couldn't turn the business around either, and eventually the unit was sold.

Gradually I learned to control myself better. But it would have been a fatal mistake to expect perfect harmony at IBM. You can't run a business well simply by announcing, "Tomorrow we're going to do A and Friday we're going to do B and next year we're going to do C." The best way to motivate people is to pit them against one another, and I was constantly looking for ways to stir up internal competition. This led me, a few years after Williamsburg, to one of my most controversial decisions. In spite of all our efforts at decentralization, the Data Processing Division, which was responsible for all our computers and punch-card machines, was just too big. It was in danger of becoming clumsy and bureaucratic. So I assigned a task force to figure out a way to break it into manageable parts. They came back to me after a month and said, "It's impossible. It's all one business. There's no way to divide it."

"All right," I said. "I'll do it for you. All products that rent for over ten thousand dollars a month will belong to one division, and all products under ten thousand dollars will belong to another division." I picked ten thousand dollars because that was our average rental price, and it made the two camps roughly equal, with about thirty thousand employees each. But apart from that, it was a very awkward split. It essentially broke our computer business into competing halves. The corporate staff had a terrible time figuring out how to divvy up our laboratories, factories, and sales force between the two new units.

Lying dead in the water and doing nothing is a comfortable alternative because it is without immediate risk, but it is an absolutely fatal way to manage a business.

I didn't think we were smart enough to manage IBM any other way. From then on we didn't have to depend on the brilliance of top management to decide what needed to be changed; when you have separate units competing against one another, to a large extent they discipline themselves. The new arrangement put the hot breath of competition into every division executive's ear and we could gauge IBM's efficiency by comparing one division with the other. I could go to the head of the Data Systems Division and instead of saying "Gee, are you sure your overhead cost is reasonable?" I could say, "How come the overhead in the General Products Division is lower than yours?" Or: "Why does it take you four years to develop a computer while it only takes General Products two years to develop a roughly comparable machine?" Much of the time it wasn't even necessary to ask. Procter & Gamble was doing something like this with consumer products—they'd develop two or three brands of detergent and let them compete against each other in the grocery stores—and of course General Motors sold several different lines of cars. But it was radical thinking to apply internal conflict to the degree IBM did. A lot of people told me it would never work, but it was one of the secrets of how we got as big as we did . . .

I believed that the only way for IBM to win was to move, move, move all the time. As the computer industry grew, we had to grow with it, no matter how fast that growth might be. I never varied from the managerial rule that the worst possible thing we could do would be to lie dead in the water with any problem. Solve it, solve it quickly, solve it right or wrong. If you solved it wrong, it would come back and slap you in the face and then you could solve it right. Lying dead in the water and doing nothing is a comfortable alternative because it is without immediate risk, but it is an absolutely fatal way to manage a business. So I never hesitated to intervene if I saw the company getting bogged down.

MICHAEL D. EISNER
1942 –

Michael D. Eisner has served as chairman and CEO of the Walt Disney Company since 1984. When he took the helm, the company was characterized as being in a state of suspended animation as was its founder, Walt Disney. (It was rumored that Disney had his body frozen when he died in 1966, hoping to have it reanimated at some later date when technology permitted.) The man who would wake the sleeping company began his career much less conspicuously as a clerk at NBC in 1964. Eisner soon sent out some two hundred résumés, looking for a more ambitious job, and reportedly received only one response—from Barry Diller, who was a programmer at ABC. Diller gave Eisner his big break.

In four short years Eisner became director of program development for the East Coast, and in 1976 he was promoted to senior vice-president for prime-time production and development. Diller, who had left ABC to become chairman of Paramount Pictures, brought Eisner in as president and chief operating officer in 1976. They churned out a string of hit movies, including *Raiders of the Lost Ark* and *Beverly Hills Cop.* In 1984 Eisner resigned from Paramount and was offered the Disney job. As for Eisner's style over the years, a colleague once said, "He is disorganized, sloppy, absent-minded, he has an optional memory, and the only way he considers a deal fair is if he wins. But . . . his instincts are solid gold." Under his leadership, Disney has grown from a $1.5 billion company in 1984 to over $22 billion in 1997. But the money is not his top priority: "If you could have great entertainment and not as great profits, or great profits and not as great entertainment, I'll take the great entertainment every time." The profits, he says, will come.

It's not all been rosy for Eisner. One criticism is that he doesn't like to share power, which has resulted in public conflicts with fellow executives. Also, Disney is constantly boycotted by groups protesting its movies, television shows, and merchandise. Finally, other media companies are always gunning for a piece of Disney's pie. These experiences have made Eisner an expert on how to grow a company while trying to avoid the many pitfalls, which he shares in *Managing a Creative Organization.*

Managing a Creative Organization

Michael D. Eisner

When I joined Disney almost 12 years ago, the company had 35,000 full-time employees. With the completion of our recent acquisition of Capital Cities/ABC we have nearly 117,000. We had about 120,000 stockholders then. We have about 1.3 million today.

I mention these statistics not to prove how majestic we are, but to show how fast we have grown. The great danger that arises out of such fast growth is that a company can sometimes lose its focus, forget its mission, take its eye off of its core competency. Not only is rapid growth a problem, but success, unless properly handled, can be toxic, too. I have watched other big corporations and have seen what can frequently happen after a long and triumphant run. The mighty stumble and fall.

Some may rise again Phoenix-like, but others just fade to shadows of their former selves. Too many tend to become self-satisfied or overconfident or arrogant or lazy or restless . . . or, in the worst case, all of the above.

Of course we are none of these. Who else would sell a 100-year bond?

How do you continue to grow and yet avoid these pitfalls?

How do you manage a company like Disney, whose principal asset is creativity, and make sure it remains young and vibrant without losing its upward trajectory or its sense of great adventure . . . so that it doesn't become so heavy with bureaucracy and rules that it crashes to the ground?

We at Disney do not have all the answers, but I would like to share with you today some of the things we think are necessary.

A response Babe Ruth once gave to a reporter sticks in my mind. "How is it," he was asked, "that you always come through in the clutch? How is it that you can come up to bat in the bottom of the 9th, in a key game with the score tied, with thousands of fans screaming in the stadium, with millions listening on the radio, the entire game on the line and deliver the game winning hit?

His answer, "I don't know. I just keep my eye on the ball."

The great danger that arises out of such fast growth is that a company can sometimes lose its focus, forget its mission, take its eye off of its core competency. Not only is rapid growth a problem, but success, unless properly handled, can be toxic, too.

Keeping one's eye on the ball is, for me, a metaphor for what we must do as a creative company.

At Disney, because of the nature of our business, everything we do is dependent on a steady stream of ideas that can be successfully transformed into film and television and radio and stage and theme park offerings. All of you have read about bold and innovative companies like Minnesota Mining and Rubbermaid and Johnson & Johnson, which are famous for their ability to create a substantial percentage of new product offerings every year, thus transforming themselves every five or six years.

We, at Disney, face the same kind challenge with the subtle but significant difference that their raw materials are of the tangible kind while ours are of the mind. They create products that people need; we create products that people cannot know they want until they have bought a ticket or tuned in.

The percentage of new products they introduce each year is in the 20 to 30 percent range; ours are closer to 80 to 90—particularly in film and television. We introduce one or more new products every week of the year. And this is why new and fresh ideas are critical to our business.

Because this is so, companies like Disney must be open to new ideas from every source, from inside and outside the company. From employees, from free-lance writers, from book and talent agents, from producers and wannabes, and yes, even from our children and most especially from our wives.

But how do you know when you have found a winning idea?

It isn't always obvious . . . and believe it or not, audience research does not help. In fact, it often misleads. In my distant past, I remember research people telling me with great certainty that *Happy Days, All in the Family* and *Roots* would all be failures on television. And just last year, there was a lot of rumbling that we were wasting too much time on *Toy Story,* the first computer-generated animated feature in history. It wouldn't work. The characters were not lifelike. People would hate it. It certainly wouldn't be worth all the effort that we were putting into it.

I'm happy to report, contrary to the naysayers and other prognosticaters, *Toy Story* is a full-blown hit, the highest grossing domestic film of 1995 with more than $185 million and on a track to do as much as 150 percent of those grosses overseas.

So, as you see, I am not a disciple of research . . . unless of course, it agrees with me. Otherwise, it is useless.

Film critic Roger Ebert of the *Chicago Sun-Times* has this to say about research: "When you're trying to decide what canned peas to buy, a focus group might be able to tell you. But movies work by surprising and amazing us."

At Disney, we also feel that the only way to succeed creatively is to fail. A company like ours must create an atmosphere in which people feel safe to fail. This means forming an organization where failure is not only tolerated, but fear of criticism for submitting a foolish idea is abolished. If not, people become too cautious. They hunker down . . . afraid to speak up, afraid to rock the boat, afraid of being ridiculed. Potentially brilliant ideas are never uttered . . . and therefore never heard.

Wayne Gretsky, the great hockey player, knows about this. Said Gretsky: "You miss 100 percent of the shots you never take."

Failing is good as long as it doesn't become a habit.

Not long after I came to Disney a bunch of us would get together with our creative executives for what we called The Gong Show. We would meet and toss ideas around . . . mostly ideas for television shows and movies. Anyone who wanted to could present an idea for a movie or a TV show. Rank had no privileges. Kinder, gentler versions of that particular activity live on.

For example, our flagship Disney Feature Animation . . . which has had a string of blockbusters . . . has its own Gong Show three times a year.

Anybody who wants to . . . and I mean anybody . . . gets a chance to pitch an idea for an animated film to a small group of executives . . . which includes, among others, me and Roy Disney, our vice chairman, and Peter Schneider, head of Feature Animation. There usually are about 40 presenters.

For this to work, you must have an environment where people feel safe about giving their ideas. And, while we do not pull our punches when people present their ideas, we create an atmosphere in which each idea can receive full and serious consideration. Yes, we tell people if we think an idea won't work. But we tell them why and we tell them how it might be improved. And, of course, we tell them when we think an idea has promise . . . and we pursue that promise.

This doesn't mean that the executives are always right . . . or that we consider ourselves infallible. Believe me, nobody is always right in the film business.

But if you take the time to listen and be honest in your reactions . . . and if you create a setting that recognizes that ideas come in all shapes and sizes . . . and are willing to follow the creative mind wherever it goes—something you can never predict—people begin to understand a basic fact:

If you have an idea you believe in and can express it, it will be considered. Let me assure you that this is more . . . much more . . . than just an exercise in employee relations. The fact is that several of our better animated features have come out of the Gong Show and some of our other major winners out of similar kinds of programs in other parts of the company.

A company like ours must create an atmosphere in which people feel safe to fail. This means forming an organization where failure is not only tolerated, but fear of criticism for submitting a foolish idea is abolished.

I love going to our gong shows. I can be the emcee, the judge and the jury. Being part of the creative process is the best part of my job.

In addition to having valuable ideas, you must have an organization that can follow through and execute that good idea. A lot of people have good ideas, but not that many do anything about them. At Disney, we do.

I am so convinced that all of us can find within ourselves hidden depths and new wellsprings of creativity that a few years ago I organized a retreat for top Disney management at the Aspen Institute, which was more accustomed to hosting charettes devoted to world political issues than to the Freudian unconscious.

The first presentation at that retreat was given by a husband-wife team who teach at the Harvard Medical School. They focused first on what it means for people to connect with their emotional depths. Being in connection with these depths, they suggested, is critical to releasing our most powerful and creative forces. Denying this deeper level—whether in one's life or in relationship to others—leads to something called "disconnection." In effect, people lose touch with fundamental aspects of who they are.

Artists produce their best and most creative work when they aren't afraid to take risks, to endure criticism or embarrassment or even failure.

The result, we were told, tends to be vulnerability, fear and denial, as well as superficiality, falseness and a mistrust of intuition—all of which can get in the way of deep, creative expression. I was especially struck by the point that fear of criticism and lack of acceptance is a primary reason that people so often censor their feelings and intuitions and shut down their depths.

It explains a lot about the difference between those who are truly creative and those who are somehow blocked, or limited or superficial. Put another way, going deeper has a very practical creative value. Artists produce their best and most creative work when they aren't afraid to take risks, to endure criticism or embarrassment or even failure.

To me, such risk-taking is the primary challenge not just for an artist, but for any truly creative executive.

Trusting one's deepest intuitions and instincts may mean overriding contrary research, peer pressure, conventional wisdom or intimidation.

Nothing matters more to me than thinking and talking about new ideas. The difference is that I can not focus solely on movies and television.

I spend a lot of my time brainstorming with people in all our divisions about potential new rides and attractions for our parks, new forms of entertainment, new expansion possibilities for The Disney Stores and our Consumer Products Division, the next great video game or magazine or book or CD ROM or record or theatrical production or cable network or sports team or maybe even an ESPN program.

I am so convinced that all of us can find within ourselves hidden depths and new wellsprings of creativity . . .

We also spend a lot of time thinking and talking about how most creatively to market and sell all of these Disney products around the world.

All of us live in an age of over-communication in which people everywhere are bombarded endlessly with thousands of pieces of information and advertising messages. As this bombardment continues to grow, people more and more tend to turn to the brands they know and trust.

The name, Disney, has become one of the single most powerful brands around the globe and we work mightily to strengthen and maintain the high level of quality with which the name has become synonymous.

And that brings me to a subject which I hesitate to even mention because it centers around the most reviled and ridiculed word in the business lexicon. It is the word most often used when companies announce a merger or acquisition; it is the justification most executives use when grilled on why the merger of two companies makes sense; it is the dreaded "S word" . . . synergy. At Disney, it is our conviction that synergy can be the single most important contributor to profit and growth in a creatively-driven company.

Having used the dreaded word, let me describe the concept more specifically. It is simply this:

When you embrace a new idea, a new business, a new product, a new film or TV show, whatever—you have to make sure that everyone throughout the company knows about it early enough so that every segment of the business can promote or exploit its potential in every other possible market, product or context.

Most of you are aware, I am sure, that there is a natural synergy in the normal product cycle of a successful film. If it does well in its initial domestic run, it almost ensures later success in international distribution, domestic and international home video, network and foreign television, pay-per-view TV and cable.

In many entertainment companies, that is where the synergy and the story ends. At Disney, as a matter of course, a well-received film will also provide profitable opportunities in our theme parks—new rides, new characters, new parades, new attractions, and in consumer products—for Disney stores, for Sears and others—toys, clothes, dolls, books, games—even children's television shows for our affiliates and owned television stations, like WLS—programming ideas for our ABC radio networks and even the Warner Brothers network which is played on Tribune stations like WGN, and others around the country.

Trusting one's deepest intuitions and instincts may mean overriding contrary research, peer pressure, conventional wisdom or intimidation.

And at Disney, we also focus on additional uses of the creative product. The successful film can also give rise to direct-to-video sequels and TV series. Our first made-for-video sequel was a highly profitable Aladdin takeoff called *The Return of Jafar*; in fact so profitable we'll release a second made-for-video Aladdin sequel this year called *Aladdin and the Prince of Thieves*.

And we go beyond that: the 1991 animated feature, *Beauty and the Beast,* has become the stage musical of the same name now playing to packed audiences in its third year on Broadway, its second year in Los Angeles, and approaching its first anniversaries in Melbourne, Toronto, Tokyo, Osaka, and Vienna with more stops to come.

This is an entirely new business for us—a giant business all by itself—emanating from one successful movie. We will be doing more stage musicals drawn from other successful movies in the years ahead. In fact, we plan to launch one new Broadway show—or should I say "Chicago Theater-type show"—each year beginning in 1997.

And now we are converting the hit animated feature, *101 Dalmatians,* into a live-action film starring Glenn Close as Cruella deVille. At the very least, this has earned us the affection of dog trainers throughout California. We think that Walt Disney Pictures live action event films such as this will be every bit as successful as our animated features.

The term, synergy, may be the object of ridicule throughout the world, but not in Burbank, California. This concept of cross-promotion and transformation of popular products into new media is an engine that helps drive our company. Whether working with Ameritech on a new video service or McDonald's to enhance both of our brands, synergy, for us, goes with creativity . . . which rhymes with selectivity . . . which means keeping one's eye on the ball.

Another key to growth and survival is rejuvenation. How?

By moving your brightest executives frequently to new responsibilities, new businesses, new contexts. A few years back, our late president Frank Wells and I looked around and decided it was "seven-year itch" time at Disney.

No, we were not thinking about the personal lives of our executives. We were concerned about the continued growth of the company. We believed—and I, obviously, still do—that a creatively-driven company such as ours has to constantly renew itself, or its ideas will dry up and its competitive edge disappear.

So we started moving our most promising executives around, exposing them to other parts of the business, increasing their responsibilities and bringing new eyes and new ideas to their new operations. All these women and men—young and younger, old and older—are the people who make the company work, but it is top management's job to make sure they are excited about that work, constantly renewed in spirit.

It is top management's job to reinvigorate them and the areas they go into.

There is an old proverb that says: "If you are planning for one year, plant rice. If you are planning for 10 years, plant trees. If you are planning for 100 years, plant people." And to that I would add . . . plant them, but don't forget to move them around every seven to ten years. New eyes give rise to new ideas and opportunities.

Earlier I talked about Chicago,* its uniqueness and its people. What I did not mention is the fact that a man named Walt Disney was born in Chicago in 1901 and later moved with his family to Marceline, Kansas. Later he moved on to Kansas City and ultimately, Southern California, seeking his fortune. I have always felt that Walt's unerring instinct for what would please and capture an American audience grew from his roots and sense of values.

Mickey Mouse, his most famous character, embodies traits—like honesty, courage, virtue, enthusiasm, optimism—that I believe most Americans still value today.

In my opinion, the company Walt and his brother, Roy, founded reflects the commitment to quality and the sense of values they learned in America's heartland and accounts in

* "Managing a Creative Organization" was a speech delivered to the Executives Club of Chicago.

no small way for the great appeal of our company's offerings around the world.

There are few places you can go on this earth where the name, Disney, is not known. Children everywhere smile when they hear the name. People of all ages everywhere flock to see a Disney-labeled product. The name, Disney, is one of the world's most powerful brands . . . and just think, it all started here in Chicago.

THANK YOU, CHICAGO.

Linda J. Wachner
1946 –

Linda J. Wachner was the highest-paid executive in the entire apparel industry in 1997, earning over $10 million. The reward reflects her achievements as chair of Warnaco, which makes lingerie and sells licensed brand names, such as Calvin Klein underwear and Chaps by Ralph Lauren. She also heads another public company, Authentic Fitness, which licenses Speedo swimwear. After graduating from the University of Buffalo with a degree in economics and business, Wachner began her career as a buyer for Foley's Federated Department Store in Houston. Her first innovation as a marketer was to bring bras out of the box. While working for Macy's in New York, she broke with tradition and displayed them on hangers. Sales skyrocketed.

Wachner worked her way up through the ranks and in 1975 became a vice-president at Warner, a Warnaco company. As for dealing with a man's world, she once said, "I never felt discriminated against. I never took the time to do that." But ten years later she was eager to run her own company and shopped around for one to buy. Eventually she made a bid for Warnaco, her old company, and in 1986 she personally borrowed $3 million to lead a leveraged buyout. The ailing company needed leadership, and she brought it. "I apply an enormous amount of pressure to get everybody moving this company in the right direction," she said. Some think too much.

Turnover has been higher than industry standards, and in 1993 *Fortune* listed her as one of America's seven toughest bosses. In response she said, "It was not the best glimpse of me. But if you've got to run a company and improve the results and the image, you're not going to be a darling." No one can argue with the results; for example, from 1991 to 1996 Warnaco stock rose 130 percent versus 46 percent for peer companies and 104 percent for the Standard & Poors 500. Wachner also admits to being a control freak who carries a notebook with her everywhere, in which she registers orders she gives to others, so she can remember to check up. Printed on the cover of the notebook is her motto *Do It Now,* a theme for change that she elaborates on in the following selection.

Do It Now!

Linda J. Wachner

When we took over,* I had worked in the company twenty-two years earlier in a much lower position, and a lot of the same people were still there. So I had to get the people comfortable with me in the first 90 seconds. At the same time I had to change things radically. The company very badly needed new direction, and it needed new thinking and enthusiasm.

What we did was impose a philosophy we call "Do it now." If we didn't make our people understand that the consumers are our bosses and make them look where the consumers are going and what they will want to buy in five years and ten years, we would not have been able to set the new direction.

So we changed. And that started at the top. The corporate office used to be 200 people—now it's seven. We invited 100 people of the existing management group to buy equity in the new Warnaco. We gave them the chance to buy stock and helped them finance their investment. You know, pay a penny and we'll loan you the rest.

Then we got them to focus on four key things. In a public company, everybody's looking at earnings per share. But in a

* Wachner led a leveraged buyout of Warnaco in 1986.

private company, a leveraged buyout like ours you're driven by cash. You've got to get your people to think about cash.

Our focus was on cash flow, EBIT (earnings before interest and taxes), innovative ideas, and distribution. Each level of management had to make objectives geared to those four goals. I didn't try to reach consensus because that's not really my way, I gave people the direction. We had a huge, huge debt to pay down. And I'm proud that in six years we've paid down over $700 million in interest and debt amortization, and we've never missed an interest payment, and we've never missed a covenant.

. . . in a private company . . . you're driven by cash. You've got to get your people to think about cash.

The biggest obstacle to change we encounter is keeping people's energy up. I have enormous energy. I'm a morning person and an afternoon person and an evening person. And I will stay up for two or three days in a row to get it done.

I don't ask others to keep my work schedule but I want to keep them focused on the same goal. When they are falling down saying "Gee, I can't do it anymore," you've got to pick them up and say, "Yes, you can, and here's why." It's getting them to dream the dream.

Once they're dreaming the dream and they see it in return on their own equity, how do you continue keeping the energy up? Success is a positive reinforcement. Every time we have a little success, we bring people together and we say "Look, this is what we've done." So we've been able to build energy and momentum in people.

This attitude has been especially important during this recession.* Every Friday night each of eight division presi-

* Wachner was writing in 1992, on the tail end of an economic downturn.

dents prepares a report on critical issues. We review these by Monday. If there's a problem, we fix it.

We know where the product is going. We have clear goals for the people. We have a "do it now" mentality. With those things in mind, we've increased production in bras from two million dozen in 1986 to 10.5 million dozen projected for next year, increased market share, and still have come up with an increase of 30 percent in sales and 140 percent in EBIT from 1986 to the present.

Don't get me wrong, getting these successes hasn't been easy. And some people felt that the pressure to succeed was too great. Some people left. So we said, "Okay, if you can't meet the goal or if you can't get under the limbo rack, goodbye, and we don't hold it against you." But of the 100 people we put in equity almost seven years ago, eighty-six are still here and have a major financial stake in the company.

One other interesting observation came out of this experience: A lot of people want to be led.

We know where the product is going. We have clear goals for the people. We have a "do it now" mentality.

There are very few leaders in life. If everybody was a leader, we'd have 22 more choices for President of the United States. We'd have 22 more choices for the job of each chief executive.

When people have a good leader who instills team spirit, and they live in an environment that demands excellence, energy, and the keeping up of momentum in order to achieve a goal, then they want to stay or, if they leave, they want to come back. While I'm pleased to say that we are building a first-rate company, it's even more exciting that we've built a world-class team.

J. Willard Marriott, Jr.

1932 –

The Marriott hotel chain was founded by Bill Marriott, Sr., who started his empire by buying an A & W Root Beer stand in 1927. The first Marriott hotel was opened in 1957. Hours before the grand opening, father and son were frantically putting on the final touches to the hotel. Marriott, Jr., who took the company's reins in 1964, learned everything about being a good host from firsthand experience. For the next fifteen years the company remained largely focused on food, and as of 1980 it had only 75 hotels, so Marriott came up with a plan to expand. He decided to build the hotels at a much faster rate, but then sell them while keeping the lucrative management contracts.

With the astounding growth comes the headache of staffing the locations with an army of housekeepers. These low-wage earners are from all over the globe and all walks of life, so absenteeism and turnover can be brutal. As incentives to improve productivity and loyalty, Marriott offers stock options for everyone, a social services referral network, day care, and welfare-to-work training classes. One program, Pathways to Independence, teaches basic living and work skills. Marriott wants all his people to feel they are in control of their life and fate; only then will they be able to provide the service required in the hotel industry.

To keep in touch, Marriott travels as many as 150,000 air miles a year to visit hotels, playing both host and boss. As Marriott makes his rounds, he notes observations and suggestions on index cards, and then gives them to his corporate staff to evaluate and act on. Business has not always been a cozy bed for Marriott. In 1990 the company laid off more than 1,000 employees when the real estate market crashed and earnings went south. The company was caught unprepared as success in the 1980s bred a certain arrogance. Upon reflection, Marriott said, "Overconfidence can cause you to misread signals about which you might normally worry." The repetitive boom-to-bust cycle in real estate, combined with managing a diverse workforce of 200,000 people, has taught Marriott a great deal about leading change, which he shares in the following selection.

Preserve Order Amid Change

J. Willard Marriott, Jr.

"The art of progress is to preserve order amid change and to preserve change amid order."

Building a business can be boring.

Heresy? Ask anyone who has been at the top of a company for more than a few years. The daily grind of business consists largely of taking care of thousands of tiny, laborious details. Very little of what a company does ever sees the light of day, much less the camera lights of press conferences, photo shoots, or commercials.

Why begin a chapter about *growth* with an unappetizing image of *hard work?*

No grunt work = no growth. No growth = no future.

Let me give you an example of the kind of no-frills work that comes with my job. Each month I join a team of Marriott executives in reviewing "red" and "yellow" hotels that are experiencing guest-service problems. The idea is to figure out how to—you guessed it—move them back into the all-systems-go "green" category.

Is this glamorous work? No. In terms of fun, does it outrank a gala opening party for a new resort? Definitely not. Is it necessary? You bet. We can't expect to add new hotels to our system successfully if we don't take care of the ones we already have.

The kind of nitty-gritty work I just described is vital to the growth of our lodging business. It's also a reflection of another kind of growth that is equally important to our health and well-being: the growth of Marriott as an *organization.*

In the past few years, the topic of "growing" a business organization has been a hot one. In spite of the wave of attention, when companies talk about growth, they are still generally referring to the process of adding units, increasing sales, improving margins, and bolstering stock prices. We're no exception. We've always been driven to make our numbers.

Between 1927 and 1957, when we opened our first hotel, Marriott's financial picture grew from the original $6,000 that my father and his partner, Hugh Colton, borrowed and pooled to more than $36 million in annual sales. The only year that didn't bring an increase in earnings was 1942, a war year. After we entered the lodging business in 1957, growth continued at a rewarding pace. We hit $1 billion in annual sales in our fiftieth anniversary year, 1977. Just before we encountered the problems of 1990, we enjoyed an unbroken string of a dozen years in which annual growth hovered around 20 percent.

Building a business can be boring. Heresy? Ask anyone who has been at the top of a company for more than a few years. . . . No grunt work = no growth. No growth = no future.

Twenty percent, in fact, became a magic number for us. We began using the shorthand 20/20 to sum up our annual growth goal: 20 percent growth in sales and 20 percent return on equity. Among other things, the catchy phrase gave our large, far-flung organization an easy-to-remember mission. One former Marriott executive—now at the helm of another major company—was always impressed that our front-line employees, located thousands of miles from corporate headquarters, could reply "20/20" when asked what their goal was for the year. He tells me that his new organization has no comparable battle cry.

To grow successfully, you must stay true *to who you are, even while working feverishly to* change *who you are.*

I was particularly pleased to hear that our 20/20 mission spread so readily to the field. Like our monthly red-yellow-green hotel review sessions, it tells me that Marriott has succeeded in putting into place key organizational mechanisms that support and sustain the growth of our businesses. Even as we've been hammering away at making our numbers, we've been growing our organization.

When you cut to the chase of what growth in all its dimensions is all about, I think the quote I selected to kick off this chapter sums it up well: "The art of progress is to preserve order amid change and to preserve change amid order."

For businesses, this translates into: To grow successfully, you must *stay true* to who you are, even while working feverishly to *change* who you are.

Businesses that hope to be around for the long haul need to find a balance between these two inherently conflicting processes. The ability to maintain order and embrace change simultaneously is no small feat. It's a little like ballet. Executed well, it looks effortless. Only when there's a misstep does it become clear that something's out of kilter.

Back in the late 1950s, one of our competitors in the lodging industry broke out of the gate fast and furiously with a terrific new product. The interstate highway system was just beginning to boom, and the company moved quickly to take advantage of the new travel market. When it came to saturating the landscape, the chain displayed a positive, go-go growth mentality and a knack for picking locations. But the company soon discovered that its internal structure wasn't sufficiently developed to handle the avalanche of growth. The organization was not able to find the critical balance between order and change. Without strong organizational systems to manage and adapt to fast-paced growth, the company tripped, lost its early lead to competitors, and never completely recovered.

Our initial experience with hotel franchising in the 1960s was a similar case of order-change imbalance. In 1968 we announced that we would begin franchising Marriott hotels on a limited basis. The fact that we were franchising at all was itself a major change for Marriott's "order." . . . my father heartily disliked franchising, because he didn't like the idea of not having day-to-day hands-on control over the management of his business.

For a company that is as systems-oriented as we are, we really fell down on developing the systems we needed to make our initial foray into franchising work. First, we jumped in too fast and had to beat a hasty retreat when we found that we had far too many unqualified applicants trying to give us a check in exchange for a Marriott franchise.

The ability to maintain order and embrace change simultaneously is no small feat. It's a little like ballet. Executed well, it looks effortless.

No sooner did we get a handle on the application process and narrow the field than we inadvertently tripped ourselves up by deciding that the franchised Marriott hotels—to be called Marriott Inns—would be specially designed to distinguish them from the company's own hotels. From today's standpoint, the decision is a strange one; one of the strengths of franchising is to have all properties appear to be part of one seamless system. Our choice also flies in the face of one of our most cherished goals: consistency.

The long and the short of it is that we soon backtracked a bit along what had been proudly touted as a new avenue of growth for Marriott. We scaled back our ambitions, opened fewer franchised hotels, and, in general, moved far more slowly than originally planned.

If I had to pick one facet of our corporate order that I maintain is absolutely vital to our future well-being, it would be hands-on management.

On the surface, it might appear that the problem stemmed from a lack of organizational capability. But I don't think knowhow was the real issue. The management systems of Marriott's "order" are so strong that we'd have found the right answers and gotten ourselves well organized before too long. After all, franchising was new to us, but running hotels was not. The real problem was one of mind-set. As an organization, we simply didn't embrace franchising as wholeheartedly as we needed to make it a success. Even as we jumped into "change" enthusiastically, a key component of our "order" resisted adapting to and supporting the change. The very fact that we didn't want to risk having the franchised hotels be confused with "real" Marriott hotels by looking too much alike probably says it all . . .

One of the most worrisome aspects of the kind of sweeping institutional change and growth I've talked about above has been its potential for endangering a key aspect of our order: our corporate culture. Our evolution from a handful of local restaurants into a huge multifaceted, global enterprise has made the care and feeding of our original culture a tremendous challenge. We've been determined not to lose the essential qualities and priorities that have defined Marriott as an organization from the very beginning.

One of our most crucial tasks is to try to maintain a family feeling in a company that now has 225,000 employees. Size alone makes it a challenge to communicate effectively with associates working at hundreds of locations around the world. Like other large companies, we also must grapple with rapid employee turnover and the negative effects of social forces that seem to fracture lives more readily than ever.

If I had to pick one facet of our corporate order that I maintain is absolutely vital to our future well-being, it would be hands-on management. In the fight to preserve the family atmosphere at Marriott, it's probably our best weapon. Every increase in the number of properties in our system means that my own visits to individual sites will be spaced farther apart, making it more difficult for me to be visible as often as I'd like. The organization will be more dependent than ever on hands-on managers in the field who can carry on the tradition that my dad started and that I've tried to continue.

Another challenge that organizational growth presents to our corporate values is in the area of quality control. Rapid changes in size and scope can cause a company to lose command of its processes and products. On this score, our long history of systems and SOPs, plus our huge internal training program, will ensure success. That doesn't mean that change won't figure in the picture; our programs will continue to evolve to stay in step with guests' and associates' needs. *How* we achieve consistency might change, but the drive for consistency itself won't.

The third point of our corporate culture—taking care of our associates—will also continue to be a top priority for us. Like hands-on management, it's a key factor in maintaining the company's family spirit. The programs and attitudes that I talked about earlier aren't apt to change anytime soon. They more likely will grow over time. In fact, a large part of the order of Marriott is and will continue to be devoted specifically to counterbalancing negative change that we think would ruin the good thing we've got going.

Underlying these challenges is something we should never lose sight of, no matter how large or prosperous the company becomes: our core values.

Henry Ford
1863 – 1947

Henry Ford, who grew up on a farm and spent his early career working for Thomas Edison's company, was forty years old when he formed the Ford Motor Company. It was his third start-up; twice before investors had pulled out for lack of faith. Finally, in 1908, he introduced the durable Model T. Over the next few years he slashed prices from $825 to $360. Dramatic improvements in production efficiencies made it possible; specifically, his implementation of the first conveyor belt assembly line in 1913, which cut production time from twelve and one-half hours to just a bit over one and one-half hours. Later he built the first vertically integrated factory, where raw materials went in one end and forty-one hours later a car came out. As Peter F. Drucker once wrote, "It was Henry Ford who provided the original example of integration on which all later industry modeled itself."

Ford was also a progressive businessman when it came to employee treatment. He established a sociological department in 1913 that taught not only personal hygiene and health but also how to avoid confidence men, to buy houses, to use banks, and essentially to live. In 1914 he doubled his workers' wages to $5 a day while reducing a shift from nine to eight hours. *The Wall Street Journal* called the move blatantly immoral. For Ford, it meant good business; he got the best of the workers and his actions held union activity at bay. He believed that "Labor union organizations are the worst thing that ever struck the earth because they take away a man's independence."

Ford's primary concern, however hokey sounding today, was to benefit mankind. Service always came before profits. "The most surprising feature of business as it was conducted was the large attention given to finance and the small attention to service," he said. "That seemed to me to be reversing the natural process. . . ." To Ford, the completion of a sale was only the beginning of his relationship with the customer, not the end. To continue to provide great service and a good product, he forever questioned the company's methods. He despised routine and bureaucracy. In the following selection, Ford shares some ideas on how to keep a business alive and growing.

How to Keep a Business Growing

Henry Ford

Suppose, walking down the street, you should pass a peanut stand. When you started your walk you had not been thinking of peanuts. You had no intention of buying peanuts, but seeing them well displayed on the stand you want a bag. The price fixed in the mind for peanuts is, say, 5 cents a bag. If this man is selling at 5 cents, you will buy without giving a thought to the price. If he asks 25 cents, you will buy if you are feeling flush—that is, feeling that the difference between 5 cents and 25 cents is not enough to bother about. Or, again, although believing that 25 cents is a deal of money for a bag of peanuts, you may buy on the representation of the seller that these are exceptionally fine peanuts and well worth the money. Or, finally, you may decide that no bag of peanuts can be worth 25 cents. Then you are out of that particular market for peanuts. If you buy at either 5 or 25 cents and the peanuts are particularly fine, you will soon buy peanuts again. But if the peanuts prove to be poor, then for a long time the sight of peanuts will not induce in you any desire to buy.

This is about all there is to buying and selling. Only the details vary. Instead of the merchant waiting for you to pass his stand, he may bring the peanuts to you. But the human element—which is what counts—does not much vary.

We cannot have a sale without a purchaser. Purchasers are made, not born. We think of certain "bread-and-butter" purchases as necessary—food, clothing, and fuel—but, although it is necessary for every human being to eat, and for those in the colder climates to have clothing and heat, yet within these divisions of absolute necessities are an infinite number of subdivisions. The food of New England is different from the food of the South. Bread does not mean as much to the average American as it does to the average Italian or Frenchman. The choice of the primary necessities is largely a matter of habit—which is only another way of saying that particular wants have been more or less unconsciously generated by environment. These habits change, although sometimes rather slowly, and also the list of necessities is being constantly added to—so much so that at any given time no one can say what is a necessity and what is not.

No new article coming into the market has purchasers ready and waiting for it. No article for which a market has already been created will continue to hold its place unless the desire to buy it continues.

Not even an individual can draw the line between his own necessities and luxuries. He may think, for instance, that he requires a certain amount of food. More than likely he would be much better off if he ate only one-quarter of the amount he considers a minimum. If he cuts down on his food by the advice of a physician or because he decides to diet, he will go about telling how fine he feels. If poverty forces him to make the same cut, he will complain that he is being starved to death. Or, again, he may fight against the purchase of what to him are really necessities. A farmer on good land may be eking out the barest sort of an existence simply because he refuses to buy proper farming machinery. What is and what is not necessary depends purely on circumstances.

No new article coming into the market has purchasers ready and waiting for it. No article for which a market has already been created will continue to hold its place unless the desire to buy it continues.

Purchasers really have to be trained and led as though they were an army. An army which is not well trained and well led will revolt. So will the purchasing army. All of which means that when purchasing falls off, when the army revolts, the sellers should look into the quantity and the quality of their own leadership. For it is the quality and the quantity of their leadership, and not the personnel of the army, which are at fault. A well-managed army never revolts.

This may seem abstract. On the contrary it is wholly concrete and of general application:

1. A man buys only because he wants to buy. His wants are constantly shifting, but always interesting.
2. He will buy only when he has confidence both in the article and in the future.
3. And he will pay only the price which seems to him reasonable. For a little while he may grumblingly pay a price which he thinks is unreasonable, but he will not do this over any long period. If the habit of buying a particular kind of article is of long standing, he will cut down his purchases of the unreasonably priced article and then either find a substitute or cut it out altogether. There is no product so firmly fixed upon the market that it cannot be dislodged by bad manufacturing or bad merchandising.
4. Lowering the quality of an article already on the market has the same effect as raising the price, excepting that the bad effects are more lasting. For if the quality is so lowered that confidence is destroyed, then the rebuilding of that market is more difficult than if the

> product were an entirely new one. Raising the quality without raising the price stimulates purchasing just as does a price reduction; but in addition it breeds a confidence which makes for free buying.

Business depends almost entirely upon human emotions. These are changing. Therefore, business is changing. We can take as a first business principle that there is nothing permanent but change.

The manufacturer can plan his production in advance and the distributor can plan his stocks, but unless all these plans are in accord with the emotions of the public, then the producer will merely pile up an unsalable mass of goods and the distributor will merely fill his shelves. They will say that business is bad, when they themselves—not business—are at fault.

In this country enough buying power always remains to keep up a fairly steady volume: people are never as rich as they feel nor as poor as they feel. The ability to buy does not fluctuate nearly so much as the desire to buy. And that desire is largely in control of the producer and distributor.

If goods are manufactured for speculation on a rising market and distributors are foolish enough to think that they can make money by outguessing the market rather than by serving people, then the prices of what is produced and offered for sale are bound to go above what the public considers a fair price. Confidence is shaken and buying lessens. Then factories close and workers are idle. The whole process of production stops because of a shortsighted attempt to make a lot of money at once out of speculation.

It is shortsighted, for the largest sums of money ever made out of speculation are trivial as compared with the sums made out of legitimate business. The profits to be gained from speculation have been overrated: when they are big usually they are only on paper. When the losses are put against them and the total cast up, it will be found that about all that has been accomplished is an interruption of business.

Really there is no saturation point in sight provided we regard business as always changing. I think of the United States and of the world as being still in the raw material stage.

We get our wealth from development; we have hardly begun that development. With the production of Ford cars going on to 10,000 cars a day, the time when all the automobiles which can be used are in use is farther away than it was 10 years ago. We are less able to keep up with the demand than we were 10 years ago when the statistics plainly showed that the automobile industry was already too big for the consuming power of the country. The automobile industry only began its growth after this country was saturated with automobiles!

Lowering the quality of an article already on the market has the same effect as raising the price, excepting that the bad effects are more lasting.

There are several reasons why the saturation point in automobiles is farther away than ever. We have by no means perfected the automobile. Nothing anywhere has been perfected. But the progress of the automobile has been rapid. The earlier automobiles not only were high-priced, but they got out of order frequently. This was inevitable because designs were so unsettled that it was not possible to make the best use of machinery in manufacture. We had not made enough motors to know exactly what we were doing. So the purchaser not only paid a price, but also brought on himself a considerable overhead for repairs. Owning an automobile was a luxury. Then, as we learned more about motors and materials, came the cars that did not easily get out of order. Instead of being just machines, automobiles became machines for service.

The roads of the country were not ready for automobile traffic. The automobile did not drop into a market eager and waiting for it. The need for a more flexible means of transportation existed, but those who needed this transportation most—that is, the farmers—did not know they had the need. They had adjusted themselves to the horse. The hardy pioneers who bought the first machines bumped over bad roads and insisted on having better ones. Better roads came and with them more automobiles.

This widening of the market permitted cheaper cars. Quickening transportation added working hours to the day. A man was able to do more in a day because he did not have to waste as much time in getting about, and also the radius in which he might work was increased.

The automobile, through increasing the productive capacity of the individual, added to the wealth of the country in much the same way as the steam engine added to the wealth of the world. Automobiles create wealth and widen their own markets. In spite of the large number of cars in use in this country, the saturation point will not be visible until there are good roads through every section, because not until then shall we have any idea as to how many machines will be required. And by that time replacements will necessarily be so large as to require a much greater industry than we now have.

A man nowadays buys an automobile with confidence. He buys the car that suits his taste and his pocketbook. No matter what car he decides on, he feels fairly safe that he is getting his money's worth. A poorly made or heavily overpriced car stands so little chance of being bought that few men will waste the time putting it on the market.

Foreign travelers think it is odd that an American workman should go to his day's labor in an automobile. They are always astonished at the miles of cars parked outside our plants. We have some 20 acres of parking space outside our River Rouge plant and as a rule it is full. They do not see that these cars increase the workers' productivity, not only by saving time in coming and going from work, but also in permitting them to live away from congested districts. It was a long time before Americans got used to seeing wage-earners go about in automobiles.

The ownership of an automobile—like the ownership of any other labor-saving device—adds to the productive capacity of the owner and hence will considerably more than pay for itself. If I thought otherwise, I should not be in the business of providing transportation.

Now, what has happened with the automobile can happen with any article the use of which will make living easier—that is, which will permit a higher production without expending greater physical effort. At no point in the past has anyone been able correctly to forecast human needs over, say, a 20-year period. The wildest estimate is, as a rule, under the mark. It has always been possible to prove that the earth was about to be overpopulated and that when this happened a great number of people would simply have to starve to death. To go back to automobiles again, it has been possible for many years past to show statistically that the industry was in excess of the consumptive capacity of the country.

All that I know about consumption in the future is this: The ordinary individual scarcely spends 1% of his time in real production. We have not really tapped human powers. Neither have we tapped natural resource. We have been mining coal for a great many years, yet we have not learned to use coal. Our great River Rouge plant uses no raw coal at all. The coal coming in there is reckoned as raw material, not as fuel. We take out everything we know how to and burn only what is left over, but still I feel we are wasting that coal. We ought to get something more out of it. We know very little about heat and the utilization of natural forces, generally.

We are using only a fraction of the available water power. And, practically, we are not using the heat of the sun or the force of the winds at all. In Southern California I came across an ingenious installation by which, through pipes on the roof, the sun's rays heated the water for the household.

An insulated tank held enough heated water to carry over at night. There is an idea in this capable of development—although, of course, not for all climates. We have a small house at Dearborn which is now lighted by electricity generated by a windmill. We get all the current we need.

In a thousand ways this country has not really started to develop. Not only have existing markets scarcely been touched, but there will be markets in the future that today we do not even dream of. These new markets and these new powers will not be developed merely by wishing for them; they will be developed as each of us looks upon his work as a service and then sees how that service may be performed. Then invention comes naturally into the picture. We are obeying the law of change, of progress.

Take, for instance, the notion that any article can be made too well—the fear that a product will last so long in use that when a man buys once he buys for all time. This fear is behind much bad business; it is easy enough to prove that if there are only a certain number of possible users of an article in the country or in the district, then in order to have a steady replacement market, the articles must wear out within a reasonable time, or at least become obsolete.

The ordinary individual scarcely spends 1% of his time in real production. We have not really tapped human powers.

Many of the changes in the styles of clothing are brought about only with the thought of making people buy in order to be uniformed like the procession. But the trouble with this theory is that it starts with a false basis—that we can possibly know the number of customers. And also it fails to take into account the force of confidence. When a man buys an article which is well made and gives the best of service, he is not out of the market but in the market. The "buyers' strike" was not wholly on prices; it was on quality, as well. People found that they were being charged high prices for inferior goods and they stopped buying anything at all. If a man is satisfied with the price of his purchase and it gives good service he becomes at once a first-class asset for all business because:

1. He will have both the confidence and the desire to buy again.
2. He will have more money with which to buy, for he does not have to spend so much on replacement.

This man may not be in the market for the particular article you have to sell, but that does not matter. He will buy something that another man has to sell and start in motion a chain of buying which will benefit you as much, if not more, than if he were buying directly from you. Every manufacturer knows how the introduction of a cheap imitation article spoils a market for years because the poor thing so destroys confidence that the good thing falls under suspicion and is not bought. Each manufacturer who turns out a good thing, each retailer who sells only honest goods, performs a service not only to himself but to every other manufacturer and retailer.

"A Thousandth of an Inch is not Accuracy . . ."

Nothing can be made too well: as it is, things wear out too quickly. In our plants for a long time we made our parts to the thousandth of an inch. Perfect fitting lessens both friction and vibration—were friction and vibration eliminated, machinery would last forever. We do not know how to do away with friction, but we can minimize both friction and vibration by being more accurate. A thousandth of an inch is not accuracy—the part must be exactly the right measurement. The only man in this country who could measure accurately was a Swedish engineer named Johannson who had devised in his home country the finest measuring instruments in the world. For some years he had a factory in New York State turning out instruments of precision, but being more scientist than salesman, his instruments were not bought as largely as they deserved to be.

Many refinements which do not add at all to durability cost money, but my own experience proves that using the very best of materials and always striving to find better ones actually decreases the cost.

We bought his plant some time ago and now the owner is working with us: We want to have the advantage of precision. This man can measure to one-millionth of an inch; we need such accuracy. We cannot manufacture to such a fraction, but we can make certain that our gages are precise.

No manufacturing is nearly so accurate as it ought to be, and hence a lot of time is wasted testing and breaking in completed machinery. A properly made machine should have its parts so accurate to size that it would not have to go through the destructive process of "limbering up." We shall not keep for our own use all of the instruments of precision turned out by Mr. Johannson's division. That would be shortsighted. The better the workmanship of the country in general, the better will be our automobile and tractor sales. Every waste cut out anywhere in business helps the whole body of business.

Quality irrespective of price is not of itself enough to market any article of general usefulness. But there need be no quarrel between quality and price. Many refinements which do not add at all to durability cost money, but my own experience proves that using the very best of materials and always striving to find better ones actually decreases the cost. In most lines of business it is the man and machine labor put upon the raw material and the marketing of the finished product that costs real money. The difference between good and bad material is in the raw state so slight as to be almost negligible in the finished costs. Indeed, much material which is believed to be cheap is really expensive because of the waste in seconds. We find that it does not pay to use anything less than the best. The best may or may not be the highest priced.

Given good quality, then, the proper price to charge the public is that sum which the public will freely pay. This is different from saying that the right price is whatever the traffic will bear. There is no objection to charging what the traffic will bear, excepting that the manufacturer or retailer who adopts this method ought to do so in the full knowledge that he is voluntarily not only limiting his volume of business but also making it exceedingly sensitive to every up and down of trade.

Many of the ups and downs of business are due solely to forgetting the customers—to forgetting the man who does the paying . . .

No one can arbitrarily say that any given price is right, for prices arise out of circumstances. For instance, it does not mean anything to me to be told how much it costs to mine coal. The detailed figures backing up the cost are of themselves nothing. A cost is something to be reduced and that is all. But regardless of costs, prices are too high when people do not pay them. If we bear in mind that the existence of every market lies at the mercy of the people who buy in that market, then at once it becomes important to know what people think of prices. If prospective purchasers believe that prices are too high—and every little while a wave of this sort of feeling comes over the country—then prices are too high and some way of cutting them has to be found.

It has been the policy of the Ford industries to turn back their profits into capital investments which will both lower costs and increase production and then to lower the price of the finished product so that this price will always be lower than people expect to pay. This policy seems to me to be the correct one. At least it has quite steadily kept orders well ahead of the capacity to fill them and has provided profits in a sufficient volume to permit us to do more or less what we please financially.

A healthy business is never satisfied with its processes. It is always striving for decreased costs and increased sales. It is always changing. Many of the ups and downs of business are due solely to forgetting the customers—to forgetting the man who does the paying—to producing not ahead of his needs but to misjudging what his needs are—making something he does not want. Perhaps the price is too high, perhaps the quality is too low, perhaps the design is unsuitable, perhaps his general confidence has been shaken. At any rate, he has not the buying emotion. You cannot serve him because he refuses to be served. Then you will have to find out how to serve him or go out of business.

If things were otherwise, business would not be interesting. Once I rode for 500 miles along a straight, perfectly level, perfectly surfaced road. The sameness grew intolerable. I had to abandon the trip. One must have change.

Chronology

Author Index

Acknowledgments

A book has little value unless it has an audience. Fortunately, my editor Ruth Mills continues to be both an enthusiastic and a critical reader of my work. For *The Book of Leadership Wisdom,* she both challenged and contributed to the ideas and the research that have made it the best possible anthology of writings by business legends. Ed Knappman, my agent, helped provide the means for feeding my family, so I thank him for his expertise.

Family, of course, is always a source of inspiration. My young children, Pierson, Alex, and Julia, are forever curious as to what Daddy is doing with the computer down in the basement dungeon. And they, as all parents know, challenge me intellectually more than anyone else. As with the first collection in this series, *The Book of Business Wisdom,* Diana, my wife, should be named as coeditor for all her help, but she will have to remain my secret weapon. My dad, who rose to the top of a Fortune 500 company himself, passed along a great deal of useful information and offered invaluable advice. He will always be the greatest businessman to me.

Such an anthology would not be possible if not for the renowned business leaders who were inspired to put their thoughts on paper. The many faceless editors and publishers who worked with such a varied and unique cast of characters must be applauded. And to the reference librarians, especially those at the Wilton and Bridgeport public libraries, whom I hope to badger and work with for years to come—thank you for your help.

Notes

The biographical sketches were drawn using the following sources.

Chester I. Barnard:

Barnard, Chester I. *The Functions of the Executive.* Cambridge, MA: Harvard University Press, 1938.

Current Biography Yearbook, 1945. New York: H. W. Wilson Company.

Olive Ann Beech:

Current Biography Yearbook, 1956. New York: H. W. Wilson Company.

Lawrence A. Bossidy:

"Larry Bossidy Won't Stop Pushing." *Fortune:* January 13, 1997.

Tulley, Shawn. "So, Mr. Bossidy, We know You Can Cut, Now Show Us How to Grow." *Fortune:* August 21, 1995.

Harry A. Bullis:

Cherne, Leo. Bullis, Harry A. "Harry A. Bullis: Portrait of the 'New Businessman.' " *Saturday Review:* January 23, 1954.

Bullis, Harry A. "The Future Belongs to the Highly Educated Man." A speech delivered in Minneapolis, Minnesota, August 18, 1955.

Sir Adrian Cadbury:

"Cadbury Trusts in Teamwork." *Management Today:* September 1996.

"Cadbury Schweppes: More than Chocolate and Tonic." Harvard *Business Review:* January–February, 1983.

Andrew Carnegie:

Carnegie, Andrew. "The Road to Business Success." Speech delivered at Curry Commercial College, June 23, 1885.

Wall, Joseph Frazier. *Andrew Carnegie.* New York: Oxford University Press, 1970.

Ben Cohen and Jerry Greenfield:

Cohen, Ben, and Jerry Greenfield. *Ben & Jerry's Double-Dip: Lead with Your Values and Make Money, Too.* New York: Simon & Schuster, 1997.

Frederick C. Crawford:
"Jet-Propelled Individualist." *Time:* April 13, 1953.

Max DePree:
DePree, Max. *Leadership Is an Art.* New York: Doubleday, 1989.
DePree, Max. *Leadership Jazz.* New York: Doubleday, 1992.

T. Coleman du Pont:
Dutton, William S. *Du Pont: One Hundred and Forty Years.* New York: Charles Scribner's Sons, 1942.
Wall, Joseph Frazier. *Alfred I. du Pont: The Man and His Family.* New York: Oxford University Press, 1990.

Thomas A. Edison:
Baldwin, Neil. *Edison: Inventing the Century.* New York: Hyperion, 1995.
Edison, Thomas A. *The Diary and Assundry Observations.* The Philosophical Library, 1948.

Michael D. Eisner:
Current Biography Yearbook, 1987. New York: H. W. Wilson Company.
Lubove, Seth, and Robert La Franco. "Why Mickey isn't doing much talking these days." *Forbes:* August 25, 1997.
"Michael Eisner Defends the Kingdom." *Business Week:* August 4, 1997.

Henry Ford:
Ford, Henry, with Samuel Crowther. *My Life and Work.* New York: Doubleday, Page & Company, 1922.
Gelderman, Carol. *Henry Ford: The Wayward Capitalist.* New York: The Dial Press, 1981.

Robert W. Galvin:
Bettner, Jill. "Underpromise, overperform." *Forbes:* January 30, 1984.
Galvin, Robert W. "Communication: The lever of Effectiveness and Productivity." *Daedalus:* Spring 1996.

Bill Gates:
Cusumano, Michael A., and Richard W. Selby. *Microsoft Secrets: How the World's Most Powerful Software Company Creates Technology, Shapes Markets, and Manages People.* New York: The Free Press, 1995.
Manes, Stephen, and Paul Andrews. *Gates: How Microsoft's Mogul Reinvented an Industry—and Made Himself the Richest Man in America.* New York: Doubleday, 1993.

Harold S. Geneen:
Araskog, Rand V. *The ITT Wars: A CEO Speaks out on Takeovers.* New York: Henry Holt and Company, 1989.
"Double the Profits, Double the Pride." *Time:* September 8, 1967.

J. Paul Getty:
Lenzner, Robert. *The Great Getty: The Life and Loves of J. Paul Getty: Richest Man in the World.* New York: Crown Publishers, 1985.
"The Do-It-Yourself Tycoon." *Time:* February 24, 1958.

A. P. Giannini:
Hector, Gary. *Breaking the Bank: The Decline of BankAmerica.* Boston: Little, Brown and Company, 1988.

Roberto C. Goizueta:
Current Biography Yearbook, 1996. New York: H. W. Wilson Co.
Morris, Betsy. "Roberto Goizueta and Jack Welch: The Wealth Builders." *Fortune:* December 11, 1995.

Katherine Graham:
Current Biography Yearbook, 1971. New York: H. W. Wilson Co.
Graham, Katherine. *Personal History.* New York: Alfred A. Knopf, 1997.

Andrew S. Grove:
Grove, Andrew S. *High Output Management.* New York: Random House, Inc., 1983.
Isaacson, Walter. "Intel's Andrew Grove." *Time:* December 29, 1997/January 5, 1998.
Ramo, Joshua Cooper. "A Survivor's Tale." *Time:* December 29, 1997/January 5, 1998.

Daniel Guggenheim:
Davis, John H. *The Guggenheim's: An American Epic.* New York: William Morrow and Company, 1978.

Robert D. Haas:
Mitchell, Russell. "Managing by Values." *Business Week:* August 1, 1994.
Mitchell, Russell. "A Mild-Mannered Maverick Puts His Brand on Levi's." *Business Week:* August 1, 1994.
"The Quiet American." *The Economist:* November 8, 1997.

William Randolph Hearst:
Hearst, William Randolph, Jr., with Jack Casserly. *The Hearsts: Father and Son.* Niwot, CO: Roberts Rinehart Publishers, 1991.

John H. Johnson:
Johnson, John H., with Lerone Bennett, Jr. *Succeeding Against the Odds.* New York: Warner Books, 1989.
Sobel, Robert, and David B. Sicilia. *The Entrepreneurs: An American Adventure.* Boston: Houghton Mifflin Company, 1986.

Ray Kroc:
"For Ray Kroc, Life Began at 50. Or Was It 60?" *Forbes:* January 15, 1973.
Kroc, Ray, with Robert Anderson. *Grinding It Out: The Making of McDonalds.* New York: St. Martin Press, 1977.
Love, John F. *McDonald's: Behind the Arches.* New York: Bantam Books, 1986.

Sandra L. Kurtzig:
Kurtzig, Sandra L., with Tom Parker. *CEO: Building a $400 Million Company from the Ground Up.* New York: W. W. Norton & Company, 1991.

Ralph Lazarus:
"Expanding with Confidence." *Nation's Business:* July 1966.
Lazarus, Ralph. "The Age of Fulfillment: Leisure Time." A speech delivered in San Francisco, November 16, 1963.

J. W. Marriott, Jr.:
Koselka, Rita. "Marriott, meet Marriott." *Forbes:* March 13, 1995.

Rene C. McPherson:
McPherson, Rene C. "Dana: Toward the Year 2000." A speech delivered before the Newcomen Society of North America, 1973.

Akio Morita:
Morita, Akio, with Edwin M. Reingold and Mitsuko Shimomura. *Made in Japan.* New York: E. P. Dutton, 1986.

Robert N. Noyce:
Hayes, Thomas C. "Chip Group Is Left with a Solid Base." *New York Times:* June 5, 1990.
Wolfe, Tom. "Robert Noyce and His Congregation." *Forbes ASAP:* August 25, 1997.

David Packard:
Packard, David. *The HP Way: How Bill Hewlett and I Built Our Company.* New York: HarperBusiness, 1995.

John H. Patterson:
Carson, Gerald. "The Machine that Kept Them Honest." *American Heritage Magazine,* August, 1966.

H. Ross Perot:
Mason, Todd. *Perot: An Unauthorized Biography.* Homewood, IL: Business One Irwin, 1990.

William Cooper Procter:
Editors of *Advertising Age. Proctor & Gamble: The House that Ivory Built.* Lincolnwood, IL: NTC Business Books, 1988.
Swasy, Alecia. *Soap Opera: The Inside Story of Procter & Gamble.* New York: Times Books, 1993.

Willard F. Rockwell, Jr.:
Heller, Mathew. "Al Rockwell's Space Odyssey." *Forbes:* December 30, 1985.
"Rockwell Trims North American." *Business Week:* January 31, 1970.
"The Rockwells Take Off for Outerspace." *Fortune:* June 1, 1967.

David Sarnoff:
Bilby, Kenneth. *The General David Sarnoff and the Rise of the Communications Industry.* New York: Harper & Row, Publishers, 1986.

Frederick W. Smith:
Grant, Linda. "Why FedEx Is Flying High." *Fortune:* November 10, 1997.
Trimble, Vance. *Overnight Success: Federal Express & Frederick Smith, Its Renegade Creator.* New York: Crown Publishers, Inc., 1993.

Louis F. Swift:
Dictionary of American Biography. New York: Charles Scribner's Sons, 1936.
Swift, Louis F. "How G. F. Swift bossed his own job." *System: The Magazine of Business:* February, 1927.

Dave Thomas:
Current Biography Yearbook, 1995. New York: H. W. Wilson Company.
Thomas, Dave, with Ron Bergman. *Well done! The Common Guy's Guide to Everyday Success.* Grand Rapids, MI: Zondervan Publishing House, 1994.

Theodore N. Vail:
Brooks, John. *Telephone: The First Hundred Years.* New York: Harper & Row, 1975.
Sobel, Robert, and David B. Sicilia. *The Entrepreneurs: An American Adventure.* Boston: Houghton Mifflin Company, 1986.
Stone, Alex. *Wrong Number: The Breakup of AT&T.* New York: Basic Books, Inc., 1989.

Lillian Vernon:
Coleman, Lisa. "I Went Out and Did It." *Forbes:* August 17, 1992.
Vernon, Lillian. *An Eye for Winners.* New York: HarperCollins Publishers, 1996.

Linda Wachner:

Dobryzynski, Judith H. "Linda Wachner: The First Woman to Buy and Head a Fortune 1000 Company." *Working Woman:* November-December 1996.

Greene, Katherine, and Richard Greene. "The 20 Best-Paid Women in Corporate America: Executive Privelege." *Working Woman:* January 1997.

An Wang:

Wang, An, with Eugene Linden. *Lessons: An Autobiography.* Reading, MA: Addison-Wesley Publishing Company, Inc., 1986.

Charles B. Wang:

Teitelbaum, Richard. "Tough Guys Finish First." *Fortune:* July 21, 1997.

Wang, Charles B. *Techno Vision: The Executive's Survival Guide to Understanding and Managing Information Technology.* New York: McGraw-Hill, Inc., 1994.

A. Montgomery Ward:

Hoge, Cecil C. *The First Hundred Years Are the Toughest: What We Can Learn from the Century of Competition Between Sears and Wards.* Berkeley, CA: Ten Speed Press, 1988.

Thomas J. Watson, Jr.:

Watson, Thomas J., Jr. with Peter Petre. *Father, Son & Co.: My Life at IBM and Beyond.* New York: Bantam Books, 1990.

John F. Welch, Jr.:

Morris, Betsy. "Roberto Goizueta and Jack Welch: The Wealth Builders." *Fortune,* December 11, 1995.

Slater, Robert. *The New GE: How Jack Welch Revived an American Institution.* Homewood, IL: Business One Irwin, 1993.

Kemmons Wilson:

Scott, Jonathan. "Family Trip Spawned Change in Travel Industry." *Memphis Business Journal:* June 24, 1996.

William Wrigley, Jr.:

Duncan-Clark, S. J. "Make a Good Product for a Fair Price—Then Tell the World." *Illustrated World:* March 1922.

Credits and Sources

"The Active Qualities of Leaders" reprinted by permission of the publisher from *Organization and Management: Selected Papers* by Chester I. Barnard. Cambridge, MA: Harvard University Press. Copyright © 1948 by the President and Fellows of Harvard College.

"The Woman Executive" by Olive Ann Beech, from the *Michigan Business Review,* May 1961.

"Reality-Based Leadership" by Lawrence A. Bossidy, from a speech before The Economic Club of Washington, Washington, D.C., June 19, 1996.

"Business and Labor" by Harry A. Bullis, from a speech delivered on CBS radio, 1952.

"Ethical Managers Make Their Own Rules" by Sir Adrian Cadbury, from *Harvard Business Review,* September–October, 1987. Reprinted by permission of *Harvard Business Review.* Copyright © 1987 by the President and Fellows of Harvard College; all rights reserved.

"The Secret of Business Is the Management of Men" by Andrew Carnegie, from a speech before The British Iron and Steel Institute, 1903.

"Lead with Your Values" from *Ben & Jerry's Doubledip* by Ben Cohen and Jerry Greenfield. Copyright © 1997 by Ben Cohen and Jerry Greenfield. Reprinted with the permission of Simon & Schuster.

"Good Human Relations: The Solution of Labor Problems" by Frederick C. Crawford, from a speech before the National Association of Manufacturers Public Relations Conference, French Lick, Indiana, August 24, 1943. Reprinted by the permission of Mrs. Frederick C. Crawford and the Western Reserve Historical Society.

"Roving Leadership" from *Leadership Is an Art* by Max DePree. Copyright © 1987 by Max DePree. Used by permission of Doubleday, a division of Bantam Doubleday Dell Publishing Group, Inc.

"Are You a Job-Holder or a Result Getter?" by T. Coleman du Pont, from *American Magazine,* November 1918.

"Machine and Progress" from *The Diary and Sundry Observations* by Thomas A. Edison. The Philosophical Library, 1948.

"Managing a Creative Organization" by Michael D. Eisner, from a speech before the Executive Club of Chicago, April 19, 1996. Reprinted by permission of the Disney Company.

"How to Keep a Business Growing" by Henry Ford, from *System: The Magazine of Business,* May 1924.

"Real Leaders Create Industries" by Robert W. Galvin, from *Research Technology Management,* November-December 1995. Copyright © 1995. Reprinted by permission of *Research Technology Management.*

"A View from Olympus" by Bill Gates, from Forbes ASAP, December 2, 1996. Reprinted by permission of FORBES ASAP Magazine © Forbes Inc., 1996.

"Leadership" from *Managing* by Harold S. Geneen and Alvin Moscow. Copyright © 1984 by Harold S. Geneen and Alvin Moscow, Inc. Used by permission of Doubleday, a division of Bantam Doubleday Dell Publishing Group, Inc.

"The Businessman at Bay" by J. Paul Getty. Copyright © by HMH Publishing Co., Inc. Reprinted from *How to be Rich* by J. Paul Getty. Permission granted by The Berkeley Publishing Group, a member of Penguin Putnam Inc. All rights reserved.

"I Answer the Telephone Myself" by A. P. Giannini, from *System: The Magazine of Business,* July 1926.

"The Real Essence of Business" by Roberto C. Goizueta, from a speech before the Executive Club of Chicago, November 20, 1996. Reprinted by permission of the Coca-Cola Company.

"If 'Business Credibility' Means Anything" by Katherine Graham, from the *Conference Board Record,* March 1976. Reprinted by permission of the Conference Board.

"Taking the Hype Out of Leadership" by Andrew S. Grove from *Fortune,* March 28, 1988. Copyright © 1988 Time, Inc. All rights reserved.

"Some Thoughts on Industrial Unrest" by Daniel Guggenheim, from the *Annals of the American Academy of Political and Social Science,* May 1915.

"Ethics: A Global Business Challenge" by Robert D. Haas, from a speech delivered to the Conference Board, May 4, 1994. Reprinted by permission of Levi Strauss and Company.

"Labor Relations: The Division of Wealth" by William Randolph Hearst, from editorials published in the Hearst Newspapers.

"Failure Is a Word I Don't Accept" by John H. Johnson, from *Succeeding Against the Odds*. Copyright © 1989 John H. Johnson. Reprinted by permission of Amistad Press, Inc.

"Self-Discipline" by Ray Kroc, from *Intellect,* November 1977.

"In the Public Eye" reprinted by permission of Harvard Business School Press, from *CEO: Building a $400 Million Company from the Ground Up* by Sandra Kurtzig with Tom Parker. Copyright ©1991, 1994 Sandra L. Kurtzig; all rights reserved.

"The Case of the Oriental Rug" by Ralph Lazarus, from the *Michigan Business Review,* November 1963.

"Preserve Order Amid Change" from *The Spirit to Serve* by J. W. Marriott, Jr. and Kathi Ann Brown. Copyright © 1997 by Marriott International, Inc. Reprinted by permission of HarperCollins Publishers, Inc.

"The People Principle" by Rene C. McPherson, from *Leaders,* March, 1980. Copyright © 1980. Reprinted by permission of *Leaders* Magazine.

"American and Japanese Styles" from *Made in Japan* by Akio Morita with Edwin M. Reingold and Mitsuko Shimomura. Copyright © 1986 by E. P. Dutton. Used by permission of Dutton, a division of Penguin Putnam, Inc.

"Innovation: The Fruit of Success" by Robert N. Noyce from *MIT's Technology Review,* February 1978. Reprinted with permission from *MIT's Technology Review,* copyright © 1998.

"Trust in People" from the *HP Way* by David Packard. Copyright © 1995 by The David and Lucile Packard Foundation. Reprinted by permission of HarperCollins Publishers, Inc.

"Business Is a Young Man's Game" by Charles W. Patterson, from *American Magazine,* June 1920.

"How I Get My Ideas Across" by John H. Patterson, from *System: The Magazine of Business,* June 1918.

"Business Leaders: It's up to Us to Recover the Industrial Leadership" by H. Ross Perot. From a speech before the Economics Club of Detroit, December 8, 1986. Reprinted by permission of H. Ross Perot.

"How We Divide with Our Men" by William Cooper Procter, from *American Magazine,* October 1919.

"Reviewing Yourself" from "The Twelve Hats of a Company President" by Willard F. Rockwell, Jr. Copyright © 1971. Reprinted with permission from Prentice Hall.

"The Fabulous Future" by David Sarnoff, from *Fortune,* January 1955. Copyright © 1955 Time, Inc. All rights reserved.

"Creating an Empowering Environment for All Employees" by Frederick W. Smith, from *The Journal for Quality and Participation,* June 1990. Reprinted with permission from *The Journal for Quality and Participation.* Copyright © 1990 The Association for Quality and Participation, Cincinnati, OH.

"G. F. Swift: I Can Raise Better Men than I Can Hire" by Louis F. Swift, from *System: The Magazine of Business,* 1927.

"The Wonder of Routine" from *Well Done!* by Dave Thomas with Ron Beyma. Copyright © 1994 by R. David Thomas. Used by permission of Zondervan Publishing House.

"The Making of a Successful Businessman" by Theodore N. Vail, from *Youth's Companion,* September 1913.

"Growth" from *An Eye for Winners* by Lillian Vernon. Copyright © 1996 by Lillian Vernon. Reprinted by permission of HarperCollins Publishers, Inc.

"Do It Now!" by Linda Wachner from *Fortune,* December 14, 1992. Copyright © 1992 Time, Inc. All rights reserved.

"Responsibility" from *Lessons: An Autobiography* by Dr. An Wang with Eugene Linden. Published by Addison-Wesley Publishing Company, Inc., 1986. Reprinted with permission of Todd L. C. Klipp, Office of the General Counsel, Boston University.

"Techno Vision" from *Techno Vision* by Charles B. Wang and published by McGraw-Hill. Copyright © 1994. Reprinted with permission of The McGraw-Hill Companies.

"The Elements of Personal Power" by A. Montgomery Ward from *Personality in Business.* Published by The System Company, 1910.

"Reorganization" from *Father, Son & Co.: My Life at IBM and Beyond* by Thomas J. Watson, Jr. and Peter Petre. Copyright © 1990 by Thomas J. Watson, Jr. Used by permission of Bantam Books, a division of Bantam Doubleday Dell Publishing Group, Inc.

"Global Competitiveness: America in the Eye of the Hurricane" by John F. Welch, Jr., from a speech before The Economic Club of Detroit, May 16, 1994. Reprinted by permission of General Electric.

"Take Your Idea and See it Through" from *Half Luck and Half Brains: The Kemmons Wilson Holiday Inn Story* by Kemmons Wilson with Robert Kerr. Published by Hambleton-Hill Publishers, 1996. Copyright © 1996. Reprinted by permission of Kemmons Wilson.

"I Never Make an Appointment" by William Wrigley, Jr., from *System: the Magazine of Business,* July 1926.

Index